ECONOMIC DEVELOPMENT FOR EVERYONE

How do we create employment, grow businesses, and build greater economic resilience in our low-income communities? How do we create economic development for everyone, everywhere – including rural towns, inner-city neighborhoods, aging suburbs, and regions such as Appalachia, American Indian reservations, the Mexican border, and the Mississippi Delta – and not just in elite communities?

Economic Development for Everyone collects, organizes, and reviews much of the current research available on creating economic development in low-income communities. Part I offers an overview of the harsh realities facing low-income communities in the US today; their many economic and social challenges; debates on whether to try reviving local economies vs. relocating residents; and current trends in economic development that emphasize high-tech industry and high levels of human capital. Part II organizes the sprawling literature of applied economic development research into a practical framework of five dynamic dimensions: empower your residents: begin with basic education; enhance your community: build on existing assets; encourage your entrepreneurs; diversify your economy; and sustain your development.

This book, assembled and presented in a unified framework, will be invaluable for students and new researchers of economic development in low-income communities, offering new perspectives for established researchers, professional economic developers and planners, and public officials. Development practitioners and community leaders will also find new ideas and opportunities, along with a broad view on how the many complex parts of economic development interconnect.

Mark M. Miller is a professor of geography at the University of Southern Mississippi, USA, with a specialty in economic development and low-income communities. He has pursued his research interests across Mississippi and the South, Arizona, Cuba, Mexico, Belize, Jamaica, and Nunavut.

ECONOMIC DEVELOPMENT FOR EVERYONE

Creating Jobs, Growing Businesses, and Building Resilience in Low-Income Communities

Mark M. Miller

Routledge
Taylor & Francis Group

LONDON AND NEW YORK

First published 2017
by Routledge
2 Park Square, Milton Park, Abingdon, Oxon OX14 4RN

and by Routledge
711 Third Avenue, New York, NY 10017

Routledge is an imprint of the Taylor & Francis Group, an informa business

© 2017 Mark M. Miller

British Library Cataloguing in Publication Data
A catalogue record for this book is available from the British Library.

Library of Congress Cataloging in Publication Data
Names: Miller, Mark M. (Mark Michael), 1957- author.
Title: Economic development for everyone : creating jobs, growing businesses, and building resilience in low-income communities / Mark M. Miller.
Description: Abingdon, Oxon ; New York, NY : Routledge, 2017. | Includes index.
Identifiers: LCCN 2016052614 | ISBN 9781138647091 (hardback) | ISBN 9781138647107 (pbk.) | ISBN 9781315627243 (ebook)
Subjects: LCSH: Community development--United States. | Economic development--United States. | Poverty--United States. | Equality--United States.
Classification: LCC HN90.C6 M55 2017 | DDC 307.1/40973--dc23
LC record available at https://lccn.loc.gov/2016052614

ISBN: 978-1-138-64709-1 (hbk)
ISBN: 978-1-138-64710-7 (pbk)
ISBN: 978-1-315-62724-3 (ebk)

Typeset in Bembo
by Taylor & Francis Books

Visit the eResources: www.routledge.com/9781138647107

To my family, my friends, and everyone else who is working to make their community a better, happier, more educated place for all

CONTENTS

ILLUSTRATIONS

Figures

Boxes

ACKNOWLEDGMENTS

I am grateful for the continued encouragement and inspiration that I have received from my many colleagues and students. I appreciate the hard work and ED insights of Chad Miller and Judson Edwards. Thanks to Andy Reese for encouraging me to complete this book. Tony Henthorne and Rick Taylor have helped fuel my interest in the tourism industry, along with my many friends and colleagues in Cuba and Jamaica. Lay Gibson, David Cochran, Joby Bass, and my other disciplinary colleagues make me proud to be a geographer. My wife Amy Miller continually inspires me to be a better teacher and a better person. I am grateful to my son Max and every other teacher who is dedicated to educating disadvantaged students. I appreciate Tim Buckner and all the other small businesspeople who serve my community and me. The support of my sangha is invaluable.

I indicate the contributions of students Mary Travis, Serena Williams Buckley, Katie Hogan, Nadine Armstrong, Nathan Satcher, and Joseph Yawn in specific sections of this book. The following students also led me to valuable resources: Brooke Boisseau, Nicole Borchert, Derek Duckworth, Jamy Galloway, Thomas Miller, Chris Ryals, and Brady Smith. Joy Foy, Garrett Harper, Robert Ingram, and Leland Speed are just a few of the many ED professionals who motivate me to put ED knowledge into community action. I am energized every time I visit a neighborhood or town in which citizens, public officials, businesspeople, and diverse social groups work together to make their community a better place to live, work, play, and raise healthy children.

INTRODUCTION

How do we create employment, grow businesses, and build greater economic resilience in our nation's low-income communities? Our low-income communities include rural towns; inner-city neighborhoods; aging suburbs surrounding most major cities today; and broad lagging regions such as American Indian reservations, the Mississippi Delta, Appalachia, and much of the border with Mexico.

Clearly, these places represent a vast diversity in terms of geographic, cultural, and social characteristics. However, they also face many similar challenges with regard to economic development (ED). Many of these communities have lost their traditional manufacturing industries and now struggle to maintain any stable economic base. Meanwhile, the loss of local retail establishments accelerates economic leakage – that is, money escaping from the community – and leaves residents without adequate access to grocery stores and other retail services. Low-income communities are highly dependent on the vicissitudes of federal and state funding for education, public sector jobs, food, housing, and other necessities of civic life. These low-income communities typically suffer from high rates of unemployment, low rates of educational attainment, large numbers of residents with criminal records, inadequate public services, and deteriorating physical infrastructure. Many of these communities have suffered from natural or man-made disasters combined with high levels of poverty, crime, drug abuse, and other social ills.

Many common misconceptions and overgeneralizations are also applied to low-income communities in the US. The populations of low-income communities are often dismissed as unemployed, dependent on public assistance, "takers" in common political discourse; in fact, the numbers of "working poor" are large and are growing larger. Although their populations are typically characterized as minority and otherwise marginalized populations, many low-income communities are predominantly White. Once a problem considered isolated in inner cities and remote rural communities, the fastest-growing low-income populations are now found in the suburbs.

These sorts of struggling communities were once a central focus of regional planning and ED – in theory, at least, and to some extent in practice and in public investment. Today, these communities find themselves, to a large extent, outside the mainstream of modern ED thought, strategy, and action. Like most fields of study, ED has progressed through a series of "waves," "phases," "paradigms," or otherwise dominant and defining models. However, the ED models of yesterday offer little guidance in the environment of today's struggling low-income communities. There is slim hope today of funding the sorts of massive, comprehensive federal programs that once targeted the lagging communities and larger regions of the US: the Tennessee Valley Authority, the Appalachian Regional Commission, the War on Poverty. To the contrary, much of the attention and best intentions from the federal government have turned away from saving low-income communities and instead have shifted toward programs intended to move people to locations where there may be available jobs: dispersing disadvantaged populations out of low-income, inner city neighborhoods, for example.

On the more private-sector-oriented side of ED, we continue "chasing smoke-stacks," or trying to attract new factories to our communities, usually with large public incentives. The remaining big prizes in this costly competition, however, such as automotive manufacturing plants, typically locate in the "greenfield" fringes of cities that are already advantaged in many ways. Our enthusiasm for enterprise zones in the 1980s and 1990s faded as we realized that these programs would not provide a low-cost cure-all for troubled regions. More recent strategies for ED – so-called "third wave" strategies that have emerged since the 1980s – emphasize highly skilled or highly educated populations, advanced technologies, ready access to research and development facilities, concentrations of innovative and creative individuals, and entrepreneurial capital: all assets that are characteristically lacking in our low-income communities.

Have we then abandoned all hope, leaving our low-income communities to wither away, their residents faced with no choice but to move or resign themselves to an ever-bleaker economic future? I do not believe that is so. To the contrary, this book documents a wide and exciting range of ideas and practical experiments in ED for low-income communities. At the same time, however, these many and disparate ideas fail to add up to an overall clear and coherent model. At this point in the twenty-first century, there is no dominant paradigm – no clear road forward – for creating ED in struggling low-income communities. Instead, community leaders face an often bewildering number of paths headed in various and sometimes even contradictory directions.

There are three purposes for this book. The first purpose is to collect, document, explain, and review, systematically in a single source, much of the published research on creating ED in low-income communities. As such, this is a book that I hope can provide a solid foundation for the research work of students (especially my own), beginning research professors, and other scholars in the years ahead.

The second purpose of this book is to help organize the sprawling literature of ED for low-income communities into a useful overall framework. I hope that a more orderly framework can help motivate more scholarly research, as well as help encourage comprehensive thought and theory-building on how our most challenged communities can create ED. As I tell my students, the first step in any scientific endeavor is classification, be it the classification of species in biology, or the types of economic activities in geography. As such, this book proposes a classification scheme, illustrated in Figure I.1, for the many possible strategies for ED in low-income communities, which provides the structure for the chapters of Part II of this book.

The third purpose of this book is to address directly those who are trying to take action on behalf of these struggling communities: ED practitioners, public officials, and other community leaders. This book seeks to provide local leaders with the broadest possible range of ideas and opportunities for serving the needs of their own communities – as well as a "big picture" perspective on how all the different concepts presented here potentially interconnect and reinforce one another.

Notes on style and method

My intention with this book is to present the material in a style that is accessible to students, working ED professionals, public officials, and others with a practical interest in ED. At the same time, I aspire to write a book that is built on a solid foundation of scholarly research, which speaks meaningfully to my academic colleagues.

The scholarly foundation of this book is a review of the best research available on this broad subject: in particular, published research from peer-reviewed journals. The intention is to survey and organize what we really know – or, at least, what we think we really know – on this broad topic. This review of the literature should

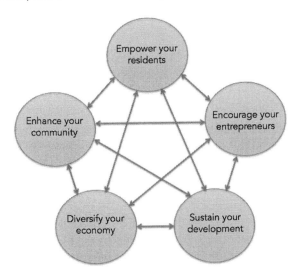

FIGURE I.1 Five dynamic dimensions of ED empowerment for all communities

also help graduate students and advanced undergraduate researchers recognize the leading researchers in fields of interest to them, along with some of the most common research methods employed in these fields of study.

The research methodology for this book is a bounded (that is, limited) literature review guided by the standards for a systematic review (Jesson, Matheson, and Lacey 2011). The core of the review consists of a complete survey of the four research journals that I have found to be most clearly focused on applied regional ED in the US: *Economic Development Quarterly, Journal of the American Planning Association, Community Development: Journal of the Community Development Society* (formerly *Journal of the Community Development Society*), and *Review of Planning Literature*. The survey extends back to 1995. I have included many key, earlier articles from these and other journals. However, the overall economic and policy environment has changed enough since 1995 that many of the earlier publications are no longer as relevant to today's challenges.

Articles in those four core journals led to a "snowball" sample of other, related literature included in this book: mainly articles from other peer-reviewed research journals, as well as books from academic publishers. I also cite several articles from the highly applied, short-lived journal *Applied Research in Economic Development*. There are many other valuable sources of information and ideas about ED: books for popular audiences, newspapers, websites, case studies, professional journals, the experiential knowledge of practitioners, and so on. This book pays respect to those sources to help illustrate sometimes-dry ED concepts. In general, though, in this book I try to hew closely to concepts that have been verified or debated by professional, scholarly researchers.

This book is inevitably influenced and biased by my own research and applied experience working in low-income communities in the US and abroad. In the US, I have worked mainly in the Southeast and Southwest, especially in my adopted home state of Mississippi. In the Developing World, I have lived, visited, taught in, and conducted ED research throughout Latin America and the Caribbean, especially in Mexico, Guatemala, Cuba, Jamaica, and Belize. I also had the opportunity to conduct research in the arctic Nunavut Territory of Canada.

While this book seeks to be comprehensive in its review of the research literature and topics related to ED in low-income communities, that goal is impossible to achieve in reality. Inevitably, I will have overlooked topics or issues that have a significant impact on ED equity or effectiveness. I will have overlooked or unintendedly omitted important articles, books, and other sources of information. Nearly every one of the many topics mentioned in this book is addressed in greater detail by more authoritative researchers specific to those topics. I purposefully omit or lightly glide over large fields of scholarship that are crucial to ED – including much from political science, public policy, sociology, economics, communications, and even my own home discipline of geography – in the interest of keeping the book as sharply focused as possible on the practical application of ED for low-income communities. And, of course, the book will be obsolete the moment I submit the manuscript for publication, as researchers will continue their work unabated.

Please contact me with any suggestions of relevant or related publications that I have overlooked or otherwise omitted – including your own work – as well as research publications that appear after this book is completed. Routledge has generously agreed to supplement the book with an online topical bibliography, which I plan to expand and update after the book's publication. I hope I will have the opportunity to incorporate all those sources into an eventual second edition of this book. Please contact me via email at m.m.miller@usm.edu, or via traditional mail at:

Mark M. Miller

Department of Geography and Geology

Box 5051

The University of Southern Mississippi

Hattiesburg, MS 39406–5051

The focus of this book

The focus of this book is a fairly specific territory within the vast literature related to "development." Above all, the focus of this book is highly applied and oriented toward ED practice, rather than more basic research or theory-building. As the subtitle of the book states, the concern is how we can go about "creating jobs, growing businesses, and building resilience in low-income communities." The book will not compete with the rich, growing, and more theoretically oriented literature on, for example, the reproduction of spatial inequality in metropolises, growing income inequalities, or theories of human capital. Instead, this book keeps its focus closer to ground level: how we might create a few more jobs in low-income communities, raise incomes for some local residents, bounce back more readily from adversity, and enable people to make more productive contributions to their home communities.

Without question, the typical low-income community has a great many and diverse needs to make progress possible, including housing, healthcare, security, leadership, political transparency, and so on: concerns which are often addressed in the broader context of "community development." The implicit assumption underlying ED and this book, however, is that the economic factor is one of the most fundamental driving forces (if not the most fundamental driving force) behind a community's progress. More businesses and better jobs in a community – especially if distributed with some reasonable degree of equity – will not solve all its problems, but some extra income and tax revenue can help a community address a great many immediate and long-term challenges.

The geographic scale of this book emphasizes ED strategies at the regional, local, and even the neighborhood level, rather than large-scale anti-poverty programs at the federal (and, to some extent, state) levels. Exceptions addressed in the book include the local impacts on low-income communities of some federally funded programs, such as Housing and Urban Development's (HUD) Moving to Opportunity initiative. One practical purpose for this relatively small-scale focus is to emphasize ED programs that are reasonably within the control of local communities themselves – and so offer some potential for citizens and their representatives to take action on their own behalf.

This book is concerned almost entirely with low-income communities in the US, rather than low-income communities in the Developing World or within other countries in the Developed World. I do draw, however, from some of the research available from elsewhere in the world that may be relevant to the US situation. In turn, I hope that lessons from this book can be considered usefully – if cautiously – in communities beyond US borders.

Organization

This book is organized into two parts. Part I – the context for ED and low-income communities – consists of the first three chapters and is intended to provide a foundation for the more action-oriented Part II. The three chapters of Part I are posed as questions, admittedly bluntly worded, about the status of low-income communities in society, policy, and ED practices today:

- Chapter 1: *Who cares? What are the realities facing low-income populations and communities in the US today?* The central thesis, or argument, of Chapter 1 is that all low-income communities are unique, as are the various ethnic, minority, and other populations that constitute those communities. However, most low-income communities share enough in common – in terms of the challenges they face and potential opportunities – that they usefully can share theories, research, and ideas regarding ED. Among the questions addressed in Chapter 1 are: What do we most appropriately call these communities? How do we define them? What are they like? How are the communities and their people similar to one another, and what are their differences? Where are they located?
- Chapter 2: *Why bother? Who cares about the future of low-income communities?* In a free-market society, why should we care at all about the economic future of particular low-income communities? Wouldn't it be more efficient to allow – even encourage – people to move to the places where economies are thriving and jobs are growing? Public policies today often focus on providing low-income people with greater access to jobs outside their home community, or even on relocating them entirely to other communities. This chapter argues that places – geographic communities – do still matter and still hold deep emotional value to the people who live there. Further, those residents may not be fully free to leave for a variety of reasons.
- Chapter 3: *What's the use? What can mainstream economic development do for low-income communities?* Chapter 3 outlines the long history of mainstream ED thought, research, and practice that has evolved and advanced over time. That mainstream has a substantial if imperfect record of attention to the needs of low-income communities. The general focus of ED today, however, has turned toward the more prosperous urban centers, creative and well-educated

populations, industrial clusters, and technology-driven development: of limited use, at best, for addressing ED in low-income communities today.

Part II of this book focuses on potential answers to the problems, or challenges, outlined in Part I. To the extent possible, the chapters of Part II emphasize actions that low-income communities and their advocates can take in order to move themselves forward. Each chapter attempts to survey a particular set of topics in as well-organized a manner as possible, including their complexities and scholarly debates. Those complexities and debates can be invaluable for a young researcher joining in the scholarship of this field, and identifying where they might be able to make their own contribution. Scholarly debates can last for decades, as we dig deeper into the layers of complexity, consider a problem from a different perspective or theory, measure variables in a different way, or consider longer-term impacts. I also find that thoughtful planners, ED professionals, and policymakers can be just as interested in some of these academic debates. Since they spend most of their time deep in the trees of professional practice and politics, they often enjoy an occasional view across the forest.

On the other hand, scholarly debates can also be frustrating, to say the least, for policymakers, planners, politicians, and professional economic developers. "Give me a one-armed economist" will be a common theme throughout the book. To address those frustrations, every chapter in Part II will end with a short, editorial section titled "Takeaway for ED action." Those "takeaway" sections will attempt to summarize conclusions and especially actions that low-income communities and their representatives can take with reasonable confidence based on the research available to date.

The chapters of Part II are titled with action-oriented, or dynamic, strategies in mind:

- Chapter 4: *Empower your residents: begin with basic education*
- Chapter 5: *Enhance your community: build on your existing assets*
- Chapter 6: *Encourage your entrepreneurs*
- Chapter 7: *Diversify your economy*
- Chapter 8: *Sustain your development*

The overall term "ED empowerment" (Figure I.1) is intended to emphasize the importance of local resources and resilience in the face of diminishing resources and attention from federal and state sources. At the same time, the book is not intended to be naïve: locally based approaches are not easy, and there have been decades of failed big ideas that were supposed to cure all the problems of low-income communities. Instead, the multifaceted strategies outlined in Part II emphasize how many different opportunities exist that can potentially make a difference – and on how many fronts communities must address their efforts to make that difference serious, strong, and sustainable. Although all of these interconnected strategies must in some way be addressed simultaneously, we can also recognize priorities among them. "Empower your residents," especially through basic education, is intentionally located top and center in Figure I.1: the strategy that should be the top priority for all communities, without which no real, sustainable, equitable ED is possible.

Emergent themes in ED for low-income communities

The following are some of the most important themes that emerge throughout the research reviewed in this book:

- *A wealth of exciting research work continues today on the development of low-income communities, along with lively debates on the most appropriate ED policies for those communities.* Debate is a sign of vitality in a scholarly field, not a sign of weakness. Many progressive public officials and ED practitioners are also eager to experiment with new ideas and innovative approaches.
- *There is no such thing as a panacea – a "cure all" – for ED in low-income communities, despite our persistent hopes over the decades, and especially not one that comes on the cheap.* The closest thing to a panacea that we have is education: widely and equitably available for all citizens, from the earliest years of age. High-quality, universally available education is certainly not cheap, and it can take decades or even generations to bear the full fruits of economic and community development. As the Chinese proverb goes, though: "The best time to plant a tree was 20 years ago. The second best time is now."
- *In the meantime, there are many realistic investments that are within the grasp of low-income communities, which can pay dividends in the near term.* One of the most consistent findings across the research reviewed in this book is the importance of building rich working networks: within your immediate community, across the greater city or region, and with organizations and agencies at the state and national levels. Those networks should include public-private-nonprofit partnerships. Time, trust, and honest dealings are the main investments necessary to turn those networks into productive social capital assets.
- *There are a few "big ideas" in ED at any given time, which tend to dominate our attention along with many other interesting, alternative "small ideas."* Don't ignore or overlook either. Currently, Michael Porter's influential work offers valuable perspectives on the importance of human capital, regional networks, and competitiveness. Richard Florida's popular theory of "creative communities" highlights the value of our creative individuals and the need to enhance local quality of life factors that can help retain them. Also, though, consider ideas that might distinguish your community from everyone else: the potential offered by local immigrants, for example, or "dark tourism."
- *Prioritize education.* Sustainable economic development starts with education, and education must begin with quality, affordable preschool and childcare. Priority goes next to providing quality education at the elementary and high school levels, and finally "second chance" job training programs for adults. Respect, support, and encourage your community's teachers.

- *Identify your community's strongest assets for ED.* Capitalize on those assets to establish a distinctive identity for your community, both to inspire local residents and attract the attention of potential outside investors. Your community's existing assets offer the most efficient path to creating ED.

- *Cultivate your local entrepreneurs.* Prioritize existing businesses over industrial recruitment. Nurture the diverse entrepreneurial potentials of local minority groups. Build on your existing base of local industry, but also build on your existing assets to diversify your economic base.

- *None of the conventional tools of ED – enterprise zones, tax increment financing, microlending programs – are likely to work well in isolation.* Instead, those programs must contribute to a larger ED strategy for your community in association with sound, transparent local governance and an overall nurturing entrepreneurial environment.

- *Sustainability can be a force for creating ED.* For too long, low-income communities worked against their environmental interests, tolerating pollution, unsightly development, abandoned buildings, and social inequities in the name of ED. Sustainable development is the new paradigm for ED: work with the natural environment and on behalf of social justice in order to create stronger and more sustainable forms of ED.

- *ED for low-income communities offers exciting opportunities for new research and practical innovation.* Virtually every topic in this book merits more attention and research. Interesting new programs and policies require careful evaluation. Unforeseen new economic, social, and other challenges, along with new and unexpected business opportunities, will transform the ED landscape. New researchers will find a wealth of established scholars cited in this book to provide inspiration and perhaps opportunities for mentoring.

Reference

Jesson, Jill, Lydia Matheson, & Fiona Lacey. 2011. *Doing Your Literature Review.* Thousand Oaks, CA: Sage.

PART I

Foundations of economic development and low-income communities

1

WHO CARES? WHAT ARE THE REALITIES FACING LOW-INCOME POPULATIONS AND COMMUNITIES IN THE US TODAY?

Where to start? What, even, to title this book and call the communities that are the concern of this book? What terminology would be meaningful, reasonably objective, but not demeaning to the residents of such communities? If possible, what terminology might even offer a hint of hope for the future?

Terms such as "poor," "poverty," and "impoverished" are powerful and continue to be used widely both in general discourse and in research (Beaulieu & Diebel 2016). However, there are many communities that would take exception to these labels for a variety of reasons. Some people may find these terms demeaning or limiting; they may see themselves as poor in income but not "poor in spirit." The terms "poverty" and "poor" have come to be associated with powerful negative images, from the downtrodden in the US (Evans & Agee 2011 [1941]), to those who are struggling simply to survive in the world's developing countries (Boo 2012), to the US War on Poverty, to infamous "welfare queens." The term "poor" also tends to sound static and perhaps even hopeless in nature: "You will always have the poor among you" (Matthew 26:11). Meanwhile, even the poorest communities may include residents who are comfortably middle-class, quite well off, or even wealthy: owners of local businesses, landowners, public officials, or perhaps some church and other civic leaders.

There are plenty of alternative academic terms from which to choose, but those terms are likely unfamiliar to residents of such communities or even to many practitioners of economic development (ED): "lagging regions," "marginalized" or "disadvantaged communities," "developing places" (as in the "Developing World"), "periphery" and "semi-periphery," "places with persistent poverty," "emerging domestic markets" (Milken Institute 2007), "economically distressed communities or neighborhoods" (Tyler-Mackey et al. 2016; Jennings 2012). The most inclusive term would be "economic development for everyone," ideally with some degree of equity, in each and every place in the US.

Ultimately, I settled on the basic term "low-income community" to designate the primary focus of this book. The term "low-income community" is not dramatic, but I believe it would sound reasonable, objective, and realistic to the leaders and residents of the sorts of communities that I had in mind as I wrote this book. A comparable term is used by the World Bank to classify countries, as in low-income countries, middle-income countries, etc. (United Nations Development Policy & Analysis Division 2016). I adopted this term for this book, including the hyphenation, albeit not the technical definition of $1,005 per capita gross national income, which would seem absurdly low in a US context. (In reality, sadly, that measure is not entirely absurd in a US context, as Edin & Shaeffer [2015] make clear in their book *$2.00 a Day: Living on Almost Nothing in America*.)

While I emphasize the term "low-income" throughout this book, I also use the terms "poor" and "poverty," especially throughout the remainder of this chapter. Those are technical terms that are used by both government agencies and scholarly researchers, so they are often unavoidable. In general, for the purposes of this book, I will reserve terms such as "poor" and "poverty" to refer to individuals, and "low-income" to refer to communities.

Finally, and importantly for this book, I believe that using the term "low-income communities" implies a call to fairly specific and focused *action*: to raise the incomes of the community's residents, as well as increase the tax revenues of the community's coffers. The typical low-income community faces an enormous number and variety of needs: education, housing, healthcare, security, leadership, political transparency, and more. Economic development – loosely defined for the purposes of this book as creating jobs, growing businesses, and building economic resilience (more on definitions of ED in Chapter 3) – won't solve all of society's problems. However, thoughtful, sustainable ED can help a community finance better schools, enable residents to afford better housing, retain local medical facilities and professionals, allow residents to lead healthier and lower-stress lives, and support a better-trained team of professional public officials.

SIDEBAR: WHAT CREATES EMPLOYMENT IN US COMMUNITIES?

In order to survive and thrive, every community must have some form of industry that brings in money from outside the community, which is the fundamental assumption of economic base theory. A basic industry is one that brings money into the community from outside: whether from another country or the community next door, the effect is largely the same. We tend to think of industry as synonymous with manufacturing, and indeed the ED profession traditionally is highly focused on attracting manufacturing industry. Internationally, the economically developed countries of the world are often referred to as the "industrialized" countries, meaning those that have advanced beyond a dependence on basic raw materials and have established a robust manufacturing sector of their economy. In economic base theory, however, "industry" refers to a very wide variety of activities and investments that generate a flow of money from outside the community.

The primary sector of an economy – "extractive" industries, or the production of raw materials – represents a critical source of income and employment for many communities, especially in rural areas (Alexander & Gibson 1979). Those industries consist of extracting or harvesting natural resource-based products for sale: grain, fiber, forage, and horticultural crops; petroleum products; and products from fishing and aquaculture, forestry, and animal husbandry.

The secondary sector of the US economy – manufacturing industries – consists of those activities that convert raw materials into something more useful for human needs: cotton into cloth, for example, or petroleum into plastics. Manufacturing may also include combining simpler manufactured goods into more complex products: e.g., cotton thread into cloth into fashion, copper tubing into an air conditioner. In any case, the manufacturing process adds value to the initial product and creates employment for local labor. Manufacturing industries encompass a broad spectrum of skill and salary levels: from rote assembly to specialized crafts to robotic engineering.

Many primary sector jobs have disappeared over the past century due, in part, to farm mechanization. As we are well aware, both our primary and secondary sector jobs have been lost to international competitors offering lower labor costs. Another very important reason for job loss in the secondary sector, though, is mechanization and other technological advancements: advanced tools, machinery, and robots that have made manufacturing much more productive per worker in developed countries such as the US (Cochrane et al. 2014).

Meanwhile, the tertiary economic sector is the fastest growing share of the US economy, and is the preferred source of employment for most US workers. The tertiary sector may simplistically be defined as sales and services: white-collar, air-conditioned office jobs. Tertiary sector employers can include schools, hotels, restaurants, accounting firms, and a wide range of government offices. As a comprehensive category, tourism is often said to be the world's largest "industry" (more in Chapter 7). The tertiary sector also covers a wide range of skill and salary levels, from the proverbial burger flipper to high-level management positions.

Some economic geographers refer to a quaternary (an academic way of saying "fourth") economic sector to convey the idea of industries that don't exactly produce anything tangible, but instead create information and exercise control. Examples include research and development centers, universities and colleges, and corporate headquarters. The quaternary sector of the economy is poorly represented in low-income communities, which highlights the lack of control that those communities generally hold over their own economies. Absentee corporate headquarters hold the decision-making power over many of the industries on which low-income communities depend – including the power over whether those local subsidiaries stay active in the community, close up shop, or leave town.

There are a number of nearly invisible "industries" in many communities. Much of the economic activity in a low-income community may be found in the "informal" economy, or black market: e.g., day laborers, shade tree mechanics, bartered transactions, labor paid in cash without reporting or withholding (more in Chapter 6). "Transfer payments" include a number of largely unrecognized flows of money into many communities, including social security payments, various forms of welfare, Medicaid, and Medicare. The federal and state governments typically represent the major sources of employment and income for many low-income communities: e.g., teachers and school administrators, post office workers, other government employees. Pensions, retirement savings, and returns from other investments can provide other quiet but important sources of income for some communities (Chapter 7).

A local basic industry, in whatever sector of the economy, not only brings outside money into the community, but that money then also multiplies within the local economy. Basic industries may buy supplies, and their employees may spend their incomes within the local community by shopping with non-basic industries, that is, local businesses that exchange money within the local economy. Examples of non-basic companies include locally owned banks, car dealerships, gas stations, restaurants, stores, and legal services. These non-basic industries, in turn, create additional employment with that revenue: bank tellers, car salespersons, lawyers, clerks, and so on.

The magnitude of the multiplier depends on a number of different factors (Gibson & Worden 1981), including the type of basic industry involved. In general, manufacturing plants tend to result in a bigger local multiplier than, say, a hotel. That's one reason why economic developers tend to focus on "bagging the buffalo," or trying to attract an auto plant or other major manufacturing facility. Typically, the biggest factor determining the size of the economic multiplier, though, is the size of the community involved. A small community offers its local businesses and residents fewer opportunities to spend their money locally than does a big city: fewer local banks, local stores, etc. That is likely to be true especially of many low-income communities, which are typically underserved by retail, banking, and other commercial services. As a result, the earnings from local basic industries "leak" out of the community almost immediately without creating many additional, non-basic jobs. Basic industries are critical, but local non-basic businesses are also important contributors to local jobs and tax revenue by helping to slow the "leakage" of local money. More ahead in Chapter 7.

How do we define a poor person, a household in poverty, or a low-income community?

What does it mean to be poor or low-income in the US today? The US Census Bureau's technical definition of individual and household poverty employs a weighting system based on the number of household members and their ages. As of 2015, the poverty income threshold for an individual under the age of 65, living alone, was $12,331 per year, or a little under $34 per day (US Census Bureau: Poverty Definitions). For a family of four including two children under the age of 18, the poverty income threshold would be $24,036. Income calculations include all cash earnings – before taxes – including "unemployment compensation, workers' compensation, Social Security, Supplemental Security Income, public assistance, veterans' payments, survivor benefits, pension or retirement income… educational assistance, alimony, [and] child support" (US Census Bureau: Poverty Definitions). Census calculations do not include non-cash benefits such as food stamps or housing subsidies.

The Census Bureau's poverty income threshold figures are updated versions of calculations and assumptions made in the 1960s (Orshansky 1965), so not surprisingly those thresholds have been criticized as simplistic, outdated, and overly narrow in scope. Internationally, the United Nations (UN) has published the *Human Development Index* since 1990, a broader measurement intended to emphasize policies that affect human lives directly instead of paying simple attention to financial accounts (United Nations Development Policy & Analysis Division 2016). Since 2010, the *Human Development Index* has also included an "Inequality-Adjusted Human Development Index" to reflect the significance of inequalities within countries and societies.

Angus Deaton (2015 Nobel Prize in Economics winner) helped develop a Human Needs Index (HNI) in a US context. Based on data provided by the Salvation Army, this HNI emphasizes the consumption of basic human needs, rather than income: in particular, the consumption of meals, groceries, clothing, furniture, housing, medical care, and energy (Jeffrey & Pasic 2015; Lilly Family School of Philanthropy 2015). Research by Christopher Wimer suggests that monetary measures of poverty alone do not tell the full extent of human suffering. Wimer suggests instead that we focus on concepts such as "hardship" or "deprivation": for example, "How often do they have trouble getting food, paying bills or getting help for a serious medical problem?" (reported by Fessler 2016).

Many researchers also use the concept of "low-income" – often calculated as twice the official poverty threshold (Mishel et al. 2012; Roberts, Povich, & Mather 2012) – to capture the population that suffers many of the pernicious impacts of poverty without meeting the technical definition. Chen & Newman (2014: 91, 93) use the terms "near poor" and "missing class" to capture the same concept: families that

> live on incomes between one and two times the poverty line.…The near poor are a much larger group than the poor. More than 50 million Americans fall into this category, compared to 37 million who are poor. That means that nearly one out of three Americans is poor or near-poor.
>
> [This category includes] 21 percent of the nation's children.…This "Missing Class" is composed of households earning roughly between $20,000 and $40,000 for a family of four.

The status of the "near poor" can place families in a precarious life situation. While they may be able to "get by" financially from month to month, a layoff, illness, car breakdown, or another unexpected circumstance can quickly relocate households from the category of near poor to the genuinely poor category – as well as place them deep into debt to credit cards or payday loan companies.

On the other side of the poverty line are those who are "deeply poor," or have incomes less than half of the official poverty level (Mishel et al. 2012). The share of the poor who meet this definition of deeply poor has increased fairly steadily (with some minor fluctuations) since the late 1970s, from below 30 percent of those in poverty to 44 percent of the poor by 2010: "The poor are getting poorer" (Mishel et al. 2012: 427).

Edin & Shaefer (2015: xv, xvi–xvii) use a measure of extremely deep poverty that is typically reserved for analysis of the Developing World. Shaefer

> borrowed inspiration from one of the World Bank's metrics of global poverty…$2 per person, per day….The official poverty line for a family of three in the United States worked out to about $16.50 per person, per day over the course of a year. The government's designation of "deep poverty" – set at half the poverty line – equated to about $8.30 per person, per day.
>
> The results of Shaefer's analysis were staggering. In early 2011, 1.5 million households with roughly 3 million children were surviving on cash incomes of no more than $2 per person, per day in any given month. That's about one out of every twenty-five families with children in America.

Shaefer's analysis defies many poverty stereotypes. Blacks and Hispanics have the highest rates of increase in the category of extreme poverty, but nearly half of the individuals living on $2 cash per day are White. Further, although single mothers are in the greatest danger of finding themselves – and their children – at that level of poverty, more than a third of the families living on $2 cash per person, per day are married couples (Edin & Shaefer 2015). Shaefer also reworks his analysis by treating Supplemental Nutrition Assistance Program (SNAP) benefits as cash – although SNAP benefits cannot legally or easily be converted to cash – and also including the value of housing subsidies: the result was still a 50 percent increase since 1996 in the level of extreme poverty.

The homeless may be found in nearly every community. Homelessness is a condition closely intertwined with poverty, mental health, domestic abuse, and a variety of other issues. The reality of homelessness is complex and fluid. According to Culhane and Metraux (2008: 112), citing numerous researchers on the subject,

> the term homeless has become a catchall term given to residents of shelters, or, in the case of people living on the streets, those opting out of such institutions….This population overlaps considerably with the poor population that is precariously housed and at imminent risk of becoming homeless….Most of the

people who are homeless were recently housed and will return to housing in a relatively short period of time.

Culhane and Metraux's (2008: 119) own research focuses on "the delivery of emergency and transitional assistance to individuals and families faced with housing emergencies" and trying to find interventions that might reduce episodes of homelessness.

The poor are commonly stereotyped as unemployed and dependent on public assistance: the "takers" of society. In reality, the numbers of "working poor" – those who hold jobs that pay wages below the official poverty level – are large and growing larger (Roberts, Povich, & Mather 2012). Many work full time, and others are employed at just below the 40 hour per week threshold that would entitle them to full employment benefits. The working near poor may also be above the threshold for – or unaware of – government benefits available to the technically poor (Newman & Chen 2007). By one calculation, as of 2011, 10.6 percent of working families in the US fell below the federal poverty income threshold, and 32.1 percent fell under the level of 200 percent of the poverty level (Roberts, Povich, & Mather 2012). By another calculation, an estimated 22 percent of total children in US households fell under the federal poverty income threshold as of 2013, with 44 percent of children in low-income households under 200 percent of the poverty level (National Center for Children in Poverty).

The distribution of working poor is in part correlated with, or related to, race, ethnicity, and gender. As of 2011, 43 percent of US workers earning poverty-level wages were Hispanic, and 36 percent were Black – well out of proportion with the overall population distribution (Mishel et al. 2012). The share of women in the working poor is high, but has fallen "dramatically from 48.0 percent in 1973 to roughly 30 percent in 2000 and was relatively stable thereafter until the rise during the recent recessionary years" (Mishel et al. 2012: 193). The rate for men overall has fluctuated, but the general trend has not been promising over the last several decades. The working poor tend to be concentrated in retail, hospitality, and other service industries, and much less so in manufacturing. Twenty-one percent of workers in "leisure and hospitality" jobs, for example, are paid poverty-level wages according to 2011 data vs. 12 percent in manufacturing industries (Mishel et al. 2012: 434).

We should recognize that there are individuals, families, and communities that choose a life of "voluntary poverty." A "vow of poverty" may be motivated by enrollment in a religious order or community, or religious beliefs may motivate a lifestyle of simplicity rather than pursuit of income (Bridger et al. 2001). Other individuals or communal groups may choose voluntary simplicity and poverty-level incomes from spiritual, ethical, social, or environmental convictions that are less explicitly religious, or from a desire to contribute the fruits of their labor to the greater good rather than to individual gain. While living close to the land, "The Farm" community in Tennessee has supported midwife training programs, a nutrition mission in Guatemala, and an ambulance service in the Bronx (Douglas Stevenson 2014; Gaskin 2002; Gaskin 1974).

To add yet one more complicating dimension to the definition of "poverty," are we considering "episodic" poverty – that is, when people fall into poverty for two or more consecutive months at a time – or poverty that is persistent, "chronic or long term" (US Census Bureau: Poverty Definitions)? Individuals and families commonly shift above and below poverty levels, depending upon jobs found and jobs lost, available housing and homelessness, marriage and divorce, good health and long-term illness, and a variety of other vicissitudes of life. Like the individual humans they consist of, communities also can relatively experience episodic or long-term periods of concentrated poverty. Communities can fall into decline after boom periods, and they can show resilience in bouncing back from periods of decline. St. Clair, Wial, and Wolman (2012: 1) use the term "chronically distressed" to characterize a region as one whose "rate of growth is slow relative to the national [or state] economy over an extended number of years."

Communities, rather than individual people or families, are the principal focus of this book, and there are technical definitions of geographically "concentrated poverty" and "poverty areas" (more on the impacts of concentrated poverty in Chapter 2). The US Census Bureau uses graduated categories of poverty areas, in which the most concentrated category has a poverty rate of 20 percent or more (Bishaw 2011). Blumenberg (2006) uses the term "extreme poverty neighborhoods" to characterize individual "census tracts with poverty rates of 40 percent or more." The more colloquial term "ghetto," with strongly loaded social and political connotations, also remains in use (Sharkey 2013).

There are a variety of other definitions for low-income communities, such as those definitions determining eligibility for federal and state grants and other forms of assistance. For example, to qualify as a federal "food desert" (Chapter 7), "[t]hey qualify as 'low-income communities', based on having: a) a poverty rate of 20 percent or greater, OR b) a median family income at or below 80 percent of the area median family income" (US Departments of Agriculture, Treasury and Health and Human Services). For research purposes, Porter and his Initiative for a Competitive Inner City (Initiative for a Competitive Inner City; much more about Porter's influence in Chapter 3) describe a specific definition of inner cities "as contiguous census tracts characterized by high poverty and unemployment relative to the metropolitan area" (Porter 2016: 106).

After all the above is said, measured, and done, however, this book is not particularly concerned with exact quantifications, definitions of, or restrictions on what constitutes geographic low-income communities – despite their importance for scientific research and the implementation of public policy. For the purposes of this book, if you think the community that you live or work in, are studying, or otherwise serve is low-income, then it probably is or at least is in need of some serious attention. If you want to provide ED-related support to such a community, then God bless you as you move forward with your mission.

Low-income: Absolute or relative? Does a rising tide lift all boats?

The broad concept of equity will be at least implicit throughout this book. The UN "Inequality-Adjusted Human Development Index," mentioned above, embraces concern with the equity of income levels and other indicators of human well-being, not simply with absolute levels in terms of a "poverty line" or some other indicator. Equity is growing as a concern in the US context as inequality continues to grow in the US, as it has especially done since the 1980s (Hartman 2014).

After a fairly steady decrease from the 1930s to the 1950s, the Gini Index for the US has climbed just as steadily from the 1970s to date, tapering off somewhat with the "Great Recession" of 2007–2009 (World Bank 2016). (The Gini Index, named after Italian sociologist Corrado Gini, is a widely and internationally used measure of inequality.) There are only a few Organisation for Economic Co-operation and Development (OECD) countries in the world today, such as Mexico, with a Gini Index as high or higher than that of the US (Mishel et al. 2012). (The OEDC represents the world's economically advanced, developed, industrialized countries.) None of the world's most developed countries – Canada, Western Europe, Japan, South Korea, Australia, New Zealand – have a higher Gini Index than ours (Dadush et al. 2012). The US has one of the highest poverty rates among the OECD countries, with poverty rate being defined as the percentage of households in the country earning less than 50 percent of the country's median income, even after accounting for taxes, welfare, and other transfer payments (Dadush et al. 2012).

Since the 1980s, economic inequality in the US has largely been a function of disproportional income growth for the upper income groups: most notoriously the "one percent," or the top one percent of households in the country (Mishel et al. 2012). Rose (2016: 11) notes increases among the "upper middle class," as well: from 1979 to 2014, the share of income held by the US "rich" grew from 0.4 to 11 percent, while the share of income held by the "upper middle class" grew from 30 to 52 percent. Income earned by all the other groups contracted over the same time period: middle class from 46 to 26 percent, lower middle class from 16 to 8 percent, and the "poor or near-poor" from 7 to 4 percent.

There are many reasoned and forceful arguments concerning the pernicious consequences of inequality (Krueger 2015; Hartman 2014; Stiglitz 2013), and there are many organizations devoted to the cause of economic and social equity: "This is equity: just and fair inclusion into a society in which all can participate, prosper, and reach their full potential. Unlocking the promise of the nation by unleashing the promise in us all" (PolicyLink). According to former Virginia senator Jim Webb, "[t]he most important – and unfortunately the least debated – issue in politics today is our society's steady drift toward a class-based system, the likes of which we have not seen since the 19th century" (Webb 2006, cited in Miller & Miller 2015).

Wilkinson and Pickett (2009) make a "spirited" argument regarding correlations between inequality levels of US states and their levels of health and mental health as well as their high school dropout and homicide rates. This correlation also holds with such other factors as obesity, life expectancy, infant mortality, and trust between fellow citizens. They also cite research suggesting that social problems such as obesity are more closely correlated with people's subjective sense of their social status than their absolute level of education or income. Jennings (2012) contends that inequality at the community level must be a component of making meaningful assessments of neighborhood distress levels.

Concerns about large and growing economic inequality in the country are exacerbated by a lack of social mobility: the tendency for people to stay "stuck" in the social class in which they are born, as opposed to the ladder of equal opportunity. Countries that are more equal in incomes tend to present greater opportunities for social mobility, while less equal countries such as the US have lower rates of movement up the social ladder (Sachs 2015). The US is among the lowest of the OECD countries in terms of social mobility, by some measures ahead only of Italy and the UK (Dadush et al. 2012). Black children, in particular, have a pattern of downward mobility (Mishel et al. 2012: 156); only 26 percent of Whites who are born into the bottom one-fifth of the US economy will end up in that category as adults, while 51 percent of Blacks born into the bottom one-fifth will remain at the bottom.

There are many plausible contributing factors to blame for our national lack of mobility. Globalization is perhaps most widely blamed for growing inequality, especially for its impacts on blue-collar workers in the US, although the evidence for this impact is not entirely clear (Dadush et al. 2012). Globalization may also be blamed for its role in driving increased technology to retain international competitiveness – and so reduce labor demands in the US. Technology may be inducing a vicious cycle of inequality, both contributing to and resulting from the "digital divide." This growing divide in access to – and ability to utilize – new technologies can have a profound impact on children's educational attainment; knowledge about opportunities for employment, healthcare, political action, housing, and so on; and ever-increasing on-the-job technical work skill requirements (Dadush et al. 2012). In addition, immigrants are perennial, politically easy targets for blame in taking American jobs, something which is also not well supported in the research (Longhi, Nijkamp, & Poot 2010; Peri 2010). Net immigration from Mexico, the country most blamed for economic harm to American workers, fell to near or below zero during the Great Recession (Passel, Cohn, & Gonzalez-Barrera 2012) and continues at relatively low levels to date.

Education is almost certainly a critical contributing factor to growing inequality: differing access to high-quality education for different social classes, differing ability to pay for higher education, and the growing importance of a college or university degree for earning a reasonable income (the subject of Chapter 4). The decline of unions is likely another contributing factor to growing economic inequality (Herzer 2016; Dadush et al. 2012). Besides their direct impact on worker wages, unions traditionally put pressure on non-union companies to maintain higher wage levels so as to prevent organizing by their own workers. Differing levels of healthcare and nutrition among different social, racial, and ethnic populations may play a contributing role as well (Putnam & Campbell 2016; Mishel et al. 2012). High incarceration rates, especially for minority groups and other residents of low-income communities, also most likely contribute to US inequality (Braman 2014; Cahn, Nash, & Robbins 2014; Raphael 2014).

The collateral consequences of mass incarceration have been profound. We ban poor women and, inevitably, their children from receiving food stamps and public housing if they have prior drug convictions. We have created a new caste system that forces thousands of people into homelessness, bans them from living with their families and in their communities, and renders them virtually unemployable. Some states permanently strip people with criminal convictions of the right to vote; as a result, in several southern states disenfranchisement among African American men has reached levels unseen since before the Voting Rights Act of 1965 (Bryan Stevenson 2014).

The exact "consequences of inequality" (Porter 2014), on the other hand, are perhaps surprisingly unclear and disputed in the academic and popular literature. Some certain level of inequality is, of course, intrinsic to the concept of capitalism, providing inspiration and motivation to climb the economic ladder. We generally accept the idea that honest labor and enterprise should be rewarded with financial gain.

Jencks (2002) and Wilkinson et al. (2009) question the extent to which inequality per se causes the wide array of social problems for which it has been blamed. Watson (2015) argues against undue attention to inequality as perhaps a distraction from root concerns with absolute poverty: "Politicians often use 'poverty' and 'inequality' interchangeably. They shouldn't. Poverty is different from inequality. One can imagine a society in which everyone was poor but there was no inequality….In the same way, one can imagine a society in which there was inequality but no poverty" (Watson 2015: 113). Further, Watson cautions against viewing education as a "cure-all" for inequality: "How do we give children the chance to move up and out of their parents' income bracket? The instinctive answer…is this: with education, the more the better….[however, education] obviously cannot move everybody to the top of the income distribution. Arithmetic forbids this" (Watson 2015: 164). Watson also notes that as technology becomes more advanced, it becomes more routinized, requiring less advanced education to maintain and utilize tools such as computers or robotic equipment.

While researchers may disagree with regard to the consequences of inequality, there is little room for doubt that inequality levels in the US are exceptionally high compared with our peer countries in the Developed World and that the disparity is continuing to grow. Overall, data indicate that low-income populations continue to rise across the US as a percentage of the overall population and that the middle class continues to shrink in terms of population percentage. The middle class now no longer constitutes a majority of the overall US population (Badger & Ingraham 2016, citing Pew Research Center 2016: America's Shrinking Middle Class).

There is general agreement that one of the greatest dangers of growing inequality is the relationship between wealth and political power: we may face continuously rising, extraordinary levels of economic inequality in the future as the upper income brackets gain increasingly greater control over political leadership and policy-making and as those in the lower income brackets increasingly become "completely detached from virtually all forms of civic life" (Putnam & Campbell 2016, citing the US Census Bureau and other sources; Porter 2014; Stiglitz 2013). Having worked for many years in Central America and the Caribbean, I personally can attest to the social instability, crime, and violence that can result from inequality levels at which the "ladder of opportunity" seems no longer to reach those on the bottom.

What are the challenges facing low-income communities today?

Stereotypes are never a safe bet, but there are several broad generalizations that can be made about most – never all – low-income communities across the US. Many low-income communities, urban and rural alike, have lost their traditional manufacturing industries and now struggle to maintain any stable economic base. Meanwhile, the loss of local retail establishments accelerates economic leakage – that is, money escaping from the community – and leaves residents without adequate access to grocery stores and other retail services. Low-income communities are highly dependent on the changing fortunes of federal and state funding for education, civil service jobs, food, housing, and other necessities of civic life, depending upon economic conditions and the prevailing political winds.

Low-income communities typically suffer from high rates of unemployment, low rates of educational attainment, large numbers of residents with criminal records, and inadequate and deteriorating infrastructure. High levels of poverty, crime, drug abuse, and other social ills tend to afflict all these communities. Although Mother Nature does not single out low-income communities for natural disasters – floods and tornados, among others – such communities are especially vulnerable to the damaging impacts of disasters and typically less resilient when it comes to recovery.

Overall, the share of equity that homeowners in the US hold in their overall home value fell from nearly 70 percent in the early 1980s to 60 percent in 2006, then tumbled to less than 40 percent over the next few years of the Great Recession (Mishel et al. 2012). Household equity is typically the major asset available for collateral for most low-income Americans, against loans for college, small business, and other means of climbing the economic ladder.

Health indicators, including life expectancy, vary widely across the US, with actual declines in many low-income communities (Murray & Ezzati 2011; Brown 2011). The US ranks at the lowest level of the OECD countries for health coverage (Dadush et al. 2012); as of 2010 (prior to the Affordable Care Act), less than 70 percent of US citizens in poverty had health insurance coverage. Immigrants, in particular, have much lower rates of health insurance coverage than the general population: "Latinos have the lowest level of health insurance coverage in the United States and, among Latinos, 57% of Mexican immigrants lack health insurance" (Becerra 2015: 466, citing Saenz 2010).

Sapolsky (2005) reviews research on the relationship between poverty and stress levels, which in turn contribute to a wide variety of mental and physical health issues: according to Putnam and Campbell (2016), "parents in poor neighborhoods are more likely to experience depression, stress, and illness, which in turn 'are associated with less warm and consistent parenting'" (Leventhal, Dupéré, & Shuey 2015). At the same time, adequate and appropriate mental healthcare is scarce for low-income populations (Camp & Trzcinski 2015).

The US has one of the highest incarceration rates in the world, and a variety of legal and social factors make it difficult, at best, for those who have served prison time to find adequate employment opportunities (Palazzolo 2015; Braman 2014; Bryan Stevenson 2014; Raphael 2014). Criminal justice issues begin early in life for many juveniles (Cahn, Nash, & Robbins 2014) both inside and outside the criminal justice system: "[A]s of 2000 about 9 percent of African American children had a father in prison or jail….[A] set of recent studies has already demonstrated a strong association between parental incarceration and children's mental health, aggressiveness, and subsequent involvement with the criminal justice system" (Sharkey 2013: 77–78).

Diet is a pervasive issue across low-income communities in terms of food scarcity, food quality, and food cost. An estimated 8.4 percent of US households face "low food insecurity," defined as "reduced quality, variety, or desirability of diet. Little or no indication of reduced food intake," and 5.6 percent of US households face "very low food security" with "multiple indications of disrupted eating patterns and reduced food intake" (US Department Agriculture, Economic Research Service: Food Security in the US). Many low-income communities – urban and rural alike – are situated in "food deserts" without ready access to supermarkets or other sources of healthy foods (Meltzer & Schuetz 2012; US Departments of Agriculture, Treasury and Health and Human Services). Where they are available, groceries – especially fresh and otherwise healthy foods – are typically more expensive in low-income communities than in more affluent communities (Otero, Pechlaner, & Gürcan 2015). "Junk food" tends to be cheaper and more readily available than fresh fruits and vegetables, and meats, and fast-food restaurants are located in high concentrations in Black neighborhoods (Otero, Pechlaner, & Gürcan 2015; Meltzer & Schuetz 2012). "Dollar stores" are taking the place of supermarkets or grocery stores in both rural and urban communities, typically offering canned and other highly processed foods, but not fresh produce.

A variety of high-interest, even "predatory" credit services are also increasingly concentrated in low-income communities (Karger 2015; Engle & McCoy 2007; more in Chapter 6), where traditional banking services are often scarce and low-income populations lack personal assets: "Interest rates on a two-week payday loan can range from 391 percent to 521 percent. In a typical 14-day $300 payday loan, a customer might pay $45 in fees and interest and receive $255 in cash" (Karger 2015: 77). If the borrower can't repay the loan by the due date, a vicious spiral of debt can quickly accumulate. The average payday service borrower is in debt for 175 days a year and spends 44 percent of their following paycheck on loan repayment (Karger 2015, citing the Center for Responsible Lending). Meanwhile, for public financial needs, states are turning to more regressive sources of taxation such as sales taxes and lotteries (Henricks & Brockett 2015): revenue sources that place a proportionately heavier burden on those at lower income levels.

Low-income communities are affected by a wide variety of national trends, transformations, and policies. Welfare reform, from the 1990s (Accordino 1998), has reduced direct assistance to low-income populations, placed more emphasis on labor force training (critiqued in Chapter 4), and expanded income support through the Earned Income Tax Credit (EITC) (Houston & Ong 2006). The Personal Responsibility and Work Opportunity Reconciliation Act (PRWORA) of 1996 established the Temporary Assistance for Needy Families, or TANF (Caputo 2015), which puts a two-year limit on benefits before recipients are required to find work (Holosko & Barner 2015). Responsibility for providing recipients with education, job training, childcare and other support services falls to the states, with wide variation in the "safety net" for the unemployed (Edin & Shaefer 2015).

Blumenberg (2002) examines the challenges that face welfare recipients seeking employment and concludes that their barriers to employment are so many and interconnected that comprehensive rather than piecemeal strategies are necessary to help people overcome them. Nationwide, labor force participation for men has fallen since at least the 1960s, from over 97 percent in 1960 to less than 88 percent today, but the rate falls to 83 percent among those with a high school degree or less education and to less than 80 percent for Black males (US President's Office 2016). Factors cited for this decline include the decline in manufacturing jobs (Cochrane et al. 2014), lower educational attainment for men than women, and steady increases in incarceration – predominantly of men, and disproportionately of minorities – since the 1970s (US President's Office 2016; Sharkey 2013), as well as a growing technology-induced "digital divide": all factors that hit low-income communities particularly hard.

White and Geddes (2002) seek to understand why some former welfare recipients – women, in particular – successfully attain employment that lifts them above the poverty level and why some do not. Mueller and Schwartz (1998) examine various strategies employed at the federal and state levels intended to facilitate the shift from welfare dependency to employment; they find that all except the EITC are inadequate to raise new workers above poverty-level wages. Seefeldt (2008) finds that women who are single mothers are especially challenged to find work paying wages above poverty level, particularly mothers with large families – in large part because of their need for scheduling flexibility to care for their children.

Immigrants – Latinos, in large measure – were singled out in the PRWORA legislation with special restrictions for documented ("legal") immigrants and prohibitions against undocumented ("illegal") immigrants receiving TANF, Medicaid, or other benefits (Becerra 2015). Many legal permanent residents (i.e., those with "green cards") "avoid applying for social welfare benefits out of fear of being labeled a 'public charge' that could affect their ability to become citizens or serve as sponsors to family members who want to immigrate to the United States" (Becerra 2015: 466).

Resilience

"Resilience" is a term that has increasingly been applied to communities as well as individuals in a variety of contexts (Wang & Gordon 1994) along with the term "grit" in terms of personal perseverance (Duckworth 2016). Resilience in the case of communities can refer to their ability to recover from natural disasters – tornados, floods, hurricanes, earthquakes – as well as their ability to withstand man-made economic disasters, such as national or more localized economic downturns in general, or specific economic calamities such as industry closures. Textile factory and paper/pulp mill shutdowns (Root & Park 2016) are among the industry closures that have hardest hit vulnerable US communities in recent decades.

Reasons for plant layoffs and outright closures have included international competition, but also automation, competition with more up-to-date plants and equipment elsewhere in the US, and product obsolescence. Root and Park (2016) note, for example, declining demand for paper in a digital age. Schmid (2012) reports that in Wisconsin alone, between 2006 and 2012, an "industry that thrived for generations on a tight, homegrown loop – from the forest to the mill to the printer and often back to the mill for recycling – finds itself at the mercy of Wall Street hedge funds and equally unforgiving global economic and political forces" (cited by Root & Park 2016).

The Great Recession and subsequent slow economic recovery not only exacerbated layoffs and industry closures, but made it more difficult for newly unemployed workers to find other employment. Residents who could once count on a living wage from a factory, with a high school degree or less, are often poorly prepared for the skills and education requirements of the new service economy – especially laid-off older workers, who must compete with biases toward younger job-seekers with more up-to-date training and skills. Aside from the obvious monetary impact of unemployment, plant closures and layoffs have a variety of other impacts on former employees and their communities. Studies have found varying levels of impacts on the physical and mental health of those who have lost their jobs (Root & Park 2016). It is common for laid-off workers to describe the experience as being comparable to the death of a family member (Minchin 2006). The social burden, in turn, strains local hospitals, counselors, and other mental health providers (Sentementes 2010, cited by Root & Park 2016).

A factory closing can strike a painful blow to the spirit as well as the economy of the entire community. The economic "multiplier effect" (Chapter 1 sidebar) of a major industry closure is likely to ripple through the entire community, hurting banks, retail, restaurants, construction, housing markets, medical providers, and downtowns alike. For individuals, a layoff can result in much lower earnings over the long term, sometimes with a loss of some or all benefits and even pension

(Root & Park 2016). Textile and paper/pulp mills are often located in rural areas, which are faced with ever-fewer ED alternatives. Meanwhile, "[a]s family farms fail while industrial agribusiness and suburban development thrive, rural communities are withering on the vine" (Beatley & Manning 1997: 150). Factories have often provided employment, sports sponsorships, and other community benefits for generations. Many former industries, however, leave behind toxic or potentially contaminated "brownfield" sites (Chapter 8), which can require extensive, long, and costly remediation.

On the other hand, a plant closure results in a prominent vacant building and surrounding land, which can potentially be available to another employer for low rent, or sometimes even be donated by the parent company (Root & Park 2016). Barnow and Hobbie (2013) examine responses from the federal and state levels, through the 2009 American Recovery and Reinvestment Act, intended to encourage individual and community resilience from the Great Recession. Resilience is possible with some combination of local "grit," creativity, persistence, and external resources.

Where are our low-income communities?

Poverty and low-income communities can be found in every state and in any type of community. Much of the geographic pattern of poverty follows the stereotypical image of impoverished, remote rural communities and of inner-city ghettos – but also accompanied with a dramatic rise in recent decades of the "suburbanization" of poverty.

Rural communities

Rural poverty today remains concentrated in the South, much as documented by James Agee and Walker Evans in the 1930s (Evans & Agee 2011), as well in American Indian reservations across the country (US Department of Agriculture, Economic Research Service: Rural Poverty and Well-Being). Rural communities tend to have higher unemployment rates and lower incomes than metropolitan centers. Rural areas also tend to be less economically resilient, as they often depend heavily on one major industry, or economic base, or often even one single factory or other employer (Federal Reserve Bank of Atlanta 2012) – and many of those factories and other sources of employment are disappearing from small, rural communities. Large numbers of rural counties in nearly every state of the US have lost population over the past decade (US Department of Agriculture, Economic Research Service: Population and Migration). Long distances combined with a lack of public transportation in rural locations present a number of employment challenges: commuting to work, but also access to job training and awareness of job opportunities (Partridge & Rickman 2006). Rural households are less likely to have broadband connections: "In today's economy, broadband access has become a necessary utility, much like electricity or running water" (Federal Reserve Bank of Atlanta 2012: 11).

PROFESSOR'S PODIUM: WHAT IS RURAL?

By "rural" in this book, I am referring to communities that are distant from major urban centers – in contrast to the "exurbs," or communities in a rural setting from which residents can commute in to work or have access to services in a major city. There are a wide range of different meanings and definitions of the term "rural." The US Census Bureau (US Census Bureau: Geography) and Flora, Flora, and Gasteyer (2015) provide some examples of standard definitions. For statistical purposes, US communities are often divided simply between metropolitan and non-metropolitan (US Department of Agriculture, Economic Research Service: Rural Poverty and Well-Being). Informally, my colleague Judson Edwards succinctly defines "rural" in terms of sewerage: if you flush your toilet and it goes into a cesspit (or less), then you know you're rural; if it flows through a pipe to a central treatment facility, you're urban.

Schaeffer, Loveridge and Weiler (2014: 4) argue in a special issue of *Economic Development Quarterly* that rural and urban communities are becoming less opposite in economic character over time: "First, urban and rural places and economies are no longer opposites but have become more similar and are two interlinked parts of the regional and national economy. Second, even in rural regions, agriculture provides a comparatively small number of jobs. On average, manufacturing...and particularly services are the most important sources of employment."

Despite some improvements in rural poverty rates through the 2000s, rural poverty persists at significantly higher rates than the US as a whole: 18.1 percent in rural areas vs. 14.1 percent in metropolitan areas according to 2014 data, and this holds true across every major region of the country (US Department of Agriculture, Economic Research Service: Rural Poverty and Well-Being). The childhood poverty rate in rural areas is 25.2 percent, and 7.7 percent of rural residents live in deep poverty – both measures, again, significantly higher than those for metropolitan populations. Duncan (2014) and Brown and Cromartie (2006) testify to not just the quantity of poverty that remains in rural areas of the US, but also to the intensity and concentration of that poverty (Lichter et al. 2008 and Lichter & Johnson 2007, cited by Harvey 2013; see also Galster 2005 and responses).

Urban communities

Urban poverty in the US grew increasingly concentrated from the 1960s through the 1980s within low-income, central city neighborhoods of metropolitan cities, including greater percentages of the urban poor population living in neighborhoods classified as "high-poverty" and "extreme-poverty" (Blumenberg 2006). Galster (2005) reviews the research literature regarding the potential impacts of concentrated poverty (more in Chapter 2). Concentrated crime, as just one example, including high homicide rates, is closely correlated with concentrated inner-city poverty (Sharkey 2013).

The economic growth years of the 1990s resulted in a decrease in inner-city poverty concentration, across the US and across ethnic groups, especially among African Americans (Bates 2010; Blumenberg 2006). Urban population growth during this period tended to move away from inner cities and toward the outer edges of cities, including into adjacent metropolitan inner-ring suburbs (Blumenberg 2006; Lee & Leigh 2005).

The 1990s economic boom typically enhanced the economies of central business districts, but generally did not extend those benefits to low-income inner-city neighborhoods (Hartley, Kaza, & Lester 2016), particularly those with minority populations (Stoll 2006). Overall inner-city employment increased by only 0.8 percent between 1995 and 2001. A 2005 study showed that residents of inner cities held only 22 percent of those jobs that did exist in the central city, primarily in low-wage positions; in-commuters held the other 78 percent of the jobs in the inner city, including a disproportionately high share of the higher-pay jobs (Bates 2010, citing Initiative for a Competitive Inner City 2005). There has been considerable discussion in the social sciences for many years regarding whether inner-city residents are excluded from inner-city jobs – either intentionally or through biases or lack of adequate networks (Reingold 1999, and responses in that issue). Kaplan and Mossberger (2012) explore the relationships among concentrated urban poverty, technological knowledge and access, and opportunities for higher-wage employment that requires technology competencies.

"Deindustrialization" refers to the massive loss of manufacturing industries – especially from the 1960s through the 1980s – from the traditional big industrial centers of the northern "rust belt" (Cochrane et al. 2014; Sharkey 2013): industries that had provided generations of urban residents with relatively low education levels with employment opportunities, and the opportunity to move to a solid middle-class lifestyle. Detroit provides just one of the most dramatic and high-profile case studies of deindustrialization and its consequences. Other former industrial powerhouse cities such as Cleveland, Pittsburgh, and Buffalo also lost not only major employers but population over this period (Singer, Hardwick, & Brettell 2008). Many of those industries relocated to smaller cities or suburbs of the South: locations that offered lower wages and non-union shops. Much of this relocation was made possible by federal and state government investments in highways and other forms of infrastructure (Sharkey 2013; Singer, Hardwick, & Brettell 2008).

Suburbia

Traditionally, suburbia represented an outpost of White flight and relative prosperity, encouraged by government subsidies for transportation infrastructure. Suburbs were largely able to cherry-pick the most desirable and tax-base-enhancing land uses, leaving many of the challenging urban issues for the central cities (Orfield 2002). Increasingly, however, especially since the 1990s, minority groups, immigrants, and low-income populations have been drawn to the suburbs by a number of factors including more affordable housing opportunities, better-funded schools, and jobs that were increasingly moving to suburban locations. Major shopping destinations, along with retail employment opportunities, shifted from metropolitan downtowns to malls and big box retail outlets along the main suburban transportation corridors (Singer, Hardwick, & Brettell 2008).

Suburban low-income populations have been growing at more than twice the rate of central city low-income populations since the 1990s. Suburbs now contain the country's largest population of the poor: one-third of all American poor and rising (Kneebone & Berube 2013): "The Great Recession exacerbated this trend, so that between 2000 and 2010 the poor population grew by an astounding 53 percent in suburbs, compared with 23 percent in cities" (Kneebone & Berube 2013: 35). No longer limited to the inner-ring suburbs, poor populations increasingly now extend out to the metropolitan exurbs, or fringes. Within suburbs, poverty was originally more dispersed than in cities, but is becoming increasingly concentrated: "By the end of the 2000s more than one-third of the suburban poor population lived in neighborhoods with poverty rates of 20 percent or higher" (Kneebone & Berube 2013: 35). The suburban poor tend to be more White than the general population of the poor, although this is a changing trend (Kneebone & Berube 2013). Inner-city Black populations were displaced in several ways to the suburbs (Chapter 2). Large numbers of Latinos and other immigrants, also, have settled in suburban locations that were once almost homogeneously White.

Straus (2013) draws a detailed case study of Compton, California, a Los Angeles suburb characterized by conflicts between growing Black and later-arriving Latino populations, emphasizing struggles for control over local public education. Ehrenhalt (2012) cites the dramatic demographic transformation of Atlanta's suburban Gwinnett County from the 1990s from its original predominantly White population. Some Gwinnett County elementary schools today are nearly 100 percent Latino and Black, with much of the Black population comprising African immigrants. The Latino population of Gwinnett County rose from 2.3 percent in 1990 to 16.2 percent in 2005, with comparable increases in neighboring Cobb and Fulton counties (Odem 2008). Gwinnett County promotes its growing Asian population as a factor in recruiting new industries from Asian countries. Li (1998, cited by Singer, Hardwick, & Brettell 2008) coins the term "ethnoburb" to describe suburban communities dominated by particular immigrant groups.

Almost twice as many immigrants today are located in suburbs as in the central cities (Ehrenhalt 2012, citing Singer, Hardwick, & Brettell 2008). In many cases, immigrants are moving directly to suburbs from abroad, instead of taking the more traditional route through central cities (Kneebone & Berube 2013; Singer, Hardwick, & Brettell 2008). As of 2009, 20 percent of the US suburban poor were foreign-born immigrants (Suro, Wilson, & Singer 2011; Odem 2008). Some suburban immigrants struggle for employment, as they face significant language and education barriers; others are highly educated and move into professional positions and achieve entrepreneurial success.

Many of the consequences and challenges of suburban poverty, as a relatively new mass phenomenon in the US, are yet to be fully understood. In many cases, minority groups, immigrants, and low-income populations have left behind their traditional central-city bases of political power, nonprofit organizations, and public-sector support services (Joassart-Marcelli & Martin 2015; Ehrenhalt 2012), and have yet to establish comparable structures in suburban communities.

Who are our low-income populations?

While poverty afflicts every ethnic and social group in the US, some are struck harder and more persistently than others. Black households in the US, for example, consistently suffer from significantly higher rates of unemployment and much lower rates of income and wealth accumulation (Mishel et al. 2012). As of 2014, the Black unemployment rate was 10.4 percent compared with 4.5 percent for Whites (Pew Research Center 2016: On Views of Race and Inequality).

Although overall household income level trends for both Blacks and Whites rose significantly since the 1960s, the income gap grew between the two populations. According to 2014 Census data, the median household income for White families was $71,300, and the median household income for Black families was $43,300. As of 2013, "the median net worth of households headed by whites was roughly 13 times that of black households ($144,200 for whites compared with $11,200 for blacks)" (Pew Research Center 2016: On Views of Race and Inequality).

Blacks and Black men in particular tend to suffer from biases in hiring, often being perceived as more likely to have criminal tendencies. This bias is especially prevalent for small businesses that lack the information resources of larger firms (Stoll 2006; Holzer, Raphael, & Stoll 2002). According to the Pew Research Center (2016: On Views of Race and Inequality: 18), "racial differences in family structure have persisted as well. While marriage rates are falling among all racial groups, the decline has been most dramatic among blacks. Non-marital births are more than twice as common among black mothers as white mothers, and black children are almost three times as likely as white children to be living with a single parent."

Latino – especially Mexican – populations tend to have the lowest skill levels of any major population group, leaving them out of job markets that increasingly require computer and other advanced skills (Stoll 2006, citing Grogger and Trejo 2002). This is exacerbated by the "digital divide," in which White and Asian populations are much more likely to have computers and Internet access at home than Black or Latino populations (Stoll 2006). Partly as a result of this divide, Latino workers tend to be concentrated in construction, basic services, and retail (Singer, Hardwick, & Brettell 2008).

The Latino population in the US, taken as a whole, has passed the US Black population to become the country's largest minority group. As of 2015, 17.6 per-cent of the US population was "Hispanic or Latino" for a total of over 56 million people (US Census Bureau: QuickFacts). "Black or African American" constitutes

13.3 percent of the population, or approximately 43 million people. "Asian" constitutes 5.6 percent of the population or 18 million people, and "American Indian and Alaska Native" constitutes 1.2 percent or close to 4 million people. "Native Hawaiian and Other Pacific Islander" makes up 0.2 percent of the US population, or approximately 650 thousand people (US Census Bureau: QuickFacts).

Grogger and Trejo (2002: xi) emphasize that "Mexican immigrants and U.S.-born Mexican Americans are distinct groups with very different skills and labor market opportunities." Grogger and Trejo's (2002) research shows large increases in both education and earnings between first- and second-generation Mexican Americans, and a similar pattern would be expected for immigrants from Central America.

PROFESSOR'S PODIUM: LATINOS AND NATIVE AMERICANS

In this book, I will generally use the term "Latino" rather than "Hispanic" to denote the US population of Latin American heritage. The two terms are similar and are often used interchangeably. Technically, though, the term "Hispanic" includes only Spanish language speakers, excluding Americans whose heritage is from Brazil or several other non-Spanish-speaking countries of Latin America.

There are many terms for Native American (the term I use in this book) populations in the US and other countries, including "American Indian" and "Indigenous." Canada commonly uses the term "First Nations." "Inuit" is the modern, correct term for the native "Eskimo" population of Alaska and arctic Canada.

Overall, Latinos are only slightly less poor than the US Black population: 24 percent of Hispanics were living in poverty as of 2014, compared with 26 percent of Blacks and 10 percent of Whites (Pew Research Center 2016: On Views of Race and Inequality). In terms of unemployment, the Latino rate in 2014 was much lower than that of Blacks, but 7.2 percent compared with 4.5 percent for Whites. On the other hand, Latinos rank lower than both Blacks and Whites in terms of pension and healthcare coverage (Mishel et al. 2012). Like all population groups in the US, Latinos live in rural areas but they are predominantly located in urban communities – and increasingly in suburbs, as mentioned earlier.

Irazábal and Farhat (2008) review our understanding of Latino settlement patterns in the US. Among the poorest Latino settlements can be found along the US–Mexico border, especially in Texas: "extremely isolated and impoverished predominantly Mexican-American and Mexican immigrant communities…known as colonias. These communities are unincorporated rural areas located outside of the official boundaries of cities and often are without electricity, paved roads, sewer systems, potable water, and access to quality education or health services" (Becerra 2015: 467).

The term "Asian" can encompass a wide range of populations, including Chinese, Korean, Vietnamese, Filipino, and Indian. The US Asian population also includes groups with wide ranges of education and income levels. Taken as a whole, Asians in 2014 had the lowest unemployment rates of any major population group (3.6 percent, compared with 4.5 percent for Whites), and were only slightly more likely to live in poverty (12 percent, compared with 10 percent for Whites) (Pew Research Center 2016: On Views of Race and Inequality). Many Asian immigrants – but certainly not all – arrive with high levels of education and high-tech skills (Singer, Hardwick, & Brettell 2008).

Immigration rose dramatically during the 1990s and shifted from White, European immigrants to those mainly from Latin America and the Caribbean (approximately 37 percent of total immigrants) and Asia (approximately 31 percent of the total) with smaller numbers from Africa and the Middle East (Blumenberg 2006). As much as 70 percent of immigrants are concentrated in six "gateway states": California, Florida, Illinois, New Jersey, New York, and Texas. Increasingly, however, immigrants are diffusing into non-traditional states such as those in the US Southeast. Singer, Hardwick, and Brettell (2008) term Atlanta an "emerging gateway city" for immigrants, along with cities such as Dallas-Fort Worth, Washington, DC, and Charlotte: cities which have experienced dramatic immigration transformations within the past 25 years. Despite large numbers of immigrants serving agriculture and other rural industries, 95 percent of immigrants in the US live in metropolitan regions – increasingly in the suburbs.

Immigrants face an especially precarious and vulnerable situation with regard to their employment status: "Workplace and community raids and deportations have a devastating impact on Mexican immigrant families in the United States....These raids and the resulting deportation of hundreds of thousands of immigrants have produced fear among undocumented immigrants and their children, which can have lasting negative effects on the psychological well-being of children" (Becerra 2015: 469).

Despite blustery political rhetoric, there is extensive research indicating that immigrants to the US make net-positive economic and fiscal contributions to most of the communities in which they reside and work (Becerra et al. 2012). In contrast to perceived stereotypes of native-born minorities, immigrants can benefit from being stereotyped as having a strong work ethic (Stoll 2006; Holzer, Raphael, & Stoll 2002). To date, largely because of their vulnerable position and diversity of languages and cultures (Ehrenhart 2012), few immigrant groups have been able to organize politically in an effective way. However, "[s]ome consider the emergence of the new ethnic groups as key political players to be merely a matter of time. In most immigrant communities in America, it is the second generation that begins to take politics seriously" (Odem 2008).

Native Americans

While Native American communities share many or most of the characteristics of other low-income communities, they are also distinct in many ways. They also reflect a large diversity among the different tribal groups and their locations:

"While some reservation lands are located in urban, even metropolitan locations, many are located in extremely remote rural locations....There are over 560 federally recognized tribes in the United States, with populations ranging from a few hundred to nearly two hundred thousand" (Dewees & Sarkozy-Banoczy 2013: 15). Reservations include the Navajo Nation's 16 million acres as well as tribal lands that are smaller than 1,000 acres; many tribes have no recognized claim to land (Friends Committee on National Legislation 2015). Reservations have a distinct political status, unlike other low-income communities; they are considered distinctive "nations" within the US: this gives reservations rights to establish independent systems of laws, regulations, and tax structures, as well as certain enterprises, such as gambling (Chapter 6.) Because of their distinctive political status, Native American tribes have many unusual opportunities – and face many special challenges – when it comes to utilizing the natural resources found on their reservations (Hibbard, Lane, & Rasmussen 2008).

According to Census Bureau data, "Native Americans have a higher poverty and unemployment rate when compared with the national average, but the rates are comparable to those of blacks and Hispanics. About one-in-four American Indians and Alaska Natives were living in poverty in 2012....The poverty rate at Standing Rock Reservation...which straddles North Dakota and South Dakota...is 43.2%, nearly triple the national average" (Pew Research Center 2014; see also Jojola & Ong 2006).

Tribes are often deeply underserved in terms of police protection, healthcare, education, and other basic services. Tribal colleges have very low graduation rates and difficulty placing graduates in successful, local careers (Butrymowicz 2014). The Native American youth suicide rate is two-and-a-half times the national average: "Many tribes [today] are working to heighten young Native Americans' sense of purpose, cultural understanding, and community belonging" (Friends Committee on National Legislation).

Cornell and Kalt (1993) draft a long list of obstacles to development in Native American communities, which include lack of access to financial investment capital; lack of education, technical and entrepreneurial skills, management experience (Cameron 1993), and other forms of human capital; "too much planning and not enough action"; lack of control over reservations' natural resources (Hibbard, Lane, & Rasmussen 2008); corruption at the federal and local levels; "non-Indian outsiders control or confound tribal decision making"; "unworkable and/or externally imposed systems of government"; racism and its detrimental impact on self-confidence; alcoholism and drug abuse; and internal factionalism. Native American communities may also have complex values and objectives with regard to planning for ED, which may include the preservation of traditional culture, sovereignty, and natural resources (Cornell & Kalt 1993).

The North American Inuit population of Alaska and northern Canada is generally considered to be distinct from other Native American populations. While the Inuit have problems of poverty and social ills similar to those of other Native Americans, they also face their own distinctive subsets of challenges and opportunities because of their extreme environment and the isolation of their traditional settlements. Some Alaskan Inuit villages are addressing rebuilding needs and even relocation due to the accelerating impacts of climate change (Barth 2016). Canada also recognizes the Métis population as a separate, distinctive group: they are historically descended from a "mix" of First Nations and French or British settlers (Andersen 2014). The creation of the enormous Nunavut Territory in 1999 on behalf of the Inuit population – driven by the Canadian Inuit themselves – is an extraordinary, ongoing political experiment (Dahl, Hicks, & Jull 2000; Duffy 1988). Nunavut has provided the Inuit with extensive control over their own governance, land use, and natural resources (Miller & Rowe 2013).

Native Hawaiians and other Pacific Island populations are often overlooked as disadvantaged groups of the US. Along with other minority groups of the US, they also have long histories of mistreatment and of losing their traditional lands and resources (Vowell 2012). Some Native Hawaiian groups continue to advocate for independence from the US and for the restoration of the Hawaiian Constitutional Monarchy (Hawaiian Kingdom).

I certainly don't want to end this chapter with a sense of despair, despite the many daunting difficulties facing disadvantaged minority and other low-income populations in the US. Part II of this book addresses the many opportunities for progress and ED for potentially all low-income communities in the US. In the case of Native American, Inuit, and Pacific Island populations, for example, their traditional lands offer some of the country's greatest natural resource assets. Chapters 5 and 7 discuss the potential for sustainably developing natural assets. Natural resources can include not just trees to be harvested or minerals to be mined, but also assets that can contribute to tourism development. The Inuit are finding new opportunities for mining and mineral exploitation as a result of climate change (Miller & Rowe 2013) as well as growing interest in arctic tourism as ED (Cohen, Hannah, & Miller 2008; Snyder & Stonehouse 2007).

References

Accordino, John. 1998. The consequences of welfare reform for central city economies. *Journal of the American Planning Association* 64(1): 11–15.

Alexander, John W., & Lay James Gibson. 1979. *Economic Geography*, 2nd ed. Englewood Cliffs, NJ: Prentice-Hall.

Andersen, Chris. 2014. *Métis: Race, Recognition, and the Struggle for Indigenous Peoplehood*. Vancouver: University of British Columbia Press.

Badger, Emily, & Christopher Ingraham. 2016. The middle class is shrinking just about everywhere in America. *Washington Post*. May 11: https://www.washingtonpost.com/news/wonk/wp/2016/05/11/the-middle-class-is-shrinking-just-about-everywhere-in-america/.

Barnow, Burt S., & Richard A. Hobbie, eds. 2013. *The American Recovery and Reinvestment Act: The Role of Workforce Programs*. Kalamazoo, MI: W.E. Upjohn Institute for Employment Research.

Barth, Brian. 2016. Before it's too late. *Planning* 82(8): 14–21.

Bates, Timothy. 2010. Alleviating the financial capital barriers impeding business development in inner cities. *Journal of the American Planning Association* 76(3): 349–362.

Beatley, Timothy, & Kristy Manning. 1997. *The Ecology of Place: Planning for Environment, Economy, and Community*, 2nd ed. Washington, DC: Island.

Beaulieu, Lionel J., & Alice Diebel. 2016. Bringing hope: Preface to the turning the tide on poverty special issue. *Community Development* 47(3): 285–286.

Becerra, David. 2015. The effects of neoliberal capitalism on immigration and poverty among Mexican immigrants in the United States, in Stephen N. Haymes, Maria V. de Haymes, & Reuben J. Miller, eds., *The Routledge Handbook of Poverty in the United States*, 463–471. New York: Routledge.

Becerra, David, David K. Androff, Cecilia Ayon, & Jason T. Castillo. 2012. Fear vs. facts: The economic impact of undocumented immigrants in the U.S. *Journal of Sociology and Social Welfare* 39(4): 111–134.

Bishaw, Alemayehu. 2011. Areas with concentrated poverty 2006–2011. U.S. Census Bureau. Retrieved March 24, 2016: http://www.census.gov/prod/2011pubs/acsbr10-17.pdf.

Blumenberg, Evelyn. 2006. Metropolitan dispersion and diversity: Implications for community economic development, in Paul Ong & Anastasia Loukaitou-Sideris, eds., *Jobs and Economic Development in Minority Communities*, 13–38. Philadelphia: Temple University Press.

Blumenberg, Evelyn. 2002. On the way to work: Welfare participants and barriers to employment. *Economic Development Quarterly* 16(4): 314–325.

Boo, Katherine. 2012. *Behind the Beautiful Forevers: Life, Death, and Hope in a Mumbai Undercity*. New York: Random House.

Braman, Donald. 2014. Race, poverty and incarceration, in Chester Hartman, ed., *America's Growing Inequality: The Impact of Poverty and Race*, 399–405. New York: Lexington.

Bridger, Jeffrey C., A.E. Luloff, Louis A. Ploch, & Jennifer Steele. 2001. A fifty-year overview of persistence and change in an old order Amish community. *Community Development* 32(1): 65–87.

Brown, David. 2011. Life expectancy in the U.S. varies widely by region, in some places is decreasing. *Washington Post*. June 15: http://www.washingtonpost.com/national/life-exp ectancy-in-the-us-varies-widely-by-region-and-in-some-places-is-decreasing/2011/06/ 13/AGdHuZVH_story.html.

Brown, Robert, & John Cromartie. 2006. Black homeplace migration to the Yazoo-Mississippi Delta: Ambiguous journeys, uncertain outcomes. *Southeastern Geographer* 46(2): 189–214.

Butrymowicz, Sarah. 2014. The failure of tribal schools. *The Atlantic*. November 26. Retrieved July 18, 2016: http://www.theatlantic.com/education/archive/2014/11/the-fa ilure-of-tribal-schools/383211/.

Cahn, Edgar S., Keri A. Nash, & Cynthia Robbins. 2014. A strategy for dismantling structural racism in the juvenile justice system, in Chester Hartman, ed., *America's Growing Inequality: The Impact of Poverty and Race*, 406–414. New York: Lexington.

Cameron, Michael W. 1993. A prototypical economic development corporation for American Indian tribes, in Stephen Cornell & Joseph P. Kalt, eds., *What Can Tribes Do? Strategies and Institutions in American Indian Economic Development*, 63–90. Los Angeles: American Indian Studies Center.

Camp, Jessica K., & Eileen Trzcinski. 2015. The rise of incarceration among the poor with mental illnesses, in Stephen N. Haymes, Maria V. de Haymes, & Reuben J. Miller, eds., *The Routledge Handbook of Poverty in the United States*, 357–366. New York: Routledge.

Caputo, Richard K. 2015. The Personal Responsibility and Work Opportunity Reconciliation Act of 1996 (PRWORA), in Stephen N. Haymes, Maria V. de Haymes, & Reuben J. Miller, eds., *The Routledge Handbook of Poverty in the United States*, 249–258. New York: Routledge.

Center for Responsible Lending. Retrieved June 28, 2016: http://www.responsiblelending.org/.

Chen, Victor, & Katherine S. Newman. 2014. The missing class: The near poor, in Chester Hartman, ed., *America's Growing Inequality: The Impact of Poverty and Race*, 90–97. New York: Lexington.

Cochrane, Steven, Sophia Koropeckyj, Aaron Smith, & Sean Ellis. 2014. Central cities and metropolitan areas: Manufacturing and nonmanufacturing employment as drivers of growth, in Susan M. Wachter & Kimberly A. Zeuli, eds., *Revitalizing America's Cities*, 65–80. Philadelphia: University of Pennsylvania Press.

Cohen, Janel, Steven Hannah, & Mark Miller. 2008. Exploring Nunavut: Extreme tourism and development. *Applied Research in Economic Development* 5(4): 32–36.

Cornell, Stephen, & Joseph P. Kalt, eds. 1993. *What Can Tribes Do? Strategies and Institutions in American Indian Economic Development*. Los Angeles: American Indian Studies Center.

Culhane, Dennis P., & Stephen Metraux. 2008. Rearranging the deck chairs or reallocating the lifeboats? Homelessness assistance and its alternatives. *Journal of the American Planning Association* 74(1): 111–121.

Dadush, Uri, Kemal Dervis, Sarah P. Milsom, & Bennett Stancil. 2012. *Inequality in America: Facts, Trends, and International Perspectives*. Washington, DC: Brookings Institution.

Dahl, Jens, Jack Hicks, & Peter Jull. 2000. *Nunavut: Inuit Regain Control of their Lands and their Lives*. Copenhagen: International Work Group for Indigenous Affairs.

Dewees, Sarah, & Stewart Sarkozy-Banoczy. 2013. Investing in the double bottom line: Growing financial institutions in native communities, in Gary P. Green & Ann Goetting, eds., *Mobilizing Communities: Asset Building as a Community Development Strategy*, 14–47. Philadelphia: Temple University Press.

Duckworth, Angela. 2016. *Grit: The Power of Passion and Perseverance*. New York: Scribner.

Duffy, R. Quinn. 1988. *The Road to Nunavut: The Progress of the Eastern Arctic Inuit since the Second World War*. Montreal: McGill-Queen's University Press.

Duncan, Cynthia M. 2014. *Worlds Apart: Poverty and Politics in Rural America*. New Haven: Yale University Press.

Edin, Kathryn, & H. Luke Shaefer. 2015. *$2.00 a Day: Living on almost Nothing in America*. Boston: Houghton Mifflin Harcourt.

Ehrenhalt, Alan. 2012. *The Great Inversion and the Future of the American City*. New York: Alfred A. Knopf.

Engle, Kathleen C., & Patricia A. McCoy. 2007. Predatory lending and community development at loggerheads, in Julia S. Rubin, ed., *Financing Low-Income Communities: Models, Obstacles, and Future Directions*, 227–262. New York: Russell Sage Foundation.

Evans, Walker, & James Agee. 2011 [1941]. *Let Us Now Praise Famous Men: The American Classic, in Words and Photographs, of Three Tenant Families in the Deep South*. Boston: Mariner.

Federal Reserve Bank of Atlanta. 2012. Wanted: Jobs 2.0 in the rural southeast. *EconSouth* 14(3): 6–11.

Fessler, Pam. 2016. Researchers find surprising results after testing a new way to measure poverty. *National Public Radio*. May 19: http://www.npr.org/2016/05/19/478643417/researchers-find-surprising-results-after-testing-a-new-way-to-measure-poverty.

Flora, Cornelia B., Jan L. Flora, & Stephen Gasteyer. 2015. *Rural Communities: Legacy and Change*, 5th ed. Boulder, CO: Westview.

Friends Committee on National Legislation. 2015. Native American advocacy: A faith voice. *Washington Newsletter*. November: 1–5.

Galster, George C. 2005. Consequences from the redistribution of urban poverty during the 1990s: A cautionary tale. *Economic Development Quarterly* 19(2): 119–125.

Gaskin, Ina Mae. 2002. *Spiritual Midwifery*, 4th ed. Summertown, TN: The Book Publishing Company.

Gaskin, Stephen. 1974. *Hey Beatnik: This Is the Farm Book.* Summertown, TN: The Book Publishing Company.

Gibson, Lay, & Marshall Worden. 1981. Estimating the economic base multiplier: A test of alternative procedures. *Economic Geography* 57(2): 146–159.

Grogger, Jeff, & Stephen J. Trejo. 2002. *Falling Behind or Moving Up: The Intergenerational Progress of Mexican Americans.* San Francisco: Public Policy Institute of California.

Hartley, Daniel A., Nikhil Kaza, & T. William Lester. 2016. Are America's inner cities competitive? Evidence from the 2000s. *Economic Development Quarterly* 30(2): 137–158.

Hartman, Chester, ed. 2014. *America's Growing Inequality: The Impact of Poverty and Race.* Lanham, MD: Lexington.

Harvey, Mark D. 2013. Consensus-based community development, concentrated rural poverty, and local institutional structures: The obstacle of race in the Lower Mississippi Delta. *Community Development* 44(2): 257–273.

Hawaiian Kingdom. Retrieved September 2, 2016: http://www.hawaiiankingdom.org/.

Henricks, Kasey, & Victoria Brockett. 2015. The house always wins: How state lotteries displace American tax burdens by class and race, in Stephen N. Haymes, Maria V. de Haymes, & Reuben J. Miller, eds., *The Routledge Handbook of Poverty in the United States,* 56–74. New York: Routledge.

Herzer, Dierk. 2016. Unions and income inequality: A panel cointegration and causality analysis for the United States. *Economic Development Quarterly* 30(3): 267–274.

Hibbard, Michael, Marcus B. Lane, & Kathleen Rasmussen. 2008. The split personality of planning: Indigenous Peoples and planning for land and resource management. *Journal of Planning Literature* 23(2): 136–151.

Holosko, Michael J., & John R. Barner. 2015. Neoliberal globalization: Social welfare policy and institutions, in Stephen N. Haymes, Maria V. de Haymes, & Reuben J. Miller, eds., *The Routledge Handbook of Poverty in the United States,* 239–248. New York: Routledge.

Holzer, Harry J., Steven Raphael, & Michael E. Stoll. 2002. *Will Employers Hire Ex-Offenders? Employer Preferences, Background Checks, and their Determinants.* Discussion Paper No. 1243–02. Institute for Research on Poverty. Retrieved May 24, 2016: http://irp.wisc.edu/publications/dps/pdfs/dp124302.pdf.

Houston, Douglas, & Paul Ong. 2006. Impacts of the new social policy regime, in Paul Ong & Anastasia Loukaitou-Sideris, eds., *Jobs and Economic Development in Minority Communities,* 40–62. Philadelphia: Temple University Press.

Initiative for a Competitive Inner City. Retrieved June 13, 2016: http://icic.org/.

Initiative for a Competitive Inner City. 2005. *State of the Inner City Economies: Small Businesses in the Inner City.* National Technical Information Service. Retrieved June 14, 2016: https://ntrl.ntis.gov/NTRL/dashboard/searchResults/titleDetail/PB2005106459.xhtml.

Irazábal, Clara, & Ramzi Farhat. 2008. Latino communities in the United States: Place-making in the pre-World War II, postwar, and contemporary city. *Journal of Planning Literature* 22(3): 207–228.

Jeffrey, David, & Amir Pasic. 2015. A better way to measure poverty. *Wall Street Journal.* October 19: http://www.wsj.com/articles/a-better-way-to-measure-poverty-1445209903.

Jencks, Christopher. 2002. Does inequality matter? *Dædalus* 131(1): 49–65.

Jennings, James. 2012. Measuring neighborhood distress: A tool for place-based urban revitalization strategies. *Community Development* 43(4): 464–475.

Joassart-Marcelli, Pascale, & Nina Martin. 2015. Migrant civil society: Shaping community and citizenship in a time of neoliberal reforms, in Stephen N. Haymes, Maria V. de Haymes, & Reuben J. Miller, eds., *The Routledge Handbook of Poverty in the United States,* 547–554. New York: Routledge.

Jojola, Ted, & Paul Ong. 2006. Indian gaming as community economic development, in Paul Ong & Anastasia Loukaitou-Sideris, eds., *Jobs and Economic Development in Minority Communities*, 213–232. Philadelphia: Temple University Press.

Kaplan, David, & Karen Mossberger. 2012. Prospects for poor neighborhoods in the broadband era: Neighborhood-level influences on technology use at work. *Economic Development Quarterly* 26(1): 95–105.

Karger, Howard. 2015. Predatory financial services: The high cost of being poor in America, in Stephen N. Haymes, Maria V. de Haymes, & Reuben J. Miller, eds., *The Routledge Handbook of Poverty in the United States*, 75–82. New York: Routledge.

Kneebone, Elizabeth, & Alan Berube. 2013. *Confronting Suburban Poverty in America*. Washington, DC: Brookings Institution.

Krueger, Alan B. 2015. The great utility of the Great Gatsby Curve. Brookings Institution. May 19: http://www.brookings.edu/blogs/social-mobility-memos/posts/2015/05/19-utility-great-gatsby-curve-krueger.

Lee, Sugie, & Nancey G. Leigh. 2005. The role of inner ring suburbs in metropolitan smart growth strategies. *Journal of Planning Literature* 19(3): 330–346.

Leventhal, Tama, Véronique Dupéré, & Elizabeth A. Shuey. 2015. Children in neighborhoods, in Richard M. Lerner, Marc H. Bornstein, & Tama Leventhal, eds., *Handbook of Child Psychology and Developmental Science, Vol. 4: Ecological Settings and Processes*, 493–533. Hoboken, NJ: Wiley.

Li, Wei. 1998. Anatomy of a new ethnic settlement: Chinese ethnoburbs in Los Angeles. *Urban Studies* 35(3): 479–501.

Lichter, David T., & Kenneth M. Johnson. 2007. The changing spatial concentration of America's rural poor population. *Rural Sociology* 72(3): 331–358.

Lichter, David T., Domenico Parisi, Michael C. Taquino, & Brian Beaulieu. 2008. Race and the micro-scale spatial concentration of poverty. *Cambridge Journal of Regions, Economy, and Society* 1(1): 51–67.

Lilly Family School of Philanthropy. 2015. Human Needs Index: A timely, multidimensional view of poverty-related need. Prepared for the Salvation Army. Retrieved March 16, 2016: http://humanneedsindex.org/wp-content/uploads/2015/10/Final-Report.pdf.

Longhi, Simonetta, Peter Nijkamp, & Jacques Poot. 2010. Joint impacts of immigration on wages and employment: Review and meta-analysis. *Journal of Geographical Systems* 12(4): 355–387.

Meltzer, Rachel, & Jenny Schuetz. 2012. Bodegas or bagel shops? Neighborhood differences in retail and household services. *Economic Development Quarterly* 26(1): 73–94.

Milken Institute. 2007. Research: Emerging domestic markets. Retrieved June 24, 2014: http://www.milkeninstitute.org/publications/view/307.

Miller, Mark M., & James Rowe. 2013. Nunavut: Potential new model for development? *Australasian Journal of Regional Studies* 19(1): 121–153.

Miller, Reuben J., & Jennifer Miller. Introduction to Part V: Organizing to Resist Neoliberal Policies and Poverty: Activism and Advocacy, in Stephen N. Haymes, Maria V. de Haymes, & Reuben J. Miller, eds., *The Routledge Handbook of Poverty in the United States*, 499–502. New York: Routledge.

Minchin, Timothy J. 2006. "Just like a death": The closing of the International Paper Company mill in Mobile, Alabama, and the deindustrialization of the South, 2000–2005. *Alabama Review* 59(1): 44–77.

Mishel, Lawrence, Josh Bivens, Elise Gould, & Heidi Shierholz. 2012. *The State of Working America*, 12th ed. Ithaca, NY: ILR.

Mueller, Elizabeth J., & Alex Schwartz. 1998. Leaving poverty through work: A review of current development strategies. *Economic Development Quarterly* 12(2): 166–180.

Murray, Christopher J.L., & Majid Ezzati. 2011. Life expectancy in most US counties falls behind world's healthiest nations. Institute for Health Metrics and Evaluation. June 15: http://www.healthdata.org/news-release/life-expectancy-most-us-counties-falls-behind-world's-healthiest-nations.

National Center for Children in Poverty. United States demographics of low-income children. Retrieved March 16, 2016: http://www.nccp.org/profiles/US_profile_6.html.

Newman, Katherine S., & Victor T. Chen. 2007. *The Missing Class: Portraits of the Near Poor in America*. Boston: Beacon.

Odem, Mary E. 2008. Unsettled in the suburbs: Latino immigration and ethnic diversity in Metro Atlanta, in Audrey Singer, Susan W. Hardwick, & Caroline B. Brettell, eds., *Twenty-First Century Gateways: Immigrant Incorporation in Suburban America*, 105–136. Washington, DC: Brookings Institution.

Orfield, Myron. 2002. *American Metropolitics: The New Suburban Reality*. Washington, DC: Brookings Institution.

Orshansky, Mollie. 1965. Counting the poor: Another look at the poverty profile. *Social Security Bulletin* 28(1): 3–29 reprinted in *Social Security Bulletin* 51(10): 25–51. Retrieved March 24, 2016: https://www.ssa.gov/policy/docs/ssb/v51n10/v51n10p25.pdf.

Otero, Gerardo, Gabriela Pechlaner, & Efe C. Gürcan. 2015. The neoliberal diet: Fattening profits and people, in Stephen N. Haymes, Maria V. de Haymes, & Reuben J. Miller, eds., *The Routledge Handbook of Poverty in the United States*, 472–479. New York: Routledge.

Palazzolo, Joe. 2015. For Americans who served time, landing a job proves tricky. *Wall Street Journal*. May 18: http://www.wsj.com/articles/for-americans-who-served-time-landing-a-job-proves-tricky-1431900037.

Partridge, Mark D., & Dan S. Rickman. 2006. *The Geography of American Poverty: Is There a Need for Place-Based Policies?* Kalamazoo, MI: W.E. Upjohn Institute for Employment Research.

Passel, Jeffrey S., D'vera Cohn, & Ana Gonzalez-Barrera. 2012. Net migration from Mexico falls to zero – and perhaps less. Pew Research Center. April 23: http://www.pewhispanic.org/2012/04/23/net-migration-from-mexico-falls-to-zero-and-perhaps-less/.

Peri, Giovanni. 2010. The effect of immigrants on U.S. employment and productivity. *Federal Reserve Board of San Francisco Economic Letter*. August 30: http://www.frbsf.org/economic-research/publications/economic-letter/2010/august/effect-immigrants-us-employment-productivity/.

Pew Research Center. 2016. America's shrinking middle class: A close look at changes within metropolitan areas. May 11. Retrieved July 12, 2016: http://www.pewsocialtrends.org/2016/05/11/americas-shrinking-middle-class-a-close-look-at-changes-within-metropolitan-areas/.

Pew Research Center. 2016. On views of race and inequality, Blacks and Whites are worlds apart. June 27. Retrieved July 12, 2016: http://www.pewsocialtrends.org/2016/06/27/on-views-of-race-and-inequality-blacks-and-whites-are-worlds-apart/.

Pew Research Center. 2014. One-in-four Native Americans and Alaska Natives are living in poverty. June 13. Retrieved July 12, 2016: http://www.pewresearch.org/fact-tank/2014/06/13/1-in-4-native-americans-and-alaska-natives-are-living-in-poverty/.

PolicyLink. Retrieved December 16, 2015: http://www.policylink.org.

Porter, Eduardo. 2014. Income equality: A search for consequences. *New York Times*. March 25: http://www.nytimes.com/2014/03/26/business/economy/making-sense-of-income-inequality.html?_r=0.

Porter, Michael E. 2016. Inner-city economic development: Learnings from 20 years of research and practice. *Economic Development Quarterly* 30(2): 105–116.

Putnam, Robert D., & David E. Campbell. 2016. *Our Kids: The American Dream in Crisis.* New York: Simon and Schuster.

Raphael, Steven. 2014. *The New Scarlet Letter? Negotiating the U.S. Labor Market with a Criminal Record.* Kalamazoo, MI: W.E. Upjohn Institute for Employment Research.

Reingold, David A. 1999. Inner-city firms and the employment problem of the urban poor: Are poor people really excluded from jobs located in their own neighborhoods? *Economic Development Quarterly* 13(4): 291–306.

Roberts, Brandon, Deborah Povich, & Mark Mather. 2012. Low-income working families: The growing economic gap. Working Poor Families Project. Policy Brief. Retrieved March 16, 2016: http://www.workingpoorfamilies.org/wp-content/uploads/2013/01/Winter-2012_2013-WPFP-Data-Brief.pdf.

Root, Kenneth A., & Rosemarie J. Park. 2016. *Surviving Job Loss: Papermakers in Maine and Minnesota.* Kalamazoo, MI: W.E. Upjohn Institute for Employment Research.

Rose, Stephen. 2016. The growing size and incomes of the upper middle class. Urban Institute. June 21. Retrieved March 16, 2016: http://www.urban.org/research/publication/growing-size-and-incomes-upper-middle-class.

Sachs, Jeffrey D. 2015. *The Age of Sustainable Development.* New York: Columbia University Press.

Saenz, Rogelio. 2010. Latinos in America 2010. Population Reference Bureau. December: Retrieved March 16, 2016: http://www.prb.org/pdf10/latinos-update2010.pdf.

Sapolsky, Robert. 2005. Sick of poverty. *Scientific American* 293: 92–99.

Schaeffer, Peter, Scott Loveridge, & Stephan Weiler. 2014. Introduction to special issue: Urban and rural: opposites no more! *Economic Development Quarterly* 28(1): 3–4.

Schmid, John. 2012. Wisconsin's place in paper industry under siege. *Milwaukee Journal Sentinel.* December 8: http://www.jsonline.com/business/paper-industry-digital-china-wisconsin-182612951.html.

Seefeldt, Kristin S. 2008. *Working after Welfare: How Women Balance Jobs and Family in the Wake of Welfare Reform.* Kalamazoo, MI: W.E. Upjohn Institute for Employment Research.

Sentementes, Gus G. 2010. The recession's psychological toll: Layoffs, workplace uncertainty stress workers and companies. *Baltimore Sun.* May 21: http://articles.baltimoresun.com/2010-05-31/business/bs-bz-worker-mental-health-20100530_1_mental-illness-health-benefits-magellan-health-services.

Sharkey, Patrick. 2013. *Stuck in Place: Urban Neighborhoods and the End of Progress toward Racial Equality.* Chicago, IL: University of Chicago Press.

Singer, Audrey, Susan W. Hardwick, & Caroline B. Brettell. 2008. *Twenty-First Century Gateways: Immigrant Incorporation in Suburban America.* Washington, DC: Brookings Institution.

Snyder, John, & Bernard Stonehouse. 2007. *Prospects for Polar Tourism.* Oxfordshire, UK: CAB International.

St. Clair, Travis, Howard Wial, & Hal Wolman. 2012. Chronically distressed metropolitan area economies. Urban Affairs Association Conference. Retrieved March 24, 2016: http://brr.berkeley.edu/wp-content/uploads/2012/06/Chronically-Distressed-Metropolitan-Area-Economies-April-2012-UAA-Conference1.pdf.

Stevenson, Bryan. 2014. *Just Mercy: A Story of Justice and Redemption.* New York: Spiegel & Grau.

Stevenson, Douglas. 2014. *The Farm Then and Now: A Model for Sustainable Living.* Gabriola Island, BC, Canada: New Society.

Stiglitz, Joseph E. 2013. *The Price of Inequality: How Today's Divided Society Endangers Our Future.* New York: W.W. Norton & Company.

Stoll, Michael A. 2006. Workforce development in minority communities, in Paul Ong & Anastasia Loukaitou-Sideris, eds., *Jobs and Economic Development in Minority Communities*, 91–118. Philadelphia: Temple University Press.

Straus, Emily E. 2013. *Death of a Suburban Dream: Race and Schools in Compton, California*. Philadelphia: University of Pennsylvania Press.

Suro, Robert, Jill H. Wilson, & Audrey Singer. 2011. Immigration and poverty in America's suburbs. Brookings Institution. August: http://www.brookings.edu/~/media/research/files/papers/2011/8/04%20immigration%20suro%20wilson%20singer/0804_immigration_suro_wilson_singer.pdf.

Tyler-Mackey, Crystal, Pamela A. Monroe, Patricia H. Dyk, Rachel Welborn, & Sheri L. Worthy. 2016. Turning the tide on poverty: Community climate in economically distressed rural communities. *Community Development* 47(3): 304–321.

United Nations Development Policy & Analysis Division. 2016. *World Economic Situation and Prospects*. Retrieved March 24, 2016: http://www.un.org/en/development/desa/policy/wesp/.

US Census Bureau. Geography: 2010 Census urban area FAQs. Retrieved June 17, 2016: https://www.census.gov/geo/reference/ua/uafaq.html.

US Census Bureau. Poverty definitions. Retrieved March 24, 2016: https://www.census.gov/hhes/www/poverty/methods/definitions.html.

US Census Bureau. QuickFacts. Retrieved June 28, 2016: http://www.census.gov/quickfacts/.

US Department of Agriculture, Economic Research Service. Food Security in the U.S. Retrieved June 29, 2016: http://www.ers.usda.gov/topics/food-nutrition-assistance/food-security-in-the-us/key-statistics-graphics.aspx.

US Department of Agriculture, Economic Research Service. Population and migration. Retrieved July 5, 2016: http://www.ers.usda.gov/topics/rural-economy-population/population-migration.aspx.

US Department of Agriculture, Economic Research Service. Rural poverty and well-being. Retrieved June 29, 2016: http://www.ers.usda.gov/topics/rural-economy-population/rural-poverty-well-being/poverty-overview.aspx.

US Departments of Agriculture, Treasury and Health and Human Services. Food deserts. Retrieved May 6, 2014: http://apps.ams.usda.gov/fooddeserts/foodDeserts.aspx.

US President's Office. 2016. *The Long-Term Decline in Prime-Age Male Labor Force Participation*. June. Retrieved June 29, 2016: https://www.whitehouse.gov/sites/default/files/page/files/20160620_cea_primeage_male_lfp.pdf.

Vowell, Sarah. 2012. *Unfamiliar Fishes*. New York: Riverhead.

Wang, Margaret C., & Edmund W. Gordon, eds. 1994. *Educational Resilience in Inner-City America: Challenges and Prospects*. Hillsdale, NJ: Lawrence Erlbaum.

Watson, William. 2015. *The Inequality Trap: Fighting Capitalism Instead of Poverty*. Toronto: University of Toronto Press.

Webb, Jim. 2006. American workers have a chance to be heard. *Wall Street Journal*. November 15: http://www.wsj.com/articles/SB116355741563823452.

White, Sammis B., & Lori A. Geddes. 2002. The impact of employer characteristics and workforce commitment on earnings of former welfare recipients. *Economic Development Quarterly* 16(4): 326–341.

Wilkinson, Richard, & Kate Pickett. 2009. *The Spirit Level: Why Greater Equality Makes Societies Stronger*. New York: Bloomsbury.

Wilkinson, Will, Lane Kenworthy, John V.C. Nye, & Elizabeth Anderson, eds. 2009. Inequality: Facts and values. *Cato Unbound*. October: http://www.cato-unbound.org/issues/october-2009/inequality-facts-values.

World Bank. 2016. *World Development Report 2016: Digital Dividends*. Retrieved September 26, 2016: http://www.worldbank.org/en/publication/wdr2016.

2

WHY BOTHER? WHO CARES ABOUT THE FUTURE OF LOW-INCOME COMMUNITIES?

Probably the most fundamental division in economic development (ED) falls between bringing "jobs to people" or "people to jobs." That is, are we trying to grow businesses and create employment in the communities where people already live? Or, are we trying to encourage even more businesses and more employment opportunities to grow in places that seem to be the most economically promising? If we emphasize the latter concept – "people to jobs" – then the residents of economically less fortunate communities must either commute or relocate to the more bustling centers of employment opportunity. Other terms used to express the same concepts include "place-based" vs. "people-based" development and "place and prosperity" vs. "people prosperity" (Bolton 1992).

The movement of people in search of job opportunities has been a norm throughout all of US history, with large migrations of people out of low-income typically rural regions toward large urban centers offering greater economic and social opportunities. Typically, this shift moves workers out of agriculture, mining, or forestry-based economic activities back home (primary sector industries: Chapter 1 sidebar) – and into secondary sector industries such as manufacturing or construction in their new location. Increasingly, in the US and many developing countries prospective workers are also being drawn to centers of tertiary sector sales and service activities, such as call centers and a variety of tourism and other service-related businesses.

Some of the greatest examples of migration within the US in post-World War II history include the migration of African Americans from the rural South to northern manufacturing cities such as Chicago and Detroit (Lemann 1992), "Okies" to California (Steinbeck 1939), and mountain folk out of Appalachia headed to Cleveland, Detroit, and other manufacturing belt destinations (Vance 2016; Eller 2008): "In one of the nation's largest internal migrations, over 3 million people left Appalachia between 1940 and 1970, seeking economic refuge in the cities of the Midwest" (Eller 2008: 20). The mechanization of mines dramatically reduced labor needs in Appalachia, like the mechanization of agriculture combined with chemical pesticides and herbicides did in the Mississippi Delta: these were precursors to labor-reducing robotics, computerization, and other labor-reducing technologies that are present in today's economy. Recent decades have seen reverse migrations from Detroit and other declining Rustbelt cities (LeDuff 2013; Granholm & Mulhern 2011; Brown & Cromartie 2006) to new construction, tourism, and other employment opportunities in Sunbelt cities such as Las Vegas (Audi 2009).

The "jobs to people" vs. "people to jobs" debate may also be couched within the larger ED "efficiency" vs. "equity" debate (credited to Okun 1975). The presumption is that it is more efficient to focus development efforts in a place that is "spatially concentrated" (that is, a very big city), rather than distributing those development efforts more widely or equitably across the countryside. This debate raged in international regional planning and development literatures from the 1950s at least through the 1970s (Friedmann & Weaver 1979). Researchers and policymakers who were concerned with the most efficient possible growth of developing countries promoted the "growth pole" model of development, attributed to French economist François Perroux around 1949: a strategy in which citizens in need of jobs would abandon the hinterlands and migrate to emerging great industrialized urban centers such as Mexico City (Friedmann & Weaver 1979). We in the US have mostly observed such large-scale policy experiments in practice from afar in policies designed to concentrate ED investments and populations in locations such as Mexico City in the 1950s (Miller 1988; Gwynne 1985) and Ciudad Guayana, Venezuela, in the 1960s (Peattie 1987). This era was filled with oil-money prosperity for some developing countries and optimism for a brighter future for all.

Meanwhile, here in the US we continue to make sensationalistic ED planning arguments from time to time on large, regional scales. Examples include an infamous proposal to vacate much of the Great Plains (Popper & Popper 1987; Bowden 2012) and suggestions not to repopulate some of New Orleans' hardest Hurricane-Katrina-hit neighborhoods (Sharkey 2013; Rivlin 2006). Neither of those proposals were realized, both having sparked outrage among the residents targeted for relocation and their advocates. Wachter and Zeuli (2014: 24) use the term "shrinking to greatness" to denote similar proposals for distressed areas of Cleveland, Detroit, and Saint Louis. Schilling and Logan (2008) refer to "right sizing" the shrinking cities of the US Rustbelt.

Today, the very popular ED strategies for creating industrial clusters and encouraging creative communities (Chapter 3) both offer implicit returns to geographic efficiency and "people to jobs" arguments. The industrial cluster theory posits that growth in particular industries occurs most strongly in concentrated geographic areas: the high-tech industry in Silicon Valley is an archetypal example of this. Meanwhile, the creative community concept theorizes that modern economic growth occurs where there are strong concentrations of human capital and creative individuals, generally within big cities. For the rest of us – living outside these tight industrial clusters and urban concentrations of vibrant creativity – the economic future seems to depend on whatever may trickle down our way from these powerhouses of economic geography. On a smaller, urban or metropolitan scale, much US urban development policy in recent decades may also be described as "people to jobs" strategies. The perceived failure of many locally based community development initiatives (Lemann 1994) drove planners to take a more regional or metropolitan perspective on solving urban problems.

Meanwhile, academics debated about whether economic geography was relevant at all anymore, as we moved into a brave new world of electronic communication, globalization, and work-from-anywhere employment environments (Blakely 2001). Is the economic geography of the world now "flat" (Friedman 2005) – a level playing-field everywhere across the globe – or still "spiky" (Florida 2005) and filled with advantaged and disadvantaged places as always? Do places still matter?

SIDEBAR: WHAT IS A "COMMUNITY"?

"'Community' is one of those words – like 'culture'… – bandied around in ordinary, everyday speech, apparently readily intelligible to speaker and listener, which, when imported into the discourse of social science, however, causes immense difficulty" (Cohen 1985: 11). According to Hamilton (1985: 7–8), "the concept of community has been one of the most compelling and attractive themes in modern social science, and at the same time one of the most elusive to define." Nasar and Julian (1995: 179) attempt to sort through the multiple meanings of "community" for local planning purposes:

> Individuals can have a psychological sense of community in a variety of contexts. They can have such a sense about a geographically defined territory like their neighborhood, or about an aspatial or extended-space community, for example, their church, job, professional group, or those committed to a certain lifestyle.…Researchers refer to the former experience as a community of place and to the latter as a community of interest.

While members of a community share something in common, at the same time they also share something which "distinguishes them in a significant way from the members of other putative groups. 'Community' thus seems to imply simultaneously both similarity and difference" (Cohen 1985: 12). As Talen (2000: 179) points out in her review of "community" in planning, "focusing on the creation of a sense of community can…breed the worst kind of social exclusion and cultural elitism."

Sociologists and kindred social scientists recognize at least three different meanings of community (Flora, Flora, & Gasteyer 2015). First, "community" can refer to a group of people who share some common identity, interests, trust, or mutual support regardless of whether or not they live in geographic proximity (Mathie & Cunningham 2003): African Americans, Latinos, advocates for environmental causes, members of the LGBTQ community, and so on. We often refer to "community spirit" in this sense of community, which Cohen (1985: 8) describes as "the sense of belonging which…is bigger than the 'family' but yet less impersonal than the bureaucracy or work organization."

Second, "community" can also refer to a more tangible system, organization, or social structure that addresses the needs of such identity groups. We often hear terms such as "breakdown of community" when a group's needs are not being met, or expected community norms are no longer being followed. A phrase like that is often followed by the terms "anymore" or "these days," as in, "folks don't look out for each other anymore," or "kids don't show any respect these days."

A third sense of "community" is the central concern of this book: the sense of community that refers to individuals who live in some sort of geographic proximity. A "community of place," to use Nasar and Julian's (1995) term, can refer to a region, a metropolis, a city, or a neighborhood.

Those three different senses of "community" were not as clearly distinguishable in the past. People generally knew and identified with their immediate neighbors. People referred to "home" in rural towns or urban neighborhoods. Typically, "home" – whether a rural town or urban neighborhood – provided a place where people could reside, but also find employment, establish a business, attend church, and shop for most of their daily needs. Today, with the advent of increased transportation, mobility regarding where people live, suburban or exurban "bedroom communities" for commuters, cultural and economic globalization, communications, and social media, there can be an increasing disconnect between the place where someone lives and the communities with which that person identifies. Some people may strongly identify with a professional or online community, for example, while they have only minimal interaction with the neighbors in their own geographic community.

On the other hand, rising interest in "sustainable development" may help encourage people to think about common concerns with their local geographic community. Sustainable development implies a community in which "the people involved have a common interest in protecting an identifiable, shared environment and quality of life" (Portney 2013: 12, citing US Environmental Protection Agency 1999: 5). Geographers and other observers note tendencies toward more concentrated communities within sprawling metropolitan areas. Garreau (1991) popularized the term "edge city" for such communities, while social scientists employ the more academic term "polycentric city" (Gordon & Richardson 1996).

Society has long been concerned with the perceived loss of sense of community – called "anomie" – at least since the appearance of the work of sociologist Emile Durkheim (2013 [1897]). Worries about social anomie – dangerous "loners," lonesome seniors, or disengaged youth – continue, if they haven't increased, to date (Putnam 2000). A literature review by Talen (2000) discusses the uses of the term "community" in a planning context and the limitations to planners' efforts to build a sense of community, place, or belonging through even the most carefully designed physical environment.

Geographic or place community – again, the central focus of this book – can vary widely in what geographers (like me) call "scale." Scales of geographic communities can range from a collection of neighboring countries such as the European Economic Community (predecessor to the European Union), to a region within a country such as the US Rustbelt or Appalachia, to the shared identity of the citizens of a particular state or a part of a particular state (Mississippi's Delta region), to an extended urban region such as a metropolis, to a particular municipality within a metropolis or a distinct rural town – and ultimately down to the level of a particular part of a city or town (e.g., downtown, "the other side of the tracks"), neighborhood, block, or even an apartment building or trailer park. Dawkins (2003) provides a history and research review of the concepts of "region" and "regional development."

This book is focused primarily on smaller regions: rural towns and municipalities within larger metropolises, right down to the level of neighborhoods. Those are the sorts of regions with which geographers are often concerned: regions that often are ambiguous in terms of clear political definition or statistics, but which have real meaning to local residents. That sense of real meaning is embodied in the extensive literature on "sense of place," "home," historical "rootedness," "place attachment," and psychological "attachment" and "place identity" written by geographers and other social scientists (Manzo & Devine-Wright 2014; McClay & McAllister 2014; Campelo et al. 2013; Dreier, Mollenkopf, & Swanstrom 2013; Manzo & Perkins 2006; Brown, Perkins, & Brown 2003; Eastman & Krannich 1995; Cuba & Hummon 1993; Buttimer 1980; Tuan 1980, 1977; Prenshaw & McKee 1979).

The geographic communities I have in mind for this book are places to which residents assign some real meaning and genuine attachment: places where many parents hope their children will live – or return to – and raise their own children. As such, the book is primarily concerned with increasing job opportunities for existing local residents of low-income communities, rather than gentrification or opening opportunities for newer, younger, or more affluent residents to move into those communities at the exclusion of existing residents.

Especially important for the purpose of this book is the fact that regions at a smaller scale can also potentially offer local residents some promise for determining their own economic destiny. Similar to the book's imprecise definition of "low-income," in Chapter 1, if residents and other interested parties are willing to work together in some manner, then they are close enough to the working definition of "community" to suit the purposes of this book. Some topics to follow in this book may serve to broaden readers' concepts of geographic "community": for example, arguments on behalf of recognizing metropolitan regions as broad and unified ED communities, rather than pitting inner cities against suburbs as competitors.

> Could it be the case that one of the chief things neglected by this pattern of ceaseless movement is precisely the opportunity for people to live dignified and purposeful lives of self-government and civic engagement, the kinds of lives that thinkers since the time of Aristotle have regarded as the highest expression of human flourishing? Is the living of such lives even conceivable in a world without "theres"?
>
> (McClay & McAllister 2014: 7)

Spatial mismatch and transportation inequity

Research, debate, and policy related to the problem of "spatial mismatch" dates at least to the 1960s (Kain 1968, cited by Chapple 2006). Spatial mismatch generally refers to the geographic (and social) distances between residents of central cities who need employment and the employment opportunities that have steadily shifted to the suburbs over recent decades. While central cities have lost many of their own manufacturing, retail, and other business establishments, suburbs experienced growth in modern manufacturing plants along with retail, hospitality, and other modern economic sectors. Jobs that remain in central cities – especially in the downtowns of major metropolises – tend to require higher education and skill levels than many nearby inner-city residents possess (Stoll 2006).

Meiklejohn (2002: 353) ponders why many African American young people in Detroit who are academically qualified for college choose instead to participate in local job training programs. She found that

> many young urban residents feel that areas and institutions in the larger White world outside their neighborhoods are hostile and potentially harmful places that they choose to avoid….With this in mind, it is important to understand that the "spatial mismatch" is not a geographic artifact of long-gone discriminatory practices but a phenomenon that is pervasive and self-reinforcing. Young people who are motivated by lack of adequate information, effective contact networks, and positive experiences in the larger White world will look hard for opportunities on their own turf. If they stay in their neighborhoods and limited occupational niches, they can only bring their friends and relatives to the same places and continue a cycle of avoiding opportunities outside of areas considered safe and familiar.

Many factors contribute to the city–suburb mismatch (Blumenberg 2006). Suburban neighborhoods often lack adequate affordable housing. Ross and Leigh (2000) review the history of exclusionary zoning and its persistence into the present day. In contrast, Schuetz, Meltzer, and Been (2009: 441) study the wide variety and possibilities of "inclusionary zoning" policies nationwide "that either require developers to make a certain percentage of the units within their market rate residential developments available at prices or rents that are affordable to specified income groups, or offer incentives that encourage them to do so."

Contributing to the challenges of bridging the spatial mismatch, many low-income residents lack reliable vehicles, especially those in Black and Latino populations and those with lower education levels (Stoll 2006). Transportation is typically the second biggest expenditure category for families behind shelter, but for low-income families the costs of transportation may exceed those of shelter (Sanchez & Brenman 2007). Mass transit systems and routes are typically designed to transport suburbanites to and from downtown centers during the standard 8 am to 5 pm working day – not the reverse, which would be to transport inner-city residents to and from widely dispersed suburban businesses, especially during after-hours shifts (Sanchez & Brenman 2007). A number of studies find that transportation access is one of the major barriers to employment for low-income populations seeking employment, which was cited both by job-seekers and employers (Sanchez & Brenman 2007). In case studies of Portland and Atlanta, Sanchez (1999) finds that access to public transportation is a significant factor limiting employment for minority residents.

While the welfare reform legislation of the 1990s was intended to move welfare recipients to employment, welfare recipients are also those who most typically have poor access to transportation. According to Sanchez and Brenman (2007, citing the US General Accountability Office 1998), about 75 percent of welfare recipients live in central cities or rural areas, and as few as six percent own motor vehicles (Sanchez & Brenman 2007, citing the US General Accountability Office 1998). Blumenberg and Manville (2004) caution against relying on inadequate public transportation policies and systems to close employment mismatches: as many as 70 percent of typical entry-level jobs are located in the suburbs, and two-thirds of those jobs are located more than a quarter-mile from a public transit stop. A literature review by Fan (2012: 164) suggests that "promoting car ownership among the socioeconomically disadvantaged is relatively more effective than other strategies in addressing the issue of spatial mismatch."

As Sanchez and Brenman 2007 remind us, transportation issues are deeply rooted in the struggles for civil rights, especially for African American communities: Rosa Parks and the Montgomery bus system boycott is just one important example. Racial discrimination has remained part and parcel of metropolitan transportation systems: "Suburban Detroit has long refused to coordinate its bus system with the separate system for the city….[Suburban counties of Atlanta], whose population is approximately 90 percent white, have refused to allow the Metropolitan Atlanta Rapid Transit System (MARTA) to be extended to them" (Ross & Leigh 2000). The term "transportation equity" today represents a variety of continuing efforts to assure fairness in a variety of transportation systems, including an effort to "[d]istribute the benefits and burdens from transportation projects equally across all income levels and communities" (Sanchez & Brenman 2007: 8).

Thompson (1997) finds that mismatch can have a particularly strong impact on women in the workforce, especially minority women, although the extent of the commuting gender gap appears to be changing over time (Crane 2007). MacDonald's (1999: 281) literature review emphasizes how many gender issues are involved in the spatial mismatch problem, commuting, and transportation needs: constraints on women's mobility "include women's generally lower wages, greater domestic responsibilities, and employment choices," while low-income women are more likely to be "sole or primary wage earners, dependent on transit, or ghettoized in particular occupations or labor markets."

Government subsidies of transportation can be strongly biased toward more affluent commuters, for example through high rates of subsidies for highway construction, subway, and commuter rail, which are most heavily used by middle-class workers, compared with bus transportation, which is most heavily used by lower-income workers: "Generally, 80 cents of every dollar spent on federal surface transportation programs is earmarked for highways, and 20 cents is earmarked for public transportation" (Sanchez & Brenman 2007: 49), with a similar pattern for state-level gasoline tax expenditures. Among the consequences of such expenditure biases has been exacerbated residential segregation by race and income level: highways as corridors to middle-class flight to the suburbs. In the process, low-income and minority neighborhoods – lacking political power – are typically most likely to be damaged or displaced due to freeway and other transportation construction projects (Sanchez & Brenman 2007).

The impacts of mismatch on inner-city residents include poor access to information about job opportunities, difficulties in reaching job applications and interviews, and added cost and time required to commute to suburban jobs if they can secure them (Stoll 2006). Mismatch tends to affect the African American populations in particular, affecting Latino populations to a somewhat lesser extent. The impacts are much less severe on White populations, even those with low education levels (Stoll 2006). The monetary costs of transportation for inner-city residents are far from trivial, and long commutes take time and energy away from families and home neighborhoods (Katz & Allen 1999, citing Elliot, Palubinsky & Tierney 1999).

Research on the Los Angeles metropolitan area by Hu (2015) presents a more complex picture of the relationship between residence and employment accessibility for the poor, and a situation in flux over time. In Hu's study, low-income Los Angeles inner-city residents may have better job accessibility today than low-income suburban residents. Other research has suggested that personal connections are more important for finding and securing employment than geographic mobility (Reingold 1999). Businesses that open in low-income urban neighborhoods often do not hire locally, opting instead to hire from outside on the basis of personal connections with existing employees. Local workers may also lack the necessary job skills to suit new local industries.

Transportation is also an essential part of educational opportunity for children and adults in low-income communities seeking higher education or skill training (Sanchez & Brenman 2007). Children from low-income families, especially in major cities, rely heavily on public transportation to travel to school. Access to public transportation becomes even more critical as many cities turn to magnet or charter schools, or school vouchers, to provide greater school choice. Charter and other private schools do not necessarily provide their student body with school bus service. As such, educational choice is often available only to students with, among other things, adequate transportation access.

Sanchez and Brenman (2007) and Hargreaves and Chang (1993) emphasize the exceptional transportation challenges facing Native American populations. Many Native Americans live in very rural and sometimes widely dispersed communities. They are often poorly served by public transportation, and reservation roads are often gravel or dirt. Motor vehicle death rates are much higher among Native Americans than for the general population.

Members of Latino and Asian minority groups who do not have a strong command of English face additional barriers to transportation access, such as not being able to obtain a driver's license or easily navigate public transportation schedules (Sanchez & Brenman 2007). Blumenberg (2004) notes that the commuting needs and patterns of low-income women, especially single mothers, may be very different from those of men and should merit specialized policy attention.

Morgan (2012), Chapple and Goetz (2011), and Sawicki and Moody (2000) review and evaluate alternative proposals for "mobility" programs intended to provide transportation for inner-city residents to greater job opportunities in the suburbs and redress spatial mismatch. Sanchez and Brenman (2007) provide an overview of the various federal acts and initiatives intended to provide for greater equity in transportation. The federal Department of Housing and Urban Development's (HUD) Bridges to Work program is one example of an effort to subsidize commutes between urban residents and suburban opportunities (US Department of Housing and Urban Development; Elliot, Palubinsky, & Tierney 1999).

Dispersal and deconcentration

Still more ambitious than inner-city-to-suburb commuting mobility programs are "people to jobs" strategies to move low-income residents entirely out of their home neighborhoods and "disperse" them into more prosperous neighborhoods of the city or suburbs (Goetz 2003a, 2003b). Demolition of major inner-city housing projects, such as Chicago's notorious Robert Taylor and Cabrini-Green Homes, drove some of the movement of the city's low-income population to suburbia (Ehrenhalt 2012). In other cases, major public works projects – examples include I-10 freeway construction in 1960s New Orleans and the 1996 Olympic Games in central Atlanta – displaced functional inner-city neighborhoods.

Rosenbaum (2009) summarizes four motivations for relocation strategies: better access to active labor markets, better schools for children, safety from crime, and a different environment of "informal social interaction." The need for change in social interaction implies that people are very strongly influenced – both positively and negatively – by the neighbors with whom they associate in their communities. Children, in particular, can be influenced negatively by delinquency in a struggling community, such as in an inner-city neighborhood. Or, they can be influenced in a positive way by manners, speech patterns, study habits, and other characteristics of peers who are likely to achieve success in society – such as might be found in a more affluent suburb. Low-income neighborhoods and communities often have more environmental toxins and other health problems (more on environmental justice in Chapter 8), poorer-quality public services, higher crime rates, and other sources of stress (Cheshire 2012). Extensive research on the impacts of living in a low-income community, termed "neighborhood effects" (Putnam & Campbell 2016; van Ham et al. 2012; Wilson 1987; Gans 1968), generally confirms that those impacts are significant and negative. Conversely, there is some evidence of the significant and positive effects of low-income children moving to higher-income neighborhoods: "In a few studies, in fact, the correlation of a student's high school learning with her classmates' family backgrounds is greater than the correlation with her own family background" (Putnam & Campbell 2016).

Debates on the importance of neighborhood effects continue in the research literature (van Ham et al. 2012): "The fundamental issue in neighbourhood effects research is causation: do poor neighbourhoods make residents poorer, or do poor people simply live in poor neighbourhoods because living in affluent ones costs too much?…The issue is whether living in a poor neighbourhood is a separate, significant additional cause of poverty" (Cheshire 2012: 267–268).

PROFESSOR'S PODIUM: CORRELATION AND CAUSALITY

"[D]o poor neighbourhoods make residents poorer, or do poor people simply live in poor neighbourhoods because living in affluent ones costs too much?" (Cheshire 2012: 267–268). This is an example of the classic "correlation does not equal causality" conundrum in the social sciences. Even if we can find statistical evidence that A is correlated with (related to) B, that does not necessarily mean that A causes B, nor that B causes A. Perhaps both are caused by a third factor C, but don't really influence each other. Quite often in the social sciences, A causes B *and* B causes A in a complex interrelationship.

These sorts of logical challenges are just one important reason why it often difficult to reach clear and simple conclusions from research on complex topics and why social scientists are often not popular among policymakers or the general public. As President Johnson said: "Give me a one-handed economist. All my economists say, 'on the one hand…on the other'." The same may be said for all the two-handed geographers, planners, and other sincere but frustrating (and sometimes frustrated) ED researchers.

The HOPE VI Program of 1993 was an experimental federal program intended to address the concerns of neighborhood effects without relocating residents by redeveloping distressed neighborhoods as mixed-income communities (Fraser & Oakley 2015). Funding for the HOPE VI Program, however, was phased out of the federal budget by 2010. Criticisms included charges that the program often led to gentrification and the forced dislocation of public housing residents instead of redevelopment for the benefit of the original residents – and otherwise placing the interests of the private real estate industry over the needs of low-income residents (Skobba, Oakley, & Farmer 2015). Goetz (2013: 347) passionately critiques the program and its legacy of putting an end to traditional public housing and the sense of community that public housing may have provided residents, citing "regressive policies of displacement, eviction, and social housing retrenchment…the forced displacement of hundreds of thousands of the poorest citizens in America."

Programs to disperse residents from low-income neighborhoods to more prosperous communities have overtaken the momentum from HOPE-VI-type redevelopment programs. In 1966, the American Civil Liberties Union (ACLU) filed a class action lawsuit in the name of Dorothy Gautreaux against the Chicago Housing Authority (CHA) on the basis of racial housing discrimination. The Supreme Court ultimately ruled against the CHA in 1976 and ordered that the City of Chicago enact a relocation program. The resulting Gautreaux Program, from 1976 to 1998, provided vouchers to African Americans living in the central city. Families who received those vouchers were provided with social services to assist them with relocation to more affluent city or suburban communities. The goals that inspired the program included greater access to job opportunities (both in terms of social networks and geographic access to modern business locations), access to better schools, a reduction in the negative social effects of low-income neighborhoods, and an increase in interaction with neighbors who have more positive social skills (van Ham et al. 2012; Goetz 2003a, 2003b; Wilson 1987).

National-scale federal housing voucher programs began with the Housing and Community Development Act of 1974 (Jacob 2015). Building on the Chicago Gautreaux Program, HUD created the Moving to Opportunity Program in the 1990s: an experimental federal program also intended to deconcentrate the urban poor from low-income inner-city neighborhoods (Sharkey 2013; Cheshire 2012; Curley 2010; McClure 2008; Briggs, Popkin, & Goering 2010; Goetz 2003a, 2003b). In many cases, public housing projects that were vacated were then demolished – and were even in some cases required to be demolished by federal regulations (Keating 2000).

Both the Gautreaux and Moving to Opportunity programs distributed vouchers to residents in a randomized manner, so as to make possible the effective evaluation of the projects' impacts. These "moving to opportunity" programs remain relatively new and are dramatic departures from anti-poverty programs of the past. As such, the body of evaluation research is still growing and evolving, in particular regarding longer-term impacts, impacts on the prospects for the second generation of families involved, and potential unintended consequences. Research studies on the results of mixed-income housing programs, in general, are – not surprisingly – complex in their findings. From their review of the research literature, Varady and Walker (2003: 17) conclude: "Research on mixed-income communities has provided little evidence that social mixing has any direct positive impacts through social interaction and/or social networks. However, the lack of research on the long-term

impacts on children, such as future improvements in their employment circumstances due to better educational attainment, makes it impossible to offer con-
clusive assessments on the connection between income mixing and social
mobility."

Other evaluations of the Gautreaux experiment are promising in many regards,
including higher rates of employment and a personal sense of efficacy (that is,
control over their own lives) for adults, together with higher rates of educational
attainment and lower rates of trouble with the law for children (DeLuca &
Rosenbaum 2010; Johnson, Ladd, & Ludwig 2002; Rosenbaum, Reynolds, &
DeLuca 2002; Rosenbaum 1995). Research by Kling, Ludwig, and Katz (2005,
cited by Cheshire 2012) suggests that girls tend to benefit significantly more than
boys from relocation; relocation may even have negative impacts for boys.

Some research suggests that children (especially girls) may benefit from relocation but that overall "moving to a more affluent neighbourhood does not improve
an adult's economic situation" (Cheshire 2012: 282). Rosenblatt and DeLuca
(2012) find that many of the residents who were relocated soon returned to their
original, home, low-income neighborhoods – within a few years – for a variety of
complex reasons. In a case study of the Minneapolis Metro region, Goetz (2004)
indicates that despite a lawsuit-mandated dispersal program that began with the
demolition of public housing, very few low-income families relocated out of their
original low-income neighborhood. Further, Gay (2012) finds that dispersing
minority and other low-income residents from their home neighborhoods may also
have the unintended effect of dispersing and reducing their voting turnout and
political power. Housing vouchers and other relocation programs have helped
contribute to the growth of poverty in the suburbs (Kneebone & Berube 2013;
Chapter 1). Low-income suburban residents may also find themselves dislocated
from social service organizations that are concentrated in urban locations (Kneebone
& Berube 2013).

Government funding opportunities for such large-scale, ambitious, and expensive
strategies, of course, are much reduced today from the comparatively lush days of
the 1990s (Cheshire 2012). Urban poverty deconcentration programs have also
been widely demonized in the popular media as dispersing crime and other social
ills (along with, implicitly, minority populations) into the suburbs. Nevertheless,
these strategies are now well established as a central component of our thought
concerning – and policy approaches towards – fighting poverty.

Gentrification

There are few terms in urban planning more loaded than "gentrification." Social
angst related to gentrification and racially mixed housing is central to two powerful,
interconnected Broadway plays: 1959's *Raisin in the Sun* (Tony Award nominee,
starring Sidney Poitier) and 2010's *Clybourne Park* (Pulitzer Prize and Tony Award
winner). Perez (2004: 139, cited in Brown-Saracino 2010: 12–13) provides a
frequently cited definition of gentrification as:

an economic and social process whereby private capital (real estate firms, developers) and individual homeowners and renters reinvest in fiscally neglected neighborhoods through housing rehabilitation, loft conversions, and the construction of new housing stocks. Unlike urban renewal, gentrification is a gradual process, occurring one building or block at a time, slowly reconfiguring the neighborhood landscape of consumption and residence by displacing poor and working-class residents unable to afford to live in "revitalized" neighborhoods with rising rents, property taxes, and new business catering to an upscale clientele.

Chapple (2015) discusses the potential consequences of gentrification as "displacement," particularly of the original, low- or middle-income resident populations of a gentrifying neighborhood: "Direct displacement occurs when new development results in demolition of older housing units, and indirect displacement is when property values in the area increase due to its new desirability, making it less likely that existing residents stay" (Chapple 2015: 143).

Downtowns in major cities as residential, commercial, and entertainment centers are experiencing redevelopment and revitalization. The target demographic is predominantly young, White professionals, raising concerns in many cases about gentrification and displacement of low-income residents. The gentrification process can also come about as a result of tourism. Gotham (2010) highlights the example of New Orleans' Vieux Carré, or French Quarter, a centuries-old residential and commercial neighborhood.

Ehrenhalt (2012) refers to the "great inversion" of return from suburban flight to the central cities. Part of the reason for this transition is the shift from manufacturing employment to service sector employment that "has permitted so many opportunities for creative reuse" of downtown and other urban buildings (Ehrenhalt 2012: 9). Such an "inversion" of central city prosperity surrounded by suburban poverty would not be unprecedented; that pattern was traditionally typical of many Latin American major cities and to some extent today's Paris.

Markley and Sharma (2016) find evidence of gentrification in suburban communities, as well as in central cities. From a study of suburban Atlanta, the researchers conclude that "in attempts to revitalize disinvested suburban spaces,…[many of these revitalization initiatives] target working-class nonwhite communities located within municipalities predominated by affluent white homeowners, displacing some of the area's most politically and socially marginalized residents" (Markley & Sharma 2016: 57). Hartley, Kaza, and Lester (2016: 139–140) cite research that focuses "on the long-term residential shifts of poor neighborhoods in U.S. metropolitan areas, which suggest that the gentrification or 'back to the city' trend may be limited or is bypassing most high-poverty neighborhoods."

We typically think of gentrification as occurring in an urban neighborhood, but gentrification can also affect a larger community as a whole. The overall character of a rural community can be affected dramatically by exurbanite commuters, tourists, or second homeowners. In many cases, exurban, tourist, or second-home communities can be torn between newcomers who want to retain the town's rustic or natural character, and locals who want more industry, logging, or other forms of ED. San Jose, California, provides an extreme example of gentrification through its transformation by Silicon Valley industry (Brown 2016).

The impacts of gentrification are complex and vary by circumstances. Residents of gentrifying neighborhoods who own homes or other properties can benefit from rising property values, although these benefits may be counteracted by rising property taxes. Low-income renters may face rising housing costs in gentrifying neighborhoods, although they may also benefit from expanding local employment opportunities in construction, retail, food and beverage, and other sectors. Gentrification may also generate improved roads, schools, and other infrastructure (Blumenberg 2006). As noted earlier, there is extensive evidence that schoolchildren can benefit from a more affluent social peer group – whether low-income students move to greater affluence, or affluence moves to low-income neighborhoods.

Atkinson and Bridge (2010: 54) summarize potential positive and negative impacts of gentrification. Among the potential negative impacts are:

- Displacement through rent/price increases
- Secondary psychological costs of displacement
- Community resentment and conflict
- Loss of affordable housing
- Price increases homelessness
- Commercial/industrial displacement
- Increased cost and changes to local services
- Displacement and housing demand pressures on surrounding poor areas.

And according to Atkinson and Bridge (2010: 54), among the potentially positive impacts for the affected local residents, as well as the community as a whole, are:

- Stabilization of declining areas;
- Increased property values [for local owners of homes, businesses, and other properties];
- Reduced vacancy rates
- Increased local fiscal revenues
- Reduction of suburban sprawl
- Increased social mix.

Florida (2010) draws a relationship between gentrification and the highly popular ED concept of the "creative community" (Chapter 3). Hertz (2016) cites several studies suggesting that the urban residents of gentrifying neighborhoods may fare better and be less likely to move than residents of neighborhoods that are not experiencing gentrification. Urban residents are leaving stagnant inner-city neighborhoods "not because of rising rents but because high-poverty neighborhoods don't provide their residents with enough of the necessities of a good life: strong schools, safe streets, access to jobs, and so on" (Hertz 2016: 52). Research by Freeman and Braconi (2004: 51) in New York City indicates

> that rather than speeding up the departure of low-income residents through displacement, neighborhood gentrification…was actually associated with a lower propensity of disadvantaged households to move….The most plausible explanation for this surprising finding is that gentrification brings with it neighborhood improvements that are valued by disadvantaged households, and they consequently make greater efforts to remain in their dwelling units, even if the proportion of their income devoted to rent rises.

Porter (2016: 107) argues: "Instead of trying to stop gentrification, economic development professionals and city leaders should focus instead on managing gentrification, with strategies that ensure maximum benefits to all residents, especially the most vulnerable." Perhaps, as Rypkema (2005: 65, cited by Walker 2009) argues, "the word gentrification has outlived its usefulness. Too many connotations no longer apply. Perhaps 'economic integration' is a better description.…[E]conomic integration is a concept that new and old residents alike can support."

Should we just give up on low-income communities?

Should we even try to save struggling towns and neighborhoods? As suggested earlier, much of the scholarly thought and public sector policy in recent decades has shifted from trying to save the struggling communities themselves and moved in the direction of trying to facilitate the movement of "people to jobs": either by providing greater mobility for inner-city–suburban commuters or outright relocation of inner-city residents to more prosperous neighborhoods or suburbs. Instead of trying to save communities, should we adopt a "survival of the fittest" strategy to weed out the communities we judge to be inefficient locations for ED? Alternatively, is it true that places don't really matter at all anymore as the US becomes a "flat" world of geography-free opportunity for telecommuting from anywhere and to anywhere (Friedman 2005)?

No. Places still matter. For many reasons, for better and for worse, our ED policies will continue to focus overwhelmingly on propping up struggling communities mainly by trying to bring jobs to people. These "place-based" practices continue to be supported by scholars who maintain that geography is still a critical component of ED in a modern world (Florida 2005; Dreier, Mollenkopf, & Swanstrom 2013; Porter 1990).

For many – probably most – residents of struggling low-income communities, the question is far from academic. These residents find themselves tightly place-bound for many compelling reasons. In real life, people – particularly those of limited means – are not necessarily free to get up and move. Low-income people often lack the networks, online search skills, transportation, or financial means that would lead them to locate or secure employment opportunities far from home.

Their home may be their only major asset. Their real property assets are not liquid in a weak economy, especially not in communities that are in economic distress.

Low-income populations face a number of "frictions" that limit their ability to move. In general, individuals who have low levels of education and job skills are less mobile, low-skill workers who are likely to depend on local word-of-mouth or local advertisements for job opportunities, and they are more likely to depend on family or friends for transportation and childcare (Partridge & Rickman 2006).

Further, a wide variety of persistent discriminatory practices – including real estate "red-lining," covenants, and outright intimidation – against low-income populations and especially against minority groups restrict mobility and job opportunities outside their home communities (Sharkey 2013; Partridge & Rickman 2006). The history of racial discrimination by the Federal Housing Administration (FHA) and Veterans Affairs (VA) in home-mortgage-lending is clearly documented, with calculations of the extensive impacts those discriminatory practices had on minority household equity that persist to this day (Sharkey 2013): wealth that could have been used for investment in higher education, housing mobility, and mobility. As a result, Blacks have a much higher tendency to live in low-income neighborhoods generation after generation than Whites: "Two out of three black children who were raised in the poorest quarter of the neighborhoods continue to live in the poorest quarter of neighborhoods as adults, and about half of black families have lived in the poorest quarter of neighborhoods over consecutive generations" (Sharkey 2013: 45). This is a situation that Sharkey refers to as "the inherited ghetto."

At the same time, psychological and social ties to place and home remain as strong as ever, in urban as well as in rural communities, no matter what the income level of the community. Goetz (2013) notes that inner-city residents' genuine attachment to even very low-income places is often left out of the discourse of urban renewal and the demolition of housing projects. The earlier mentioned play *Clybourne Park* wrestles with those deep connections to place, the pain of breaking those connections, and the highly charged racial challenges that may be entangled with those issues.

Residents remain passionate and deeply emotional about their roots in home-towns and local neighborhoods. Alumni attend hometown high school football games, and class reunions can continue even after the schools themselves are long closed down. In Mississippi, many communities still host regular class reunions for schools that were closed or reorganized in the course of desegregation. People may simply find their greatest comfort level and sense of belonging in the community in which they were raised, or a comparable community, regardless of the income or class they may attain (Sharkey 2013). Many people wish for their children and grandchildren to live and be able to prosper nearby in their own hometown.

From an ED perspective, a distinctive sense of place can provide a critical element of "destination branding" for tourism development and a variety of other initiatives (Campelo et al. 2013; Phillips 2002). The extensive literature on social capital reinforces the practical planning and ED-related importance of bonds within local communities, extended families, civic organizations, and churches (Hutchinson &

Vidal 2004; Saegert, Thompson, & Warren 2001; Chapter 5). Church congregations in low-income communities can be very closely connected to particular small geographic locations.

Political power is also largely place-based (Manville 2012; Partridge & Rickman 2006; Sawicki & Moody 2000). City council members, county superintendents, state senators and representatives, and national congressional members are all elected on behalf of particular places, and they answer to constituencies connected to those places.

Prejudicial views toward the poor and minorities can make place-based policies more palatable than relocating poor persons of color into wealthier, Whiter neighborhoods (Manville 2012). It may be difficult to untangle concerns about property values from racial prejudices (Tighe 2010): "Investing in troubled cities, then, could sidestep political landmines associated with racial attitudes, including White suburbanites' fear about the arrival of racial minorities" (Manville 2012: 3103).

Most ED-related professionals, as well, are employed by specific communities or regional organizations, and their performances are evaluated in terms of the economic returns to those particular places. Their job security depends on local ribbon-cuttings and local employment rates. Even those working at the level of state ED agencies must answer to state legislators, mayors, and other constituents representing specific communities (Granholm & Mulhern 2011). Besides, how many of us have the courage to face a town meeting or neighborhood association and say: "Face the facts: if you want a job, you'll just have to leave." Sharkey (2013: 169) argues for "urban policy *and* place-based policy", seeing the two as complementary and not as a matter of "either/or."

For the sake of small and struggling communities all across our country, we will continue plowing ahead on their behalf, whether economically efficient or not, no matter what the odds. The next chapter reviews the many ways we have attempted to do, and continue to do, just that.

References

Atkinson, Rowland, & Gary Bridge. 2010. Globalization and the new urban colonialism, in Japonica Brown-Saracino, ed., *The Gentrification Debates*, 51–61. New York: Routledge.

Audi, Tamara. 2009. As boom times sour in Vegas, upward mobility goes bust. *Wall Street Journal*. July 20, 2009: http://online.wsj.com/article/SB124804383363363397.html.

Blakely, Edward J. 2001. Competitive advantage for the 21st-century city. *Journal of the American Planning Association* 6(2): 133–141.

Blumenberg, Evelyn. 2006. Metropolitan dispersion and diversity: Implications for community economic development, in Paul Ong & Anastasia Loukaitou-Sideris, eds., *Jobs and Economic Development in Minority Communities*, 13–39. Philadelphia: Temple University Press.

Blumenberg, Evelyn. 2004. En-gendering effective planning: Spatial mismatch, low-income women, and transportation policy. *Journal of the American Planning Association* 70(3): 269–281.

Blumenberg, Evelyn, & Michael Manville. 2004. Beyond the spatial mismatch: Welfare recipients and transportation policy. *Journal of Planning Literature* 19(2): 182–205.

Bolton, Roger. 1992. "Place prosperity vs people prosperity" revisited: An old issue with a new angle. *Urban Studies* 29(2): 185–203.

Bowden, Charles, with photographs by Eugene Richards. 2012. North Dakota, the emptied prairie. *National Geographic.* January. Retrieved February 1, 2012: http://ngm.nationa lgeographic.com/2008/01/emptied-north-dakota/bowden-text.html.

Briggs, Xavier de Souza, Susan J. Popkin, & John Goering. 2010. *Moving to Opportunity: The Story of an American Experiment to Fight Ghetto Poverty.* Oxford: Oxford University Press.

Brown, Barbara B., Douglas Perkins, & Graham Brown. 2003. Place attachment in a revitalizing neighborhood: Individual and block levels of analysis. *Journal of Environmental Psychology* 23(3): 259–271.

Brown, Eliot. 2016. Neighbors clash in Silicon Valley. *Wall Street Journal.* June 7: http://www.wsj.com/articles/neighbors-clash-in-silicon-valley-1465291802.

Brown, Robert, & John Cromartie. 2006. Black homeplace migration to the Yazoo-Mississippi Delta: Ambiguous journeys, uncertain outcomes. *Southeastern Geographer* 46(2): 189–214.

Brown-Saracino, Japonica, ed. 2010. *The Gentrification Debates.* New York: Routledge.

Buttimer, Anne. 1980. Home, reach, and the sense of place, in Anne Buttimer & David Seamon, eds., *The Human Experience of Space and Place*, 166–187. New York: St. Martin's.

Campelo, Adriana, Robert Aitken, Maree Thyne, & Juergen Gnoth. 2013. Sense of place: The importance for destination branding. *Journal of Travel Research* 53(2): 154–166.

Chapple, Karen. 2015. *Planning Sustainable Cities and Regions: Towards More Equitable Development.* New York: Routledge.

Chapple, Karen. 2006. Overcoming mismatch: Beyond dispersal, mobility, and development strategies. *Journal of the American Planning Association* 72(3): 322–336.

Chapple, Karen, & Edward G. Goetz. 2011. Spatial justice through regionalism? The inside game, the outside game, and the quest for the spatial fix in the United States. *Community Development* 42(4): 458–475.

Cheshire, Paul. 2012. Are mixed community policies evidence-based? A review of the research on neighbourhood effects, in Maaten van Ham, David Manley, Nick Bailey, Ludi Simpson, & Duncan Maclennan, eds., *Neighbourhood Effects Research: New Perspectives*, 267–294. Dordrecht, The Netherlands: Springer.

Cohen, Anthony. 1985. *The Symbolic Construction of Community.* London: Routledge.

Crane, Randall. 2007. Is there a quiet revolution in women's travel? Revisiting the gender gap in commuting. *Journal of the American Planning Association* 73(3): 298–316.

Cuba, Lee, & David M. Hummon. 1993. Constructing a sense of home: Place affiliation and migration across the life cycle. *Sociological Forum* 8(4): 547–569.

Curley, Alexandra. 2010. Relocating the poor: Social capital and neighborhood resources. *Journal of Urban Affairs* 32(1): 79–103.

Dawkins, Casey J. 2003. Regional development theory: Conceptual foundations, classic works, and recent developments. *Journal of Planning Literature* 18(2): 131–172.

DeLuca, Stefanie, & James E. Rosenbaum. 2010. Residential mobility, neighborhoods, and poverty: Results from the Chicago Gautreaux Program and the Moving to Opportunity experiment, in Chester Hartman & Gregory D. Squires, eds., *The Integration Debate: Competing Futures for American Cities*, 185–198. New York: Routledge.

Dreier, Peter, John Mollenkopf, & Todd Swanstrom. 2013. *Place Matters: Metropolitics for the Twenty-First Century*, 2nd ed. Lawrence, KS: University Press of Kansas.

Durkheim, Emile. 2013 [1897]. *Suicide: A Study in Sociology.* Snowball Publishing: www.snowballpublishing.com.

Eastman, Clyde, & Richard S. Krannich. 1995. Community change and persistence: The case of El Cerrito, New Mexico. *Journal of the Community Development Society* 26(1): 41–51.

Ehrenhalt, Alan. 2012. *The Great Inversion and the Future of the American City*. New York: Alfred A. Knopf.

Eller, Ronald D. 2008. *Uneven Ground: Appalachia since 1945*. Lexington, KY: University Press of Kentucky.

Elliot, Mark, Beth Palubinsky, & Joseph Tierney. 1999. *Overcoming Roadblocks on the Way to Work*. Bridges to work field report. Philadelphia: Public/Private Ventures. Retrieved May 24, 2016: http://eric.ed.gov/?id=ED432671.

Fan, Yingling. 2012. The planners' war against spatial mismatch: Lessons learned and ways forward. *Journal of Planning Literature* 27(2): 153–169.

Flora, Cornelia B., Jan L. Flora, & Stephen Gasteyer. 2015. *Rural Communities: Legacy and Change*, 5th ed. Boulder, CO: Westview.

Florida, Richard. 2010. Building the creative community, in Japonica Brown-Saracino, ed., *The Gentrification Debates*, 345–354. New York: Routledge.

Florida, Richard. 2005. The world is spiky. *Atlantic Monthly*. October: 48–51.

Fraser, James C., & Deirdre Oakley. 2015. Mixed-income communities and poverty amelioration, in Stephen N. Haymes, Maria V. de Haymes, & Reuben J. Miller, eds., *The Routledge Handbook of Poverty in the United States*, 268–274. New York: Routledge.

Freeman, Lance, & Frank Braconi. 2004. Gentrification and displacement. *Journal of the American Planning Association* 70(1): 39–52.

Friedman, Thomas L. 2005. *The World Is Flat: A Brief History of the Twenty-First Century*. New York: Farrar, Straus & Giroux.

Friedmann, John, & Clyde Weaver. 1979. *Territory and Function: Evolution of Regional Planning*. London: Hodder & Stoughton Educational.

Gans, Herbert J. 1968. Culture and class in the study of poverty: an approach to antipoverty research, in Daniel P. Moynihan, ed., *On Understanding Poverty: Perspectives from the Social Sciences*, 201–228. New York: Basic Books.

Garreau, Joel. 1991. *Edge City: Life on the New Frontier*. New York: Doubleday.

Gay, Claudine. 2012. Moving to Opportunity: The political effects of a housing mobility experiment. *Urban Affairs Review* 48(2): 147–179.

Goetz, Edward G. 2013. The audacity of HOPE VI: Discourse and the dismantling of public housing. *Cities* 35: 342–348.

Goetz, Edward G. 2004. Desegregation lawsuits and public housing dispersal. *Journal of the American Planning Association* 70(3): 282–299.

Goetz, Edward G. 2003a. *Clearing the Way: Deconcentrating the Poor in Urban America*. Washington, DC: Urban Institute.

Goetz, Edward G. 2003b. Housing dispersal programs. *Journal of Planning Literature* 18(1): 3–16.

Gordon, Peter, & Harry W. Richardson. 1996. Beyond polycentricity: The dispersed metropolis, Los Angeles, 1970–1990. *Journal of the American Planning Association* 63(3): 289–295.

Gotham, Kevin F. 2010. Tourism gentrification: The case of New Orleans' Vieux Carré (French Quarter), in Japonica Brown-Saracino, ed., *The Gentrification Debates*, 145–174. New York: Routledge.

Granholm, Jennifer, & Dan Mulhern. 2011. *A Governor's Story: The Fight for Jobs and America's Economic Future*. New York: Public Affairs.

Gwynne, Robert N. 1985. *Industrialization and Urbanization in Latin America*. London: Croom Helm.

Hamilton, Peter. 1985. Foreword, in Anthony Cohen, *The Symbolic Construction of Community*, 1–9. London: Routledge.

Hargreaves, Margaret B., & Hedy N. Chang. 1993. The impact of welfare reform in Indian Country: The Family Support Act of 1988 and the Rosebud Reservation, in Stephen

Cornell & Joseph P. Kalt, eds., *What Can Tribes Do? Strategies and Institutions in American Indian Economic Development*, 239–300. Los Angeles: American Indian Studies Center.

Hartley, Daniel A., Nikhil Kaza, & T. William Lester. 2016. Are America's inner cities competitive? Evidence from the 2000s. *Economic Development Quarterly* 30(2): 137–158.

Hertz, Daniel K. 2016. The displacement factor. *Planning* 82(3): 52.

Hu, Lingqian. 2015. Job accessibility of the poor in Los Angeles. *Journal of the American Planning Association* 81(1): 30–45.

Hutchinson, Judy, & Avis C. Vidal, eds. 2004. Symposium: Using social capital to help integrate planning theory, research, and practice. *Journal of the American Planning Association* 70(2): 142–192.

Jacob, Anupama. 2015. Countering urban poverty concentration in the United States: The people versus place debate in housing policy, in Stephen N. Haymes, Maria V. de Haymes, & Reuben J. Miller, eds., *The Routledge Handbook of Poverty in the United States*, 275–284. New York: Routledge.

Johnson, Michael P., Helen F. Ladd, & Jens Ludwig. 2002. The benefits and costs of residential mobility programmes for the poor. *Housing Studies* 17(1): 125–138.

Kain, John F. 1968. Housing segregation, negro employment, and metropolitan decentralization. *Quarterly Journal of Economics* 82(2): 175–197.

Katz, Bruce, & Katherine Allen. 1999. Help wanted: Connecting inner-city job seekers with suburban jobs. *Brookings Review* 17(4): 31–35.

Keating, Larry. 2000. Redeveloping public housing: Relearning urban renewal's immutable lessons. *Journal of the American Planning Association* 66(4): 384–397.

Kling, Jeffrey R., Jens Ludwig, & Lawrence F. Katz. 2005. Neighbourhood effects on crime for female and male youth: Evidence from a randomized housing voucher experiment. *Quarterly Journal of Economics* 120(1): 87–130.

Kneebone, Elizabeth, & Alan Berube. 2013. *Confronting Suburban Poverty in America.* Washington, DC: Brookings Institution.

LeDuff, Charlie. 2013. *Detroit: An American Autopsy.* New York: Penguin.

Lemann, Nicholas. 1994. The myth of community development. *New York Times Magazine.* January 29: 27.

Lemann, Nicholas. 1992. *The Promised Land: The Great Black Migration and How It Changed America.* New York: Vintage.

MacDonald, Heather I. 1999. Women's employment and commuting: Explaining the links. *Journal of Planning Literature* 13(3): 267–283.

Manville, Michael. 2012. People, race and place: American support for person- and place-based urban policy, 1973–2008. *Urban Studies* 49(14): 3101–3119.

Manzo, Lynne C., & Douglas D. Perkins. 2006. Finding common ground: The importance of place attachment to community participation and planning. *Journal of Planning Literature* 20(4): 335–350.

Manzo, Lynne C., & Patrick Devine-Wright. 2014. *Place Attachment: Advances in Theory, Methods and Applications.* London: Routledge.

Markley, Scott, & Madhuri Sharma. 2016. Gentrification in the revanchist suburb: The politics of removal in Roswell, Georgia. *Southeastern Geographer* 56(1): 57–80.

Mathie, Alison, & Gord Cunningham. 2003. From clients to citizens: Asset-based community development as a strategy for community-driven development. *Development in Practice* 13(5): 474–486.

McClay, Wilfred M., & Ted V. McAllister, eds. 2014. *Why Place Matters: Geography, Identity, and Civic Life in Modern America.* New York: New Atlantis.

McClure, Kirk. 2008. Deconcentrating poverty with housing programs. *Journal of the American Planning Association* 74(1): 90–99.

Meiklejohn, Susan T. 2002. Overqualified minority youth in a Detroit job training program: Implications for the spatial and skills mismatch debates. *Economic Development Quarterly* 16(4): 342–359.

Miller, Mark M. 1988. *Managing the Maelstrom: Decentralization Planning for the Mexico City Metropolis*. Unpublished Ph.D. dissertation. Tucson: University of Arizona.

Morgan, Jonathan Q. 2012. Regional clusters and jobs for inner-city workers: The case of transportation, distribution, and logistics. *Community Development* 43(4): 492–511.

Nasar, Jack L., & David A. Julian. 1995. The psychological sense of community in the neighborhood. *Journal of the American Planning Association* 61(2): 178–184.

Okun, Arthur M. 1975. *Equality and Efficiency: The Big Tradeoff*. Washington, DC: Brookings Institution.

Partridge, Mark D., & Dan S. Rickman. 2006. *The Geography of American Poverty: Is there a Need for Place-Based Policies?* Kalamazoo, MI: W.E. Upjohn Institute for Employment Research.

Peattie, Lisa. 1987. *Planning: Rethinking Ciudad Guayana*. Ann Arbor: University of Michigan Press.

Perez, Gina. 2004. *The Near Northwest Side Story: Migration, Displacement, and Puerto Rican Families*. Berkeley: University of California Press.

Phillips, Rhonda. 2002. *Concept Marketing for Communities: Capitalizing on Underutilized Resources to Generate Growth and Development*. Westport, CT: Praeger.

Popper, Frank J. & Deborah E. Popper. 1987. The Great Plains: From dust to dust. *Planning* 53(12): 12–18.

Porter, Michael E. 2016. Inner-city economic development: Learnings from 20 years of research and practice. *Economic Development Quarterly* 30(2): 105–116.

Porter, Michael E. 1990. *The Competitive Advantage of Nations*. New York: Free Press.

Portney, Kent E. 2013. *Taking Sustainable Cities Seriously: Economic Development, the Environment, and Quality of Life in American Cities*, 2nd ed. Cambridge: MIT Press.

Prenshaw, Peggy W., & Jesse O. McKee. 1979. *Sense of Place: Mississippi*. Jackson, MS: University Press of Mississippi.

Putnam, Robert D. 2000. *Bowling Alone: The Collapse and Revival of American Community*. New York: Simon & Schuster.

Putnam, Robert D., & David E. Campbell. 2016. *Our Kids: The American Dream in Crisis*. New York: Simon & Schuster.

Reingold, David A. 1999. Inner-city firms and the employment problem of the urban poor: Are poor people really excluded from jobs located in their own neighborhoods? *Economic Development Quarterly* 13(4): 291–306.

Rivlin, Gary. 2006. All parts of city in rebuild plan of New Orleans. *New York Times*. January 8: http://www.nytimes.com/2006/01/08/national/nationalspecial/08orleans.html.

Rosenbaum, James E. 2009. Can residential mobility programs improve human capital?, in Maude Toussaint-Comeau & Bruce D. Meyer, eds., *Strategies for Improving Economic Mobility of Workers*, 125–150. Kalamazoo, MI: W.E. Upjohn Institute for Employment Research.

Rosenbaum, James E. 1995. Changing the geography of opportunity by expanding residential choice: Lessons from the Gautreaux Program. *Housing Policy Debate* 6(1): 231–269.

Rosenbaum, James E., Lisa Reynolds, & Stephanie DeLuca. 2002. How do places matter? The geography of opportunity, self-efficacy and a look inside the black box of residential mobility. *Housing Studies* 17(1): 71–82.

Rosenblatt, Peter, & Stefanie DeLuca. 2012. "We don't live outside, we live in here": Neighborhood and residential mobility decisions among low-income families. *City & Community* 11(3): 254–284.

Ross, Catherine L., & Nancey G. Leigh. 2000. Planning, urban revitalization, and the inner city: An exploration of structural racism. *Journal of Planning Literature* 14(3): 367–380.

Rypkema, Donovan D. 2005. *The Economics of Historic Preservation: A Community Leader's Guide*. Washington, DC: National Trust for Historic Preservation.

Saegert, Susan, J. Phillip Thompson, & Mark R. Warren, eds. 2001. *Social Capital and Poor Communities*. New York: Russell Sage Foundation.

Sanchez, Thomas W. 1999. The connection between public transit and employment: The cases of Portland and Atlanta. *Journal of the American Planning Association* 65(3): 284–296.

Sanchez, Thomas W., & Marc Brenman. 2007. *The Right to Transportation: Moving to Equity*. Chicago: Planners.

Sawicki, David S. & Mitch Moody. 2000. Developing transportation alternatives for welfare recipients moving to work. *Journal of the American Planning Association* 66(3): 306–318.

Schilling, Joseph, & Jonathan Logan. 2008. Greening the Rust Belt: A green infrastructure model for right sizing America's shrinking cities. *Journal of the American Planning Association* 74(4): 451–466.

Schuetz, Jenny, Rachel Meltzer, & Vicki Been. 2009. 31 flavors of inclusionary zoning: Comparing policies from San Francisco, Washington, DC, and suburban Boston. *Journal of the American Planning Association* 75(4): 441–456.

Sharkey, Patrick. 2013. *Stuck in Place: Urban Neighborhoods and the End of Progress toward Racial Equality*. Chicago: University of Chicago Press.

Skobba, Kimberly, Deirdre Oakley, & Dwanda Farmer. 2015. Privatizing the housing safety net: HOPE VI and the transformation of public housing in the United States, in Stephen N. Haymes, Maria V. de Haymes, & Reuben J. Miller, eds., *The Routledge Handbook of Poverty in the United States*, 285–295. New York: Routledge.

Steinbeck, John. 1939. *The Grapes of Wrath*. New York: Viking.

Stoll, Michael A. 2006. Workforce development in minority communities, in Paul Ong & Anastasia Loukaitou-Sideris, eds., *Jobs and Economic Development in Minority Communities*, 91–118. Philadelphia: Temple University Press.

Talen, Emily. 2000. The problem with community in planning. *Journal of Planning Literature* 15(2): 171–183.

Thompson, Mark A. 1997. The impact of spatial mismatch on female labor force participation. *Economic Development Quarterly* 11(2): 138–145.

Tighe, J. Rosie. 2010. Public opinion and affordable housing: A review of the literature. *Journal of Planning Literature* 25(1): 3–17.

Tuan, Yi-Fu. 1980. Rootedness versus sense of place. *Landscape* 24(1): 3–8.

Tuan, Yi-Fu. 1977. *Space and Place*. Minneapolis: University of Minnesota Press.

US Department of Housing and Urban Development. Bridges to work. Retrieved May 24, 2016: http://portal.hud.gov/hudportal/HUD?src=/programdescription/bridges.

US Environmental Protection Agency. 1999. *EPA's Framework for Community-Based Environmental Protection*. National Service Center for Environmental Publications. Retrieved June 17, 2016: https://nepis.epa.gov.

US General Accountability Office. 1998. *Welfare Reform: Transportation's Role in Moving from Welfare to Work*. RCED-98–161. Retrieved June 21, 2016: http://www.gao.gov/products/RCED-98-161.

van Ham, Maarten, David Manley, Nick Bailey, Ludi Simpson, & Duncan Maclennan, eds. 2012. *Neighbourhood Effects Research: New Perspectives*. Dordrecht, The Netherlands: Springer.

Vance, J.D. 2016. *Hillbilly Elegy: A Memoir of a Family and Culture in Crisis*. New York: Harper.

Varady, David P., & Carole C. Walker. 2003. Housing vouchers and residential mobility. *Journal of Planning Literature* 18(1): 17–30.

Wachter, Susan M., & Kimberly A. Zeuli, eds. 2014. *Revitalizing American Cities*. Philadelphia: University of Pennsylvania Press.

Walker, Philip L. 2009. *Downtown Planning for Smaller and Midsized Communities*. Chicago: Planners.

Wilson, William J. 1987. *The Truly Disadvantaged: The Inner City, the Underclass, and Public Policy*. Chicago: University of Chicago Press.

3

WHAT'S THE USE? WHAT CAN MAINSTREAM ECONOMIC DEVELOPMENT CONTRIBUTE TO LOW-INCOME COMMUNITIES?

Economic development (ED) scholars take pride in tracing their roots to the Founding Fathers, beginning perhaps with Alexander Hamilton's First Bank of the United States in 1792 (Cohen & DeLong 2016). Hamilton's model of "ED" apparently served the young nation well, at least through the eras of canal- and railroad-based development (Immergluck 2004). Like most fields of study or practice, ED strategy has progressed through a series of dominant styles or models in particular eras (Miller 2009).

This chapter is intended to provide a historical overview of and general context for mainstream ED as it is studied and practiced professionally in the US today (also Dawkins 2003). Many of the various ED strategies in use today were inspired by the needs of low-income communities, and many of those strategies are still employed to support those communities. The main argument of this chapter, however, is that none of these traditional strategies provide a clear model for the development of low-income communities today.

Public sector emphasis: Big government to the rescue

Two of our largest federally funded epics of regional development focused on severely lagging rural regions: the Tennessee Valley Authority (TVA), followed a few decades later by the Appalachian Regional Commission (ARC). The TVA targeted a region notoriously characterized at that time by poverty, unemployment, deforestation, erosion of agricultural land, and lack of industrialization (Lilienthal 1954): "Even by Depression standards, the Tennessee Valley region was in sad shape in 1933. Much of the land had been farmed too hard for too long, eroding and depleting the soil. Crop yields had fallen along with farm incomes" (Tennessee Valley Authority: History).

The federal Tennessee Valley Authority Act of 1933 established the TVA as a comprehensive development planning program "[t]o improve the navigability and to provide for the flood control of the Tennessee River; to provide for reforestation and the proper use of marginal lands in the Tennessee Valley; to provide for the agricultural and industrial development of said valley…and for other purposes" (Tennessee Valley Authority: Tennessee Valley Authority Act, 1933). The Tennessee Valley region included some existing federal assets, especially chemical plants from World War I, which were repurposed for fertilizer production. The designation of this region also was consistent with the regional planning emphasis of the time on natural resource development, particularly water resources (Friedmann and Weaver 1979).

PROFESSOR'S PODIUM: ED TERMINOLOGY AND JARGON

I have adapted for this book a fairly standard combination of business management and scholarly research terms that will be familiar to most researchers and ED practitioners. As suggested earlier, I believe the most fundamental division in ED can be described as the debate between creating ED at the local level ("jobs to people") and encouraging people to move where ED is being created ("people to jobs"), as is illustrated in Figure 3.1. We can think of those two, broad, highest-level classifications of ED as being "core values," a fairly vague management term which is used in a number of different ways. Does your ED-related organization most value the creation of jobs in the local community, or most value the ability of people to move out of their community to places with better prospects for good jobs? Neither value is necessarily right or wrong – although "jobs to people" is obviously the interest of the present book. Both sides of the great debate value trying to improve people's lives. Yet, the two core values can result in very different efforts, even efforts that can work in opposition – as discussed in Chapter 2.

Beyond fundamental core values, the highest level in the standard business hierarchy is a firm's "mission," which, in the corporate world, is the purpose for a company's existence and its long-term, most fundamental objectives (Barney & Hesterly 2011). The same strategic concepts apply – perhaps even more so – to nonprofit organizations (Drucker 1990) including community and ED organizations.

The term "mission" might be a bit awkward and unfamiliar in an ED context, so I am also using the term "emphasis." As shown in Figure 3.1, I have again divided the classification into "public sector emphasis" vs. "private sector emphasis." The use of the word "emphasis" helps to underscore that the differences between the two missions are not entirely clear and distinct. The archetypal example of public sector emphasis would be the original concept of the federally funded TVA. Most states and cities today have ED organizations that emphasize the private sector, attracting and otherwise promoting private sector industries. In reality, the lines between these two types of organizations have been blurry since the beginning and have grown increasingly so. Most of the organizations on both sides of the divide today would consider themselves "public-private partnerships," which combine public funding and grants with private sector initiatives. The differences in this regard are a matter of degree, rather than clearly one or the other.

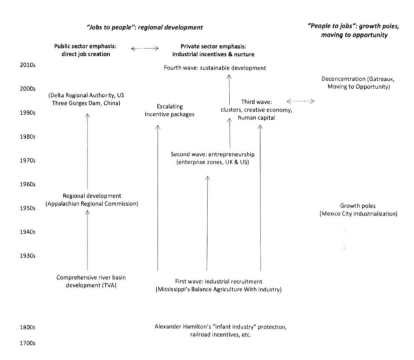

FIGURE 3.1 Mainstream strategies of ED
Adapted from Miller 2009

In the case of a public-sector-emphasis ED organization, such as the original TVA, the emphasis is to mobilize investment capital and other resources primarily from the public sector to create jobs, wealth, and so on. The emphasis of most state and municipal ED organizations is to mobilize capital and resources from the private sector to accomplish good things – generally along with material or political support from the public sector. Business firms and well-managed non-profit organizations typically express their mission in a succinct "mission state-ment." Ideally, rather than some generic platitudes, a mission statement will clarify just how the firm is unique, distinctive, and competitive in its market.

The next level of the hierarchy in most business management schema, below the "mission" level, is that of "objectives," which are generally understood as specific and measurable performance targets (Barney & Hesterly 2011) and which should follow clearly from the firm's mission. In ED practice, the role of "objectives" (not shown in Figure 3.1) is typically filled by concepts such as "benchmarking," "scorecards," and "dashboards" (Simms, Freshwater, & Ward 2014; Huggins & Izushi 2009; Wilkins et al. 2009).

Only now, at last, do we come to the much beloved term "strategy." Ideally – by definition, really – only after completing and publicly stating its mission and measurable objectives should an ED organization state its "strategy," which is the specific way in which it seeks to accomplish its mission and meet its objectives. Tactics or policies, at the final level of the hierarchy, are the tools that are used to implement an organization's strategy or strategies.

Strategy is sometimes defined by the scientific term "theory": a strategy is a well-researched plan or model of how firms – or non-governmental organizations (NGOs) or ED organizations – believe they can achieve success in their efforts (Barney & Hesterly 2011: 3, who credit Drucker 1994). This is the point where the academic researcher typically enters: to evaluate those strategies/theories critically to determine whether or not they have been successful. This book, mainly in Part II, summarizes much of this sort of evaluation research. Note that this sort of evaluative research makes academic researchers unpleasant and unpopular with practitioners and policymakers, since we seem to take such delight in shooting down preferred strategies.

There is one last technical term to look at, "paradigm," which forms part of the related expression "paradigm shift" – a fancy term that is tossed around freely. By dictionary definition, paradigm can mean simply a model or a pattern, but the term also has a more specific and significant meaning for academic researchers. In his highly influential 1962 book *The Structure of Scientific Revolutions*, Thomas Kuhn (1962) describes a paradigm as the normal way of doing things in a field of science at a particular time, and maybe as the only acceptable way of doing things. Everything proceeds smoothly, orderly, and stepwise – until "normal science" finds itself upended by a "revolution" (in Kuhn's terms), or a dramatic, abrupt, and even shocking shift from one paradigm, or standard way of doing things, to another. Then, after a period of painful and chaotic transition, scientists settle back again into the new paradigm – until the next revolution.

My long experience with the ED field suggests that the patterns of professional practice are similar to those of academic practice: periods of "normal" ED, followed by abrupt and dramatic changes. In the case of ED, I use the term "paradigms" to refer to "normal" ways of doing ED business and following ED strategies. For example, it was once considered quite normal to create massive federal programs such as the TVA or ARC. Both organizations still exist, but neither would be considered "normal" models of ED today.

Another "normal" that emerged around the same time, around the 1930s and 1940s, was the use of incentives to attract private industry. That paradigm has never left us, even as new paradigms arise (enterprise zones, industrial clusters, sustainable development). Fresh new paradigms get more attention, but often they serve to reframe the old "normal": for example, huge incentives to attract industries are justified today because they propose to attract not just a single industry, but a new industrial cluster.

So, armed now with all that context and terminology, let us walk through the recent history of ED thought and practice – and then begin to explore some brave new strategies and perhaps even contemplate future paradigm shifts.

The region was notoriously characterized at that time by poverty, unemployment, deforestation, erosion of agricultural land, and lack of industrialization (Lilienthal 1954). However, the enabling legislation makes direct mention neither of poverty nor of unemployment. The emphasis of the times was on making use of wasted resources, in particular natural resources such as hydroelectric power, navigation, agricultural land, and an undereducated labor force. President Roosevelt viewed the TVA as a model for other such authorities across the US, with each one to be focused on a region defined as a river basin and its resources (Friedmann & Weaver 1979). Part of the reason for the emphasis on river basin development was practical, and part was political: precedent for federal intervention was already well established for the use of waterways for navigation.

The strategy of river basin development became well established in regional development scholarship and policymaking, although in practical application less in the US than internationally. Grand examples abroad include Mexico (Barkin & King 1970; Lilienthal 1954), and Venezuela's Ciudad Guayana project (Peattie 1987). China's Three Gorges Dam project today presents much of the same justification as the original TVA project, integrating power-generation with flood control for farmlands and improved navigation for the region (China Three Gorges Corporation). Incidentally, there is plenty both to applaud and criticize about ED efforts in the US – the topic of this chapter – but also plenty of both with regard to ED projects in the Developing or Third World (Easterly 2007).

In the US, the concept of a regional development authority was adapted most successfully to another severely lagging region, although it was nearly the opposite of a river basin: it was applied to the Appalachian mountain region through the ARC (Isserman & Rephann 1995; Eller 2008; Appalachian Regional Commission: History). The creation of the ARC was much more explicitly and primarily grounded in concerns over poverty and unemployment than was the TVA:

As of the mid-1960s:

- One of every three Appalachians lived in poverty;
- Per capita income was 23 percent lower than the US average; and
- High unemployment and harsh living conditions had forced more than 2 million Appalachians to leave their homes and seek work in other regions (Appalachian Regional Authority: History).

The foundational report for the ARC emphasizes the use of regional resources, but with greater emphasis on the region's human resources: "An unfilled job is more than a man unemployed, it is an opportunity lost" (Appalachian Regional Commission 1964: 49). The work of the ARC today can be summarized by four goals identified in the Commission's strategic plan:

- Increase job opportunities and per capita income in Appalachia to reach parity with the nation.

- Strengthen the capacity of the people of Appalachia to compete in the global economy.
- Develop and improve Appalachia's infrastructure to make the Region economically competitive.
- Build the Appalachian Development Highway System to reduce Appalachia's isolation.

(Appalachian Regional Commission: About)

Both the TVA (Hargrove 2001; Neuse 1983; Drucker 1980; Lilienthal 1954; Jacobs 1984) and the ARC (Isserman & Rephann 1995; Widner 1990; Bradshaw 1992; Gauthier 1973; Hansen 1966) have been the subject of extensive critique regarding their leadership, goals, effectiveness, and efficiency as ED programs. Eller (2008: 193) emphasizes public criticism that the ARC's "growth center strategy...exacerbated the poverty and depopulation of rural areas and facilitated the continued drain of wealth from the region by absentee industries. Education and health programs were designed to encourage out-migration from rural areas rather than to improve public services where people lived, and the ARC had failed to justify the expenditure of almost 80 percent of its budget on an uncompleted highway system."

In the cases of both the TVA and the ARC, the focus on low-income communities has been somewhat tenuous from the beginning. The TVA's enabling legislation makes direct mention neither of poverty nor of unemployment (Tennessee Valley Authority: Tennessee Valley Authority Act, 1933). Much of the early emphasis of the ARC focused on the development of regional growth poles, or larger urban centers with the greater promise for industrial development and regional service provision. Only secondarily were ARC programs expanded to address the needs of more distressed communities of the region (Bradshaw 1992; Widner 1990). The successes of the ARC were uneven, at best, with many "hardcore pockets of poverty" remaining, still characterized by "despair, scarcity, and frustration" (Eller 2008: 217–218).

Partly in response to such large-scale, top-down models of regional development, Stöhr & Taylor (1981) and Friedmann and Weaver (1979) proposed alternative models of "development from within" or "development from below." Those models are primarily focused on regions of the Developing World and have inspired relatively little academic or applied follow-up (Nel, Hill & Binns 1997; Riker 1994). There seems to be little connection between the "development from below" concept of international development and the "bottom-up" concept of development planning in a US context (Martinez-Cosio & Bussell 2012; Ross & Usher 1986).

Critiques of large-scale, federally funded regional ED initiatives are largely moot, however, given today's budgetary constraints. Bradshaw (1992) describes the federally funded TVA as something of a period piece, relevant mainly to its particular historical setting. The long-established ARC has struggled to justify its work and sustain its federal funding level since the Reagan Administration (Eller 2008).

The concept lingers on in spirit and periodic policy proposals, regardless. The Delta Regional Authority, for example, was established in 2000 as a federal development partnership with eight states in the lower Mississippi River Delta region, including many of the poorest counties and parishes in the US (Delta Regional Authority). The Denali Commission is another federal-state partnership established in 1998 to address the ED needs of rural and remote communities throughout Alaska (Denali Commission). The Obama Administration's National Commission on Fiscal Responsibility and Reform has questioned the return on federal investment provided by both of these relatively new regional programs, as well as the ARC (Sullivan 2012).

Among the first, instinctive responses to the widespread destruction of Hurricane Katrina was to suggest a regional commission (Hogue 2005), but the idea was neither enacted nor seriously pursued. Instead, even in the darkest moments following Katrina, the overwhelming concern of the local communities and the nation was to reverse the displacement of population from the Gulf Coast region by rebuilding, repopulating, and re-establishing the economies of these severely damaged communities in both New Orleans (Blakely 2011; Waugh & Smith 2006; Campanella 2006; Olshansky 2006) and the Mississippi Gulf Coast (Talen 2008; Mississippi Renewal Forum).

Private sector to the rescue

The modern history of ED practice has progressed through three or four overlapping "waves" (Bradshaw & Blakely 1999; Herbers 1990), more recently renamed "phases," of strategies (Leigh & Blakely 2013). The first of these waves, or phases, is the use of incentives and other tactics to attract industry to our community. As Leigh & Blakely (2013: 58) note, the phases are "both chronological and overlapping," and indeed the first phase continues today as probably the most utilized strategy in the ED profession's toolkit – despite decades of scholarly and popular criticism.

SIDEBAR: WHAT IS "ECONOMIC DEVELOPMENT"?

As in the complex case of defining a seemingly simple term like "community" in the sidebar of Chapter 2, there are also many different definitions of "development" in general and "economic development" in particular. Those definitions can include everything from "the creation of wealth" (American Economic Development Council 1984) to "choice" to "freedoms" and "capabilities" (Sen 1999) and even "happiness" (Graham 2011).

A longstanding standard definition of ED comes from the American Economic Development Council (AEDC):

> The process of creating wealth through the mobilization of human, financial, capital, physical and natural resources to generate marketable goods and services. The economic developer's role is to influence the process for the benefit of the community through expanding job opportunities and the tax base.

> *(Swager 1991; American Economic Development Council 1984)*

ED is both a process and a practice, as suggested in the definition above. The process of ED occurs naturally in the form of business growth and transformation over time: local businesses grow and expand, primarily financed by private banks; local entrepreneurs start up new businesses; and the industrial mix and character of the community changes over the years. The practice of ED begins when professionals attempt to intervene in the process in order to facilitate local ED or target a particular type of ED on behalf of the community they represent.

Many ED scholars emphasize the difference between economic growth and economic development, along with a number of different ways to characterize those differences. Generally speaking, economic growth reflects a simple expansion in the output or earnings of a local economy. Economic development implies a transformation of that economy, with positive consequences for local employment levels and wage levels, and a wide variety of quality of life considerations.

We broaden and modernize the standard ED definition a bit in the University of Southern Mississippi's Economic Development program, in order to include sustainability and quality of life considerations, as

> the management of public-private investment collaborations to facilitate sustainable growth in the economy as typically measured by job creation, increased citizen wealth, a greater tax base, and improved quality of life. The three legs of ED are business attraction, business retention and expansion, and entrepreneurship development that start from a base of community development.

A mnemonic device we have long used for students for the four ways of creating ED is the acronym ACRE:

- Attraction: industrial incentives, marketing, and other tools for attracting new industries to locate in your community.
- Creation: encouraging local entrepreneurship.
- Retention: making sure your existing local industries are content, healthy, and not about to close or leave your community. (This should be the top priority among the four ways.)
- Expansion: working with local industries to expand production, exports, earnings, and especially employment. (Ideally this should be the second priority on the list.)

The International Economic Development Council (IEDC, which subsumed the old AEDC) elaborates on the concept of ED with a nod to the challenges inherent in defining the term:

> No single definition incorporates all of the different strands of economic development. Typically economic development can be described in terms

of objectives. These are most commonly described as the creation of jobs and wealth, and the improvement of quality of life. Economic development can also be described as a process that influences growth and restructuring of an economy to enhance the economic well-being of a community.

As there is no single definition for economic development, there is no single strategy, policy, or program for achieving successful economic development. Communities differ in their geographic and political strengths and weaknesses. Each community, therefore, will have a unique set of challenges for economic development.

(International Economic Development Council)

Servon (2007: 97) suggests that ED and poverty alleviation are very different in terms of their objectives: "Those who are interested in economic development tend to look at outcomes such as job creation, tax base enhancement, and business growth (in terms of revenues and employees, for example). Those who concern themselves with poverty alleviation, on the other hand, are more interested in changes in individual and household income, the acquisition of particular skills (education and soft skills), and issues such as health insurance."

Long one of my favorite scholarly definitions of the concept of development in general is that of Lewis. Although frequently cited, this quote comes from an appendix to his 1955 book *The Theory of Economic Growth*:

The advantage of economic growth is not that wealth increases happiness, but that it increases the range of human choice. It is very hard to correlate wealth and happiness. Happiness results from the way one looks at life, taking it as it comes, dwelling on the pleasant rather than the unpleasant, and living without fear of what the future may bring. Wealth would increase happiness if it increased resources more than it increased wants, but it does not necessarily do this, and there is no evidence that the rich are happier than the poor, or that individuals grow happier as their incomes increase. Wealth decreases happiness if in the acquisition of wealth one ceases to take life as it comes, and worries more about resources and the future. There is, indeed some evidence that this is the case.

(Lewis 1955: 420)

Sen follows a similar line of logic in his 1999 book *Development as Freedom*, in which he develops the theory of development "capabilities," or the abilities of people to function in their own interests: a theory that is now embodied in the United Nations' Human Development Index (Jeroslow 2015; United Nations Development Programme 2015). In his classic text, Sen emphasizes the inter-relationship between economic freedom and other necessary components of a free society:

> (1) Political freedoms, (2) economic facilities, (3) social opportunities, (4) transparency guarantees and protective security....Political freedoms (in the form of free speech and elections) help promote economic security. Social opportunities (in the form of education and health facilities) facilitate economic participation. Economic facilities (in the form of opportunities for participation in trade and production) can help to generate personal abundance as well as public resources for social facilities. Freedoms of different kinds can strengthen each other.
>
> *(Sen 1999: 10–11)*

Citing the work of Lewis, Sen, and others, Todaro and Smith (2014: 22–23), in their standard textbook on ED, assert, primarily from an international perspective, that "development in all societies must have at least the following three objectives":

1. To increase the availability and widen the distribution of basic life-sustaining goods such as food, shelter, health, and protection
2. To raise levels of living, including, in addition to higher incomes, the provision of more jobs, better education, and greater attention to cultural and human values, all of which will serve not only to enhance material well-being but also to generate greater individual and national self-esteem
3. To expand the range of economic and social choices available to individuals and nations by freeing them from servitude and dependence not only in relation to other people and nation-states but also to the forces of ignorance and human misery

Chapter 8 of this book will focus on the concept of "sustainable development" and specifically on "sustainable economic development." The classic definition of sustainable development comes from the Brundtland Commission (World Commission on Environment and Development 1987), as "development which meets the needs of current generations without compromising the ability of future generations to meet their own needs." Sachs (2015) lists the three concerns of sustainable development more broadly as:

*   Economic development,
*   Social inclusion, and
*   Environmental sustainability.

The science of "happiness" (Graham 2011; Diener & Biswas-Diener 2009; Layard 2006) continues to grow and fill entire dedicated, multidisciplinary journals (e.g., Cox 2012; Leung et al. 2011), and it is also finding its way into more traditional planning and development journals (Pfeiffer & Cloutier 2016).

It seems intuitively obvious that there is some relationship between ED, happiness, and equity. It's difficult for someone to be happy when they can't afford the basic needs for themselves or their family. There is considerable evidence, however, that various traditional economic measures provide only weak and indirect – at best – proxies for happiness. More money does not necessarily guarantee happiness, as Lewis notes above. So, why not attempt to measure happiness levels more directly in humans and in human societies – and study more precisely what it is that makes us happier? Research shows that ED can create more human happiness, especially for disadvantaged populations, as it allows them to enjoy health, shelter, nutrition, dignity, and other basic human necessities for individuals and their families. There are also other ways to create happiness, however, particularly education for its own sake and improved access to mental healthcare.

The very broad field of "community development" (Phillips & Pittman 2015) and the slightly narrower field of "community economic development" (Shaffer, Deller, & Marcouiller 2006), as applied to low-income communities, can encompass everything from housing, to healthcare, to community organizing. All of these elements have vital relationships to ED – as causes, effects, and intermediaries of ED – although this book focuses explicitly and directly on growing the economy of a community.

Ratner and Markley (2014) edit a special issue of *Community Development* devoted to "rural wealth creation," a term that harks back to the earliest and most basic definitions of ED presented in this chapter. The authors in that issue, however, explore a relatively new framework that they argue can synthesize economic and community development with an emphasis on the sustainability of that development (more in Chapter 8).

For the present, this book – as promised in the title – will emphasize three pragmatic, old-school, mundane, but reasonably concrete and measurable dimensions of ED: (1) jobs created, (2) businesses established, and (3) resilience, or the ability of a community to bounce back from an economic shock such as a local plant closure or a natural disaster. This book particularly emphasizes research on ED strategies that *explicitly* target low-income communities. Almost any sort of ED could potentially have some application for, or impact on, low-income communities: the promise of "trickle-down" economics. However, as mentioned earlier, the emphasis of this book is on ED programs that are within the immediate grasp and potential action of local communities themselves.

"First-wave" ED: Manufacturing attraction and industrial incentives

This first wave, or phase, of ED is credited to the "Balance Agriculture with Industry" program originating in our nation's poorest state of Mississippi (Mississippi Historical Society; Hopkins 1944), luring northern industries to Mississippi with offers of buildings, job training, and other incentives. The strategy quickly diffused across the country, as communities both poor and wealthy joined the ever-escalating and near-ubiquitous "smokestack chasing," an old pejorative term for the practice.

The critiques of industrial incentives as ED strategy are legion, dating from the earliest years of such programs (Clark 1927). Broad categories of critiques include questioning the effectiveness of incentives for attracting investment and creating jobs (Florida 2012; Peters & Fisher 2002), the ever-escalating competition among states, the resulting ever-increasing costs (Markusen 2007), and the growing challenges of competing for manufacturing in a globalized economy. (Walcott 2011). Whitacre, Shideler, & Williams (2016) provide a detailed case study analysis among communities participating in an industrial incentives program in Oklahoma, a program that had mixed outcomes at best.

The above critiques of industrial incentives apply to all communities in the competition, but all the more so for the scarce development resources and many competing needs of low-income communities. The use of the practice has grown more sophisticated since the 1930s, with a number of efforts to evaluate more effectively and transparently the net returns on these often massive incentive packages. The Pew Center on the States (2012: 13) notes some states that have taken a leading role in rigorous evaluation to help guide ED policy (Arizona, Iowa, Oregon, Washington) and many others that either conduct evaluation analysis but fall "short in using the data to inform policy," or do "not review all major tax incentives or use data to inform policy choices." Many communities also complement or temper their use of incentive offers with other ED strategies such as support for existing small businesses (Zheng & Warner 2010).

Low-income communities, again, typically will not have the resources necessary to evaluate incentive offers thoroughly. Further, those low-income communities are often in a situation of economic desperation that makes them unwilling or unable to negotiate effectively with prospective industries. Zheng & Warner (2010) find that communities with "stagnating or declining economies" and relatively low tax bases tend to be most dependent on industrial incentives.

Academic critiques notwithstanding, traditional first-wave ED strategies – offering financial, material, tax, or other incentives to attract manufacturing investment in a community – remain the primary strategy for many rural and other low-income communities today (Levy 1990). Both scholars (Reese 2014; Markusen 2007; Peters & Fisher 2004; Buss 2001) and investigative journalists alike (Story 2012a, 2012b, 2012c) have strongly suggested for decades that the impacts of industrial incentives for communities are largely minor, at best, as the cost of competing continues to rise. The largest prizes in the incentive competition – such as large automotive manufacturing plants – may be "attractable" to low-income states, but they tend to locate in areas of the states that are already relatively advantaged: e.g., Mercedes near Tuscaloosa, Alabama; Nissan near Nashville, Tennessee; Nissan near Jackson, Mississippi; and Toyota near Tupelo, Mississippi. Low-income communities are often left targeting industrial facilities with a mixed record of economic, environmental, and social outcomes, such as waste disposal plants, or public and privately operated prisons (Burayidi & Coulibaly 2009).

There is growing evidence that overall employment in the manufacturing sector – traditionally the working-class ladder to middle-class lifestyles – is following the service sector in the creation of low-wage, low-benefit jobs: "A third (34 percent) of the families of frontline manufacturing production workers are enrolled in one or more public safety net programs. For those workers employed through staffing agencies, the percentage of families utilizing safety net programs is 50 percent – similar to the rate for fast-food workers and their families" (Jacobs et al. 2016; see also Wolman, Stokan, & Wial 2015). Union membership fell from 27 percent in 1973 to 13 percent in 2011, and "[t]his falling rate of unionization has lowered wages, not only because there is less pressure on nonunion employers to raise wages; the spillover or threat effect of unionism and the ability of unions to set labor standards have both declined" (Mishel et al. 2012: 269). Overall, the outlook for employment in the manufacturing sector is not good for at least the decade ahead (US Department of Labor, Bureau of Labor Statistics 2013). Even in the developing countries, where manufacturing has long been viewed as the natural next stage from natural-resource-based economies in the development process to join the ranks of the "industrialized" countries; even that near-gospel process now seems questionable (Zhong 2015).

A focus issue of *Economic Development Quarterly* provides a perspective on "deindustrialization, manufacturing job loss, and economic development policy" (Wolman, Wial, & Hill 2015). In that issue, Wolman, Stokan, & Wial (2015) attempt to separate out fact from misconception on the phenomenon of deindustrialization and its impacts on different regions of the US. According to Blumenberg (2006: 21),

> total manufacturing employment has been remarkably stable over time.... Productivity growth in the manufacturing sector has been tremendous, but because much of this growth is owed to improved technology and capital goods, it has not resulted in a corresponding surge in employment....Manufacturing is in decline not because of its failure to grow but because its meager rate of growth has been swamped by the dramatic expansion of employment in the service sector....The steady increase in service-sector employment has been accompanied by a growth in low-wage jobs, many of which offer few benefits and are part time.

Adkisson and Ricketts (2016) emphasize that manufacturing is a very broadly diverse economic sector, ranging from paper mills to airplane factories, with very different prospects for different sub-sectors and potentially for different parts of the country. More effective use of regional cooperation and networking – a common thread that will run throughout this book – also offers some promise for more effective manufacturing-based ED. In a study of Illinois, Gordon (2007: 73) finds that ED agencies express their willingness to cooperate with other agencies in their region, although "the inherently competitive nature of economic development" often prevails. She argues that "[s]pecific examples of successful interactions – marketing, tourism, and agriculture – have demonstrated that collaborations with a specific purpose may work better than vague notions of cooperating."

"Second-wave" ED: Enterprise zones, etc.

The "second wave" of ED thought and practice included a broad range of programs that refocused on retaining and expanding existing businesses (Bradshaw & Blakely 1999). In particular, it was the enterprise zone concept that captured a great deal of political and policy attention. Sir Peter Hall was inspired by his observations of the bustling entrepreneurship in the developing Asian economic centers such as Hong Kong, Singapore, South Korea, and Taiwan (the "Tigers of Asia"), which he theorized was driven by low taxes and low levels of government regulation. In Hall's original conception, "small, selected areas of inner cities would be simply thrown open to all kinds of initiative, with minimal control. In other words, we would aim to recreate the Hong Kong of the 1950s and 1960s inside inner Liverpool or inner Glasgow" (Hall 1982: 417).

The enterprise zone concept was rapidly and widely embraced across the UK and the US (Turner & Cassell 2007) and implemented at state and local levels in the US from the late 1970s into the 1980s and at the federal level beginning in 1994 (Rich & Stoker 2014; Wallace 1999) – racing well ahead of empirical evidence on whether or not the strategy was effective (Boarnet 2001). Originally targeting the development of lagging central cities, the concept was soon adapted to struggling rural regions (US Department of Housing and Urban Development). Under the so-called "Renewal Community Initiative," the George W. Bush Administration shifted the emphasis from block grant funding to cities, to tax cuts and employment tax credits (Rich & Stoker 2014).

As data on designated enterprise zones (and comparable "empowerment zones") became available through the 1990s, evaluative research results were discouraging. At a minimum, the strategy was certainly not the panacea for distressed communities that many politicians had proclaimed it would be. There is evidence that designated enterprise zones can increase economic activity in a distressed locality (Wilder & Rubin 1996). A case study evaluation of Louisville's enterprise zone program by Zhang (2015: 347) finds that the "program has significantly increased the growth of manufacturing and service activities, and the program achieved its expected goals in the long run."

However, other studies find no significant positive impact and, in some cases, even negative impact on the number of jobs available in designated zones or on the employment rate of local residents (Neumark & Kolko 2010; Elvery 2009; Lambert & Coomes 2001; Greenbaum & Engberg 2000; Dowall 1996). Instead, evidence suggests that firms tend to move to such zones from nearby locations to take advantage of incentives, with little impact on employment for zone residents (Stoll 2006, citing Ladd 1994). Greenbaum (2004) finds that states may fail to designate the most distressed neighborhoods for enterprise zone designation and favor neighborhoods with more existing business activity. In a study of California's system of enterprise zones, Dowall (1996: 364) concludes that the credits offered "simply do not offset the many negative economic factors (real and perceived) affecting zone businesses."

Research by Peters and Fisher (2002) and Dewar (2013) suggests that jobs created within enterprise zones in distressed communities are often taken by outsiders who commute in, rather than local residents. Dewar concluded from her research on "paying employers to hire local workers in distressed places" in a Detroit empowerment zone case study that "the major way of recruiting new workers for job openings…was through referrals from social networks, especially among current workers, and resulted in few hires of nearby residents in industrial districts and segregation by race and ethnicity….The stereotypes held by industrial district employers about workers from nearby neighborhoods, likely partially valid, also made such connections difficult" (Dewar 2013: 297, citing Hanson & Pratt 1992).

A national employment subsidy program, the Work Opportunity Tax Credit (WOTC) program, "began in 1996 as part of the Personal Responsibility and Work Opportunity Reconciliation Act, as an incentive for employers to hire eligible workers from eight different target groups that are normally considered 'unemployable'" (Ajilore 2012: 231). Those eight groups include various categories of people receiving welfare assistance, young people living within an empowerment zone, ex-felons, and people "receiving vocational rehabilitation." The results of Ajilore's evaluation were mixed, but he did find an increase in employment for long-term welfare recipients, at least over the short term.

Meanwhile, enterprise zones – along with the tax breaks and other incentives offered – proliferated in number and geographic size, including communities well beyond those that were distressed, to the point of becoming just more tools of general ED (Peters & Fisher 2002) – not easily distinguished from other kinds of economic incentives. Rich & Stoker (2014: 223) find large variation in the outcomes of enterprise zones in several major US cities. They conclude from their analysis that

> governance matters. EZ cities that practiced good governance produced better outcomes; cities with poor governance produced worse outcomes. Local capacity, meaningful community participation, and program integrity are the elements of good governance…EZ cities that practiced good governance overcame unfavorable trends and conditions, while cities that practiced poor governance squandered favorable trends and conditions.

Although the initial excitement over enterprise zone strategies has subsided since the 1980s and 1990s, "[e]nterprise zone programs continue to be a popular way to package and deliver economic development incentives in the United States" (Greenbaum 2004: 78). The general concept also reappears under slightly new names, such as "economic freedom zones" (McCabe 2014).

A small ED movement called "economic gardening" – which has a strong appeal to ED students – also emphasizes entrepreneurship and especially growing local businesses by providing market research, training, and other technical support. Chris Gibbons, as Director of Business/Industry Affairs in Littleton, Colorado, is credited with originating the term: "Our council became concerned about our future being controlled by an out-of-state company....It isn't that we didn't like them, but we were told to work with local companies to create local jobs" (Gibbons 2010, quoted by Calabrese 2012).

Gibbons emphasizes, however, that Littleton – a relatively affluent enclave within metropolitan Denver – holds a relatively advantaged geographic and economic position for such a strategy. Under new leadership, and responding to fairly flat growth in recent years, Littleton has now reduced its emphasis on the economic gardening approach (City of Littleton 2013). Meanwhile, the concept has gained broader attention from academics (Florida Economic Gardening Institute; Taylor & Miller 2010), government (Quello & Toft 2006), and foundations (Edward Lowe Foundation; Kauffman Foundation).

"Third-wave" ED: Michael Porter's industrial cluster and related concepts

ED's "third wave," emerging in the 1990s, broadened our perspective to incorporate the greater local or regional environment in support of ED, including networks and partnerships, involving both public and private partners, as well as a greater emphasis on the quality of human capital and the role of technology (Bradshaw and Blakely 1999; Herbers 1990; Ross & Friedman 1990).

Again, it was one particular strategy – Michael Porter's theory of competitive advantage and the industrial cluster concept – that dominated much of ED policy discourse in this era. In very brief explanation, Porter's (2000, 1998, 1990, 1985) original empirical work (that is, his observations in the US and worldwide) examines communities and regions that are already economically outstanding, with high levels of human capital and technological development. Those are, of course, factors in which low-income communities are typically, almost by definition, in short supply. Classic examples presented by Porter (1990) include computer technology in California's Silicon Valley, fashion footwear in Italy, fabricated steel products in Sweden, robotics in Japan, and chemicals in Germany. San Diego's biotechnology cluster is another prominent example in the US (Walcott 2002). Clusters can potentially form around major centers of higher education, or in areas with a high concentration of immigrant entrepreneurs (Saxenian 2002), or they can form for less tangible reasons, either simply by chance or through distinctive regional variations in tastes, behaviors, or in other characteristics (Cortright 2002).

Porter identifies several interrelated characteristics of thriving industrial centers, which he organizes into a memorable "diamond"-shaped diagram. The four facets of this diamond configuration consist of (Porter 1990):

- A dynamic competitiveness among local businesses, centered on a particular industrial theme;

- "Sophisticated and demanding local customers" for locally made products;
- "Related and supporting industries" capable of supplying the needs of the local core industry; and
- Factor, or input, conditions. (Traditionally, this would have emphasized industrial inputs such as coal or steel; Porter now emphasizes the critical role of skilled, educated, and experienced human resources.)

Over the course of the 1990s, the ED profession came under the thrall of the cluster concept – in a familiar pattern, ahead of the evidence that thriving industrial clusters could be created by deliberate efforts. Wolman and Hincapie (2015: 135) offer a literature review of "how clusters work to bring about economic growth and whether policies put in place to build or strengthen clusters actually achieve the desired result." In the skeptical words of a theoretical "competitor" with Porter, Richard Florida (2010a: 345), in a section titled "Beyond Nerdistan":

> When they are not trying to lure firms, many cities around the country seek to emulate the Silicon Valley model of high-tech economic development. City after city has tried to turn itself into a clone of the Valley by creating R&D parks, office complexes, technology incubators and the like….This is essentially betting the future on an economic development model from the past.

Porter (2016, 2005, 1997) subsequently argues that the concept of competitive advantage and economic clustering can be applied to inner-city contexts as well, strongly emphasizing investment by the private sector, building on potential competitive advantages of the inner city such as central location in the metropolitan region. Porter argues that the inner city's geographic potential for supply chain and other networking within the region can provide lucrative investment markets to the private sector – particularly with enough information to overcome market failures. Porter (2016: 112) does not dismiss the importance of addressing social needs in the inner city, maintaining that "[i]nclusive growth will require both economic and social progress."

Porter's application of his theory to an inner-city context has met with skepticism and empirical challenges. Critiques of Porter's work in this regard include that he presents an oversimplification of the root causes of inner-city poverty, including pervasive social discrimination against minority residents (Bates 1997); an underappreciation of the role that government organizations and NGOs (such as community development corporations) have taken in ED in general and ED in inner cities (Harrison & Glasmeier 1997); and an overlooking of decades of vigorous scholarship and debate on policies that he proposes as being fresh (Sawicki & Moody 1997). Bradshaw (2007) points out decades of research suggesting that existing geographic agglomerations of investment are self-reinforcing in many ways and are difficult to reverse; the corollary is that there are many reasons why place poverty is just as self-reinforcing.

Bates (2010, more in Chapter 6) maintains that the competitive advantages of the inner city heralded by Porter are not great enough to support profitable business development lending, except under certain specific conditions. Rubin (2011: 182) critiques the related research work of the Milken Institute regarding what it terms "emerging domestic markets" (Milken Institute) as being overly simplistic: "First, it treats all underserved communities as interchangeable, ignoring that they differ in important ways….Second, it claims that underserved communities lack access to capital primarily as a result of information failure, overlooking numerous other obstacles that discourage investment in such communities."

Porter founded and chairs the Initiative for a Competitive Inner City for the purposes of research, publication, and advising on practice (Initiative for a Competitive Inner City). A special issue of the *Economic Development Quarterly* commemorates the twentieth anniversary of Porter's (1997) original paper in the journal (Qian & Zeuli 2016) with introductory commentary by Porter (2016) and other articles still engaging with the influential strategy. Porter (2016: 110) reconsiders and updates the work of his organization, and provides a generally positive reappraisal. Porter reassesses the following competitive advantages of the inner city:

- Underserved local demand, in the form of both concentrated population as well as an exceptionally diverse population.
- Strategic location, particularly with regard to "proximity to major transportation hubs…and quality of transportation infrastructure."
- Connections to regional clusters: in particular, clusters that represent the competitive advantages of the inner city "include Apparel, Performing Arts, Environmental Services, Jewelry and Precious Metals, Leather and Related Products, Music and Sound Recording, and Tobacco," as well as local clusters including "health services, hospitality, and retail."

An underutilized workforce represents one competitive advantage that no longer seems to hold true as of Porter's 2016 reconsideration. Persistent unemployment and underemployment in the inner city, combined with rising skill levels required in the modern workforce, "raises the stakes for continuing to improve education and training in inner cities" (Porter 2016: 111).

Delgado & Zeuli (2016: 129) examine industrial clusters within the inner city and their relationship to clusters within the larger metropolitan region; they conclude that, consistent with Porter's (1997) argument, "industries located in inner cities with a strong cluster in the inner city or in the nearby region exhibit greater employment growth, a finding that is robust across many cluster categories." Significant inner-city clusters identified in their analysis "include Music and Sound Recording, Footwear, Business Services, Metalworking Technology, Apparel, and Transportation and Logistics" (Delgado & Zeuli 2016: 129). They also confirm higher employment growth for industries that locate in inner cities within a pre-existing initial industrial cluster.

Porter (2016: 111–112) suggests several directions for enhancing the business environment for inner-city business growth as of 2016, including what his research indicates as "the top five disadvantages facing inner-city businesses[:]...parking and traffic problems, the perception of high crime, negative perceptions of the inner city, actual crime, and higher costs for office space." Porter also notes the importance of more fully engaging "anchor institutions," or major industries such as hospitals and universities that are often located in inner cities (Chapter 6).

Richard Florida's creative communities

Not long after Porter's theories caught fire in the ED community, Richard Florida emerged with another highly influential ED theory: the "creative class" and the strategy of attempting to build "creative communities" (Florida 2014, 2010a, 2010b, 2003a, 2003b; Creative Class Group). In a short synopsis, Florida's data analysis suggests that cities with the fastest rates of economic growth are those with the greatest concentrations of what he termed the "creative class": those who work in knowledge-based and creative industries. In Dreher's slightly sarcastic summation, "be creative − or die: cities must attract the new 'creative class' with hip neighborhoods, an arts scene and a gay-friendly atmosphere − or they'll go the way of Detroit" (Dreher 2002: 1, quoted in Peck 2005). The creative class starts with a "super-creative" core of innovative artists, designers, and others working in a variety of media activities (Liu et al. 2010; Florida 2002). In addition, a population of creative professionals includes those in knowledge-based industries such as education, healthcare, and law.

Florida (2003a: 10) argues that this creative class is attracted to places that exhibit concentrations of "the three T's of economic development: Technology, Talent, and Tolerance": high *technology* infrastructure and industries, *talent* in the form of people with university degrees or other skill sets, and *tolerance* for diverse ethnicities, races, and sexual orientations. Florida gained particular attention for his "Bohemian" and "Gay" Indices, which he claims correlate economic growth most closely with high concentrations of artists and especially LGBTQ populations.

Like any substantial theory, there is much to study and critique with regard to the creative class concept. Eduardo Porter (2014: 202) notes that Florida's "ideas have been misappropriated and misunderstood; politicians have justified everything from 'cool cities' to bigger stadiums and everything in between in the name of 'magnetizing' the creative class" (see Peck's 2005 biting critique). In most cases, the creative class will find these concentrations of "T's" in major cities, usually in central cities: "Rural areas are generally not locations of new knowledge production. Few patents go to rural areas (Barkley, Henry, & Lee 2006); research universities in the USA are largely urban, as are industrial R&D activities" (McGranahan, Wojan, & Lambert 2011: 3). As Florida (2013) himself concedes,

> [t]he past couple of decades have seen America sort itself into two distinct nations, as the more highly skilled and affluent have migrated to a relatively small number of cities and metro areas....On close inspection, talent clustering provides little in the way of trickle-down benefits. Its benefits flow

disproportionately to more highly-skilled knowledge, professional and creative workers whose higher wages and salaries are more than sufficient to cover more expensive housing in these locations. While less-skilled service and blue-collar workers also earn more money in knowledge-based metros, those gains disappear once their higher housing costs are taken into account....There is a rising tide of sorts, but it only lifts about the most advantaged third of the workforce, leaving the other 66 percent much further behind.

In theory, attractive rural locations could provide such a creative environment. There are at least some limited examples of rural artist colonies such as Marfa, Texas (Visit Marfa; Seman 2008), and efforts to promote high-tech infrastructure in small cities and rural communities such as LaGrange, Georgia (Gallardo 2016; Edwards 2009; Youtie 2000). The ED profession has been rife for many years with anecdotes about wizened old farmers speaking up at rural town meetings to ask: "How do we get some of those gay boys to move into our downtown?" Rural and other low-income communities, however, often carry at least the reputation of inadequate *technology* infrastructure, scarcity of highly educated *talent*, and in-*tolerance* for diverse populations. In one study of rural communities, Crowe et al. (2015) found no relationship between income levels and traditional measures of the creative class.

Like with many ED theories, creative class causality is unclear, at best. That is, even if there is a statistically significant relationship between high populations of artists and LGBTQ people, how do we know that their presence helped grow the economy – rather than that population being attracted to an economically healthy location? The reality is probably some interdependent combination of both. Regardless, it remains unclear – to my mind – whether or not the theory can be applied normatively: that is, can communities lacking strong endowments of the three "T's" somehow create creative communities? It is even less clear whether the concept can be extended from fairly affluent creative centers to typical low-income communities (Sands & Reese 2008). In a now-familiar pattern of ED strategies, a lack of evidence of success did little to slow the strategy's widespread and enthusiastic application across urban and rural communities alike (Hatcher, Oyer, & Gallardo 2011). The concept has also been closely intertwined with asset-based ED strategies, especially those centered on local art and other cultural traditions (Chapter 5).

Major cities, despite their many advantages in this regard, also find challenges in creative-class-based ED. As Scott (2006: 15) notes, "large cities today may well harbor unprecedented creative capabilities, but they are also places where striking social, cultural, and economic inequalities prevail." According to Thomas & Darnton (2006: 165–166), who reviewed the literature on "social diversity and economic development in the metropolis," "for policy makers, it is indeed important to attract highly educated and creatively talented people to metropolitan areas and to be tolerant in many different ways to encourage free thought, but it is also important to recognize that existing social inequalities must be addressed in a more effective manner than in the past."

Data analysis by Sands & Reese (2008: 18) on mid-sized Canadian cities reveals what "appears to be little connection between the various creativity measures and generally accepted metrics of economic well-being.…It is not just the causal chain that is imperceptible; it was not possible to find even a respectable level of correlation." Zimmerman (2008), Malone and Richard (2007), and Ley (2003) address concerns with the gentrification of low-income, artistic/bohemian communities, in which rising housing costs drive out the creative residents that may have originally driven the vitality of the local community.

New urbanism, smart growth, smart code

The concepts of "new urbanism" and "smart growth" gained widespread attention and popularity within the planning and architecture professions at roughly the same time that Florida's creative community concept caught fire within ED. Prior to that time, in my own professional experience, the fields of planning and ED were often suspicious and even hostile to one another. Since the emergence of the third wave of ED, the fields seem now to recognize the mutually dependent relationships among land use planning, architectural design, and ED (Kim 2011).

The smart growth movement emerged by that name during the economic boom of the 1990s (Goetz 2004) from roots in previous decades. Early advocates represented smart growth as an antidote to uncontrolled economic and land-use growth at any cost in favor of a more thorough evaluation of fiscal, environmental, and quality of life factors in considering the costs and benefits of new growth (Ye, Mandpe, & Meyer 2015; Smart Growth America; Smart Growth Network). Meanwhile, smart growth was often viewed with contempt by ED professionals as simply anti-growth and anti-development.

Meanwhile, the new urbanism movement was popularized by Duany, Plater-Zyberk, and Speck's (2000) highly influential book *Suburban Nation: The Rise of Sprawl and the Decline of the American Dream*. New urbanism harks back to traditional characteristics of urban life: development that was concentrated in city centers; design that facilitates pedestrian and bicycle traffic; and a mixture of residential, commercial, and retail land uses in the same neighborhoods. Suburban and exurban sprawl, segregated land uses, and social isolation are seen as the antitheses of such traditional values.

Through the 2000s, the smart growth and new urbanism movements seemed nearly to merge in terms of concept and terminology. Duany and his colleagues codified the principles of new urbanism into a land ordinance template known as "smart code" (Duany & Speck 2009). The smart code created a new system of mixed-use "transect zoning" (Duany & Talen 2002) as an alternative to the accustomed, nearly ubiquitous system of segregated land use called "Euclidean zoning" (named after a 1926 key court case involving Euclid, Ohio; see Williams 1980). Florida's creative community concept is not directly related to new urbanism and smart growth, but they are all largely compatible with it. New urbanist design and smart codes are generally consistent with the urban life that is considered attractive to the young professionals of the creative class.

One of the first examples of new urbanist design was the affluent community of Seaside, Florida. A lack of affordable housing in communities such as Seaside helped encourage criticism of new urbanism as elitist. There is evidence and concern – acknowledged by Florida – that cities with high levels of creative class population also tend toward high levels of economic inequality (Donegan & Lowe 2008, citing Florida 2005). Leigh and Hoelzel (2012) express concern also that smart growth policies may fail to protect industrial-zoned land, which in turn can compromise communities' manufacturing base.

On the other hand, many new urbanist colleagues under Duany's leadership donated thousands of hours of consulting on the Mississippi Gulf Coast's 2005 Hurricane Katrina recovery and rebuilding efforts (Mississippi Renewal Forum; Talen 2008). I had the privilege of working with the team that developed an inspirational plan for the low-income, largely African American community of Moss Point, Mississippi (Mississippi Renewal Forum: Moss Point). Cabrera and Najarian (2013) and Deitrick and Ellis (2004) are among the researchers who are exploring the potential for applying new urbanist design and smart growth development to inner cities and low-income populations.

"Fourth wave" ED: Sustainable economic development

More recently, we have entered the "fourth wave" of mainstream ED (Leigh & Blakely 2013). Comparable terminology includes "sustainable development" (Jepson 2001), "sustainable local economic development" (Newby 1999), and "green economy" (Barbier & Markandya 2013).

A precise definition of sustainable development remains difficult to pin down, despite long and extensive discussion (Elliott 2012; Jepson 2001) and implementation (Godschalk & Malizia 2014) of the concept. According to the World Bank,

> sustainable development recognizes that growth must be both inclusive and environmentally sound to reduce poverty and build shared prosperity for today's population and to continue to meet the needs of future generations. It is efficient with resources and carefully planned to deliver both immediate and long-term benefits for people, planet, and prosperity.
>
> *(World Bank)*

Newby (1999: 68) argues that a sustainable local economic development (SLED) perspective has the potential to redress some of the deficiencies of traditional, modern ED: "a single-minded focus on global trade and attracting inward investment…tends to be blind to wider social and economic issues.…These include:

- *economic vulnerability*, because reliance on global businesses with no local attachment leaves local economies vulnerable to changes in local market conditions;
- *a tendency to bypass marginalized communities*, because the jobs created may not be accessible to those who most need them in disadvantaged areas;

- *environmental damage….*
- *a failure to develop local skills, entrepreneurship and businesses,* which could otherwise generate local jobs and wealth and lead to more self-reliant and diverse local economies."

Does "sustainable" in actual ED practice really mean anything, or just new, slightly greener wrapping for mostly more of the same (Gunder and Hillier 2009)? Can ED professionals overcome their biases toward traditional "pro-business" and incentive-centered policies in favor of more broadly stated metrics that include environmental protection and social equity (Grodach 2011)?

Instead of viewing environmental or social concerns as luxuries or costs to the economic bottom line, the fourth wave of ED suggests that not only should all three dimensions be considered in evaluating an ED project, but the three dimensions – if considered in totality – can potentially enhance one another and lead to a larger bottom line for everyone concerned. Roberts and Cohen (2002) and others promote "triple value adding" or the "triple bottom line" as a means of institutionalizing and quantifying sustainable development in government, business, planning, and ED practice (Elkington 1994, Savitz 2006; Slaper & Hall 2011).

There are a host of challenges – and also promising opportunities – for realizing this latest strategic wave of ED: truly sustainable development that grows economies along all dimensions, including support for struggling people and communities (Reese & Sands 2007). Chapter 8 expands on the potential for sustainable solutions for ED in low-income communities. There may be hope for low-income communities, after all, within the growing and evolving strategies of mainstream ED.

References

Adkisson, Richard V., & Comfort F. Ricketts. 2016. Exploring the redistribution of manufacturing employment among the American states in the face of overall declines in employment. *Economic Development Quarterly* 30(3): 215–231.

Ajilore, Olugbenga. 2012. Did the Work Opportunity Tax Credit cause subsidized worker substitution? *Economic Development Quarterly* 26(3): 231–237.

American Economic Development Council. 1984. *Economic Development Today.* Chicago: American Economic Development Council.

Appalachian Regional Commission. 1964. *Appalachia: A Report by the President's Appalachian Regional Commision.* Retrieved May 28, 2014: http://files.eric.ed.gov/fulltext/ED076290.pdf.

Appalachian Regional Commission. About ARC. Retrieved May 28, 2014: http://www.arc.gov/about/index.asp.

Appalachian Regional Commission. History. Retrieved December 21, 2016: https://www.arc.gov/about/ARCHistory.asp.

Barbier, Edward B., & Anil Markandya. 2013. *A New Blueprint for a Green Economy.* London: Routledge.

Barkin, David, & Timothy King. 1970. *Regional Economic Development: The River Basin Approach in Mexico.* Cambridge: Cambridge University Press.

Barkley, David L., Mark S. Henry, & Doohee Lee. 2006. Innovative activity in rural areas: The importance of local and regional characteristics. *Community Development Investment Review* 2(3): 1–14.

Barney, Jay B., & William S. Hesterly. 2011. *Strategic Management and Competitive Advantage: Concepts*, 4th ed. Englewood Cliffs, NJ: Prentice Hall.

Bates, Timothy. 2010. Alleviating the financial capital barriers impeding business development in inner cities. *Journal of the American Planning Association* 76(3): 349–362.

Bates, Timothy. 1997. Response: Michael Porter's conservative urban agenda will not revitalize America's inner cities: What will? *Economic Development Quarterly* 11(1): 39–44.

Blakely, Edward J. 2011. *My Storm: Managing the Recovery of New Orleans in the Wake of Katrina*. Philadelphia: University of Pennsylvania Press.

Blumenberg, Evelyn. 2006. Metropolitan dispersion and diversity: Implications for community economic development, in Paul Ong & Anastasia Loukaitou-Sideris, eds., *Jobs and Economic Development in Minority Communities*, 13–39. Philadelphia: Temple University Press.

Boarnet, Marlon G. 2001. Enterprise zones and job creation: Linking evaluation and practice. *Economic Development Quarterly* 15(3): 242–254.

Bradshaw, Michael. 1992. *The Appalachian Regional Commission: Twenty-Five Years of Government Policy*. Lexington, KY: University Press of Kentucky.

Bradshaw, Ted K. 2007. Theories of poverty and anti-poverty programs in community development. *Community Development* 38(1): 7–25.

Bradshaw, Ted K., & Edward J. Blakely. 1999. What are "third-wave" state economic development efforts? From incentives to industrial policy. *Economic Development Quarterly* 13(3): 229–244.

Burayidi, Michael A., & Mamadou Coulibaly. 2009. Image busters: How prison location distorts the profiles of rural host communities and what can be done about it. *Economic Development Quarterly* 23(2): 141–149.

Buss, Terry F. 2001. The effect of state tax incentives on economic growth and firm location decisions: An overview of the literature. *Economic Development Quarterly* 15(1): 90–105.

Cabrera, Joseph F., & Jonathan C. Najarian. 2013. Can new urbanism create diverse communities? *Journal of Planning Education and Research* 33(3): 427–441.

Calabrese, Dan. 2012. States re-examine how they use incentives to attract business. *Area Development Online*. Winter. Retrieved June 24, 2014: http://www.areadevelopment. com/taxesincentives/winter2012/states-business-attraction-incentives-reexamined-662 52555.shtml.

Campanella, Thomas J. 2006. Urban resilience and the recovery of New Orleans. *Journal of the American Planning Association* 72(2): 141–146.

China Three Gorges Corporation. Retrieved July 25, 2016: http://www.ctgpc.com/.

City of Littleton. 2013. *Economic Plan 2013*. Retrieved July 26, 2016: http://www.lit tletongov.org/Home/ShowDocument?id=2176.

Clark, John F. 1927. Keeping up with Jonesville. *The Saturday Evening Post*. September 10. Reprinted in *Economic Development Review* 17(2): 5–17.

Cohen, Stephen S., & J. Bradford DeLong. 2016. *Concrete Economics: The Hamilton Approach to Economic Growth and Social Policy*. Boston: Harvard Business Review.

Cortright, Joseph. 2002. The economic importance of being different: Regional variations in tastes, increasing returns, and the dynamics of development. *Economic Development Quarterly* 16(1): 3–16.

Cox, Keith. 2012. Happiness and unhappiness in the developing world: Life satisfaction among sex workers, dump-dwellers, urban poor, and rural peasants in Nicaragua. *Journal of Happiness Studies* 13(1): 103–128.

Creative Class Group. Retrieved October 9, 2013: http://www.creativeclass.com.

Crowe, Jessica A., Ryan Ceresola, Tony Silva, & Nicholas Recker. 2015. Rural economic development under devolution: A test of local strategies. *Community Development* 46(5): 461–478.

Dawkins, Casey J. 2003. Regional development theory: Conceptual foundations, classic works, and recent developments. *Journal of Planning Literature* 18(2): 131–172.

Deitrick, Sabina, & Cliff Ellis. 2004. New urbanism in the inner city. *Journal of the American Planning Association* 70(4): 426–442.

Delgado, Mercedes, & Kimberly Zeuli. 2016. Clusters and regional performance: Implications for inner cities. *Economic Development Quarterly* 30(2): 117–136.

Delta Regional Authority. Retrieved July 25, 2016: http://dra.gov/.

Denali Commission. Retrieved July 25, 2016: https://www.denali.gov/.

Dewar, Margaret. 2013. Paying employers to hire local workers in distressed places. *Economic Development Quarterly* 27(4): 284–300.

Diener, Ed, & Robert Biswas-Diener. 2009. *Happiness: Unlocking the Mysteries of Psychological Wealth.* Hoboken, NJ: Wiley-Blackwell.

Donegan, Mary, & Nichola Lowe. 2008. Inequality in the creative city: Is there still a place for "old-fashioned" institutions? *Economic Development Quarterly* 22(1): 46–62.

Dowall, David E. 1996. An evaluation of California's enterprise zone programs. *Economic Development Quarterly* 10(4): 352–368.

Dreher, Christopher. 2002. Be creative – or die. *Salon.* June 6: http://www.salon.com/2002/06/06/florida_22/.

Drucker, Peter F. 1994. The theory of business. *Harvard Business Review* 72(5): 95–105.

Drucker, Peter F. 1990. *The Non-Profit Organization.* New York: Routledge.

Drucker, Peter F. 1980. The deadly sins in public administration. *Public Administration Review* 40(2): 103–106.

Duany, Andrés, Elizabeth Plater-Zyberk, & Jeff Speck. 2000. *Suburban Nation: The Rise of Sprawl and the Decline of the American Dream.* New York: North Point.

Duany, Andrés, & Emily Talen. 2002. Transect planning. *Journal of the American Planning Association* 68(3): 246–266.

Duany, Andrés, & Jeff Speck. 2009. *The Smart Growth Manual.* New York: McGraw-Hill Education.

Easterly, William. 2007. *The White Man's Burden: Why the West's Efforts to Aid the Rest Have Done So Much Ill and So Little Good.* New York: Penguin.

Edwards, Judson. 2009. *Digital Deliverance: Dragging Rural America, Kicking and Screaming, into the Information Economy.* Lanham, MD: University Press of America.

Edward Lowe Foundation. Economic gardening. Retrieved July 26, 2016: http://edwardlowe.org/entrepreneurship-programs/economic-gardening/.

Elkington, John. 1994. Towards the sustainable corporation: Win-win-win business strategies for sustainable development. *California Management Review* 36(2): 90–100.

Eller, Ronald D. 2008. *Uneven Ground: Appalachia since 1945.* Lexington, KY: University Press of Kentucky.

Elliott, Jennifer. 2012. *An Introduction to Sustainable Development*, 4th ed. New York: Routledge.

Elvery, Joel. 2009. The impact of enterprise zones on resident employment. *Economic Development Quarterly* 23(1): 44–59.

Florida Economic Gardening Institute. University of Central Florida. Retrieved July 26, 2016: http://www.growfl.com.

Florida, Richard. 2014. The creative class and economic development. *Economic Development Quarterly* 28(3): 196–205.

Florida, Richard. 2013. More losers than winners in America's new economic geography. *The Atlantic.* January 30: http://www.theatlanticcities.com/jobs-and-economy/2013/01/more-losers-winners-americas-new-economic-geography/4465/.

Florida, Richard. 2012. The uselessness of economic development incentives. *The Atlantic.* December 7: http://www.citylab.com/work/2012/12/uselessness-economic-development-incentives/4081/.

Florida, Richard. 2010a. Building the creative community, in Japonica Brown-Saracino, ed., *The Gentrification Debates*, 345–354. New York: Routledge.

Florida, Richard. 2010b. *The Flight of the Creative Class: The New Global Competition for Talent.* New York: HarperCollins.

Florida, Richard. 2005. *The Flight of the Creative Class.* New York: HarperCollins.

Florida, Richard. 2003a. Cities and the creative class. *City & Community* 2(1): 3–19.

Florida, Richard. 2003b. *The Rise of the Creative Class.* New York: Basic Books.

Florida, Richard. 2002. Bohemia and economic geography. *Journal of Economic Geography* 2(1): 55–71.

Friedmann, John, & Clyde Weaver. 1979. *Territory and Function: Evolution of Regional Planning.* London: Hodder & Stoughton Educational.

Gallardo, Roberto. 2016. *Responsive Countryside: The Digital Age and Rural Communities.* Mississippi State University Extension Service.

Gauthier, Howard L. 1973. The Appalachian development highway system: Development for whom? *Economic Geography* 4(2): 103–108.

Gibbons, Chris. 2010. Littleton's economic gardening strategy. *Nation's Cities Weekly.* January 11: 4–6. Retrieved June 24, 2014: http://www.nlc.org/File%20Library/Utility%20Navigation/News%20Center/NCW/2010/NCW011110.pdf.

Godschalk, David R., & Emil E. Malizia. 2014. *Sustainable Development Projects: Integrating Design, Development, and Regulation.* Chicago: Planners.

Goetz, Edward G. 2004. The big tent of growth management: Smart growth as a movement. Proceedings of a Symposium at the Society for Conservation Biology 2004 Annual Meeting. Retrieved July 29, 2016: http://www.nrs.fs.fed.us/pubs/gtr/gtr_nc265/gtr_nc265_045.pdf.

Gordon, Victoria. 2007. Partners or competitors? Perceptions of regional economic development cooperation in Illinois. *Economic Development Quarterly* 21(1): 60–78.

Graham, Carol. 2011. *The Pursuit of Happiness: An Economy of Well-Being.* Washington, DC: Brookings Institution.

Greenbaum, Robert T. 2004. Siting it right: Do states target economic distress when designating enterprise zones? *Economic Development Quarterly* 18(1): 67–80.

Greenbaum, Robert T., & John Engberg. 2000. An evaluation of state enterprise zone policies. *Review of Policy Research* 17(2–3): 29–45.

Grodach, Carl. 2011. Barriers to sustainable economic development: The Dallas–Fort Worth experience. *Cities* 28(4): 300–309.

Gunder, Michael, & Jean Hillier. 2009. *Planning in Ten Words or Less: A Lacanian Entanglement with Spatial Planning.* Farnham, UK: Ashgate.

Hall, Peter. 1982. Enterprise zones: A justification. *International Journal of Urban & Regional Research* 6(3): 416–421.

Hansen, Niles. 1966. Some neglected factors in American regional development policy: The case of Appalachia. *Land Economics* 62(1): 1–9.

Hanson, Susan, & Geraldine Pratt. 1992. Dynamic dependencies: A geographic investigation of local labor markets. *Economic Geography* 68(4): 373–405.

Hargrove, Erwin C. 2001. *Prisoners of Myth: The Leadership of the Tennessee Valley Authority, 1933–1990.* Princeton: Princeton University Press.

Harrison, Bennett, & Amy K. Glasmeier. 1997. Response: Why business alone won't redevelop the inner city: A friendly critique of Michael Porter's approach to urban revitalization. *Economic Development Quarterly* 11(1): 39–44.

Hatcher, William, Matt Oyer, & Roberto Gallardo. 2011. The creative class and economic development as practiced in the rural US South: An exploratory survey of economic development professionals. *The Review of Regional Studies* 41(2–3): 139–159.

Herbers, John. 1990. A third wave of economic development. *Governing* 3(9): 43–50.

Hogue, Henry B. 2005. Federal hurricane recovery coordinator: Appointment and oversight issues. Congressional Research Service. November 28. Retrieved July 25, 2016: http://www.au.af.mil/au/awc/awcgate/crs/rs22334.pdf.

Hopkins, Ernest J. 1944. *Mississippi's BAWI Plan: An Experiment in Industrial Subsidization.* Atlanta: Federal Reserve Bank of Atlanta.

Huggins, Robert, & Hiro Izushi. 2009. Regional benchmarking in a global context: Knowledge, competitiveness, and economic development. *Economic Development Quarterly* 23(4): 275–293.

Immergluck, Daniel. 2004. *Credit to the Community: Community Reinvestment and Fair Lending Policy in the United States.* Armonk, NY: M.E. Sharpe.

Initiative for a Competitive Inner City. Retrieved June 13, 2016: http://icic.org/.

International Economic Development Council. *Economic Development Reference Guide.* Retrieved February 1, 2016: http://www.iedconline.org/clientuploads/Downloads/IEDC_ED_Reference_Guide.pdf.

Isserman, Andrew, & Terance Rephann. 1995. The economic effects of the Appalachian Regional Commission. *Journal of the American Planning Association* 61(3): 345–364.

Jacobs, Jane. 1984. Why TVA failed. *New York Review of Books.* May 10: 41–47.

Jacobs, Ken, Zohar Perla, Ian Perry & Dave Graham-Squire. 2016. Producing poverty: The public cost of low-wage production jobs in manufacturing. University of California Berkeley Labor Center. May 10: http://laborcenter.berkeley.edu/producing-poverty-the-public-cost-of-low-wage-production-jobs-in-manufacturing/.

Jepson, Jr., Edward. 2001. Sustainability and planning: Diverse concepts and close associations. *Journal of Planning Literature* 15(4): 499–510.

Jeroslow, Phyllis. 2015. Creating a sustainable society: Human rights in the U.S. welfare state, in Stephen N. Haymes, Maria V. de Haymes, & Reuben J. Miller, *The Routledge Handbook of Poverty in the United States,* 559–566. New York: Routledge.

Kauffman Foundation. Economic gardening. Retrieved July 26, 2016: http://www.kauffman.org/what-we-do/resources/policy/economic-gardening.

Kim, Jae H. 2011. Linking land use planning and regulation to economic development: A literature review. *Journal of Planning Literature* 26(1): 35–47.

Kuhn, Thomas S. 1962. *The Structure of Scientific Revolutions.* Chicago: University of Chicago Press.

Ladd, Helen F. 1994. Spatially targeted economic development strategies: Do they work? *Cityscape* 1(1): 193–218.

Lambert, Thomas E., & Paul A. Coomes. 2001. An evaluation of the effectiveness of Louisville's enterprise zone. *Economic Development Quarterly* 15(2): 168–180.

Layard, Richard. 2006. *Happiness: Lessons from a New Science.* London: Penguin.

Leigh, Nancey G., & Edward J. Blakely. 2013. *Planning Local Economic Development: Theory and Practice,* 5th ed. Thousand Oaks, CA: Sage.

Leigh, Nancey G., & Nathanael Z. Hoelzel. 2012. Smart growth's blind side. *Journal of the American Planning Association* 78(1): 87–103.

Leung, Ambrose, Cheryl Kier, Tak Fung, Linda Fung, & Robert Sproule. 2011. Searching for happiness: The importance of social capital. *Journal of Happiness Studies* 12(3): 443–462.

Levy, John. 1990. What local economic developers actually do: Location quotients versus press releases. *Journal of the American Planning Association* 56(2): 183–190.

Lewis, W. Arthur. 1955. Appendix: Is growth desirable? *The Theory of Economic Growth.* Homewood, IL: Richard D. Irwin.

Ley, David. 2003. Artists, aestheticisation and the field of gentrification. *Urban Studies* 40(12): 426–441.

Lilienthal, David E. 1954. *TVA: Democracy on the March.* New York: Harper.

Liu, Cathy Y., Ric Kolenda, Grady Fitzpatrick, & Tim N. Todd. 2010. Re-creating New Orleans: Driving development through creativity. *Economic Development Quarterly* 24(3): 261–275.

Malone, Ken, & Brian Richard. 2007. Linking high tech, arts, & affordable housing – Winston-Salem case study. *Applied Research in Economic Development* 4(1): 112–123.

Markusen, Ann. 2007. *Reining in the Competition for Capital.* Kalamazoo, MI: W.E. Upjohn Institute for Employment Research.

Martinez-Cosio, Maria, & Mirle R. Bussell. 2012. Private foundations and community development: Differing approaches to community empowerment. *Community Development* 4(4): 416–429.

McCabe, Sean. 2014. Kentucky death march. *Rolling Stone.* May 22: 68–75.

McGranahan, David, Timothy R. Wojan, & Dayton M. Lambert. 2011. The rural growth trifecta: Outdoor amenities, creative class and entrepreneurial context. *Journal of Economic Geography* 11(3): 529–557.

Milken Institute. Research: Emerging domestic markets. Retrieved June 24, 2014: http://www.milkeninstitute.org/research/research.taf?cat=cedm.

Miller, Mark M. 1988. *Managing the Maelstrom: Decentralization Planning for the Mexico City Metropolis.* Unpublished Ph.D. dissertation. Tucson: University of Arizona.

Mishel, Lawrence, Josh Bivens, Elise Gould, & Heidi Shierholz. 2012. *The State of Working America,* 12th ed. Ithaca, NY: ILR.

Mississippi Historical Society. Economic development in the 1930s: Balance agriculture with industry. *Mississippi History Now.* Retrieved July 25, 2016: http://mshistorynow.mdah.state.ms.us/articles/224/economic-development-in-the-1930s-balance-agriculture-with-industry.

Mississippi Renewal Forum. Retrieved May 28, 2014: http://www.mississippirenewal.com.

Mississippi Renewal Forum. Moss Point. Prepared by the HOK Planning Group: Steve Schukraft, Todd Meyer, & Dhaval Barbhaya. Retrieved July 29, 2016: http://mississippirenewal.com/documents/Pres_MossPoint.pdf.

Nel, Etienne L., Trevor Hill, & Tony Binns. 1997. Development from below in the 'New' South Africa: The case of Hertzog, Eastern Cape. *Geographical Journal* 163(1): 57–64.

Neumark, David, & Jed Kolko. 2010. Do enterprise zones create jobs? Evidence from California's enterprise zone program. *Journal of Urban Economics* 68(1): 1–19.

Neuse, Steven. 1983. TVA at age fifty – reflections and retrospect. *Public Administration Review* 43(6): 491–499.

Newby, Les. 1999. Sustainable local economic development: A new agenda for action? *Local Environment* 4(1): 67–72.

Olshansky, Robert B. 2006. Planning after Hurricane Katrina. *Journal of the American Planning Association* 72(2): 147–153.

Peattie, Lisa. 1987. *Planning: Rethinking Ciudad Guayana.* Ann Arbor, MI: University of Michigan Press.

Peck, Jamie. 2005. Struggling with the creative class. *International Journal of Urban and Regional Research* 29(4): 740–770.

Peters, Alan H., & Peter S. Fisher. 2004. The failures of economic development incentives. *Journal of the American Planning Association* 70(1): 27–37.

Peters, Alan H., & Peter S. Fisher. 2002. *State Enterprise Zone Programs: Have They Worked?* Kalamazoo, MI: W.E. Upjohn Institute for Employment Research.

Pew Center on the States. 2012. *Evidence Counts: Evaluating State Tax Incentives for Jobs and Growth.* Retrieved July 26, 2016: http://www.pewtrusts.org/~/media/legacy/uploadedfiles/wwwp ewtrustsorg/reports/economic_mobility/pewevaluatingstatetaxincentivesreportpdf.pdf.

Pfeiffer, Deirdre, & Scott Cloutier. 2016. Planning for happy neighborhoods. *Journal of the American Planning Association* 82(3): 267–279.

Phillips, Rhonda, & Robert H. Pittman, eds. 2015. *An Introduction to Community Development,* 2nd ed. New York: Routledge.

Porter, Eduardo. 2014. Income equality: A search for consequences. *New York Times.* March 25: http://www.nytimes.com/2014/03/26/business/economy/making-sense-of-income-inequality.html?_r=0.

Porter, Michael E. 2016. Inner-city economic development: Learnings from 20 years of research and practice. *Economic Development Quarterly* 30(2): 105–116.

Porter, Michael E. 2005. The competitive advantage of the inner city. *Harvard Business Review* 73(3): 55–71.

Porter, Michael E. 2000. Location, competition, and economic development: Local clusters in a global economy. *Economic Development Quarterly* 14(1): 15–34.

Porter, Michael E. 1998. Clusters and the new economics of competition. *Harvard Business Review* 76(6): 77–90.

Porter, Michael E. 1997. New strategies for inner-city economic development. *Economic Development Quarterly* 11(1): 11–27.

Porter, Michael E. 1990. *The Competitive Advantage of Nations.* New York: Free Press.

Porter, Michael E. 1985. *Competitive Advantage: Creating and Sustaining Superior Performance.* New York: Free Press.

Qian, Haifeng, & Kimberly Zeuli. 2016. Introduction to special issue: Inner-city economic development. *Economic Development Quarterly* 30(2): 103–104.

Quello, Steve, & Graham Toft. 2006. Economic gardening, in *The Small Business Economy.* Small Business Administration, 159–194. Retrieved March 4, 2013: http://www.sba. gov/advocacy/849/6282.

Ratner, Shanna, & Deborah Markley. 2014. Rural wealth creation as a sustainable economic development strategy: Introduction to the special issue. *Community Development* 45(5): 435–442.

Reese, Laura A. 2014. The alchemy of local economic development. *Economic Development Quarterly* 28(3): 206–219.

Reese, Laura A., & Gary Sands. 2007. Sustainability and local economic development in Canada and the United States. *International Journal of Sustainable Development Planning* 2(1): 25–43.

Rich, Michael J., & Robert P. Stoker. 2014. *Collaborative Governance for Urban Revitalization: Lessons from Empowerment Zones.* Ithaca, NY: Cornell University Press.

Riker, James V. 1994. Linking development from below to the international environmental movement: Sustainable development and state-NGO relations in Indonesia. *Journal of Business Administration* 22–23: 157–188.

Roberts, Brian, & Michael Cohen. 2002. Enhancing sustainable development by triple value adding to the core business of government. *Economic Development Quarterly* 16(2): 127–137.

Ross, David P., & Peter J. Usher. 1986. *From the Roots Up: Economic Development as if Community Mattered.* New York: Bootstrap.

Ross, Doug, & Robert E. Friedman. 1990. The emerging third wave: New economic development strategies. *Entrepreneurial Economy Review* 9: 3–10.

Rubin, Julia S. 2011. Countering the rhetoric of emerging domestic markets: Why more information alone will not address the capital needs of underserved communities. *Economic Development Quarterly* 25(2): 182–192.

Sachs, Jeffrey D. 2015. *The Age of Sustainable Development.* New York: Columbia University Press.

Sands, Gary, & Laura A. Reese. 2008. Cultivating the creative class: And what about Nanaimo? *Economic Development Quarterly* 22(1): 8–23.

Savitz, Andrew. 2006. *The Triple Bottom Line: How Today's Best-Run Companies Are Achieving Economic, Social and Environmental Success – and How You Can Too.* San Francisco: Jossey-Bass.

Sawicki, David, & Mitch Moody. 1997. Déjà-vu all over again: Porter's model of inner-city redevelopment, in Thomas Boston & Catherine Ross, eds., *The Inner City*, 75–94. New Brunswick, NJ: Transaction.

Saxenian, AnnaLee. 2002. Silicon Valley's new immigrant high-growth entrepreneurs. *Economic Development Quarterly* 16(1): 20–31.

Scott, Allen J. 2006. Creative cities: Conceptual issues and policy questions. *Journal of Urban Affairs* 28(1): 1–17.

Seman, Michael. 2008. No country for old developers: The strange tale of an arts boom, bohemians, and "Marfalafel" in the High Desert of Marfa, Texas. *Applied Research in Economic Development* 5(3): 25–31.

Sen, Amartya. 1999. *Development as Freedom.* New York: Knopf.

Servon, Lisa. 2007. Making US microenterprise work: Recommendations for policy makers and the field, in Julia S. Rubin, ed., *Financing Low-Income Communities: Models, Obstacles, and Future Directions*, 95–120. New York: Russell Sage Foundation.

Shaffer, Ron, Steve Deller & Dave Marcouiller. 2006. Rethinking community economic development. *Economic Development Quarterly* 20(1): 59–74.

Simms, Alvin, David Freshwater, & Jamie Ward. 2014. The Rural Economic Capacity Index (RECI): A benchmarking tool to support community-based economic development. *Economic Development Quarterly* 28(4): 351–363.

Slaper, Timothy F., & Tanya J. Hall. 2011. The triple bottom line: What is it and how does it work? *Indiana Business Review* 86(1): 4–8.

Smart Growth America. Retrieved July 29, 2016: http://www.smartgrowthamerica.org/.

Smart Growth Network. Retrieved July 29, 2016: http://www.smartgrowth.org/.

Stöhr, Walter B., & D. R. Fraser Taylor. 1981. *Development from Above or Below? Dialectics of Regional Planning in Developing Countries.* Hoboken, NJ: Wiley.

Stoll, Michael A. 2006. Workforce development in minority communities, in Paul Ong & Anastasia Loukaitou-Sideris, eds., *Jobs and Economic Development in Minority Communities*, 91–118. Philadelphia: Temple University Press.

Story, Louise. 2012a. Michigan town woos Hollywood, but ends up with a bit part. *New York Times.* December 3: http://www.nytimes.com/2012/12/04/us/when-hollywood-comes-to-town.html?ref=todayspaper&_r=0.

Story, Louise. 2012b. Lines blur as Texas gives industries a bonanza. *New York Times.* December 2: http://www.nytimes.com/2012/12/03/us/winners-and-losers-in-texas.html?pagewanted=all&_r=0.

Story, Louise. 2012c. As companies seek tax deals, governments pay high price. *New York Times.* December 1: http://www.nytimes.com/2012/12/02/us/how-local-taxpayers-bankroll-corporations.html.

Sullivan, Bartholomew. 2012. Is Delta Regional Authority on chopping block? *Commercial Appeal.* December 22: http://www.commercialappeal.com/news/2012/dec/22/is-delta-regional-authority-on-chopping-block/.

Swager, Ronald J., ed. 1991. *Economic Development Tomorrow: A Report from the Profession*. Chicago: American Economic Development Council.

Talen, Emily. 2008. New urbanism, social equity, and the challenge of post-Katrina rebuilding in Mississippi. *Journal of Planning Education and Research* 27(3): 277–293.

Taylor, Davis F. & Chad R. Miller. 2010. Rethinking local business clusters: The case of food clusters for promoting community development. *Community Development* 41(1): 108–120.

Tennessee Valley Authority. History. Retrieved December 14, 2011: http://www.tva.gov/econdev/index.htm.

Tennessee Valley Authority. Tennessee Valley Authority Act, 1933. Retrieved June 20, 2012: http://www.tva.com/abouttva/pdf/TVA_Act.pdf.

Thomas, June M., & Julia Darnton. 2006. Social diversity and economic development in the metropolis. *Journal of Planning Literature* 21(2): 153–168.

Todaro, Michael P., & Stephen C. Smith. 2014. *Economic Development*, 12th ed. Englewood Cliffs, NJ: Prentice Hall.

Turner, Robert C., & Mark K. Cassell. 2007. When do states pursue targeted economic development policies? The adoption and expansion of state enterprise zone programs. *Social Science Quarterly* 88(1): 86–103.

United Nations Development Programme. 2015. *Human Development Report 2015: Work for Human Development*. Retrieved March 24, 2016: http://hdr.undp.org/sites/default/files/2015_human_development_report_1.pdf.

University of Southern Mississippi, Department of Economic Development, Tourism and Sport Management. About – Master of Science in Economic Development. Retrieved September 5, 2016: https://www.usm.edu/business/eco-dev-tourism-sport-management/about-master-science-economic-development.

US Department of Housing and Urban Development. Welcome to the Community Renewal Initiative. Retrieved June 26: 2016: http://www.hud.gov/offices/cpd/economicdevelopment/programs/rc/index.cfm.

US Department of Labor, Bureau of Labor Statistics. 2013. Industry employment and output projections to 2022. *Monthly Labor Review*. December: http://www.bls.gov/opub/mlr/2013/article/industry-employment-and-output-projections-to-2022.htm.

Visit Marfa. Retrieved July 28, 2016: http://www.visitmarfa.com/.

Walcott, Susan M. 2011. The furniture foothills and the spatial fix: Globalization in the furniture industry. *Southeastern Geographer* 51(1): 6–30.

Walcott, Susan M. 2002. Analyzing an innovative environment: San Diego as a bioscience beachhead. *Economic Development Quarterly* 16(2): 99–114.

Wallace, Sherri L. 1999. Life on "EZ" street: Linking community economic development to the empowerment zones and enterprise community policy goals. *Community Development* 30(2): 154–177.

Waugh, Jr., William, & R. Brian Smith. 2006. Economic development and reconstruction on the Gulf after Katrina. *Economic Development Quarterly* 20(3): 211–218.

Whitacre, Brian E., David Shideler, & Randi Williams. 2016. Do incentive programs cause growth? The case of the Oklahoma Quality Jobs Program and community-level economic growth. *Economic Development Quarterly* 30(1): 62–74.

Widner, Ralph R. 1990. Appalachian development after 25 years: An assessment. *Economic Development Quarterly* 4(4): 291–312.

Wilder, Margaret G., & Barry M. Rubin. 1996. Rhetoric versus reality: A review of studies on state enterprise zone programs. *Journal of the American Planning Association* 62(4): 473–491.

Wilkins, Joy, Dana King, Blair Garvey, & Andrea Lytle. 2009. *Benchmarking Excellence among Accredited Economic Development Organizations*. Washington, DC: International Economic Development Council.

Williams, Jr., Norman. 1980. *American Land Planning Law*. New Brunswick, NJ: Center for Urban Policy Research.

Wolman, Harold, & Diana Hincapie. 2015. Clusters and cluster-based development policy. *Economic Development Quarterly* 29(2): 135–149.

Wolman, Harold, Eric Stokan, & Howard Wial. 2015. Manufacturing job loss in U.S. deindustrialized regions – its consequences and implications for the future: Examining the conventional wisdom. *Economic Development Quarterly* 29(2): 102–112.

Wolman, Harold, Howard Wial, & Edward Hill. 2015. Introduction to focus issue on deindustrialization, manufacturing job loss, and economic development policy. *Economic Development Quarterly* 29(2): 99–101.

World Bank. Sustainable development overview. Retrieved June 25, 2014: http://www.worldbank.org/en/topic/sustainabledevelopment/overview.

World Commission on Environment and Development. 1987. *Our Common Future (The Brundtland Report)*. Retrieved April 7, 2016: http://www.un-documents.net/wced-ocf.htm.

Ye, Lin, Sumedha Mandpe, & Peter B. Meyer. 2015. What is "Smart Growth?" – Really? *Journal of Planning Literature* 19(3): 301–315.

Youtie, Jan. 2000. Field of dreams revisited: Economic development and telecommunications in LaGrange, Georgia. *Economic Development Quarterly* 14(2): 146–153.

Zhang, Sumei. 2015. Impacts of enterprise zone policy on industry growth: New evidence from the Louisville program. *Economic Development Quarterly* 29(4): 347–362.

Zheng, Lingwen, & Mildred Warner. 2010. Business incentive use among U.S. local governments: A story of accountability and policy learning. *Economic Development Quarterly* 24(4): 325–336.

Zhong, Raymond. 2015. Manufacturing bust: For poor countries, well-worn path to development turns rocky. *Wall Street Journal*. November 24: http://www.wsj.com/articles/for-poor-countries-well-worn-path-to-development-turns-rocky-1448374298.

Zimmerman, Jeffrey. 2008. From brew town to cool town: Neoliberalism and the creative city development strategy in Milwaukee. *Cities* 25(4): 230–242.

PART II

Five dynamic dimensions of economic development for low-income communities

4

EMPOWER YOUR RESIDENTS: BEGIN WITH BASIC EDUCATION[1]

More than anything else that we *think* we know about economic development (ED), be it in low-income communities or not, be it in the US or anywhere else in the world, we can state with bold confidence that education is the driving force behind the creation of true ED (Todaro & Smith 2014; Organisation for Economic Co-operation and Development 2010; Hanushek & Wößmann 2010; Checchi 2006; Heckman 2006). This relationship is widely recognized in the literature and the conventional wisdom of development both internationally and in the US.

The ED success of South Korea has been widely credited to the country's investment in, emphasis on, and performance in public education (Severin & Capota 2011; Hanushek 2002; Boyer 1991), all of which it sustained, it should be strongly noted, over the course of several decades. Not only does education correlate with average income in a country, but there is evidence that "income inequality tends to be lower in countries where average educational achievement is higher" (Checchi 2006: 5).

In contrast with the reputations of South Korea and other developing Asian countries (Hanushek 2002) for economic success through education, research suggests a relationship between lower access to education in Latin America and that region's comparative economic stagnation and inequalities, at least into the 1990s (Checchi 2006; Brandolini & Rossi 1998). Sturm (1993: xi) summarizes his review of the international literature thus: "Education and training are clearly connected to economic performance. Regardless of the particular method used to measure this contribution, education and its effects on labor quality are generally found to be among the most important contributors to economic growth." Here in the US, a number of noted researchers – including Timothy Bartik (2011), Nobel laureate James Heckman (2006), and Dimitriy Masterov (Heckman & Masterov 2007) – conclude that the returns to investment in education are especially high when those investments target low-income, disadvantaged populations.

Within ED theory, beginning with the "third wave" of ED in the 1990s (Chapter 3), education in indirect terms such as "human capital" (Johansen & Arano 2016; Pink-Harper 2015; Hornbeck & Salamon 1991; Becker 1964) and "capabilities" (Sen 1999) has been assigned a much more central role. An extensive and growing body of theory and empirical analysis focuses on these concepts as applied to countries of the Developing World. Mathur (1999) provides a concise review of the human capital literature and argues for its relevance to ED in the US. Based on their analysis of 223 communities in the US, Reese and Ye (2011) argue that the relationship between education and economic health among communities outweighs the effects of any other traditional ED strategy. Education can also build individual and community resilience against economic and other hardships (Perna 2014; Rothwell & Berube 2011; Berube 2010).

Human resources are among the most important of Porter's (2000, 1990; Chapter 3) "factors" driving ED: taking the foremost place from traditional ED factors such as raw materials, land, and financial capital resources. Florida's (2003a, 2003b; Chapter 3) theories of ED success are entirely built around the critical importance of "creative" human capital. Most members of his creative class are defined by the level and character of their education – mainly higher education (Moretti 2012).

Indeed, the relationship between education and economic success seems so obvious as to be trivial. When a student and I began a research project starting with the question "Does education create ED at the local level?" some other academic colleagues were surprised that we would be pursuing such a self-evident question. On an individual basis, educational achievement seems clearly to be related to higher earnings (Checchi 2006), along with a wide variety of other personal benefits including increased health, better consumer choices, higher levels of savings, as well as wider and more efficient job searches (Wolfe & Haveman 2002). As with nearly any aspect of community or economic development, however, the relationship is far more complicated than first instincts would suggest, both in terms of individual, personal benefits from education and in terms of the benefits that society may gain from investing in public education.

In terms of individual, personal benefits from education, Card and Krueger (2011) and Heckman and Krueger (2003) argue that there is a positive relationship between "school quality" at the grade school level and student earnings. Card & Krueger (2011: 12) conclude that "much of the gain in black-white relative earnings over the past century has been attributed to growth in the relative quality of black schooling" (see also Smith & Welch 1989). In terms of what does seem to pay off most for individuals, Card and Kreuger (2011: 13) find that "rates of return are higher for individuals who attended schools with lower pupil/teacher ratios and higher relative teacher salaries." On the other hand, the results of studies on the relationship between investment in public education and outcomes for society are deeply complex and sometimes appear to be contradictory: "The large literature on the effect of school resources on student achievement generally finds ambiguous, conflicting, and weak results" (Card & Krueger 2011: 122).

PROFESSOR'S PODIUM: MORE CHALLENGES OF SOCIAL SCIENCE

Much of the difficulty here – as is the case with so much social science research – is the difficulty of "operationalizing" abstract concepts such as "investment" and "outcomes." Operationalizing means to turn those abstract and often vague concepts into something solid enough to be measured or otherwise studied with rigor. "Investment," for example, sounds like a pretty concrete concept, but what exactly are we spending our money on? Better schools? More computers? Higher teacher salaries? Fewer students per classroom? Card and Krueger (2011: 8), for example, operationalize "school quality" in terms of "pupil-teacher ratio, average term length, and the relative pay of teachers."

Next, how are we operationalizing results? Higher earnings by the students in the future? Test scores? High school graduation rates? Percentage of students who progress on to college? Success of the students' children? Some researchers study the characteristics of "resilience" in children, which can include factors such as social competence, problem-solving skills, independence, a sense of purpose, and the ability to adapt to stressful life events (Wang, Haertel, & Walberg 1994). As you can see, some of these outcome measures – such as test scores – are readily available, but other measures can take years or even a generation to yield the data we need for meaningful analysis. Further, are we comparing school districts within individual states? In-depth case studies of particular schools or school districts (e.g., Straus 2013; Tough 2008)? Comparisons among different states? Comparisons of the US with other countries? Besides all that, what levels of education are we studying? High schools? Elementary schools? Kindergartens or Pre-Ks? All of the above? You can see some of the challenges and the reasons for the difficulties of comparing outcomes from many different studies.

We also face the age-old question of correlation vs. causality. If there is a relationship between higher teacher salaries and higher student test scores, for example, which "causes" which? Sometimes these quandaries can be sorted out with longitudinal studies, or research work that is conducted over a long period of time: when did teachers receive raises, for example, and when did test scores improve? Longitudinal studies, though, are expensive, slow, and time-consuming.

Sometimes, we have the opportunity to study what are called "natural experiments," or analyses of events that occurred outside the researchers' control. One example mentioned above is Card and Krueger's (2011) historical analysis of the effects on earnings for African Americans resulting from the desegregation of schools, especially in the South. Obviously, no researcher would deliberately and severely deprive huge numbers of students of adequate school resources in order to compare them with students who are not deprived. But, of course, that did occur in our history, and happily it also was reversed (to at least some extent) over time.

Researchers – and those who have the task of interpreting research results – also face the challenge of "generalizability." (There is nothing we academics like better than a long, awkward, word that is difficult to pronounce.) That is, can we be confident that the results from one study – perhaps a study of a few particular school districts or a few particular years – will apply to a different school district or another time period? Results during economic booms may not be the same, for example, as results during recessions, and vice versa. Researchers will often address the issue in a research paper's conclusion: to what extent the results can be generalized, and to what extent the results have "limitations" when it comes to being generalized to other circumstances.

Perhaps the biggest problem of them all is what is known, among other terms, as "confounding variables." For example, tests scores, high school graduation rates, or college matriculation rates may be much higher in one district than in another. We are tempted to praise the superiority of the better-performing district and condemn the failure of others. On the other hand, how many other factors could be involved? We would expect that the students in a wealthier district would have superior performance: their parents are more likely to pay for tutoring, have computers available at home, and be role models of educational and career success. Similarly, we would expect a school with a high proportion of students with English as a second language to face extra challenges. Wealthier school districts can typically provide higher pay for teachers and hire better-qualified administrators. The parents in lower-income school districts will typically have lower levels of education themselves, so they may not be able to help their children with homework or advise them on college applications. Again, a serious researcher will attempt to "control" for the many other factors, or "variables," that might influence the results – but it is very difficult and expensive to account fully for them all.

In a longitudinal analysis (1992 through 2002) of data at the state level, Deskins, Hill, and Ullrich (2010) find no statistical relationship between state levels of K–12 education spending and economic growth measured either as gross state product (GSP) or employment growth. Even that result is better, though, than the finding of a statistically significant *negative* economic impact from state spending on higher education, both in terms of GSP and employment growth. Based on their review of previous work, Deskins, Hill, and Ullrich (2010) suggest that these results are largely due to the tax impacts of financing education expenditures. Alternatively, instead of raising revenues entirely through tax increases, states may choose to increase education funding by cutting expenditures in other areas of the budget that are also critical for ED, such as transportation, transfer payments, healthcare, ports, or other branches of state government.

Just a few of the potentially confounding factors, or variables, discussed in the "Professor's podium" include the education level and employment status of the students' parents, the nature of the community or neighborhood in which the students live (recall "neighborhood effects" from Chapter 2), students' access to positive social networks, and the various effects of discrimination. According to Checchi (2006: 215–216), "there is a vast empirical evidence to the effect that the children of educated parents are more likely to acquire education." Young people raised by relatively wealthy, well-educated parents and who live in relatively affluent communities are more likely to have both high educational achievement and high earnings in their future. Checchi (2006) notes a wide variety of factors that may contribute to the success of students who have well-resourced and educated parents, including imitation, a higher awareness of the importance of education, information about school quality and options, and higher incomes allowing more investment in extracurricular tutoring and other resources. Not only will more affluent parents be able to afford more expensive grade school and university edu-cations for their children, but their children will be endowed with more extensive and higher-level social networks, as well as a wealth of social "soft skills." Children acquire attitudes toward education through observing their own parents as role models: educational attainment, reading habits, vocabulary in conversation, etc. (Checchi 2006). Even for children attending essentially free public school, wealthier parents can afford to live in communities or neighborhoods that provide access to schools with plentiful resources and higher-achieving students: "Schools work with what parents give them….Successful schools build on the efforts of successful families" (Heckman & Masterov 2007: 447–448). As such, important impacts of education also may be most apparent only over very long time frames, such as decades or generations (Bartik 2011).

We naturally tend to think of investment in monetary terms, but there are also many other types of investment that potentially yield positive results for education – and apparently do so in other countries as well. The Scandinavian countries are noted as some of the world's wealthiest countries per capita, possessing some of the highest levels of quality of life by various measures and, most likely not coin-cidentally, some of the world's highest-quality education systems. Surely these nations can afford to invest well financially in their schools, but they also invest their teachers with levels of respect and professional regard that we in the US would typically reserve for doctors, lawyers, and perhaps university professors (Sahlberg 2014). South Korea treats top teachers with near rock-star reverence – and remuneration (Fifield 2014).

Sorting out causes and effects between educational investment and ED makes for complicated reasoning, and causalities can often be circular. Within the US, for example, states with high levels of investment in public education not surprisingly tend to be wealthier, and vice versa (Reese & Ye 2011; US Census Bureau 2015). The relationship is not a perfect correlation, but relatively wealthy states (both in per capita and absolute terms) such as Connecticut, New York, Vermont, and New Jersey spend more than double per student than some of the lower-income states such as Alabama and Mississippi. To the extent that educational investment yields ED benefits for individual states, those wealthy states should be able to invest even more in the future – perpetuating an economic "virtuous cycle" for those fortunate states. The lower-income states, on the other hand, risk perpetuating a "vicious cycle" relative to wealthier competing states.

Ironically, when a community is successful in its ED efforts, that can have the effect of discouraging residents from pursuing higher levels of educational achievement – and so, potentially, stagnating at that level of ED and other aspects of development. Demand for higher education can decrease, for example, when relatively low-skill jobs are widely available (Donaldson & O'Keefe 2013). This effect is similar to the so-called "curse of natural resources," in which countries or communities that have the richest natural endowment of economic wealth often have low levels of development, and vice versa (Chapter 7 sidebar). It is a truism of higher education that enrollments tend to rise in periods of economic decline, and vice versa – although this relationship has not been as clear cut during the Great Recession and times of rising college tuition costs.

As such, education has the potential to serve as a double-edged sword for ED: a powerful tool for ED on behalf of individuals and communities, but also an instrument for exacerbating inequality among communities and segments of society. As noted above, educational success is highly "inheritable" from one's family (Hartman 2014). Meanwhile, there is clear evidence of a persistent, growing, perhaps even accelerating resegregation of schools in the US along class and racial lines (Putnam & Campbell 2016; McArdle, Osypuk, & Acevedo-Garcia 2014).

Ultimately, growing class segregation across neighborhoods, schools, and marriages (and probably also civic associations, workplaces, and friendship circles) means that rich Americans and poor Americans are living, learning, and raising children in increasingly separate and unequal worlds, removing the stepping-stones to upward mobility – college-going classmates or cousins or middle-class neighbors who might take a working-class kid from the neighborhood under their wing. Moreover, class segregation means that members of the upper middle class are less likely to have firsthand knowledge of the lives of poor kids and therefore less able to even recognize the growing opportunity gap (Putnam & Campbell 2016).

Brain drain

One of the most frustrating "perverse" (or negative, unintended) consequences of education can be "brain drain": when educational achievement contributes to the out-migration of a community's brightest, best educated, highest skilled, and often most entrepreneurial people toward places with greater opportunities for employment, higher education, greater freedoms, and other quality of life attractions (Docquier & Rapoport 2012; Kaba 2007). Bright, ambitious, educated, and skilled young people typically move from rural communities to cities (Weber et al. 2007), from small cities to big cities, or from dull communities to more exciting "creative" communities. Motivating factors involved can include higher wages, broader job opportunities, Florida's "three T's" (Chapter 3), the excitement and amenities of a big city, recreation amenities, opportunities for continued higher education, family ties, and climate. Some of those factors can be influenced by or promoted through

ED efforts, and some are simply the luck of location (Hansen, Ban, & Huggins 2003). As a result, low-income communities hemorrhage much of their most valuable "human capital" (Weber et al. 2007) and so, ironically, help to subsidize the communities that are already thriving economically.

The term "brain drain" is attributed to a study of the UK's loss of its engineers, scientists, and other members of its technically skilled labor force in the 1960s, especially to the US (Committee on Manpower Resources for Science and Technology 1967). Since that time, the term has been applied more commonly to countries of the Developing World (Gibson & McKenzie 2012) as well as to rural and other low-income communities of the US (Artz 2003).

Economic Development Quarterly devotes a special issue to the topic of brain drain and its implications for ED (Gottleib 2011a, 2011b). Waldorf (2011) studies the location patterns in the US of international immigrants, toward a better understanding of potentially attracting well-educated and skilled immigrants. Although the challenges of brain drain can affect any community, rural areas are typically struck the hardest (Weber et al. 2007). Historically, vast rural regions of the US such as Appalachia (Eller 2008) and the Mississippi Delta (Lemann 1992) have lost large shares of their best, brightest, most ambitious, and most highly educated and skilled population to urban areas. Artz and Yu (2011) study graduates of Iowa State University, a land-grant university, and the extent to which they live in rural communities after graduation. They conclude that most rural graduates are motivated by their values and roots in rural communities, and economic incentives are unlikely to provide a significant influence one way or another. Graduates who return to their rural communities are significantly more likely than graduates as a whole to be entrepreneurs. Theodori and Theodori (2015) study rural youth in Texas and the factors that seem to influence their decisions to migrate or remain in their home communities.

Kaba (2007) refers to the "dual brain drain" of African Americans in the US owing both to traditional brain drain and also to health scourges such as HIV/AIDS. The same might be applied to the LGBTQ (lesbian, gay, bisexual, trans, and queer) population of many developing, and sometimes unaccepting, communities – contrary to the key role for gay populations in Florida's theory of the creative community (2003a, 2003b; see also McGranahan, Wojan, & Lambert 2011).

Meanwhile, the brain drain effect can deepen the local unemployment rate for a low-income community: "The more education a person has, the more mobile she is. College graduates have the highest mobility, workers with a community college education are less mobile, high school graduates are even less, and high school dropouts come at the bottom of the list" (Moretti 2012: 156, citing Wozniak 2010).

All is not necessarily lost through brain drain, however, and communities should not abandon their commitment to education for fear of losing their youngsters. Writing particularly about urban communities, Bartik (2011: 45, citing Schweinhart, Barnett, & Belfield 2005) assures us that "[s]tate and local policies that invest in early childhood programs are not doomed to fail to help local economic development because everyone leaves. This is confirmed by real-world early childhood programs. For example, in the famous Perry Preschool program, 82 percent of the former program participants still lived in the state of Michigan as of age 40." Moretti (2012) observes that the brain drain problem helps make a stronger case for federal-level financing of education. A larger share of federal, and to some extent state, financing for education would assure more of a direct return on investment: federal spending on education, for example, yields returns to that investment no matter where students may choose to move and work in the US.

Successful migrants will very often send "remittances" back to the family members that they have left behind: money or other gifts from their earnings (World Bank 2016). These remittances may be spent on upgraded housing, computers, or luxury items, but quite frequently money is sent back home for investment in a family business to which the migrant hopes to return in the future. At least, that is the pattern that has been well studied in a Developing World context. Remittances from migrants can constitute a large – sometimes even the largest – share of a developing country's economy.

The traditional migration pattern, in both the Developing and Developed Worlds, flows from rural areas to towns to small cities and ultimately to the largest cities. Enormous "mega-cities" in the Developing World such as Mexico City, Sao Paulo, and Mumbai provide ample evidence of this continuing effect. Plane, Henrie, and Perry (2005), however, note that this pattern has become less clear in the US in recent decades, with population migrating both up and down the "urban hierarchy" of city sizes, providing some hope, perhaps, for smaller cities that talented population will not necessarily be lost irretrievably to the bright lights of the bigger cities.

Postsecondary education: Colleges and universities

Not surprisingly, academic research on education and ED has a bias toward higher education, especially toward the role of universities. Indeed, universities do play an important and well-documented role in growing the world's modern, technological, global economies (Johansen & Arano 2016; Lane & Johnstone 2012). However, major universities can be very remote from the lives of disadvantaged populations, rural towns, American Indian reservations, and low-income urban communities.

Lane and Johnstone (2012), Vogel and Keen (2010), and Blackwell, Cobb, and Weinberg (2002) describe a wide range of contributions of colleges and universities to national, state, and local economies. Those contributions can include the direct local economic impacts of a higher education as a relatively well-paying and stable "industry." Other well-recognized impacts for local, regional, and state ED include a highly skilled workforce, research grant funding, industry consulting, patents, business spin-offs from university research, technology parks, and university-based business incubators. Yet another contribution of a local college to a community, resilience, may be due to the "reinvention hypothesis," which suggests that a highly educated population is better prepared to adapt to a changing economic environment and negative economic shocks such as local industry closings. For example, better-educated residents may be better able to adapt by creating new local businesses or adjusting to different types of employers (Kodrzycki & Muñoz 2014).

According to Moretti (2012: 194–196), the presence of a university can increase the local

> supply of college graduates, by educating some and attracting others from outside....[However,] the fact that college-educated Americans are so mobile makes the states' efforts [to fund higher education] less effective...[M]y research suggests that the presence of a university is on average associated with a better-educated labor force and higher local wages. But at the same time, mayors and local policy-makers should realize that a university – even a good one – is no guarantee of economic success.

The benefits of an institution of higher education can depend on the scale of analysis, like with any other form of educational or policy research. Reese and Ye (2011: 227), in their community-level study, conclude:

> Surprisingly, having an institution of higher education located within a municipality...appears to be negatively related to economic health. This may be the case for several reasons including the tax exempt status of public universities and increased pressure on local services related to students, traffic, parking problems, and so on. Having a major university nearby, however, is positively associated with economic health. Hospitals appear to function in a similar manner.

On an individual level of analysis, Hershbein and Hollenbeck (2015) review the many concerning issues associated with rising levels of student debt incurred from higher education, including potential negative impacts on credit ratings for future financial stability, disposable income, and other future borrowings for home and business. Student debt is a particular problem for students who do not manage to complete their bachelor's degree (Gicheva & Thompson 2015). The documentary *Starving the Beast: The Battle to Disrupt and Reform America's Public Universities* examines the national political movement to shift the costs of higher education from the public sector to individual students, as well as shift university curricula from liberal arts to STEM (science, technology, engineering, and math) subjects (Mims 2016; Mangan 2016). The editors at *Scientific American* (Scientific American 2016), however, argue on behalf of the vital importance of university humanities-based curricula.

The promise of economic success with a college degree is real, but not guaranteed. Real entry-level wage levels of college graduates have fallen steadily over the past two decades. As of 2011, "[r]eal hourly wages have declined for roughly 70 percent of the college-educated workforce since 2000....Perhaps more astonishing is that wages of college graduates at the 90th percentile were lower in 2011 than in 2002.

Since 2000, the vast majority of college graduates have not been winners from technological change, or in general" (Mishel et al. 2012: 302–303). Continuing research by Bartik and Hershbein (2016) suggests that increases in career earnings from a college education are much lower for graduates who grew up in a low-income family.

Meanwhile, the racial gap in higher education pay-off persists: "The income of blacks at all levels of educational attainment lags behind that of their white counterparts….Blacks…lag behind whites in college completion, but even among adults with a bachelor's degree, blacks earned significantly less in 2014 than whites ($82,300 for households headed by a college-educated black compared with $106,600 for comparable white households)" (Pew Research Center 2016: 18 and 8). In the past, minority students have tended to concentrate in historically Black and other traditionally minority-serving institutions of higher education – which, in turn, are likely to serve economically challenged rural and urban communities (O'Brien & Zudak 1998). These institutions were historically under-resourced in the US South, a situation from which they still struggle to recover.

Latinos have recently emerged as the largest minority group in the US enrolled in four-year colleges and universities: a result both of growing overall population numbers, as well as Latino educational progress (Fry & Taylor 2013). However, as a percentage of the US population attending or graduating with a four-year degree, Latinos still lag behind Asians, Whites, and Blacks (Martone 2015): "Among Hispanics, the share with a bachelor's degree has tripled since 1971, when data for this group first became available. Now about 15% are college graduates. Even so, the Hispanic-white gap in college completion has persisted; whites today are more than twice as likely as Hispanics to have a college degree, as was the case in the early 1970s" (Pew Research Center 2016: 21).

From an ED standpoint, Watson (2015), among others, cautions that university education will not necessarily provide the engine for economic progress and mobility in the future that it has for earlier generations. For one reason, inasmuch as undergraduate education has become more widely available, it has become an increasingly less scarce commodity that is less capable of driving demand from employers.

Adult job, technical, and workforce training programs

Workforce development and technical training programs – provided through community colleges, technical schools, and other institutions – have garnered a great deal of attention in the literature as well as in public policy (Shrock 2014; Besharov & Cottingham 2011). These institutions are said to provide "second chance education" because of their roles in GED (general educational development) certification and technical training for students who are unemployed or who are facing a layoff.

Case study research on specific job training programs suggests some opportunities for success. The common denominator for success stories at this level appears to be effective and extensive networking, such as that between public sector organizations – such as community and technical colleges – and employers (Harper-Anderson 2008; Green & Galetto 2005; Meléndez & Harrison 1998; Harrison & Weiss 1998). Meléndez et al. (2015) assess some of the common, critical barriers to workforce development program collaboration across regions.

Successful training programs also appear to include at least some of the following elements: building connections between employers and employment seekers (Meléndez & Harrison 1998), especially to help reduce biases against minority groups; training in relevant and current job skills and meeting particular standardized skill sets; programs that combine basic education with specific job skill training; and continued support after employment, including the continued enhancement of on-the-job skills and the addressing of problems that contribute to absenteeism such as childcare and transportation issues (Stoll 2006).

Garmise (2009) provides an overview of the wide (and often fragmented) range of workforce development programs and intermediary organizations in the US – the latter seeking to bridge the gap between employers and job-seekers (Giloth 2003). An important consideration in this regard is the "mismatching" of skills with anticipated job demand, for example, the rising demand for healthcare and other service occupations (Autor 2010). Workforce development strategies tend to bifurcate between "sector-based" and "place-based" programs: "Sector-based practitioners begin where the good jobs are and then work backward to creating connections to low-income communities and skill-building pathways" (Giloth 2000: 342). Place-based programs, however, typically target specific neighborhoods in need, or perhaps "dislocated workers" in a community that has recently suffered an economic shock such as a factory closing (Giloth 2000: 343).

Workforce training programs can also be divided into the "basic education" vs. "work-first" approaches (Stoll 2006). The former was a primary focus of earlier federally funded training programs, emphasizing basic skills such as reading, writing, and math and including high school degree programs. The latter has become the principal focus of more recent federal programs, emphasizing immediate needs for assistance in job searches, specific employment skills training, and on-the-job training. Evaluation research suggests that "work-first" approaches can be more effective in creating employment over the short term, but not necessarily beyond the first year or two (Stoll 2006, citing Strawn 1998). A combination of basic education and employment skills training appears necessary for sustained employment prospects (Stoll 2006).

Much of the funding for workforce training flows from federal sources. The three major federal programs supporting job training have been the Comprehensive Employment and Training Act (1973–1982), the Job Training and Partnership Act (1982–1998), and the Workforce Investment Act (1998 to date; Besharov & Cottingham 2011; Stoll 2006). The programs, however, are largely devised and implemented at the regional and local levels, reflecting local or regional labor markets and politics (Giloth 2004). A wide spectrum of actors is typically involved, ranging from the job-seekers to trainers to intermediaries to government entities to employers (Stone & Worgs 2004). The diverse nature of local workforce programs, actors, and experimentation lends itself well to case-study research. For example, Shrock (2013: 166) describes Chicago's efforts to create a sector program focused on manufacturing and low-wage services but also integrate "the program directly into the city's federally funded WIA [Workforce Investment Act] service delivery infrastructure" to make the program work on behalf of disadvantaged populations. In an earlier case study of the California-based Center for Employment Training, Meléndez and Harrison (1998) similarly credit the program's success with its ability to serve effectively as an intermediator and network between industry employers and job-seekers among disadvantaged (primarily Latino) populations. They credit the organization's credibility with Latino populations to its association with local Latino social movements.

Ample criticism of these programs can also be found with regard to the effectiveness and return on public investment provided by technical training programs. Those critiques can be found in the academic literature (Giloth 2000; Heckman & Lochner 2000; Shrock 2013; Bloom et al. 1996; Heckman 1994), think tank reports (Barnow & Smith 2009), government studies (US General Accountability Office 2011), and the general press (Williams 2014; Goodman 2010; Goldstein 2012). Partly in response to this, the training concept has been broadened from "job training" to a wider scope of "workforce training," which can include "substantial employer engagement, deep community connections, career advancement, integrative human service supports, contextual and industry-driven education and training, and the connective tissue of networks" (Giloth 2000: 342). These diverse programs, as mentioned above, are sometimes termed "second chance" programs, to supplement the "first chance" of traditional education, more traditional technical school training, and higher education tracks (Giloth 2004). Training programs can also target the workforce obstacles of "soft skills," including attitudes, perspectives, and cultural competencies (Stone & Worgs 2004).

Research by Barnow and Smith (2009) on the Job Corps suggests that the program can be effective in terms of reducing criminal behavior in the short term, educational attainment, and "substantial earnings impacts for 20- to 24-year old participants, but not for younger participants. As a result, because of its high cost, the program does not come close to passing a cost-benefit test (which includes the impacts on crime) for younger participants but does come close for 20- to 24-year-olds" (Barnow & Smith 2009: 168). Successful sector-based programs are accused of "creaming" the best and most promising of a community's labor force and leaving behind those most in need of a leg-up on the job ladder (Shrock 2013; Meléndez & Harrison 1998). According to Giloth (2004: 20, citing Stone & Worgs 2004),

> the disconnection between the hardest to employ and the mainstream economy is so substantial that job training alone is not enough. This disconnection has been characterized as the "two worlds" problem. One world is made up of business culture and expectations that hard work is rewarded. The other world is made up of people who have been marginalized by the mainstream over

generations and face the labor market with cynicism, loss of hope, and few positive expectations. Bridging these two worlds is an enormous challenge.

Barnow and Smith (2009) suggest some potential for combining conventional job training programs with programs such as subsidized employment to help launch trainees into the workforce. Dewar (2013) warns that subsidized employment programs can be ineffective for low-skilled workers, who are overwhelmed by a lack of hiring networks, segregation, and other common issues facing a low-income labor force. Intermediary organizations can potentially provide networks capable of making employment programs more effective (Fitzgerald 2004). In a somewhat related vein, Chirinko and Wilson (2014) assess the potential for job creation tax credit programs.

High school

There is strong evidence that student success at the higher education level is highly dependent on preparation at the high school level, whether measured through advanced placement courses, grade point average, or scores on college entrance exams. According to Putnam & Campbell (2016: 187), "enrolling in college is one thing, but getting a degree is quite another. The class gap in college completion, which was already substantial 30 to 40 years ago, has steadily expanded. This matters hugely, because completing college is much more important than entering college on all sorts of levels: socioeconomic success, physical and mental health, longevity, life satisfaction, and more." Kuh et al. (2007: 34) argue that "the quality of the academic experience and intensity of the high school curriculum affect almost every dimension of success in postsecondary education."

A similar relationship should be expected for success in community college, technical schools, and other training programs (McCabe 2003). Success in nearly any form of adult education requires basic foundational skills in literacy, math, analytical thinking, as well as the social "soft skills" noted earlier – particularly in the increasingly technology-dependent workplace of the modern economy. It also requires taking childhood experiences into account (Helfield 2001). General education skills can help foster more adaptability and resilience: "Jobs created in recent recoveries looked nothing like those that were lost, and the people hired for those new positions looked nothing like the people laid off from the old ones" (Carnevale, Smith, & Stohl 2010, cited by Perna 2014). Business surveys consistently project an increasing demand for postsecondary education in future job markets and declining employment opportunities for those with a high school diploma or less (Perna 2014; Deskins, Hill, & Ullrich 2010).

Among the barriers to low-income populations progressing from high school to college are that many of them are first-generation college students who do not benefit from the advice and experience of parents or relatives. They must rely, instead, on high school counselors, who may be subject to biases in their advice, depending on the student's racial, ethnic, or other profile (Martone 2015). Student success at progressing to the college level is also highly correlated with the educational attainment of the student's parents. That is, students who are academically ill-prepared for college tend to come from families with parents who have a high school diploma or less (Arum & Roksa 2011). This relationship is particularly pronounced for students from minority groups: "Only 21 percent of African American high school graduates, 33 percent of Hispanics, and 33 percent of students from families with annual incomes below $30,000 have college-level reading skills" (Kuh et al. 2007: 23, citing the American College Testing Program 2006). In 1996, for example, "high school completers' enrollment rates in postsecondary education ranged from 45 percent for those with parents who had less than a high school education to 85 percent for those students with parents with a bachelor's degree or higher" (Kuh et al. 2007: 30; see also Choy 2001).

African American and Latino students tend to be much more concentrated in high schools with predominantly minority or predominantly low-income fellow students; 41 percent of Latino students and 38 percent of African American students attend high schools with predominantly minority student populations, compared with two percent for White students (Arum & Roksa 2011). In turn, segregated schools tend to have lower levels of academic resources and less ability to focus on high academically achieving students (Orfield, Bachmeier, & Eitle 1997). Students who are Black, Latino, and/or low-income tend to be in classrooms with less-experienced teachers (Martone 2015, citing Kalogrides, Loeb, & Béteille 2013). These same challenges – as well as other, unique challenges – also confront many Native American students (O'Brien & Zudak 1998).

High school completion is also critical to success in the job market for individuals who don't continue on to higher education: "Since many of the desirable qualities and skills [for employment] cannot be directly observed, employers use 'credentials' – such as attainment of a high school diploma, previous work experience, and references – to gain information" (Stoll 2006: 93). And yet despite the importance of high school completion, Heckman & LaFontaine (2008) note with concern that

> it is surprising and disturbing that, at a time when the premium for skills has increased and the return to high school graduation has risen, the high school dropout rate in America is increasing. America is becoming a polarized society. Proportionately more American youth are going to college and graduating than ever before. At the same time, proportionately more are failing to complete high school.

Over the past decade, "the white-black gap in high school completion rates has almost disappeared...though blacks are still significantly less likely than whites to graduate from college" (Pew Research Center 2016: 18). Latinos continue to lag far behind, with a 67 percent high school completion rate vs. 93 percent for Whites and 88 percent for Blacks (Pew Research Center 2016). Grogger & Trejo (2002: viii), however, note that "Mexican Americans experience dramatic gains in education and earnings between the first and second generations. On average,

U.S.-born Mexican Americans have three and a half years more schooling and at least 30 percent higher wages than do Mexican immigrants."

Research by Harding (2003, cited by Sharkey 2013), controlling for other factors, suggests that a child growing up in a high-poverty neighborhood is twice as likely to drop out of high school as a child growing up in a low-poverty neighborhood. Between 1980 and 2010, the hourly average wages of men, in 2011 dollars, fell by 14 percent for high school dropouts. Meanwhile, the wages of those with a high school diploma fell also by 8 percent, which is also a decrease, but one that is still better than that for dropouts (Pew Research Center 2016).

Despite all these challenges and more, success at the high school level is important not just for the individual but for the ED success of the community as a whole. Reese & Ye (2011: 229) find that a variety of policy-related variables are generally poorly related to community economic health. However, among the policy variables they studied, "[h]igher graduation rates are significantly correlated to [community economic] health....[Of the variables analyzed,] graduation rate from the local public schools is the strongest correlate of economic health."

Checchi (2006) cites research that states that educational attainment is correlated to future job success measured by earnings – however, he fails to find a clear relationship between job success and specific knowledge gained in school. Checchi (2006: 170) speculates that "firms may prefer educated individuals because they are self-selected according to their ability to identify with authority, or, even more simply, because they believe that achieving educational degrees is a signal of non-cognitive ability" such as the job applicant's health or reliability.

Most ED professionals view education and educational attainment measures as critical for attracting industrial investment. Several educational measurements are included in the International Economic Development Council's (IEDC, which absorbed the old American Economic Development Council (AEDC)) Site Selection Data Standards, which are widely utilized by ED professionals. The Standards are intended to guide communities in preparing the data that "a site selection consultant looks for in determining what communities to recommend to their client" (International Economic Development Council). IEDC Standards for secondary schools in a community include nearly 30 data points in 14 categories ranging from student-teacher ratios in elementary schools to percentage of high school seniors attending college, although high school graduation rates are not included.

Beyond direct economic benefits from a well-educated population, Heckman & Krueger (2003) also argue for indirect community impacts. And according to Heckman and Masterov (2007: 455), "increasing high school graduate rates is a major crime prevention strategy." Education "lowers the probability of being involved in criminal activities....And the effect is even larger for African Americans" (Moretti 2012: 229, citing Lochner & Moretti 2004). In addition, "single parenthood is much more prevalent for high school dropouts" (Heckman & Masterov 2007: 463). Further, "more educated voters make the democratic process work better" (Heckman & Krueger 2003: 14–15). Recall Lewis' and Sen's emphasis on development as expanding the range of human choice, freedoms, and capabilities – with education being central to making those opportunities possible (O'Hearn 2009).

How do we go about making high school success more equitably distributed? Among others, Schweke (2004: 44) argues for improving the high-school-to-work transition through programs such as "apprenticeships, tech prep education, career academies, and school-based enterprises." Lynch (2000) calls attention to the extensive use of vocational apprenticeships by German students to facilitate the transition from school to labor force. Other approaches include youth leadership programs; Proweller and Monkman (2015) provide a literature review. The job-market value of a GED vs. a traditional high school diploma is disputed, but Grogger and Trejo (2002: ix) note that "[t]he labor market payoff to acquiring a high school diploma through an equivalency exam such as the GED, rather than through the usual coursework, is substantially higher for Mexican immigrants than for the U.S.-born workers of any race/ethnicity."

The highly politicized voucher, open enrollment, and charter school concepts currently dominate much of the public discussion about school success (Addonizio & Kearney 2012; Fryer 2012; Rand Gulf States Policy Institute): all three of them are free-market-centered options that have been especially attractive in post-Katrina New Orleans and other communities with limited public resources (Louisiana Association of Charter Schools). School choice programs can be limited by low-income students' problems with transportation (Chapter 2), as well as some low-income parents' time constraints and limited access to information about available programs. We await further research on the relationship between such "choice" programs and community population growth, ED outcomes, and especially their ability to serve low-income populations. Based on a relatively early study by King (2005: 363), "for the school choice variables, charter schools were found to be a positive and significant contributing factor to population growth. Vouchers and open enrollment were found to be insignificant." According to Putnam and Campbell (2016), "careful studies have concluded that charter schools are no panacea and generally do not narrow the class gap, in part because more educated parents are better able to manage the process of choosing a good school and transporting their kids to that school" (citing Angrist et al. 2012; Zimmer et al. 2011; Gleason et al. 2010; Hoxby & Muraka 2009; and Abdulkadiroglu et al. 2009).

Much research attention has focused on the Kalamazoo Promise, a program funded by anonymous donors that pledges full tuition and fees to any Michigan university or college for a student who completes K–12 education in the Kalamazoo school system, and a lesser amount for students who graduate after attending at least four years in the system (Kalamazoo Promise; Miller-Adams 2009). The program is exceptional although not unique: the similar Clemens Foundation program was established in the smaller town of Philomath, Oregon, in 1959.

According to the Kalamazoo Public Schools Superintendent, "this is not an educational decision. This is an economic development, quality of life, community-building decision" (quoted in Miller-Adams 2009: 17). At the time of the donation, Kalamazoo was suffering from many of the ills of other cities in the Rustbelt, and

Michigan in particular: a hemorrhage of population and economic activity from the central city (particularly in the middle class), manufacturing plant closings, declining housing values, city-suburb segregation, rising poverty rates, and a high school dropout rate over 20 percent. The "promises" of the Kalamazoo Promise included to retain middle-class population, attract new residents, and provide those residents with increasing housing values and more disposable income (e.g., money that otherwise might have been saved or borrowed for college). The Promise was coupled with other programs intended to mitigate some of the educational concerns noted earlier in this chapter: a local internship program was expanded, for example, that was intended to connect college students with employment opportunities at local businesses (Miller-Adams 2009).

Initiated in 2005, early evaluations of the program suggest increases in enrollment, test scores, and percentage of students continuing to higher education. There are also indications that the program has helped retain students in the Greater Kalamazoo area and attracted several hundred more students into the local public school system, who were overall less disadvantaged than the original student body (Hershbein 2013; Bartik & Lachowska 2012). The impact on local housing prices remains inconclusive, perhaps overwhelmed by other economic problems facing Kalamazoo and Michigan in subsequent years (Miller-Adams 2009). The majority of the students accepting Promise scholarships have attended local colleges, which has kept that money in the community (Miller-Adams 2009).

Meanwhile, other communities have adopted similar programs, joined in a loose association called "PromiseNet" (Cities of Promise). Miller-Adams (2015) evaluates the success of three other place-based scholarship programs at the Denver; Pittsburgh; and El Dorado, Arkansas, public school systems. Davenport, Iowa; Akron, Ohio; and hapless Flint, Michigan, are among the communities that attempted and failed to implement Promise scholarship programs.

Elementary school

Education at the grade school level is not as well represented in the standard ED texts or research agenda in the US, in comparison with the attention given to higher education, adult skills training, high school, and even preschool (Phillips & Pittman 2015; Leigh & Blakely 2013; Elliott 2013). Together with preschool, however, elementary school is part of an essential foundation for all modern ED (Bartik 2014, 2011; Schweke 2004).

Much of the current research literature and policy guidelines on education emphasizes that grades four through six are already too late for effective intervention in education (National Governors Association 2013; Annie E. Casey Foundation 2010). Special attention to grade 3 and below is critical to our individuals, society, and ED: "The U.S. has a thick lower tail of essentially illiterate and innumerate persons, who are a drag on productivity and a source of social and economic problems" (Heckman & Masterov 2007: 452). Carneiro and Heckman (2003: 86–87) state that evidence suggests that factors operating during the early childhood years and culminating in adolescence in the form of crystallized cognitive abilities, attitudes, and social skills play far more important roles than tuition or family credit constraints during the college-going years in explaining minority-majority gaps in socioeconomic attainment. It suggests that tuition reduction may be much less effective in increasing college attendance rates than policies that foster cognitive abilities.

Bartik's (2011: 340) research shows significant, substantial, and positive ED impacts at the state level from improved elementary test scores: "The improvement in secondary test scores has about the same economic development benefits as the improvement in elementary test scores. However, the secondary improvement is probably harder to accomplish."

How to meet these needs, especially for low-income communities? "Additional resources invested in education can take different forms: fewer students per teacher, better-paid teachers…a greater share of GDP on education, a greater share of educational resources invested in buildings and equipment.…In all these cases, with the exception of teachers' pay…we do not find strong evidence of positive effects arising from more resources being allocated to primary enrollment.…The case of teachers' pay is inclusive: for a given level of resources, having better-paid teachers necessarily implies having fewer teachers, fewer or more crowded classes" (Checchi 2006: 67).

Financial investment at the elementary school level is critical, but there are also limits to what can be accomplished in school. In studies of low-income children over summer breaks, for example, "the achievement level of children from low-income families either fell or stagnated during the summer, whereas that of children from higher income families continued to improve" (Heckman & Krueger 2003, citing Entwhistle, Alexander, & Olson 1997). And "it is important to remember…that the interventions conducted by such programs only alleviate and do not reverse early damage caused by bad family environments" (Carneiro & Heckman 2003: 181). Research by Freiberg (1994: 156) suggests that the development of resilience for children largely results from contact with other resilient children – "resilient cohorts" – together with "interdependence [within the community] and family-based orientation to achievement."

Preschool

Extensive work by Bartik (2014, 2011) and Heckman (2006) indicates strong, positive returns to public investment in preschool programs – especially for children in "disadvantaged environments" (Heckman & Masterov 2007; Barnett & Ackerman 2006). Preschool programs can enhance fundamental, life-long cognitive skills at an especially critical period for brain development (Bradbury et al. 2015; Knudsen et al. 2006): "A large body of empirical work at the interface of neuroscience and social science has established that fundamental cognitive and noncognitive skills are produced in the early years of childhood, long before children start kindergarten. The technology of skill formation developed by economists shows that learning and motivations are dynamic, cumulative processes" (Heckman & Masterov 2007: 487). Putnam & Campbell (2016: 111) synthesize the findings of various researchers in this regard:

> Research has shown that so-called noncognitive skills (grit, social sensitivity, optimism, self-control, conscientiousness, emotional stability) are very important for life success. They can lead to greater physical health, school success, college enrollment, employment, and lifetime earnings, and can keep people out of trouble and out of prison. These skills are at least as important as cognitive skills in predicting such measures of success, and may be even more important in our postindustrial future than in the preindustrial and industrial past.

Bartik (2011: 1) summarizes the overall takeaway from his own economic analysis on the topic: "Local economic development strategies in the United States should include extensive investments in high-quality early childhood programs, such as prekindergarten (pre-K) education, child care, and parenting assistance." Danziger and Waldfogel (2000: 13, italics in the original), summarizing the findings of their edited volume on investing effectively in children, prescribe "*early childhood interventions that target the most disadvantaged children, who are at highest risk of school failure.* Much evidence documents the effectiveness of early childhood interventions in improving a range of developmental outcomes. We cannot afford to wait until children reach elementary school to undertake investments to improve their school achievement and other outcomes." Bradbury et al. (2015) emphasize that most of the achievement gap among students is already in place by the time they start school; as such, they recommend not only investment in preschool educational programs but also investment in effective parenting programs. Bartik (2011: 210) points out the potential benefits of pre-K programs to parents: "Comprehensive programs that include assistance to parents directly increase short-term benefits.... Early childhood programs may increase the rate of return of adult job training programs, and adult job training programs may increase the rate of return of early childhood programs. Experimentation should explore such possibilities."

Public benefits from quality preschool programs include better school performance and higher test scores, lower dropout rates, higher rates of high school graduation and college attendance, as well as lower rates of crime and welfare dependency. And "the best estimates suggest that high-quality early childhood programs can provide a state's residents with substantial economic development benefits. These economic development benefits are of similar magnitude to the benefits of high-quality business incentive programs. Early childhood programs have particularly strong benefits in the long run" (Bartik 2011: 110).

One of the challenges in developing these programs remains the relatively low prestige and salary for pre-K teachers (Whitebrook 2013): "My priority list of education and training initiatives would include...fully funding Head Start and

Early Head Start so every eligible child can participate" (Krueger 2002: 28; see also Krueger 2003). Jenkins (2014) reviews the very wide variety of early childhood education programs as developed across the "laboratory of states." Heckman (2006: 1902) summarizes the issue of investing in early childhood education thus:

> Investing in disadvantaged young children is a rare public policy initiative that promotes fairness and social justice and at the same time promotes productivity in the economy and in society at large. Early interventions targeted toward disadvantaged children have much higher returns than later interventions such as reduced pupil-teacher ratios, public job training, convict rehabilitation programs, tuition subsidies, or expenditure on police.
>
> Although investments in older disadvantaged individuals realize relatively less return overall, such investments are still clearly beneficial. Indeed, the advantages gained from effective early interventions are sustained best when they are followed by continued high-quality learning experiences....Stated simply, early investments must be followed by later investments if maximum value is to be realized.

Bartik (2011: 144–145) cautions that investment should be targeted thoughtfully to be most effective: "The available research suggests that having children spend more hours in pre-K increases economic development benefits. However, it may not always increase economic development benefits by more than the increased costs. This is particularly true for spending more hours per day in pre-K education." He also says that "lower class size in a pre-K program or child care center probably significantly improves program effects" (Bartik 2011: 135) and that "children from disadvantaged backgrounds will benefit from being placed in pre-K classrooms with children from more advantaged backgrounds who have higher test scores" (Bartik 2011: 140).

Childcare

There is no clear distinction between preschool education and progressive childcare. Warner (2006a, 2006b) groups preschool educational programs with childcare in general as "early care and education" (ECE), emphasizing the important role of both categories for developing life-long cognitive and social skills at a critical young age. According to Putnam and Campbell (2016: 129), "well-educated parents have long invested more resources than less educated parents in high-quality day care for their 4–6-year-olds, but in recent years upper-class parents have extended that investment edge into an even younger stage of life (0–4) – precisely the stage that the latest brain science suggests is so critical developmentally."

Warner (2006a, 2006b) broadens the ED perspective to recognize childcare centers as community businesses. ECE centers also play vital ED roles in helping to raise children as productive members of the community's future labor force, and they enable parents – especially mothers and most especially single mothers

(Kimmel 2006) – to participate more fully in a local labor force. In this context, childcare is necessary not just during traditional school hours, but also after school to accommodate non-standard shiftwork hours (Meyers & Jordan 2006), and summers (Kimmel 2006). Pratt and Kay (2006), Warner (2006b), and Warner and Liu (2006) argue that childcare contributes to local economies in terms of both backward and forward linkages to more traditional industries in a community. As such, childcare centers merit ED interventions to facilitate their growth (Warner & Liu 2006) – especially since childcare centers are primarily private sector businesses in the US.

To the extent that childcare programs are subsidized from state and federal programs (Kimmel 2006), those programs also represent basic, or "export" industries bringing new money into a community. Low-income and minority workers typically rely more on family than they do on outside childcare providers – but that may be less a matter of preference and more a matter of financial and availability constraints (Kimmel 2006; Meyers & Jordan 2006). Currently, the availability of quality childcare facilities is skewed toward more affluent communities and neighborhoods (Meyers & Jordan 2006).

TAKEAWAY FOR ED ACTION: EDUCATION AND HUMAN CAPITAL RESOURCES

What the best and wisest parent wants for his own child, that must the community want for all of its children. Any other ideal for our schools... destroys our democracy.

(Dewey 1915: 3, quoted by Addonizio & Kearney 2012: 259)

Each of the five chapters of Part II of this book concludes with a section titled "Takeaway for ED action." This section is intended to briefly summarize and emphasize the lessons that we can fairly safely conclude from the chapter and apply to ED practice in low-income communities with reasonable confidence that we are acting appropriately. Even the points listed here come with qualifications, cautions, detractors, and remaining unknowns. But, I believe the following points indicate actions that prudent community members, ED professionals, and policymakers can take to heart and begin putting into practice.

- *ED starts with education.* Education is not simply a critical factor contributing to the ED of a community. Modern, sustainable, equitable ED is simply impossible without quality education at all levels, widely and fairly available. A better-educated population is also more resilient to a variety of possible future economic changes.
- *Drive home the connection between ED and education.* Many communities emphasize the importance of education, and most communities emphasize the importance of ED. Some communities pay lip service to the connection with tired phrases such as "building the workforce of tomorrow." Make the

connection, explain the connection, and keep driving home the connection to policymakers and the general public.

- *Start with, and prioritize, preschool education.* One of the most efficient ED investments we can make as a community is in preschool and the lowest levels of elementary education. Those investments yield high returns in terms of individual students' advancement, as well as in terms of economic and social contributions to the community: "Missing from discussions of education and training policy is any consideration of priorities, or even recognition of the need to prioritize....[T]he current returns to policies in place indicate that the best policy is to invest more in the very young to improve their basic learning and socialization skills, to invest less in mature adults" (Heckman & Lochner 2000: 49).

- *Don't ignore grades 4 through 12.* The higher elementary school grades and the high school grades provide the advanced reading, math, social studies, critical thinking, and social soft skills necessary to succeed in the modern job market or move ahead to college or university study. High school dropouts are increasingly unable to make economically substantial contributions to the community; instead, they are more likely to contribute to crime, teen pregnancies, incarceration, and other social problems. Educational success at the high school level is vital for industrial recruitment and most other ED strategies.

- *Childcare empowers ED.* Quality childcare complements preschool programming. Available, affordable childcare also empowers more of your potential labor force to participate in the market, especially single mothers and low-income populations.

- *Not all investments in education require money.* Show your teachers respect, recognize the importance of their profession, and demonstrate community support for schools and educators. Encourage your best students to pursue teaching as a valued career.

- *Make better choices regarding school choice.* We need much more research and public information regarding the costs and benefits of "school choice" options with regard to impacts on both individual students and our communities.

- *Build connections with local institutions of higher education.* Colleges and universities are often isolated from their local communities, especially low-income populations. Colleges and universities can provide important sources of employment for nearby low-income communities and neighborhoods; potential linkages for local businesses; and outreach to support local schools, business development, and social welfare.

- *Help make college more affordable.* Few communities will have deep-pocket scholarship donors such as the Kalamazoo Promise. To the extent possible, help provide scholarship opportunities to your young people who show promise and need financial support. Deep student loan debts drain both individuals and the community as a whole.

- *Adult technical training programs should not be a first priority.* They are termed "second chance" programs with good reason. Prioritize students' "first chances." Technical training programs can provide results, under certain conditions – especially by emphasizing network-building – but they must build on a solid foundation of basic education.
- *You can't always keep them home on the farm.* "Brain drain" reflects a chicken-and-egg situation for low-income communities: you can't expect bright young people to stay in the community without job opportunities and other community assets, but you can't create modern industry and lively communities without a well-educated population. Some will stay, especially if there is evidence that the community is working toward change and progress. Some will leave, gain more education, skills, and experience elsewhere, then return to contribute to their home community. Create an accepting environment that welcomes a creative diversity of native sons and daughters as the community's possible assets for ED.
- *Don't blame your schools and teachers.* "The fact that schools as organizations today have a mixed and modest impact on the opportunity gap does not mean that reforms in schools might not be an important part of the solution to the gap. On the contrary, even if schools didn't cause the growing opportunity gap – and there's little evidence that they have – they might well be a prime place to fix it. Americans concerned about the opportunity gap must not make the all too common mistake of blaming schools for the problem. Instead, we should work with schools to narrow the gap. School is, after all, where the kids are" (Putnam & Campbell 2016: 182–183).
- *ED also ends with education.* What is the ultimate purpose of ED? Successful, prosperous communities are able to help provide their residents with richer, happier, more fulfilling lives with good neighbors, parks and other amenities, cultural and learning enrichment for adults, and especially ever-better educational opportunities for local children. Better-educated citizens can more effectively help create a just and equitable society, and help assure that local ED remains sustainable and resilient for generations to come.

Note

1   I'd like to thank Serena Williams Buckley, University of Southern Mississippi undergraduate honor student, for her thesis research, which contributed to this chapter.

References

Abdulkadiroglu, Atila, Joshua Angrist, Susan Dynarski, Thomas J. Kane, & Parag Pathak. 2009. *Accountability and Flexibility in Public Schools: Evidence from Boston's Charters and Pilots.* National Bureau of Economic Research Working Paper No. 15549. Retrieved September 25, 2016: http://www.nber.org/papers/w15549.

Addonizio, Michael F. & C. Philip Kearney. 2012. *Education Reform and the Limits of Policy: Lessons from Michigan*. Kalamazoo, MI: W.E. Upjohn Institute for Employment Research.

American College Testing Program. 2006. *Reading Between the Lines: What the ACT Reading Test Reveals about College Readiness in Reading*. Washington, DC: American Association for Higher Education. Retrieved November 19, 2014: http://www.act.org/research/poli cymakers/reports/reading.html.

Angrist, Joshua D., Susan M. Dynarski, Thomas J. Kane, Parag A. Pathak, & Christopher R. Walters. 2012. Who benefits from KIPP? *Journal of Policy Analysis and Management* 31(4): 837–860.

Annie E. Casey Foundation. 2010. *Early Warning! Why Reading by the End of Third Grade Matters*. Retrieved October 14, 2015: http://www.aecf.org/resources/early-warning-why-reading-by-the-end-of-third-grade-matters/.

Artz, Georgeanne. 2003. Rural area brain drain: Is it a reality? *Choices* 18(4): 11–15.

Artz, Georgeanne, & Li Yu. 2011. How ya gonna keep 'em down on the farm: Which land grant graduates live in rural areas? *Economic Development Quarterly* 25(4): 341–352.

Arum, Richard, & Josipa Roksa. 2011. *Academically Adrift: Limited Learning on College Campuses*. Chicago: University of Chicago Press.

Autor, David. 2010. *The Polarization of Job Opportunities in the U.S. Labor Market: Implications for Employment and Earnings*. The Center for American Progress and The Hamilton Project. Retrieved September 11, 2016: http://economics.mit.edu/files/5554.

Barnett, W. Steven, & Debra J. Ackerman. 2006. Costs, benefits, and long-term effects of early care and education programs: Recommendations and cautions for community developers. *Community Development* 37(2): 86–100.

Barnow, Burt S., & Jeffrey A. Smith. 2009. What we know about the impacts of workforce investment programs, in Maude Toussaint-Comeau & Bruce D. Meyer, eds., *Strategies for Improving Economic Mobility of Workers*, 165–178. Kalamazoo, MI: W.E. Upjohn Institute for Employment Research.

Bartik, Timothy J. 2014. *From Preschool to Prosperity: The Economic Payoff to Early Childhood Education*. Kalamazoo, MI: W.E. Upjohn Institute for Employment Research.

Bartik, Timothy J. 2011. *Investing in Kids: Early Childhood Programs and Local Economic Development*. Kalamazoo, MI: W.E. Upjohn Institute for Employment Research.

Bartik, Timothy J., & Brad Hershbein. 2016. Degrees of poverty: Family income background and the college earnings premium. *Employment Research Newsletter* (W.E. Upjohn Institute for Employment Research) 23(3): 1–3.

Bartik, Timothy J., & Marta Lachowska. 2012. *The Short-Term Effects of the Kalamazoo Promise Scholarship on Student Outcomes*. W.E. Upjohn Institute for Employment Research Working Paper No. 186. Kalamazoo, MI. Retrieved December 19, 2013: www.aeaweb.org/aea/2013conference/program/retrieve.php?pdfid=166.

Becker, Roger S. 1964. *Human Capital: A Theoretical and Empirical Analysis, with Special Reference to Education*. Chicago: University of Chicago Press.

Berube, Alan. 2010. Educational attainment, in Brookings Institution, ed., *The State of Metropolitan America*, 104–117. Retrieved September 25, 2016: https://www.brookings.edu/multi-chapter-report/the-state-of-metropolitan-america/.

Besharov, Douglas J., & Phoebe H. Cottingham, eds. 2011. *The Workforce Investment Act: Implementation Experiences and Evaluation Findings*. Kalamazoo, MI: W.E. Upjohn Institute for Employment Research.

Blackwell, Melanie, Steven Cobb, & David Weinberg. 2002. The economic impact of educational institutions: Issues and methodology. *Economic Development Quarterly* 16(1): 88–95.

Bloom, Larry L., Howard S. Bell, Stephen H. Doolittle, Fred Lin, & George Cave. 1996. *Does Training for the Disadvantaged Work? Evidence from the National JTPA Study.* Washington, DC: Urban Institute.

Boyer, Ernest L. 1991. Elementary and secondary education, in David W. Hornbeck, & Lester M. Salamon, eds., *Human Capital and America's Future: An Economic Strategy for the 90s*, 168–192. Baltimore: Johns Hopkins University Press.

Bradbury, Bruce, Miles Corak, Jane Waldfogel, & Elizabeth Washbrook. 2015. *Too Many Children Left Behind: The U.S. Achievement Gap in Comparative Perspective.* New York: Russell Sage Foundation.

Brandolini, Andrea, & Nicola Rossi. 1998. Income distribution and growth in industrial countries, in Vito Tanzi & Ke-Young Chu, eds., *Income Distribution and High-Quality Growth*, 69–105. Cambridge, MA: MIT Press.

Camp, Jessica K., & Eileen Trzcinski. 2015. The rise of incarceration among the poor with mental illnesses, in Stephen N. Haymes, Maria V. de Haymes, & Reuben J. Miller, eds., *The Routledge Handbook of Poverty in the United States*, 357–366. New York: Routledge.

Card, David, & Alan B. Krueger. 2011. *Wages, School Quality, and Employment Demand.* Edited by Randall K.Q. Akee & Klaus F. Zimmerman. Oxford: Oxford University Press.

Carneiro, Pedro, & James J. Heckman. 2003. Human capital policy, in James J. Heckman & Alan B. Krueger, eds., *Inequality in America: What Role for Human Capital Policies?* 77–240. Cambridge: MIT Press.

Carnevale, Anthony, Nicole Smith, & Jeffrey Stohl. 2010. *Help Wanted: Projections of Job and Education Requirements Through 2018.* Georgetown University: Center on Education and the Workforce.

Checchi, Daniele. 2006. *The Economics of Education: Human Capital, Family Background, and Inequality.* New York: Cambridge University Press.

Chirinko, Robert S., & Daniel J. Wilson. 2014. Job creation tax credits: Still worth consideration? *Employment Research* 21(3): 4–6.

Choy, Susan P. 2001. *Students whose Parents Did Not Go to College: Postsecondary Access, Persistence, and Attainment.* National Center for Educational Statistics. Retrieved November 19, 2014: http://nces.ed.gov/pubs2001/2001072_Essay.pdf.

Cities of Promise. Retrieved September 12, 2016: https://citiesofpromise.com/.

Committee on Manpower Resources for Science and Technology. 1967. *The Brain Drain: Report of the Working Group on Migration.* London: Her Majesty's Stationery Office.

Corley, John. 2015. To Pell and back: Federal government eases restrictions against the most effective rehabilitative and anti-recidivism tool. *The Angolite.* May/June-July: 28–35.

Danziger, Sheldon, & Jane Waldfogel, eds. 2000. *Securing the Future: Investing in Children from Birth to College.* New York: Russell Sage Foundation.

Deskins, John, Brian Hill, & Laura Ullrich. 2010. Education spending and state economic growth: Are all dollars created equal? *Economic Development Quarterly* 24(1): 45–59.

Dewar, Margaret. 2013. Paying employers to hire local workers in distressed places. *Economic Development Quarterly* 27(4): 284–300.

Dewey, John. 1915. *The School and Society.* Chicago: University of Chicago Press.

Docquier, Frédéric, & Hillel Rapoport. 2012. Globalization, brain drain, and development. *Journal of Economic Literature* 50(3): 681–730.

Donaldson, Caitlin Cullen, & Suzanne O'Keefe. 2013. The effects of manufacturing on educational attainment and real income. *Economic Development Quarterly* 27(4): 316–324.

Eller, Ronald D. 2008. *Uneven Ground: Appalachia since 1945.* Lexington, KY: University Press of Kentucky.

Elliott, Jennifer. 2013. *An Introduction to Sustainable Development*, 4th ed. New York: Routledge.

Entwhistle, Doris, Karl Alexander, & Linda Olson. 1997. *Children, Schools, and Inequality.* Boulder, CO: Westview.

Fifield, Anna. 2014. In education-crazy South Korea, top teachers become multimillionaires. *Washington Post.* December 30: http://www.washingtonpost.com/world/asia_pacific/in-education-crazy-south-korea-top-teachers-become-multimillionaires/2014/12/29/1bf7e7ae-849b-11e4-abcf-5a3d7b3b20b8_story.html.

Fitzgerald, Joan. 2004. Moving the workforce intermediary agenda forward. *Economic Development Quarterly* 18(1): 3–9.

Florida, Richard. 2003a. Cities and the creative class. *City & Community* 2(1): 3–19.

Florida, Richard. 2003b. *The Rise of the Creative Class.* New York: Basic Books.

Freiberg, H. Jerome. 1994. Understanding resilience: Implications for inner-city schools and their near and far communities, in Margaret C. Wang & Edmund W. Gordon, eds., *Educational Resilience in Inner-City America: Challenges and Prospects,* 151–166. Hillsdale, NJ: Lawrence Erlbaum.

Fry, Richard, & Paul Taylor. 2013. Hispanic high school graduates pass whites in rate of college enrollment: High school drop-out rate at record low. Pew Research Center, *Hispanic Trends.* May 9: http://www.pewhispanic.org/2013/05/09/hispanic-high-school-graduates-pass-whites-in-rate-of-college-enrollment/.

Fryer, Jr., Roland G. 2012. *Learning from the Successes and Failures of Charter Schools.* Brookings Institution. Retrieved December 19, 2013: http://scholar.harvard.edu/files/fryer/files/hamilton_project_paper_2012.pdf.

Garmise, Sheri. 2009. Building a workforce development system as an economic development strategy: Lessons from US programs. *Local Economy* 24(3): 211–223.

Gibson, John, & David McKenzie. 2012. The economic consequences of "brain drain" of the best and brightest: Microeconomic evidence from five countries. *Economic Journal* 122 (560): 339–375.

Gicheva, Dora, & Jeffrey Thompson. 2015. The effects of student loans on long-term household financial stability, in Brad Hershbein & Kevin M. Hollenbeck, eds., *Student Loans and the Dynamics of Debt,* 287–316. Kalamazoo, MI: W.E. Upjohn Institute for Employment Research.

Giloth, Robert P., ed. 2004. *Workforce Development Politics: Civic Capacity and Performance.* Philadelphia: Temple University Press.

Giloth, Robert P. 2003. *Workforce Intermediaries for the 21st Century.* Philadelphia: Temple University Press.

Giloth, Robert P. 2000. Learning from the field: Economic growth and workforce development in the 1990s. *Economic Development Quarterly* 14(4): 340–359.

Gleason, Philip, Melissa Clark, Christina Clark Tuttle, & Emily Dwoyer. 2010. *The Evaluation of Charter School Impacts: Final Report* (NCEE 2010–4029), National Center for Education Evaluation and Regional Assistance. Retrieved September 25, 2016: http://ies.ed.gov/ncee/pubs/20104029/.

Goldstein, Amy. 2012. Job retraining for the unemployed: A popular fix that might not work. *Washington Post.* February 17: http://www.washingtonpost.com/opinions/job-retraining-for-the-unemployed-a-popular-fix-that-might-not-work/2012/02/15/gIQAbpc3JR_story.html.

Goodman, Peter S. 2010. The new poor: After training, still scrambling for employment. *New York Times.* July 18: http://www.nytimes.com/2010/07/19/business/19training.html.

Gottlieb, Paul D. 2011a. Introduction to EDQ special issue on "brain drain." *Economic Development Quarterly* 25(4): 299–302.

Gottlieb, Paul D. 2011b. Supply or demand, make or buy: Two simple frameworks for thinking about a state-level brain drain policy. *Economic Development Quarterly* 25(4): 303–315.

Green, Gary P., & Valeria Galetto. 2005. Employer participation in workforce development networks. *Economic Development Quarterly* 19(3): 225–231.

Grogger, Jeff, & Stephen J. Trejo. 2002. *Falling Behind or Moving Up? The Intergenerational Progress of Mexican Americans.* San Francisco: Public Policy Institute of California.

Hansen, Carolyn Ban, & Leonard Huggins. 2003. Explaining the "brain drain" from older industrial cities: The Pittsburgh region. *Economic Development Quarterly* 17(2): 132–147.

Hanushek, Eric A. 2002. *The Long Run Importance of School Quality.* National Bureau of Economic Research Working Paper No. 9071. Retrieved December 3, 2014: http://www.nber.org/papers/w9071.pdf.

Hanushek, Eric A., & Ludger Wößmann. 2010. Education and Economic Growth, in Penelope Peterson, Eva Baker, & Barry McGaw, eds., *International Encyclopedia of Education,* Vol. 2, 245–252. Amsterdam: Elsevier.

Harding, David J. 2003. Counterfactual models of neighborhood effects: The effect of neighborhood poverty on dropping out and teenage pregnancy. *American Journal of Sociology* 109(3): 676–719.

Harper-Anderson, Elsie. 2008. Measuring the connection between workforce development and economic development: Examining the role of sectors for local outcomes. *Economic Development Quarterly* 22(2): 119–135.

Harrison, Bennett, & Marcus Weiss. 1998. *Workforce Development Networks: Community-Based Organizations and Regional Alliances.* Thousand Oaks, CA: Sage.

Hartman, Chester, ed. 2014. *America's Growing Inequality: The Impact of Poverty and Race.* Lanham, MD: Lexington.

Heckman, James J. 2006. Skill formation and the economics of investing in disadvantaged children. *Science* 312(5782): 1900–1902.

Heckman, James J. 1994. Is job training oversold? *Public Interest* 115: 91–115.

Heckman, James J., & Alan B. Krueger. 2003. *Inequality in America: What Role for Human Capital Policies?* Cambridge: MIT Press.

Heckman, James J., & Dimitriy V. Masterov. 2007. The productivity argument for investing in young children. *Review of Agricultural Economics* 29(3): 446–493.

Heckman, James J., & Lance Lochner. 2000. Rethinking education and training policy: Understanding the sources of skill formation in a modern economy, in Sheldon Danziger & Jane Waldfogel, eds., *Securing the Future: Investing in Children from Birth to College,* 47–86. New York: Russell Sage Foundation.

Heckman, James J., & Paul A. LaFontaine. 2008. *The Declining American High School Graduation Rate: Evidence, Sources, and Consequences.* National Bureau of Economic Research Reporter: Research Summary 2008 No. 1. Retrieved October 21, 2015: http://www.nber.org/reporter/2008number1/heckman.html.

Helfield, Isa. 2001. *Poisonous Pedagogy.* Presentation delivered at the International Conference on Women and Literacy. January. Retrieved December 22, 2016: http://whale.to/v/helfield.html.

Hershbein, Brad J. 2013. *A Second Look at Enrollment Changes after the Kalamazoo Promise Year.* W.E Upjohn Institute Working Paper No. 13–200. Retrieved September 4, 2013: http://research.upjohn.org/up_workingpapers/200/.

Hershbein, Brad J., & Kevin M. Hollenbeck. 2015. *Student Loans and the Dynamics of Debt.* Kalamazoo, MI: W.E. Upjohn Institute for Employment Research.

Hornbeck, David W., & Lester M. Salamon, eds. 1991. *Human Capital and America's Future.* Baltimore: Johns Hopkins University Press.

Hoxby, Caroline M., & Sonali Muraka. 2009. *Charter Schools in New York City: Who Enrolls and How they Affect their Students' Achievement.* National Bureau of Economic Research Working Paper No. 14852. Retrieved September 25, 2016: http://www.nber.org/papers/w14852.

International Economic Development Council. *Site Selection Data Standards*. Retrieved September 28, 2016: http://www.iedconline.org/web-pages/resources-publications/site-selection-data-standards/.

Jenkins, Jade M. 2014. Early childhood development as economic development: Considerations for state-level policy innovation and experimentation. *Economic Development Quarterly* 28(2): 147–165.

Johansen, Tom, & Kathleen Arano. 2016. The long-run economic impact of an institution of higher education: Estimating the human capital contribution. *Economic Development Quarterly* 30(3): 203–214.

Kaba, Amadu J. 2007. The Black world and the dual brain drain: A focus on African Americans. *Journal of African American Studies* 11(1): 16–23.

Kalamazoo Promise. Retrieved December 19, 2013: https://www.kalamazoopromise.com.

Kalogrides, Demetra, Susanna Loeb, & Tara Béteille. 2013. Systematic sorting: Teacher characteristics and class assignments. *Sociology of Education* 86(2): 103–123.

Kimmel, Jean. 2006. Child care, female employment, and economic growth. *Community Development* 37(2): 71–85.

King, Kerry A. 2005. The impacts of school choice on regional economic growth. *Review of Regional Studies* 35(3): 356–368.

Knudsen, Eric I., James J. Heckman, Judy L. Cameron, & Jack P. Shonkoff. 2006. Economic, neurobiological, and behavioral perspectives on building America's future workforce. *Proceedings of the National Academy of Sciences* 103(27): 10155–10162.

Kodrzycki, Yolanda K., & Anna P. Muñoz. 2014. Lessons from resurgent mid-sized manufacturing cities, in Susan M. Wachter & Kimberly A. Zeuli, eds., *Revitalizing America's Cities*, 83–104. Philadelphia: University of Pennsylvania Press.

Krueger, Alan B. 2003. Inequality, too much of a good thing, in James J. Heckman & Alan B. Krueger, eds., *Inequality in America: What Role for Human Capital Policies?* 1–75. Cambridge: MIT Press.

Krueger, Alan B. 2002. *Inequality, Too Much of a Good Thing*. Center for Economic Policy Studies Working Paper No. 87. Retrieved September 12, 2016: https://www.princeton.edu/ceps/workingpapers/87krueger.pdf.

Kuh, George D., Jillian Kinzie, Jennifer A. Buckley, Brian K. Bridges, & John C. Hayek. 2007. *Piecing Together the Student Success Puzzle: Research, Propositions, and Recommendations*. ASHE *Higher Education Report*. Hoboken, NJ: Wiley.

Lane, Jason E., & D. Bruce Johnstone. 2012. *Universities and Colleges as Economic Drivers*. Albany, NY: State University of New York Press.

Leigh, Nancey G., & Edward J. Blakely. 2013. *Planning Local Economic Development: Theory and Practice*, 5th ed. Thousand Oaks, CA: Sage.

Lemann, Nicholas. 1992. *The Promised Land: The Great Black Migration and How It Changed America*. New York: Vintage.

Lochner, Lance, & Enrico Moretti. 2004. The effect of education on crime: Evidence from prison inmates, arrests and self-reports. *American Economic Review* 94(1): 155–189.

Louisiana Association of Charter Schools. Retrieved December 19, 2013: http://lacharterschools.org.

Lynch, Lisa. 2000. Trends in and consequences of investments in children, in Sheldon Danziger & Jane Waldfogel, eds., *Securing the Future: Investing in Children from Birth to College*, 19–46. New York: Russell Sage Foundation.

Mangan, Katherine. 2016. After public colleges suffer many blows, a film fires back. *Chronicle of Higher Education*. August 30: http://www.chronicle.com/article/After-Public-Colleges-Suffer/237616.

Martone, Jessica. 2015. Students that lag or a system that fails? A contemporary look at the academic trajectory of Latino students, in Stephen N. Haymes, Maria V. de Haymes, & Reuben J. Miller, eds., *The Routledge Handbook of Poverty in the United States*, 218–225. New York: Routledge.

Mathur, Vijay K. 1999. Human capital-based strategy for regional economic development. *Economic Development Quarterly* 13(3): 203–216.

McArdle, Nancy, Theresa Osypuk, & Dolores Acevedo-Garcia. 2014. Segregation and exposure to high-poverty schools in large metropolitan areas, 2008–2009, in Chester Hartman, ed., *America's Growing Inequality: The Impact of Poverty and Race*. Lanham, MD: Lexington.

McCabe, Robert H. 2003. *Yes We Can! A Community College Guide for Developing America's Underprepared*. Lanham, MD: Rowman & Littlefield.

McGranahan, David, Timothy R. Wojan, & Dayton M. Lambert. 2011. The rural growth trifecta: Outdoor amenities, creative class and entrepreneurial context. *Journal of Economic Geography* 11(3): 529–557.

Meléndez, Edwin, Ramon Borges-Mendez, M. Anne Visser, & Anna Rosofsky. 2015. The restructured landscape of economic development: Challenges and opportunities for regional workforce development collaborations. *Economic Development Quarterly* 29(2): 150–166.

Meléndez, Edwin, & Bennett Harrison. 1998. Matching the disadvantaged to job opportunities. *Economic Development Quarterly* 12(1): 3–11.

Meyers, Marcia K., & Lucy P. Jordan. 2006. Choice and accommodation in parental child care decisions. *Community Development* 37(2): 53–70.

Miller-Adams, Michelle. 2015. *Promise Nation: Transforming Communities through Place-Based Scholarships*. Kalamazoo, MI: W.E. Upjohn Institute for Employment Research.

Miller-Adams, Michelle. 2009. *The Power of a Promise: Education and Economic Renewal in Kalamazoo*. Kalamazoo, MI: W.E. Upjohn Institute for Employment Research.

Mims, Steve, dir. 2016. *Starving the Beast: The Battle to Disrupt and Reform America's Public Universities* [video documentary].

Mishel, Lawrence, Josh Bivens, Elise Gould, & Heidi Shierholz. 2012. *The State of Working America*, 12th ed. Ithaca, NY: ILR.

Moretti, Enrico. 2012. *The New Geography of Jobs*. Wilmington, MA: Mariner.

National Governors Association. 2013. *A Governor's Guide to Early Literacy: Getting All Students Reading by Third Grade*. Retrieved October 14, 2015: http://www.nga.org/files/live/sites/NGA/files/pdf/2013/1310NGAEarlyLiteracyReportWeb.pdf.

O'Brien, Eileen M., & Catherine Zudak. 1998. Minority-serving institutions: An overview. *New Directions for Higher Education* 26(2): 5–15.

O'Hearn, Denis. 2009. Amartya Sen's *Development as Freedom*: Ten years later. *Policy & Practice* 8: 9–15.

Orfield, Gary, Mark D. Bachmeier, David R. James, & Tamela Eitle. 1997. Deepening segregation in American public schools: A special report from the Harvard Project on School Equity. *Excellence in Education* 30(2): 5–24.

Organisation for Economic Co-operation and Development. 2010. *The High Cost of Low Educational Performance*. Retrieved December 19, 2013: http://www.oecd.org/pisa/44417824.pdf.

Perna, Laura W. 2014. Promoting workforce readiness for urban growth, in Susan M. Wachter & Kimberly A. Zeuli, eds., 242–255. *Revitalizing America's Cities*, Philadelphia: University of Pennsylvania Press.

Pew Research Center. 2016. On views of race and inequality, Blacks and Whites are worlds apart. June 27: http://www.pewsocialtrends.org/2016/06/27/on-views-of-race-and-inequality-blacks-and-whites-are-worlds-apart/.

Phillips, Rhonda, & Robert H. Pittman, eds. 2015. *An Introduction to Community Development*, 2nd ed. New York: Routledge.

Pink-Harper, Stephanie A. 2015. Educational attainment: An examination of its impact on regional economic growth. *Economic Development Quarterly* 29(2): 167–179.

Plane, David A., Christopher J. Henrie, & Marc J. Perry. 2005. Migration up and down the urban hierarchy and across the life course. *Proceedings of the National Academy of Sciences* 102: 15313–15318. Retrieved July 20, 2016: http://www.pnas.org/content/102/43/15313.

Porter, Michael E. 2000. Location, competition, and economic development: Local clusters in a global economy. *Economic Development Quarterly* 14(1): 15–34.

Porter, Michael E. 1990. *The Competitive Advantage of Nations*. New York: Free Press.

Pratt, James E., & David L. Kay. 2006. Beyond looking backward: Is child care a key economic sector? *Community Development* 37(2): 23–37.

Proweller, Amira, & Karen Monkman. 2015. From the self to the social: Engaging urban youth in strategies for change, in Stephen N. Haymes, Maria V. de Haymes, & Reuben J. Miller, eds., *The Routledge Handbook of Poverty in the United States*, 538–546. New York: Routledge.

Putnam, Robert D., & David E. Campbell. 2016. *Our Kids: The American Dream in Crisis*. New York: Simon & Schuster.

Rand Gulf States Policy Institute. *Are Charter Schools a Good Option in the Gulf States?* Retrieved November 30, 2012: http://www.rand.org/gulf-states/policy-spotlights/charter-schools.html.

Raphael, Steven. 2014. *The New Scarlet Letter? Negotiating the U.S. Labor Market with a Criminal Record*. Kalamazoo, MI: W.E. Upjohn Institute for Employment Research.

Reese, Laura A., & Minting Ye. 2011. Policy versus place luck: Achieving local economic prosperity. *Economic Development Quarterly* 25(3): 221–236.

Rothwell, Jonathan, & Alan Berube. 2011. Education, demand, and unemployment in metropolitan America. Washington, DC: Brookings Institution. Retrieved September 25, 2016: https://www.brookings.edu/research/education-demand-and-unemployment-in-metropolitan-america/.

Sahlberg, Pasi. 2014. Opinion: Why Finland's schools are top-notch. *CNN*. October 6: http://www.cnn.com/2014/10/06/opinion/sahlberg-finland-education/index.html?hpt=hp_c2.

Schweinhart, Lawrence J., W. Steven Barnett, & Clive R. Belfield. 2005. *Lifetime Effects: The High/Scope Perry Preschool Study Through Age 40*. Ypsilanti, MI: High/Scope.

Schweke, William. 2004. *Smart Money: Education and Economic Development*. Washington, DC: Economic Policy Institute.

Scientific American. 2016. STEM education is vital – but not at the expense of the humanities. October: https://www.scientificamerican.com/article/stem-education-is-vital-but-not-at-the-expense-of-the-humanities/.

Sen, Amartya. 1999. *Development as Freedom*. New York: Knopf.

Severin, Eugenio, & Christine Capota. 2011. The use of technology in education: Lessons from South Korea. *International Development Bank Education* 10. November: http://idb docs.iadb.org/wsdocs/getdocument.aspx?docnum=36419815.

Sharkey, Patrick. 2013. *Stuck in Place: Urban Neighborhoods and the End of Progress toward Racial Equality*. Chicago: University of Chicago Press.

Shrock, Greg. 2014. Connecting people and place prosperity: Workforce development and urban planning in scholarship and practice. *Journal of Planning Literature* 29(3): 257–271.

Shrock, Greg. 2013. Reworking workforce development: Chicago's sectoral workforce centers. *Economic Development Quarterly* 27(3): 163–178.

Smith, James P., & Finis R. Welch. 1989. Black economic progress after Myrdal. *Journal of Economic Literature* 27(2): 519–564.

Stoll, Michael A. 2006. Workforce development in minority communities, in Paul Ong & Anastasia Loukaitou-Sideris, eds., *Jobs and Economic Development in Minority Communities*, 91–118. Philadelphia: Temple University Press.

Straus, Emily E. 2013. *Death of a Suburban Dream: Race and Schools in Compton, California.* Philadelphia: University of Pennsylvania Press.

Strawn, Julie. 1998. *Beyond Job Search or Basic Education: Rethinking the Role of Skills in Welfare Reform.* Washington, DC: Center for Law and Social Policy. Retrieved May 24, 2016: http://eric.ed.gov/?id=ED418281.

Stone, Clarence, & Donn Worgs. 2004. Poverty and the workforce challenge, in Robert Giloth, ed., *Workforce Development Politics: Civic Capacity and Performance*, 249–278. Philadelphia: Temple University Press.

Sturm, Roland. 1993. *How do Education and Training Affect a Country's Economic Performance? A Literature Survey.* Rand Corporation. Retrieved December 3, 2014: http://www.rand.org/content/dam/rand/pubs/monograph_reports/2007/MR197.pdf.

Su, Xuejuan. 2004. The allocation of public funds in a hierarchical educational system. *Journal of Economic Dynamics and Control* 28(12): 2485–2510.

Theodori, Ann E., & Gene L. Theodori. 2015. The influences of community attachment, sense of community, and educational aspirations upon the migration intentions of rural youth in Texas. *Community Development* 46(4): 380–391.

Todaro, Michael P., & Stephen C. Smith. 2014. *Economic Development*, 12th ed. Englewood Cliffs, NJ: Prentice Hall.

Tough, Paul. 2008. *Whatever It Takes: Geoffrey Canada's Quest to Change Harlem and America.* Boston: Houghton Mifflin Harcourt.

Tyler, John H., & Jillian Berk. 2009. Correctional programs in the age of mass incarceration, Maude Toussaint-Comeau & Bruce D. Meyer, eds., *Strategies for Improving Economic Mobility of Workers: Bridging Research and Practice*, 177–195. Kalamazoo, MI: W.E. Upjohn Institute for Employment Research.

US Census Bureau. 2015. *Public Education Finances: 2013.* June: http://www2.census.gov/govs/school/13f33pub.pdf.

US General Accountability Office. 2011. *Multiple Employment and Training Programs: Providing Information on Colocating Services and Consolidating Administrative Structures Could Promote Efficiencies* (GAO-11–92). January: http://gao.gov/assets/320/314551.pdf.

Vogel, Richard, & W. Hubert Keen. 2010. Public higher education and NY State's economy. *Economic Development Quarterly* 24(4): 384–393.

Waldorf, Brigitte. 2011. The location of foreign human capital in the United States. *Economic Development Quarterly* 25(4): 330–340.

Wang, Margaret C., Geneva D. Haertel, & Herbert J. Walberg. 1994. Educational resilience in inner cities, in Margaret C. Wang, & Edmund W. Gordon, eds., *Educational Resilience in Inner-City America: Challenges and Prospects*, 45–72. Hillsdale, NJ: Lawrence Erlbaum.

Warner, Mildred E. 2006a. Overview: Articulating the economic importance of child care for community development. *Community Development* 37(2): 1–6.

Warner, Mildred E. 2006b. Putting child care in the regional economy: Empirical and conceptual challenges and economic development prospects. *Community Development* 37(2): 7–22.

Warner, Mildred E., & Zhilin Liu. 2006. The importance of child care in economic development: A comparative analysis of regional economic linkage. *Economic Development Quarterly* 20(1): 97–103.

Watson, William. 2015. *The Inequality Trap: Fighting Capitalism Instead of Poverty.* Toronto: University of Toronto Press.

Weber, Bruce, Alexander Marre, Monica Fisher, Robert Gibbs, & John Cromartie. 2007. Education's effect on poverty: The role of migration. *Review of Agricultural Economics* 29(3): 437–445.

Whitebrook, Marcy. 2013. Preschool teaching at a crossroads. *Employment Research Newsletter* (W.E. Upjohn Institute for Employment Research) 20(3): 1–3. Retrieved September 4, 2013: research.upjohn.org/cgi/viewcontent.cgi?article=1211&context=empl_research.

Williams, Timothy. 2014. Seeking new start, finding steep cost: Workforce Investment Act leaves many jobless and in debt. *New York Times.* August 17: http://www.nytimes.com/2014/08/18/us/workforce-investment-act-leaves-many-jobless-and-in-debt.html.

Wolfe, Barbara L., & Robert H. Haveman. 2002. Social and nonmarket benefits from education in an advanced economy. *Proceedings from an Economic Conference on Education in the 21st Century* 47: 97–142. Retrieved December 17, 2014: http://www.bostonfed.org/economic/conf/conf47/conf47g.pdf.

World Bank. 2016. *Migration and Remittances Factbook 2016*, 3rd ed. Retrieved July 21, 2016: http://siteresources.worldbank.org/INTPROSPECTS/Resources/334934-1199807908806/4549025-1450455807487/Factbookpart1.pdf.

Wozniak, Abigail. 2010. Are college graduates more responsive to distant labor market opportunities? *Journal of Human Resources* 45(4): 944–970.

Zimmer, Ron, Brian Gill, Kevin Booker, Stéphane Lavertu, & John Witte. 2011. Charter schools: Do they cream skim, increasing student segregation? in Mark Berends, Marisa Cannata, & Ellen B. Goldring, eds., *School Choice and School Improvement*, 215–232. Cambridge: Harvard Education Press.

5

ENHANCE YOUR COMMUNITY: BUILD ON YOUR EXISTING ASSETS

This chapter covers a broad range of strategies assembled under the general heading of "asset-based strategies." Such strategies are also termed "strength-based approaches" (Jakes et al. 2015) and asset-based community development (resulting in the memorable acronym of ABCD). Advocates of asset-based development argue that most conventional development strategies are needs-based, or deficiency-based. Needs-based strategies focus on the shortcomings of a community, namely, what is missing, what is in short supply, or what is broken (Phillips & Pittman 2015). Kretzmann and McKnight (1993: 3) argue that a needs-based approach can shape the overall orientation of community residents "as fundamentally deficient, victims incapable of taking charge of their lives, and of their community's future." A needs-based approach may also tend to steer the path of development toward greater dependence on outside direction and resources in order to fill those needs or deficiencies.

Contrast that traditional approach with asset-based development, which builds on the existing "capacities, skills and assets of lower income people and their neighborhoods" (Kretzmann & McKnight 1993: 5). Asset-based development, as a result,

> is by necessity "internally focused." That is, the development strategy con-
> centrates first of all upon the agenda building and problem-solving capacities
> of local residents, local associations and local institutions....This intense and
> self-conscious internal focus is not intended to minimize either the role
> external forces have played in helping to create the desperate conditions of
> lower income neighborhoods, nor the need to attract additional resources to
> these communities. Rather this strong internal focus is intended simply to
> stress the primacy of local definition, investment, creativity, hope, and control.
>
> *(Kretzmann & McKnight 1993: 9)*

Advocates argue that the asset-based approach can positively influence a community's overall perspective on its potential and possibilities for development: "A positive starting narrative is more likely to lead to perceptions of a hopeful future. A community that focuses on its strengths perceives a positive future as more probable; this, in turn, acts in a way that makes the positive future more likely to happen" (Jakes et al. 2015: 394).

Foundations of asset-based development

The practical applications of asset-based development for ED are built on an expansive body of theory and methodology. In this section, I attempt to map out some of those theories and methods, and provide the interested reader with beginning points for reading more deeply. Academic readers who come from a strong theoretical foundation – in social capital, for example – will recognize this section as a brief overview, at best, which is intended to set the stage for practical application.

Social capital

Sociologist Robert Putnam brought social capital theory to the attention of a wide audience through his scholarly writing (Putnam 1995, 1993), his popular 2000 book *Bowling Alone: The Collapse and Revival of American Community*, and his subsequent elaborations on the topic (Putnam & Campbell 2016; Putnam & Feldstein 2014; Putnam & Campbell 2012). Social capital theory emphasizes the networks among humans and their organizations: a common thread that runs throughout this book. As defined in brief by Putnam (1995: 67), the study of social capital is concerned with "social organization such as networks, norms, and social trust that facilitate coordination and cooperation for mutual benefit" (cited by Rohe 2004).

Planners (Hutchinson & Vidal 2004), community developers (Flora & Allen 2006; Rohe 2004), and ED scholars (Oh, Lee, & Bush 2014) have subsequently interpreted and extended the theory, applying it in their own fields. Social capital theory is commonly applied to low-income or otherwise disadvantaged communities, both urban and rural (Light 2004; Rohe 2004; Saegert, Thompson, & Warren 2001).

SIDEBAR: THE MANY FORMS OF CAPITAL

Economic developers are readily familiar with the concept of "capital." The most familiar form is "financial capital": access to money for investment in businesses, housing projects, etc. Also familiar is physical, built, or real capital: real estate; available buildings; business equipment; and a wide variety of infrastructure and utilities including water, electricity, storm and sanitary sewers; and high-speed Internet access.

"Political capital" is just as real to any practicing ED professional: working relationships with all levels of government officials, as well as many and various professional associations and individual colleagues across the community. "Human capital" is another form of development capital (Chapters 3 and 4) that has become much more prominent and familiar since the "third wave" of ED in the 1990s: the capabilities of educated, creative, trained, and otherwise skilled individuals (Leigh & Blakely 2013). Human capital can include everything from the knowledge of an electrical engineer to the skills of a self-taught blues musician. "Natural capital" (Emery & Flora 2006; Flora, Flora, & Gasteyer 2015), or "natural assets" (Green 2013b), may be less familiar phrases, but they are phrases that are likely to be heard more often as sustainable development becomes central to the field of ED (Chapter 8).

The concept of "cultural capital," however, is probably not nearly as familiar. It has been defined as "high cultural knowledge that can be turned to the owner's socioeconomic advantage" (Light 2004: 146). When we substitute terms such as "social skills" or "soft skills" (Chapter 4), though, the significance of cultural capital is obvious to any developer, businessperson, or teacher, for it includes the command of spoken and written English, manners, punctuality, appropriate dress, and grooming. In all these cases, of course, we are referring to the dominant culture of those who possess the other forms of capital: employers, bankers, customers, clients, teachers, police, and so on. Cultural capital can also include traditions and skills that translate into business opportunities such as arts and crafts or tourism (Phillips & Shockley 2013; Chapter 7). Flora, Flora, and Gasteyer (2015) are widely credited for building the "community capitals framework," which attempts to identify and connect together all the forms of potential community capital. Pigg et al. (2013) and Emery and Flora (2006) build on that framework.

Finally, we come to "social capital." A concise definition of social capital is "relationships of trust embedded in social networks" (Light 2004: 146). This idea may sound abstract or academic until we substitute concepts such as "networking" that are applied every day in ED practice. As such, Putnam's (1993: 35) somewhat expanded definition might resonate with practicing developers. In his view, social capital refers to "features of social organization, such as networks, norms, and trust, that facilitate coordination and cooperation for mutual benefit. Social capital enhances the benefits of investment in physical and human capital."

There are three different forms, or geographic scales, of social capital, which vary a bit depending on the author. "Bonding capital" refers to trusting relationships among people who are similar to one another (Putnam 2004). Classic examples include a closely knit neighborhood or an engaged church congregation. In many low-income communities, the church can be an especially powerful bonding force, providing mutual support for members in difficult circumstances, informing members about political issues, and organizing the congregation to address political or social concerns (Putnam 1993). On the other hand, bonding social capital can also potentially constrain a tightly knit community from developing beyond a certain point, to the extent that it limits members' willingness to build links to the larger world of politics and resources.

If we think of bonding capital as trusting relationships with people who are similar to us, then "bridging capital" refers to expanding trusting relationships to those in the larger community who are different from us. Examples include a low-income neighborhood working with city agencies, nonprofit organizations, or regional initiatives with other neighborhoods or communities.

"Linking capital" refers to networks with those beyond your own local community – especially those that can provide greater resources or political influence than the extended community itself can provide. Examples might include links to state or federal government agencies, national non-governmental organizations (NGOs), regional or national church associations, and other major grant providers.

Putnam (1993: 38) connects the theory of social capital to a number of topics that are raised throughout this book. Regarding the ubiquitous concept of the industrial cluster, popularized by Porter (Chapter 3), he states that "studies of highly efficient, highly flexible 'industrial districts' (a term coined by Alfred Marshall, one of the founders of modern economics) emphasize networks of collaboration among workers and small entrepreneurs. Such concentrations of social capital, far from being paleo-industrial anachronisms, fuel ultra-modern industries from the high tech of Silicon Valley to the high fashion of Benetton." Many low-income communities may be strong in certain forms of social capital, but they also typically lack the types of social capital that can readily translate into job connections, business loans, or other development opportunities (Putnam 1993, citing Wilson 1987).

Putnam (1993) relates social capital to entrepreneurship (Chapter 6), examples of such a connection being the Chinese concept of *guanxi*, or personal connections, that has driven much of the economic growth in China, or the entrepreneurial investment associations among ethnic Chinese here in the US. Putnam (crediting Hirshman 1984, also Couto & Davidson 2010) also uses the term "moral resource" as a characteristic of social capital, meaning "a resource whose supply increases rather than decreases through use and which (unlike physical capital) becomes depleted if not used" (Putnam 1993: 4; see "sustainable development" in Chapters 3 and 8).

A special issue of *Community Development* (Beaulieu & Diebel 2016) addresses the ways in which a wide variety of social and community capitals can be brought to bear on "turning the tide of poverty" in a community (Dyk et al. 2016; Tyler-Mackey et al. 2016). Monroe et al. (2016) in that issue explore the potential for those forms of capital to sustain community engagement in local development efforts. Asset-based development is highly "relationship-driven," partly as a result of its close association with social capital theory. According to Kretzmann and McKnight (1993: 9), to be successful asset-based development depends on building and maintaining "the relationships between and among local residents, local associations and local institutions" (see also Oh, Lee, & Bush 2014).

Much of the practical application of social capital theory to ED has focused internationally, especially in the Developing World (World Bank 2013; Portes &

Landolt 2005; Nel & McQuaid 2002). In turn, much of this international work has focused in particular on the volatile tourism industry in the Developing World. A study by Henthorne, George, and Swamy (2006), for example, considers the role of social capital in the resilience of Indian communities struck by the 2004 Indian Ocean tsunami. The researchers conclude that the residents of a community whose economy was dominated by a major tourism resort had lost many of their traditional relationships and that they were therefore slower to respond to local needs after the disaster.

In the US context, Saegert, Thompson, and Warren (2001) present many possible practical development applications of social capital theory to low-income communities. Marré and Weber (2010) study the measurement of social capital and its relationship to development in rural communities in Canada and the US. Gittell and Thompson 2001 relate the social capital concept specifically to ED, especially for low-income neighborhoods and communities in the US. Research by Rupasingha, Goetz, and Freshwater (2000) suggests a connection between the social capital levels of counties and their levels of per capita income growth. In a study of rural Canadian communities, Tiepoh and Reimer (2004) find a relationship between social capital levels and household income, while Crowe (2008) finds mixed results with regard to social capital and the development of businesses and industries in rural communities in the northwestern US.

In a study of rural communities in the Great Plains, Bridger and Alter (2006) conclude that social capital can promote positive community ED outcomes: specifically, they find "bridging capital" – or the networks that a community builds with outside organizations – to be most relevant to development potential for those communities. Vidal (2004) also emphasizes the importance of bridging capital in a community planning context, compared with bonding capital – or relationships within a small community. In a similar vein, Chapple (2002) examines the challenges that many low-income women face, who frequently lack the extensive professional networks of many well-educated and career-oriented women.

Capacity-building

The broad concept of "capacity-building" is often applied to healthcare, resilience from disasters, and other areas of community development. Related terms and concepts (Vidal 2004) include building "community social capacity" (Chazdon & Lott 2010) and ABCD (Mathie & Cunningham 2003; Green & Haines 2012). Perhaps capacity-building can be thought of as a framework for operationalizing social capital, or for putting social capital into practice, particularly as applied to community and economic development. As defined by Chaskin et al. (2001: 7) in their foundational text,

> community capacity is the interaction of human capital, organizational resources, and social capital existing within a given community that can be leveraged to solve collective problems and improve or maintain the well-being

of that community. It may operate through informal social processes and/or organized efforts by individuals, organizations, and social networks that exist among them and between them and the larger systems of which the community is a part.

Lyons and Reimer (2006, cited in Marré & Weber 2010) offer a succinct, applied definition of capacity as "the ability of people to organize their assets and resources to achieve objectives they consider important." Other researchers focus on more specific aspects of a community's capacity, such as "capacity for community efficacy: the ability of a local population to come together and act collectively in pursuit of a generalized interest" (Parisi et al. 2002: 19). Chaskin (2001: 292–293) acknowledges the variety of definitions of capacity and capacity-building, and offers a systematic explanation of the concept as incorporating, at minimum, "(1) the existence of resources (ranging from the skills of individuals to the strength of organizations to access financial capital), (2) networks of relationships…(3) leadership…, and (4) support for some kind of mechanism for or processes of participation by community members in collective action and problem solving."

Marré and Weber (2010) note that most of the foundational work on community capacity was focused on urban neighborhoods, but they apply a social capital / community capacity framework to an analysis of rural communities in Oregon and across a diverse range of rural communities across Canada. Haverkampf and Loden (2010) offer a case study of Wisconsin communities for the use of "community resource teams" in assessing local capacities for development. Parisi et al. (2002) apply the framework to 296 communities in Mississippi in their analysis of capacity for community efficacy. Markley, Lyons, and Macke (2015) apply the concept of capacity-building to community entrepreneurship development in studies of Kansas and Australia.

Sustainable livelihoods

"Sustainable livelihoods" is a framework for community asset analysis that emerged from the UK:

A livelihood comprises the capabilities, assets (including both material and social resources) and activities required for a means of living. A livelihood is sustainable when it can cope with and recover from stresses and shocks, maintain or enhance its capabilities and assets, while not undermining the natural resource base.

(Scoones 1998: 5)

The research on sustainable livelihoods to date has focused largely on international applications, especially in the Developing World (Mazibuko 2013; Scoones 1998; Ashley & Carney 1999; Carney n.d.) and, to some extent, in lagging regions within the Developed World such as northern Australia (Nikolakis & Grafton 2015).

Ashley and Carney (1999: 7; see also Carney n.d.) suggest core principles of sustainable livelihoods, emphasizing that "poverty-focused development activity should be people-centered, responsive and participatory, multi-level in its perspective, conducted in partnership, sustainable, and dynamic" in its responsiveness to changing environments for development. Citing work by Chambers (1999) and Chambers and Conway (1992), Mazibuko (2013: 176) identifies five key concepts for development in low-income regions, which are central to the sustainable livelihoods framework: (1) well-being, (2) livelihood security, (3) people's capabilities, (4) equity, (5) and sustainability. These concepts are consistent with those emphasized by Sen's (1999) "capabilities" framework (mentioned in Chapter 3), which has provided a foundation for the United Nations' modern approach to global development (United Nations Development Programme 2015; Jeroslow 2015).

Participatory research, action research, and participatory mapping

Participatory research is a broad, multidisciplinary concept that includes research on an organization or a social movement in which the researcher is an active member, participant, or advocate. Davidoff (1965: 331) was an early champion of the concept in the field of planning: "Planning action cannot be prescribed from a position of value neutrality." Davidoff coined the term "advocacy planning" in this regard – a term that Benner and Pastor (2015) apply to the regional equity movement (following in this chapter). Prior (2015: 56) cites Norman Krumholz's (2015, 1991) overriding mission as the influential planning director of Cleveland (1969–1979) as "providing a wide range of choices for those…residents who have few, if any, choices." "Choice" here harks back to the use of the term by Lewis (1955) (which we saw in Chapter 3).

Some of the extensive applications of the concept may be found in community health (Minkler & Wallerstein 2008) and a wide range of other disciplines around the world. Wallerstein and Duran (2008) credit the work of Brazilian philosopher and education theorist Paulo Freire (2000, originally published in English in 1970) as an early inspiration in the field. In the field of planning, "[a]dvocacy planning gained popularity in many professional schools during the 1970s, and some planners who pursued goals of social equity and redistribution sought to implement this new vision *within* government….This became known as *equity planning*" (Metzger 1996: 113). A wide variety of other related terms have been employed for synonymous, similar, or at least closely related concepts (Wallerstein & Duran 2008). Harvey (2013, see also Harvey & Beaulieu 2013) uses the term "consensus-based community development." The use of yet another term, "community-based participatory research," adds emphasis to the importance placed on "research that is *community*-based, rather than merely *community* placed" (Minkler & Wallerstein 2008: 5, italics in original).

Research in this general field typically emphasizes combining the strengths of academic researchers with those outside the academy, especially those with particular knowledge of the community to be studied: "A key strength…is the integration of researchers' theoretical and methodological expertise with nonacademic participants' real-world knowledge and experiences into a mutually reinforcing partnership" (Cargo & Mercer 2008: 327, cited by Minkler & Wallerstein 2008). Typically, participatory research includes a concern for social justice issues involving low-income communities or other populations that may be vulnerable or not fully empowered – and this is especially true of research that is intended to help facilitate community action or social change on behalf of those populations: "[P]articipatory research fundamentally is about who has the right to speak, to analyze and to act" (Hall 1992: 22, cited by Minkler & Wallerstein 2008; see also Prokopy & Castelloe 1999). Honadle (1996) applies participatory research methods to her research on the sensitive topic of municipal school consolidation. Seltzer and Mahmoudi (2012) update the concept of citizen participation to include "crowdsourcing" technologies.

Over the years, the term and the concept have been expanded to "participatory *action* research" (Minkler & Wallerstein 2008), which seems nearly to be synonymous with "action research." Wallerstein & Duran (2008: 26) refer to a "convergence of principles" involving these two concepts, in which participation is one of the "working principles" of action research.

It is difficult to find a specific definition of action research. Instead, it is typically explained through its basic principles. According to Stringer (2014), the fundamental "working principles" of action research are relationships, communication, participation, and inclusion. Stringer (2014: 15) also characterizes action research, in part, by the following "participatory approaches to inquiry: democratic, equitable, liberating (from 'oppressive, debilitating conditions'), and life enhancing for those involved." According to Oden, Hernandez, and Hidalgo (2010: 21–22), "[i]n essence, PAR [participatory action research] acknowledges the expertise of researchers and participants and encourages partnership throughout all phases of research....By having participants play an active role in research, a desired outcome of PAR is enhancing their sense of empowerment." Stringer (2014: 10) includes an anecdote in his standard textbook on action research methodology:

> A colleague approached me after listening to my report on one of the action research projects in which I had been involved. "You know," she said, "the difference with your work is that you expect something to actually happen as a result of your research activities."

Oden, Hernandez, and Hidalgo (2010) apply the methods of PAR to the needs of a community's disabled population. Woodyard, Przybyla, and Hallam (2015) present a case study of "community-based participatory research" applied to community health needs in the Mississippi Delta region. Vorley and Williams (2015: 559) employ a "participatory action research case study" to study entrepreneurial education in the UK school system.

Yet another dimension of the participatory-research-related framework is participatory *mapping* (O'Looney 1998). The term "asset mapping" is used extensively in asset-based development, but it is often used more in the sense of an inventory of assets – data which may or may not be collected in a fully participatory manner, and may or may not be mapped out geographically. In the case of "participatory mapping," the process involves drawing an actual geographic map, either on paper or increasingly by utilizing a geographic information system (GIS, or mapping in a computerized database) for that purpose.

Cochran (2009) provides an overview and literature review of participatory mapping in the Developing World as well as in the US. Talen (2000, 1998) reviews the literature related to participatory GIS mapping in a variety of planning applications. Cochran, Reese, and Liu (2009: 425) engage residents of Honduras' coastal region in better assessing – through the use of participatory maps – how residents "understand and respond to tropical cyclones and how landscape change influences the vulnerability of a coastal area." Duval-Diop, Curtis, and Clark (2010) apply participatory GIS in a case study of faith-based organizations and their role in New Orleans' recovery from Hurricane Katrina.

Appreciative inquiry

Appreciative inquiry (AI) is a research perspective that originated in the fields of organizational behavior and management (Ludema, Cooperrider, & Barrett 2001; Srivastva & Cooperrider 1990). Similar in attitude to that of asset-based development, AI research deliberately and almost exclusively focuses on what is *right* rather than what is *wrong* about an organization (i.e., what is missing or broken). Bushe & Kassam (2005) offer a critical overview of AI case studies concerned with a wide variety of businesses and organizations. Bushe (2007: 1) concludes that AI can be transformational: "When successful, AI generates spontaneous, unsupervised, individual, group and organizational action toward a better future....When AI is transformational it has both these qualities: it leads to new ideas, and it leads people to choose new actions."

The AI methodology has been extended in the literature to include research on communities. A guidebook by Whitney and Trosten-Bloom (2010) concerns both organizational and community applications of AI. In some writings on the topic, AI is directly connected with community-related concepts already addressed in this chapter, such as action research (Stowell 2013) and capacity-building (Barrett & Fry 2005). Consistent with those earlier concepts, David Cooperrider, one of the founders of AI, offers this definition:

> Appreciative Inquiry is the cooperative...search for the best in people, their organizations, and the world around them. It involves systematic discovery of what gives life to an organization or community when it is most effective and most capable in economic, ecological, and human terms....Instead of negation, criticism, and... diagnosis, there is discovery, dream, and design. AI involves the art and practice of asking unconditionally positive questions.
>
> *(Cooperrider & Whitney 2005: 8)*

Koster and Lemelin (2009) apply AI to a case study of rural tourism development in western Canada. Once again, much of the applied development-related research on AI is focused internationally, especially in the Developing World. Based on her research on indigenous NGOs in three African countries, Michael concludes that there

were three clear benefits to using AI....Interviewees

- were eager to tell their stories;
- offered dynamic and unrehearsed information; and
- spoke more openly, with less defensiveness or fear of reprisal.

....Time and time again I had people telling me that this was the most fun they'd ever had in an interview, that this was the first interview at which they'd been unable to guess what question I was going to ask next, that I didn't ask any of the questions they were expecting me to ask.

(Michael 2005: 226–227)

In an intriguing contribution to the ABCD and appreciative inquiry methodologies, Pstross, Talmage, and Knopf (2014) employ "community catalytic storytelling" to capture the values and aspirations of a diverse population in a Phoenix, Arizona, study.

Asset-based development in practice[1]

The application of asset-based development, asset mapping, and many related concepts has been widely embraced in practice as a tool for local ED in the US. To be concise, I will use the memorable acronym ABCD (asset-based community development) in this section to represent all these various tools. Asset-based ED typically involves community members working with outside organizers and facilitators, usually to create a "capacity inventory" or an "asset map" document. An asset inventory or map details what the community prizes or what might be useful for helping it to attract investment or development.

Much of the applied literature of ABCD focuses, once again, on the Developing World (Jakes et al. 2015; Mengesha, Meshelemiah, & Chuffa 2015) – as well as on applications outside ED, healthcare in particular (African Religious Health Assets Programme 2006). O'Leary, Burkett, and Braithwaite (2011) apply an ABCD perspective across much of the English-speaking Developed World. For US practitioners, there are a number of applied, practical step-by-step guides to conducting an ABCD project, including Green and Haines (2012), Advancement Project (2012), Kretzmann et al. (2005), and Kretzmann and McKnight (1993). In my own practical experience with asset-based development, I have found the concept to be tightly associated in many practitioners' minds with Florida's concept of creative communities (Chapter 3) – particularly with regard to musical and other artistic assets that might contribute to tourism development.

Harvey (2013) and others suggest that the ABCD approach represents an evolution away from more traditional community organizing and political confrontation characterized by the self-professed radical Saul Alinsky (1969). Instead, ABCD approaches work toward "consensus-building" within a community, making the approach attractive especially to government agencies at the local and state levels (Saegert 2006): "Looking outside [the community] for resources and assistance can create additional problems. Technical assistance may not match the need in the local setting. Providers of technical assistance frequently have a generic response to community issues. They have little, if any, knowledge or understanding of the local context" (Green 2013a: 3).

The transition toward ABCD approaches has been encouraged by the reduced flow of community development funding from the federal level, leaving localities with more responsibility for identifying and managing their own limited resources (Green 2013a; Mathie & Cunningham 2003). Instead of fighting for a "piece of the pie" from federal funding, low-income communities are increasingly left to bake their own pie with the ingredients, or assets, they have available.

I have engaged several university classes in ABCD mapping projects, working with local communities and the state ED authority. At a minimum, ABCD offers a process that is potentially useful for creating local community engagement in the development process, forging connections among local organizations and with outside organizations, and promoting outside awareness of a sometimes-neglected community. Santilli, Wong, and Ickovics (2011) engage local grade-school students in neighborhood-level healthcare asset-mapping projects in the US and abroad. Andresen (2012) employs ABCD research to identify factors to help rural communities in Michigan's Upper Peninsula region retain and attract young people. Andresen also designs a 10-year evaluation plan to measure the success of the effort.

A number of challenges inherent in the ABCD process have been recognized nearly since its inception. Among the most important issues, as identified by Mathie and Cunningham (2003), are the needs to assure that the ABCD process truly (1) is driven by the community itself, making use of outside organizations' knowledge and resources but still fostering community ownership; (2) encourages inclusive community participation; (3) nurtures community leadership; and (4) recognizes that community organizations and informal networks are fluid in their nature and their interrelationships.

Harvey (2013: 258) cautions against the view of ABCD as a panacea, in which, "as argued by Kretzmann and McKnight (1993: 6), every place, no matter how distressed, possesses the 'individuals, associations, and institutions' necessary to play the lead role in its own transformation." Harvey argues that the nature of distinctive and powerful "political and economic environments" in various communities can strongly influence the outcomes of an ABCD-based development initiative. In particular, Harvey (2013) cites the "invisible elephant of institutional racism" in his study of rural communities of the Mississippi Delta – a concern that my own students and professional colleagues have come to recognize in their own work in that challenging region.

A relatively new development in the ABCD-related literature is termed "collective impact," or combining what might be termed community "organizational assets." Walzer, Weaver, and McGuire (2016) devote a special issue of *Community Development* to "collective impact approaches and community development issues." Kania and Kramer (2011: 37–38) describe the concept in an early, seminal article as

> the commitment of a group of important actors from different sectors to a common agenda for solving a specific social problem....Unlike most collaborations, collective impact initiatives involve a centralized infrastructure, a dedicated staff, and a structured process that leads to a common agenda, shared measurement, continuous communication, and mutually reinforcing activities among all participants.

Often-overlooked community assets

The rest of this chapter focuses on categories of community assets that may typically be found in low-income communities, but that too often may be overlooked as potential assets for ED. Such potentially overlooked assets include historical and natural resources, churches and faith-based organizations, the community's location within a larger metropolis or other region, returned criminal offenders, and immigrant populations.

Local history and natural amenities

Barton and Leonard (2010) employ the Mississippi Delta region's history of racism and discrimination as a "dark asset" on which to build a particular type of tourism that is based on social justice and reconciliation. I believe I am coining the term "dark asset" based on the existing term "dark tourism" – or tourism based on an unpleasant aspect of a place's history (Chapter 7). Barton and Leonard focus their study on no less than memorial planning in Tallahatchie County for the death of Emmett Till, which was among the darkest and most notorious episodes in the history of the civil rights struggle. Blejwas (2013) applies the ABCD approach to a comparable region: Alabama's Black Belt region (named for the rich black soil that supported local cotton production). Kretzmann and Puntenney (2013) apply ABCD principles to low-income urban communities on Chicago's West Side.

On the more positive side of the community asset spectrum, natural amenities – such as trees, parks, proximity to bodies of water or mountains, and recreational facilities – can also contribute to a community's economic base in addition to its quality of life. A substantial literature examines the direct economic impacts of tourism on rural regions (Bergstrom et al. 1990). Natural amenities can also provide indirect economic benefits by attracting more "creative workers" (McGranahan, Wojan, & Lambert 2011). Reese and Ye (2011) refer to "place luck," or the fortune of some communities that are blessed with good climates and/or note-worthy cultural resources (e.g., music or art traditions). However, this "luck" must also be recognized and nurtured as an ED asset.

Churches and faith-based organizations

We have addressed churches earlier in this chapter as an important source of a community's social capital. Much of the research regarding churches and ED has focused on economically challenged urban communities. Reese (2004: 51) sum-marizes research work on a variety of urban "faith-based organizations" (FBOs):

> Although FBOs initially focused their efforts on housing and social services, some now include workforce and entrepreneurial training, business incubators, consulting support, and loans among their development activities....Faith-based entrepreneurial efforts in central cities include cooperative restaurants, con-struction cooperatives... recycling operations, and day care centers....Initial research suggests that larger churches are more likely to operate businesses (bakeries, restaurants, and restoration companies) and job training programs, and churches with predominantly African American congregations appear more likely to offer financial services such as credit unions to their congregants.

Reese and Shields (2000) observe that churches may be among the very few remaining institutions available in hard-hit low-income urban neighborhoods. Religious institutions "are often a hidden asset, despite the long history and influence of Christian churches in American society, and are the single most important source of social capital" in many low-income communities (Choi 2010: 374). Because of their congregations and physical infrastructure, churches serve important roles, also, as "anchors" of their communities and potential promotors of "place-based" development (Welch 2012; Chapter 2).

Based on her case study of the Catholic Archdiocese of Philadelphia, Welch (2012) says that churches can play a potential "mediating" role between low-income neigh-borhoods and government policies in the tradition of bridging social capital. Foley, McCarthy, and Chaves (2001) identify specific sorts of social capital resources that FBOs can provide to low-income communities, including access to information, free use of space, political connections, and legitimacy in the community.

While the majority of churches or FBOs engage in some sort of community service, Reese (2004) suggests that relatively few engage in ED-related activities. Choi (2010) presents a case study of a church that serves an ethnic urban com-munity, a Korean church in an ethnic neighborhood of Los Angeles, which emphasizes support for local small business development as ED: "Since the estab-lishment of the [Oriental Mission Church] in 1970, pastors and members have emphasized labor and education to immigrants. Members have been encouraged to help each other by starting small businesses....Business owners were even encour-aged to advertise in the church's newsletter. Church members started small businesses such as gas stations, restaurants, tailor shops, and body shops" (Choi 2010: 379).

Duval-Diop, Curtis, and Clark (2010) work with a coalition of churches at the local and national level, applying participatory GIS to support their efforts to support New Orleans' recovery from Hurricane Katrina. Lacho, Parker, and Carter (2005) take another view of faith-based ED in New Orleans in a case study of the historic, low-income, African American Treme neighborhood.

Regionalism and regional equity

One of the most powerful potential assets for any community is the greater region in which it is located: either the larger metropolis for an urban neighborhood, or the greater surrounding area for a rural community. The basic concept of regionalism is not new. The Tennessee Valley Authority (TVA) was founded in the 1930s on the concept of a "natural region" for development. More recently, one of the major emphases of the "third wave" of ED from the 1990s has been regional clustering and enhanced regional cooperation to grow the economic pie for all communities involved. For decades, ED professionals have acknowledged the merit of regional approaches for creating a "win-win" development situation for all cooperating communities in the region (Dickes & Robinson 2013; Gordon 2009; Olberding 2002).

The regional sword can also cut both ways. Local rivalries, jealousies, and political turf-protection too often prevail over regional cooperation (Lackey, Freshwater, & Rupasingha 2002). Inner-city neighborhoods notoriously tend to be economically isolated – or "ghettoized" – from the larger, more prosperous metropolitan region (Blair & Carroll 2007). In Aiken's (1990) study of the Mississippi Delta, unhealthy regional dependencies can develop as small rural town economies wither away and the remaining shopping and employment opportunities become increasingly concentrated in a few larger cities in the region – leaving behind what Aiken terms "rural ghettos."

A number of researchers have issued calls for greater regional cooperation and equity within metropolitan regions. Rusk (1999) expresses frustration with the inadequate success of working strictly with small, low-income neighborhoods within larger, more prosperous metropolitan regions – what he terms the "inside game." Rusk advocates complementing local efforts with an "outside game": building cooperative alliances between central city neighborhoods and more affluent suburbs. The argument anticipates the various forms of bonding, bridging, and linking social capital presented earlier in this chapter. Manuel Pastor and his colleagues, in particular, champion "regional equity," especially within metropolitan regions (Benner & Pastor 2012; Pastor, Benner, & Matsuoka 2009; Pastor, Brenner, & Rosner 2003; Pastor, Lopez-Garza, & Drier 2000). Pastor, Benner, and Matsuoka (2006) also use the term "community-based regionalism." In his introduction to a special issue of *Community Development* devoted to regional equity, Rubin (2011: 434–435) states: "In the broadest sense, regional equity is a framework for social change that is nestled within, and inseparable from, the quest for economic and social justice in America." Benner and Pastor (2015) incorporate "advocacy planning" in describing regional equity as an activist social movement. Pastor, Brenner, and Rosner (2003) present a "regional audit" case study of California's Central Coast region (between Santa Cruz and Monterey). The regional audit method they demonstrate includes an inventory of regional economic assets, which include industrial cluster opportunities. The audit also addresses the most pressing needs of vulnerable populations in the region. In their case study, housing emerged as the outstanding issue to be addressed by the region.

Nowak (1997) argues that neighborhood-level development must be addressed within a regional context: "The persistence and acceleration of poverty, in the very areas where so much community development activity takes place, reveal the limitations of the approach: limitations of *scale and perspective*. The scale problem is self-explanatory. Just take a drive through the most blighted sections of Philadelphia, Baltimore, or Detroit, and it becomes clear that massive development intervention is required to restore the ordinary mechanisms of the marketplace and make the area a place in which anyone with choice will want to remain or locate" (Nowak 1997: 4, italics in original).

A literature review by Chapple and Goetz (2011) highlights the regional nature of equitable housing efforts, efforts to create access for the poor to job opportunities outside low-income neighborhoods, and the deconcentration of poverty within a metropolis. Morgan and Shetty (2011) address the need to include low-income inner-ring suburbs, as well as the traditional inner-city communities, within a regional perspective. Henderson and Weiler (2010) address the need for isolated entrepreneurs – in rural communities, especially – to make regional linkages.

Low-income communities are not just dependent on their greater region; research reinforces the fact that all communities in a region are economically interdependent: "Even if the most acute problems associated with urban decline do not arise in the suburbs, central city decline is likely to be a long-run, slow drain on the economic and social vitality of the region" (Voith 1992, quoted by Hartley, Kaza, & Lester 2016: 139). Pastor, Benner, and Matsuoka (2009) make the argument that the overall region has the potential for greater economic growth if all elements of the region's workforce and market are incorporated.

Returned criminal offenders

High incarceration rates have had a disproportionate impact on low-income and minority populations, as well as their communities (Chapter 1). *The Angolite: The Prison News Magazine* – produced by inmates of Louisiana's notorious Louisiana State Penitentiary, more commonly known as Angola Prison – provides the interested outsider with a sympathetic view of prisoners' efforts to rehabilitate themselves with continuing education, skills training, and a variety of self-help and spiritual programs (e.g., Corley 2015). Offenders who are released to their communities – many after serving long mandatory sentences – face a variety of barriers to productive employment, including business policies and employer prejudices. Over half of those who have been incarcerated have not completed high school (Raphael 2014).

There are a number of promising model programs across the US, along with a need – as usual – for much more evaluation research of those programs, so they can be effectively utilized by other communities (Raphael 2014; Redcross et al. 2009). The Center for Employment Opportunities "is one of the nation's largest and most well-regarded employment programs for ex-offenders....The employment effects of CEO participation are not impressive....On the other hand, the effects of CEO on recidivism appear to be rather substantial" at least for certain groups (Tyler & Berk 2009: 185–186).

Camp & Trzcinski (2015) and Slate, Buffington-Vollum, and Johnson (2013) offer perspectives on the complex relationship between incarceration and mental illness. That connection is exacerbated by the stresses of life in poverty (Sapolsky 2005) and the shortage of appropriate mental health facilities in most low-income communities.

Immigrants as community assets

"Despite studies that found immigrant families to be less dependent on welfare than U.S.-born families and that immigrants tend to contribute more to local, state, and federal budgets than they consume in services, rhetoric about the economic drain of immigrants in the United States has persisted" (Becerra 2015, citing Becerra et al. 2012).

Blumenberg (2006) notes that most initiatives to revitalize central city downtowns and other neighborhoods tend to focus on attracting relatively high-income, young, White populations: the classic creative class community. Lin (1998) offers an alternative approach: we should build on the natural tendency of immigrants to re-invent and re-energize neighborhoods and local economies. In the words of Blumenberg (2006: 31–32), "revitalization efforts can...take another path by supporting and enhancing existing minority, immigrant, and low-income communities...simultaneously revitalizing the neighborhood while benefiting working- and middle-class minority families."

Howland and Nguyen (2010: 100–101) review the research on the relationship between immigrants and local labor markets: "A review of this literature indicates that foreign immigrants are not simply competing with native-born workers for a fixed number of jobs....A number of labor market studies find that immigration has little or no negative impact on the employment rate and wages of natives.... Muller (1993) argues that immigrants have shaped the structure of cities by creating growth in particular industries, including apparel, despite the industry's national decline." Howland and Nguyen's (2010: 107) own research on metropolitan labor markets confirms those conclusions: "How can policy makers use this information to make better decisions? Cities attracting large numbers of low-skilled immigrants can expect to also attract or retain footloose industries that depend on low-skilled workers. This analysis shows that fruit and vegetable processing, apparel, and leather and leather products manufacturing retain more jobs where there are Hispanic immigrants."

Hartley, Kaza, and Lester (2016: 140) emphasize the contribution of immigrants in keeping inner-city neighborhoods competitive in a modern economy: "Some scholars highlight the positive impact of immigration for inner-city neighborhoods. For example…neighborhoods with a higher share of foreign-born residents have lower rates of violent crime. Also…high levels of social capital in tight immigrant-ethnic enclaves can lead to greater entrepreneurship among some immigrant groups. As Bates (2011) points out, however, significant barriers remain, such as access to capital, that limit immigrant and minority entrepreneurship." Trabalzi and Sandoval (2010), in an Iowa case study, explore the role of immigrants in reshaping community identities – or "re-branding," in marketing terminology. They caution, however, that "[c]ommunity development multicultural policies should appreciate cultural diversity but not transform it into a museum curiosity for the locals" (Trabalzi & Sandoval 2010: 76): "the exotic other." Waldorf (2011) analyzes the location patterns of highly educated international immigrants in the US. One of the study's purposes is to provide a better understanding of how communities might potentially attract well-educated and skilled migrants to add to their existing pool of human capital. Singer, Hardwick, and Brettell (2008: 314) summarize their research findings with three recommendations to empower immigrant populations to take roles as contributing citizens and fully productive members of their communities:

- *Implementing an English-Learning Campaign.…*This recommendation calls for a coordinated effort among the state community college board, businesses, educators, and immigrant advocates to create, fund, and implement a campaign to offer English instruction where immigrants live and work.
- *Ensuring that Immigrants and Refugees Can Access State Services.…*Many local governments across the country already offer services and material in languages of local immigrant groups, provide translation services, and hire multilingual staff.…
- *Helping Eligible Legal Permanent Residents Attain U.S. Citizenship.* When immigrants naturalize, they take on the rights and responsibilities of being a full member of U.S. society: they can vote, hold public office, serve on juries, and participate in other civic activities.

TAKEAWAY FOR ED ACTION: COMMUNITY ASSETS AND ED

- *Carefully consider your community's assets.* Raise awareness of local assets within the community, and market those assets outside the community. Like education (Chapter 4), we give lip service to building on existing community assets, but often fail to seriously focus on that dimension in our

ED initiatives. Instead, we tend to rely on the same generic strategies that all the other communities are using.

- *Focus first on your community's assets, then your community's (many) needs.* Beginning with a focus on assets can create a more positive context for community engagement in the ED process. Focusing on assets can help your community build a collective identity, and perhaps a clearer and more specific strategy for moving forward. Community needs can then be addressed in the context of working toward that strategy.

- *There are many different terminologies and frameworks within the general concept of asset-based development.* They may have slightly different emphases, but they complement much more than they contradict one another. Embrace a terminology and framework that seems most appropriate to your community, and work with it.

- *Above all other assets, focus on building "social capital," or networks throughout your community, as well as on linking your community to assets outside its boundaries.* These networks can include better, more trusting, and productive relationships within your own community ("bonding capital"); networks with government offices, businesses, nonprofit organizations, and more prosperous neighboring communities within your greater region ("bridging capital"); and networks with government agencies and other organizations at the state or federal level.

- *All forms of social capital, or network building, are valuable, but "bridging capital" appears to be the most valuable.* Build networks between your neighborhood and the larger metropolis, or between your rural community and the larger region.

- *Effective network building can and should be a "win-win" proposition.* All communities, low-income as well as wealthy, can contribute to the mutual prosperity of the greater region.

- *Don't overlook those assets that are "hidden in plain sight."* Work with experienced outsiders, from state agencies or local universities, for example, who may be able to identify assets that are so familiar to locals that they may be overlooked: natural amenities, neighboring communities, churches, immigrants, and others.

- *Recognize and develop all possible pools of human capital.* Residents who have returned from incarceration represent a significant human capital asset for many low-income communities. Providing them with education and training opportunities, and reducing their barriers to employment, can help grow ED in the community while helping to lower the likelihood that they will return to prison. By helping to keep them outside jails and prisons, fathers and mothers can much more effectively raise, educate, and provide role models for their children. Immigrants are often disparaged (especially during election years), but they can provide a community with a wide variety of skills, entrepreneurial energy, and cultural vitality.

Note

1   Mary Travis, a University of Southern Mississippi undergraduate honors student, contributed research from her class project and thesis titled "Delta Hands for Hope: A Force for Reconciliation and Sustainable Development in the Delta?" Joy Foy, Director of the Community Asset Development Division of the Mississippi Development Authority, and her team provided me with practical experience in community asset mapping.

References

AdvancementProject. 2012. *Participatory Asset Mapping: A Community Research Lab Toolkit.* Retrieved December 9, 2015: http://communityscience.com/knowledge4equity/Asset MappingToolkit.pdf.

African Religious Health Assets Programme. 2006. *Appreciating Assets: The Contribution of Religion to Universal Access in Africa.* Retrieved November 11, 2015: http://www.arhap. uct.ac.za/pub_WHO2006.php.

Aiken, Charles S. 1990. A new type of Black ghetto in the Plantation South. *Association of American Geographers* 80(2): 223–246.

Alinsky, Saul D. 1969. *Reveille for Radicals.* New York: Random House.

Andresen, William. 2012. Evaluating an asset-based effort to attract and retain young people. *Community Development* 43(1): 49–62.

Ashley, Caroline, & Diana Carney. 1999. *Sustainable Livelihoods: Lessons from Early Experience.* Department for International Development, UK. Retrieved February 2, 2016: http:// www.eldis.org/vfile/upload/1/document/0902/DOC7388.pdf.

Barrett, Frank J., & Ronald E. Fry. 2005. *Appreciative Inquiry: A Positive Approach to Building Cooperative Capacity.* Cleveland: CreateSpace Independent Publishing Platform. Retrieved September 14, 2016: http://www.pdf.net/assets/uploads/publications/Appreciative% 20InquiryTxt_SAMPLE_chp1.pdf.

Barton, Alan W., & Sarah J. Leonard. 2010. Incorporating social justice in tourism planning: Racial reconciliation and sustainable community development in the Deep South. *Community Development* 41(3): 298–322.

Bates, Timothy. 2011. Minority entrepreneurship. *Foundations and Trends in Entrepreneurship* 7(3–4): 151–311.

Beaulieu, Lionel J., & Alice Diebel. 2016. Bringing hope: Preface to the Turning the Tide on Poverty special issue. *Community Development* 47(3): 285–286.

Becerra, David. 2015. The effects of neoliberal capitalism on immigration and poverty among Mexican immigrants in the United States, in Stephen N. Haymes, Maria V. de Haymes, & Reuben J. Miller, eds., *The Routledge Handbook of Poverty in the United States,* 463–471. New York: Routledge.

Becerra, David, David K. Androff, Cecilia Ayon, & Jason T. Castillo. 2012. Fear vs. facts: The economic impact of undocumented immigrants in the U.S. *Journal of Sociology and Social Welfare* 39(4): 111–134.

Benner, Chris, & ManuelPastor, Jr. 2015. Collaboration, conflict, and community building at the regional scale: Implications for advocacy planning. *Journal of Planning Education and Research* 35(3): 307–322.

Benner, Chris, & ManuelPastor, Jr. 2012. *Just Growth: Inclusion and Prosperity in America's Metropolitan Regions.* Abingdon, UK: Routledge.

Bergstrom, John C., H. Ken Cordell, Gregory A. Ashley, & Alan E. Watson. 1990. Economic impacts of recreational spending on rural areas. *Economic Development Quarterly* 4(1): 29–39.

Blair, John P., & Michael C. Carroll. 2007. Inner-city neighborhoods and metropolitan development. *Economic Development Quarterly* 21(3): 263–277.

Blejwas, Emily. 2013. Asset-based community development in Alabama's Black Belt: Seven strategies for building a diverse community movement, in Gary P. Green & Ann Goetting, eds., *Mobilizing Communities: Asset Building as a Community Development Strategy*, 48–67. Philadelphia: Temple University Press.

Blumenberg, Evelyn. 2006. Metropolitan dispersion and diversity: Implications for community economic development, in Paul Ong & Anastasia Loukaitou-Sideris, eds., *Jobs and Economic Development in Minority Communities*, 13–38. Philadelphia: Temple University Press.

Bridger, Jeffrey C., & Theodore R. Alter. 2006. Place, community development, and social capital. *Community Development* 37(1): 5–18.

Bushe, Gervase R. 2007. Appreciative Inquiry is not (just) about the positive. *OD Practitioner* 39(4): 30–35.

Bushe, Gervase R., & Aniq F. Kassam. 2005. When is Appreciative Inquiry transformational? A meta-case analysis. *Journal of Applied Behavioral Science* 41(2): 161–181.

Camp, Jessica K., & Eileen Trzcinski. 2015. The rise of incarceration among the poor with mental illnesses, in Stephen N. Haymes, Maria V. de Haymes, & Reuben J. Miller, eds., *The Routledge Handbook of Poverty in the United States*, 357–366. New York: Routledge.

Cargo, Margaret, & Shawna L. Mercer. 2008. The value and challenges of participatory research: Strengthening its practice. *Annual Review of Public Health* 29: 325–350.

Carney, Diana. *Sustainable Livelihoods Approaches: Progress and Possibilities for Change*. Department for International Development, UK. Retrieved February 2, 2016: http://www.eldis.org/vfile/upload/1/document/0812/sla_progress.pdf.

Chambers, Robert. 1999. *Whose Reality Counts? Putting the First Last*, 2nd ed. London: Intermediate Technology.

Chambers, Robert, & Gordon Conway. 1992. *Sustainable rural livelihoods: Practical concepts for the 21st century*. OpenDocs. Retrieved July 29, 2016: http://opendocs.ids.ac.uk/opendocs/handle/123456789/775#.VqfYdvEupXx.

Chapple, Karen. 2002. "I name it and I claim it – In the name of Jesus, this job is mine": Job search, networks, and careers for low-income women. *Economic Development Quarterly* 16(4): 294–313.

Chapple, Karen, & Edward G. Goetz. 2011. Spatial justice through regionalism? The inside game, the outside game, and the quest for the spatial fix in the United States. *Community Development* 42(4): 458–475.

Chaskin, Robert J. 2001. Building community capacity: A definitional framework and case studies from a comprehensive community initiative. *Urban Affairs Review* 36(3): 291–323.

Chaskin, Robert J., Prudence Brown, Sudhir Venkatesh, & Avis Vidal. 2001. *Building Community Capacity*. New York: Aldine de Gruyter.

Chazdon, Scott A., & Stephanie Lott. 2010. Ready for engagement: Using key informant interviews to measure community social capacity. *Community Development* 41(2): 156–175.

Choi, Hyunsun. 2010. Religious institutions and ethnic entrepreneurship: The Korean ethnic church as a small business incubator. *Economic Development Quarterly* 24(4): 372–383.

Cochran, Jr., David M. 2009. Placing geographic power in the hands of the people: The potential for participatory GIS in ED. *Applied Research in Economic Development* 6(2): 64–77.

Cochran, Jr., David M., Carl A. Reese, & Kam-biu Liu. 2009. Tropical Storm Gamma and the Mosquitia of eastern Honduras: A little-known story from the 2005 hurricane season. *Area* 41(4): 425–434.

Cooperrider, David L., & Diana Whitney. 2005. *Appreciative Inquiry: A Positive Revolution in Change*. San Francisco: Berrett-Koehler.

Corley, John. 2015. To Pell and back: Federal government eases restrictions against the most effective rehabilitative and anti-recidivism tool. *The Angolite*. May/June-July: 28–35.

Couto, Richard A., & John Davidson. 2010. Social and economic development, in Richard A. Couto, ed., *Political and Civic Leadership: A Reference Handbook*, 219–228. Thousand Oaks, CA: Sage.

Crowe, Jessica A. 2008. Economic development in the nonmetropolitan West: The influence of built, natural, and social capital. *Community Development* 39(4): 51–70.

Davidoff, Paul. 1965. Advocacy and pluralism in planning. *Journal of the American Institute of City Planners* 31(4): 331–338.

Dickes, Lori A., & Kenneth Robinson. 2013. Community partnerships as a tool to reduce regional labor gaps: A South Carolina regional case study. *Community Development* 44(1): 127–143.

Duval-Diop, Dominique; Andrew Curtis, & Annie Clark. 2010. Enhancing equity with public participatory GIS in hurricane rebuilding: Faith-based organizations, community mapping, and policy advocacy. *Community Development* 41(1): 32–49.

Dyk, Patricia H., Pamela A. Monroe, Crystal Tyler-Mackey, & Rachel Welborn. 2016. Turning the tide on poverty: History, theoretical frameworks, and methods. *Community Development* 47(3): 287–303.

Emery, Mary, & Cornelia Flora. 2006. Spiraling-up: Mapping community transformation with community capitals framework. *Community Development* 37(1): 19–35.

Flora, Cornelia B., Jan L. Flora, & Stephen Gasteyer. 2015. *Rural Communities: Legacy and Change*, 5th ed. Boulder, CO: Westview.

Flora, Jan, & Beverlyn L. Allen, eds. 2006. Introduction: Community development and social capital. *Community Development* 37(1): 1–4.

Foley, Michael W., John D. McCarthy, & Mark Chaves. 2001. Social capital, religious institutions, and poor communities, in Susan J. Saegert, Phillip Thompson, & Mark R. Warren, eds., *Social Capital and Poor Communities*, 215–245. New York: Russell Sage Foundation.

Freire, Paulo. 2000. *Pedagogy of the Oppressed*, 30th anniversary ed. London: Bloomsbury Academic.

Gittell, Ross, & J. Phillip Thompson. 2001. Making social capital work: Social capital and community economic development, in Susan J. Saegert, Phillip Thompson, & Mark R. Warren, eds., *Social Capital and Poor Communities*, 115–135. New York: Russell Sage Foundation.

Gordon, Victoria. 2009. Perceptions of regional economic development: Can win-lose become win-win? *Economic Development Quarterly* 23(4): 317–328.

Green, Gary P. 2013a. Community assets: Building the capacity for development, in Gary P. Green & Ann Goetting, eds., *Mobilizing Communities: Asset Building as a Community Development Strategy*, 1–13. Philadelphia: Temple University Press.

Green, Gary P. 2013b. Natural amenities and asset-based development in rural communities, in Gary P. Green & Ann Goetting, eds., *Mobilizing Communities: Asset Building as a Community Development Strategy*, 130–145. Philadelphia: Temple University Press.

Green, Gary P., & Anna Haines. 2012. *Asset Building and Community Development*, 3rd ed. Thousand Oaks, CA: Sage.

Hall, Budd. 1992. From margins to center? The development and purpose of participatory research. *American Sociologist* 23(4): 15–28.

Hartley, Daniel A., Nikhil Kaza, & T. William Lester. 2016. Are America's inner cities competitive? Evidence from the 2000s. *Economic Development Quarterly* 30(2): 137–158.

Harvey, Mark D. 2013. Consensus-based community development, concentrated rural poverty, and local institutional structures: The obstacle of race in the lower Mississippi Delta. *Community Development* 44(2): 257–273.

Harvey, Mark D., & Lionel J. Beaulieu. 2013. Implementing community development in the Mississippi Delta: The effect of organizations on resident participation, Gary P. Green & Ann Goetting, eds., *Mobilizing Communities: Asset Building as a Community Development Strategy*, 146–176. Philadelphia: Temple University Press.

Haverkampf, Kelly, & Connie C. Loden. 2010. Community resource teams: A collaborative, multi-disciplinary team approach to community problem solving in Wisconsin. *Community Development* 41(2): 192–208.

Henderson, Jason, & Stephan Weiler. 2010. Entrepreneurs and job growth: Probing the boundaries of time and space. *Economic Development Quarterly* 24(1): 23–32.

Henthorne, Tony L., Babu P. George, & G. Anjaneya Swamy. 2006. Social capital and local community support for post-tsunami economic recovery in India. *Applied Research in Economic Development* 3(1): 34–48.

Hirshman, Albert O. 1984. Against parsimony: Three easy ways of complicating some categories of economic discourse. *American Economic Association Papers and Proceedings* 74(2): 89–96.

Honadle, Beth W. 1996. Participatory research for public issues education: A strategic approach to a municipal consolidation study. *Journal of the Community Development Society* 27(1): 56–77.

Howland, Marie, & Doan Nguyen. 2010. The impact of immigration on four low-wage industries in the 1990s. *Economic Development Quarterly* 24(2): 99–109.

Hutchinson, Judy, & Avis C. Vidal, eds. 2004. Symposium: Using social capital to help integrate planning theory, research, and practice. *Journal of the American Planning Association* 70(2): 142–192.

Jakes, Susan, Annie Hardison-Moody, Sarah Bowen, & John Blevins. 2015. Engaging community change: The critical role of values in asset mapping. *Community Development* 46(4): 392–406.

Jeroslow, Phyllis. 2015. Creating a sustainable society: Human rights in the U.S. welfare state, in Stephen N. Haymes, Maria V. de Haymes, & Reuben J. Miller, eds., *The Routledge Handbook of Poverty in the United States*, 559–566. New York: Routledge.

Kania, John, & Mark Kramer. 2011. Collective impact. *Stanford Social Innovation Review*. Winter: 36–41.

Koster, Rhonda L.P., & Raynald H. Lemelin. 2009. Appreciative Inquiry and rural tourism: A case study from Canada. *Tourism Geographies* 11(2): 256–269.

Kretzmann, John P., & Deborah Puntenney. 2013. Neighborhood approaches to asset mobilization: Building Chicago's West Side, in Gary P. Green & Ann Goetting, eds., *Mobilizing Communities: Asset Building as a Community Development Strategy*, 112–129. Philadelphia: Temple University Press.

Kretzmann, John P., & John L. McKnight. 1993. *Building Communities from the Inside Out: A Path toward Finding and Mobilizing a Community's Assets*. Chicago: ACTA.

Kretzmann, John P., John L. McKnight, Sarah Dobrowolski, & Deborah Puntenney. 2005. *Discovering Community Power: A Guide to Mobilizing Local Assets and Your Organization's Capacity*. Retrieved December 9, 2015: http://www.abcdinstitute.org/docs/kel loggabcd.pdf.

Krumholz, Norman. 2015. An optimistic comment. *Journal of Planning Education and Research* 35(3): 343–346.

Krumholz, Norman. 1991. Equity and local economic development. *Economic Development Quarterly* 5(4): 291–300.

Lacho, Kenneth J., Tammy Parker, & Kristie Carter. 2005. Economic development initiatives of African-American churches in Treme: The oldest African-American neighborhood in the United States. *Journal of Economics & Economic Education Research* 6(2): 83–106.

Lackey, Steven B., David Freshwater, & Anil Rupasingha. 2002. Factors influencing local government cooperation in rural areas: Evidence from the Tennessee Valley. *Economic Development Quarterly* 16(2): 138–154.

Leigh, Nancey G., & Edward J. Blakely. 2013. *Planning Local Economic Development: Theory and Practice*, 5th ed. Thousand Oaks, CA: Sage.

Lewis, W. Arthur. 1955. Appendix: Is growth desirable? in W. Arthur Lewis, *The Theory of Economic Growth*, 420–435. Homewood, IL: Richard D. Irwin.

Light, Ivan. 2004. Social capital's unique accessibility. *Journal of the American Planning Association* 70(2): 145–151.

Lin, Jan. 1998. Globalization and the revalorization of ethnic places in immigration gateway cities. *Urban Affairs Review* 34(2): 313–339.

Ludema, James D., David L. Cooperrider, & Frank J. Barrett. 2001. Appreciative Inquiry: The power of the unconditional positive question, in Peter Reason & Hilary Bradbury, eds., *Handbook of Action Research*, 189–199. Thousand Oaks, CA: Sage.

Lyons, Tara, & Bill Reimer. 2006. A literature review of capacity frameworks: Six features of comparison. Paper presented at the National Rural Research Network Conference, Twillingate, Newfoundland, Canada, June 8.

Markley, Deborah M., Thomas S. Lyons, & Donald W. Macke. 2015. Creating entrepreneurial communities: Building community capacity for ecosystem development. *Community Development* 46(5): 580–598.

Marré, Alexander W. & Bruce A. Weber. 2010. Assessing community capacity and social capital in rural America: Lessons from two rural observatories. *Community Development* 41(1): 92–107.

Mathie, Alison, & Gord Cunningham. 2003. From clients to citizens: Asset-based community development as a strategy for community-driven development. *Development in Practice* 13(5): 474–486.

Mazibuko, Sibonginkosi. 2013. Understanding underdevelopment through the sustainable livelihoods approach. *Community Development* 44(2): 173–187.

McGranahan, David, Timothy R. Wojan, & Dayton M. Lambert. 2011. The rural growth trifecta: Outdoor amenities, creative class and entrepreneurial context. *Journal of Economic Geography* 11(3): 529–557.

Mengesha, Semalegne K., Jacquelyn C.A. Meshelemiah, & Kasaw A. Chuffa. 2015. Asset-based community development practice in Awramba, Northwest Ethiopia. *Community Development* 46(2): 64–179.

Metzger, John T. 1996. The theory and practice of equity planning: An annotated bibliography. *Journal of Planning Literature* 11(1): 112–126.

Michael, Sarah. 2005. The promise of affirmative inquiry as an interview tool for field research. *Development in Practice* 15(2): 222–230.

Minkler, Meredith, & Nina Wallerstein, eds. 2008. *Community-Based Participatory Research for Health*, 2nd ed. San Francisco: Jossey-Bass.

Monroe, Pamela A., Crystal Tyler-Mackey, Patricia H. Dyk, Rachel Welborn, Sheri L. Worthy, Catherine H. Lowe, & Natalie J. Pickett. 2016. Turning the tide on poverty: Sustainability of community engagement in economically distressed communities. *Community Development* 47(3): 358–374.

Morgan, Jane, & Sujata Shetty. 2011. Regional equity through community development planning: The Metro Detroit Regional Investment Initiative. *Community Development* 42(4): 511–524.

Muller, Thomas. 1993. *Immigrants and the American City*. New York: New York University Press.

Nel, Etienne L., & Ronald W. McQuaid. 2002. The evolution of local economic development in South Africa: The case of Stutterheim and social capital. *Economic Development Quarterly* 16(1): 60–74.

Nikolakis, William, & R. Quentin Grafton. 2015. Putting Indigenous water rights to work: The sustainable livelihoods framework as a lens for remote development. *Community Development* 46(2): 149–163.

Nowak, Jeremy. 1997. Neighborhood initiative and the regional economy. *Economic Development Quarterly* 11(1): 3–10.

Oden, Kristin, Brigida Hernandez, & Marco Hidalgo. 2010. Payoffs of participatory action research: Racial and ethnic minorities with disabilities reflect on their research experiences. *Community Development* 41(1): 21–31.

Oh, Youngmin, In Won Lee, & Carrie B. Bush. 2014. The role of dynamic social capital on economic development partnerships within and across communities. *Economic Development Quarterly* 28(3): 230–243.

Olberding, Julie C. 2002. Diving into the "Third Waves" of regional governance and economic development strategies: A study of regional partnerships for economic development in U.S. metropolitan areas. *Economic Development Quarterly* 16(3): 251–272.

O'Leary, Tara, Ingrid Burkett, & Kate Braithwaite. 2011. *Appreciating Assets*. International Association for Community Development. Retrieved February 25, 2016: http://www.ia cdglobal.org/files/Carnegie_UK_Trust_-_Appreciating_Assets_FINAL-1.pdf.

O'Looney, John. 1998. Mapping communities: Place-based stories and participatory planning. *Community Development* 29(2): 201–236.

Parisi, Domenico, Steven M. Grice, Michael Taquino, & Duane A. Gill. 2002. Building capacity for community efficacy for economic development in Mississippi. *Journal of the Community Development Society* 33(2): 19–38.

Pastor, Jr., Manuel, Chris Benner, & Martha Matsuoka. 2009. *This Could Be the Start of Something Big: How Social Movements for Regional Equity Are Reshaping Metropolitan America*. Ithaca, NY: Cornell University Press.

Pastor, Jr., Manuel, Chris Benner, & Martha Matsuoka. 2006. The regional nexus: The promise and risk of community-based approaches to metropolitan equity, in Paul Ong & Anastasia Loukaitou-Sideris, eds., *Jobs and Economic Development in Minority Communities*, 63–88. Philadelphia: Temple University Press.

Pastor, Jr., Manuel, Chris Benner, & Rachel Rosner. 2003. An "option for the poor": A research audit for community-based regionalism in California's Central Coast. *Economic Development Quarterly* 17(2): 75–192.

Pastor, Jr., Manuel, Marta Lopez-Garza, & Peter Drier. 2000. *Regions that Work: How Cities and Suburbs Can Grow Together*. Minneapolis: University of Minnesota Press.

Phillips, Rhonda. 2002. *Concept Marketing for Communities: Capitalizing on Underutilized Resources to Generate Growth and Development*. Westport, CT: Praeger.

Phillips, Rhonda, & Gordon Shockley. 2013. Linking cultural capital conceptions to asset-based community development, in Gary P. Green & Ann Goetting, eds., *Mobilizing Communities: Asset Building as a Community Development Strategy*, 92–111. Philadelphia: Temple University Press.

Phillips, Rhonda, & Robert H. Pittman, eds. 2015. *An Introduction to Community Development*, 2nd ed. New York: Routledge.

Pigg, Kenneth, Stephen Gasteyer, Kenneth E. Martin, Kari Keating, & Godwin P. Apaliyah. 2013. The community capitals framework: An empirical examination of internal relationships. *Community Development* 44(4): 492–502.

Portes, Alejandro, & Patricia Landolt. 2005. Social capital: Promise and pitfalls of its role in development. *Journal of Latin American Studies* 32(2): 529–547.

Prior, Garet. 2015. Planning's role in social justice. *Planning*. December: 56.

Prokopy, Joshua, & Paul Castelloe. 1999. Participatory development: Approaches from the Global South and the United States. *Community Development* 30(2): 213–231.

Pstross, Mikulas, Craig A. Talmage, & Richard C. Knopf. 2014. A story about storytelling: Enhancement of community participation through catalytic storytelling. *Community Development* 45(5): 525–538.

Putnam, Robert D. 2004. Preface to Judy Hutchinson et al., eds. Symposium: Using social capital to help integrate planning theory, research, and practice. *Journal of the American Planning Association* 70(2): 142–143.

Putnam, Robert D. 2000. *Bowling Alone: The Collapse and Revival of American Community.* New York: Simon & Schuster.

Putnam, Robert D. 1995. Bowling alone: America's declining social capital. *Journal of Democracy* 6(1): 65–78.

Putnam, Robert D. 1993. The prosperous community: Social capital and public life. *American Prospect* 4(13): 35–42.

Putnam, Robert D., & David E. Campbell. 2016. *Our Kids: The American Dream in Crisis.* New York: Simon & Schuster.

Putnam, Robert D., & David E. Campbell. 2012. *How Religion Divides and Unites US.* New York: Simon & Schuster.

Putnam, Robert D., & Lewis Feldstein. 2014. *Better Together: Restoring the American Community.* New York: Simon & Schuster.

Raphael, Steven. 2014. *The New Scarlet Letter? Negotiating the U.S. Labor Market with a Criminal Record.* Kalamazoo, MI: W.E. Upjohn Institute for Employment Research.

Redcross, Cindy, Dan Bloom, Gilda Azurdia, Janine Zweig, & Nancy Pindus. 2009. *Transitional Jobs for Ex-Prisoners: Implementation, Two-Year Impacts, and Costs of the Center for Employment Opportunities (CEO) Prisoner Reentry Program.* Urban Institute. Retrieved July 22, 2016: http://www.urban.org/uploadedpdf/1001362_transitional_jobs.pdf.

Reese, Laura A. 2004. A matter of faith: Urban congregations and economic development. *Economic Development Quarterly* 18(1): 50–66.

Reese, Laura A. & Gary Shields. 2000. Faith-based economic development. *Review of Policy Research* 17(2–3): 84–103.

Reese, Laura A., & Minting Ye. 2011. Policy versus place luck: Achieving local economic prosperity. *Economic Development Quarterly* 25(3): 221–236.

Rohe, William M. 2004. Building social capital through community development. *Journal of the American Planning Association* 70(2): 158–164.

Rubin, Victor. 2011. Guest editor's introduction: Special issue on regional equity. *Community Development* 42(4): 434–436.

Rupasingha, Anil, Stephan J. Goetz, & David Freshwater. 2000. Social capital and economic growth: A county-level analysis. *Journal of Agricultural and Applied Economics* 32(2): 565–572.

Rusk, David. 1999. *Inside Game / Outside Game: Winning Strategies for Saving Urban America.* Washington, DC: Brookings Institution.

Saegert, Susan J. 2006. Building civic capacity in urban neighborhoods: An empirically grounded analysis. *Journal of Urban Affairs* 28(3): 275–294.

Saegert, Susan J., Phillip Thompson, & Mark R. Warren, eds. 2001. *Social Capital and Poor Communities.* New York: Russell Sage Foundation.

Santilli, Alycia, Amy Carroll-Scott, Fiona Wong, & Jeannette Ickovics. 2011. Urban youths go 3000 miles: Engaging and supporting young residents to conduct neighborhood asset mapping. *American Journal of Public Health* 101(12): 2207–2210.

Sapolsky, Robert. 2005. Sick of poverty. *Scientific American.* December: 92–99.

Scoones, Ian. 1998. *Sustainable Rural Livelihoods: A Framework for Analysis.* Institute of Development Studies Working Paper 72. Retrieved December 16, 2015: http://mobile.op endocs.ids.ac.uk/opendocs/bitstream/handle/123456789/3390/Wp72.pdf?sequence=1.

Seltzer, Ethan, & Dillon Mahmoudi. 2012. Citizen participation, open innovation, and crowdsourcing: Challenges and opportunities for planning. *Journal of Planning Literature* 28(1): 3–18.

Sen, Amartya. 1999. *Development as Freedom*. New York: Knopf.

Singer, Audrey, Susan W. Hardwick, & Caroline B. Brettell. 2008. *Twenty-First Century Gateways: Immigrant Incorporation in Suburban America*. Washington, DC: Brookings Institution.

Slate, Risdon N., Jacqueline K. Buffington-Vollum, & W. Wesley Johnson. 2013. *The Criminalization of Mental Illness: Crisis and Opportunity for the Justice System*. Durham, NC: Carolina Academic Press.

Srivastva, Suresh, & David L. Cooperrider. 1990. *Appreciative Management and Leadership: The Power of Positive Thought and Action in Organizations*. San Francisco: Jossey-Bass.

Stowell, Frank. 2013. The appreciative inquiry method – a suitable candidate for action research? *Systems Research and Behavioral Science* 30(1): 15–30.

Stringer, Ernest T. 2014. *Action Research*, 4th ed. Thousand Oaks, CA: Sage.

Talen, Emily. 2000. Bottom-up GIS: A new tool for individual and group expression in participatory planning. *Journal of the American Planning Association* 66(3): 279–294.

Talen, Emily. 1998. Visualizing fairness. *Journal of the American Planning Association* 64(1): 22–38.

Tiepoh, M. Geepuh Nah, & Bill Reimer. 2004. Social capital, information flows, and income creation in rural Canada: A cross-community analysis. *Journal of Socio-Economics* 33(4): 427–448.

Trabalzi, Ferro, & Gerardo Sandoval. 2010. The exotic other: Latinos and the remaking of community identity in Perry, Iowa. *Community Development* 41(1): 76–91.

Tyler, John H. & Jillian Berk. 2009. Correctional programs in the age of mass incarceration, Maude Toussaint-Comeau & Bruce D. Meyer, eds., *Strategies for Improving Economic Mobility of Workers: Bridging Research and Practice*, 177–195. Kalamazoo, MI: W.E. Upjohn Institute for Employment Research.

Tyler-Mackey, Crystal, Pamela A. Monroe, Patricia H. Dyk, Rachel Welborn, & Sheri L. Worthy. 2016. Turning the tide on poverty: Community climate in economically distressed rural communities. *Community Development* 47(3): 304–321.

United Nations Development Programme. 2015. *Human Development Report 2015: Work for Human Development*. Retrieved March 24, 2016: http://hdr.undp.org/sites/default/files/2015_human_development_report_1.pdf.

Vidal, Avis. 2004. Building social capital to promote equity. *Journal of the American Planning Association* 70(2): 164–168.

Voith, Richard. 1992. City and suburban growth: Substitutes or complements? *Business Review* September/October. Retrieved August 2, 2016: https://www.phil.frb.org/research-and-data/publications/business.../brso92rv.pdf.

Vorley, Tim, & Nick Williams. 2015. Creating and sustaining a model of community-based enterprise learning: A participatory case study of ready hubs. *Community Development* 46(5): 559–579.

Waldorf, Brigitte. 2011. The location of foreign human capital in the United States. *Economic Development Quarterly* 25(4): 330–340.

Wallerstein, Nina, & Bonnie Duran. 2008. The theoretical, historical, and practice roots of CBPR, in Meredith Minkler, & Nina Wallerstein, eds., *Community-Based Participatory Research for Health*, 2nd ed., 25–46. San Francisco: Jossey-Bass.

Walzer, Norman, Liz Weaver, & Catherine McGuire. 2016. Collective impact approaches and community development issues. *Community Development* 47(2): 156–166.

Welch, Bethany J. 2012. A dual nature: The archdiocesan community development corporation. *Community Development* 43(4): 451–463.

Whitney, Diana, & Amanda Trosten-Bloom. 2010. *The Power of Appreciative Inquiry: A Practical Guide to Positive Change*, 2nd ed. Oakland, CA: Berrett-Koehler.

Wilson, William J. 1987. *The Truly Disadvantaged: The Inner City, The Underclass, and Public Policy*. Chicago: University of Chicago Press.

Woodyard, Catherine Dane, Sarahmona Przybyla, & Jeffrey S. Hallam. 2015. A community health needs assessment using principles of community-based participatory research in a Mississippi Delta community: A novel methodological approach. *Community Development* 46(2): 84–99.

World Bank. 2013. Social capital. Retrieved January 26, 2016: http://www.worldbank.org/en/webarchives/archive?url=httpzzxxweb.worldbank.org/archive/website01360/WEB/0__MEN-2.HTM&mdk=23354653.

6

ENCOURAGE YOUR ENTREPRENEURS

When you buy from a small business, you're not helping a CEO buy a 3rd holiday home. You're helping a little girl get dance lessons, a little boy his team jersey, moms and dads put food on the table. Shop local.

(Sign outside a restaurant, posted as a web meme)

Teachers will always top my personal list, but I consider local, small business entrepreneurs among the top assets of any community, especially for low-income communities. Not everyone is cut out to be an entrepreneur, certainly not me. Not only are successful entrepreneurs responsible for managing all the affairs of a business, they typically serve as the labor force for the business along with perhaps a few other employees or family members. Entrepreneurs, by definition, bear most of the worry and financial risk of the business. They provide the community with employment opportunities, taxes, revitalization of buildings, and inspiration for other potential local entrepreneurs. They sponsor local sports teams, school events, and festivals. They can provide a sense of hope for a community: evidence that legitimate local success is possible.

It can be very difficult and expensive to attract outside industries to a low-income community. And this may be due to misconceptions and biases, or real issues including inadequate infrastructure, low-skilled workers, or high crime rates. It is usually easier and more efficient to keep a local business in place than recruit a new business from outside. Nurturing local businesses, though, can also still be a difficult and often frustrating process (Anderson 2012).

Many books, academic journals, and magazines are devoted to entrepreneurship in general. This chapter is focused more specifically on research about entrepreneurship within low-income communities and disadvantaged populations. Servon et al. (2010) use the term "disadvantaged entrepreneurs." Chapters 7 and 8 will focus on specific sectors of potential business opportunities for entrepreneurs in low-income communities, such as tourism and the "green economy." This chapter, then, will focus on creating an overall ED environment to help encourage entrepreneurship in those communities.

SIDEBAR: THE ROLE OF SMALL BUSINESS

I am biased personally toward small businesses: the underdogs of the local economy. There is substantial research on the important role of small business in growing the employment numbers and economies of local communities. Komarek and Loveridge (2014) conclude from their research "on local firm size distribution and economic growth in U.S. counties and high-poverty rural regions" that counties that tend toward smaller firms tend to have better job growth than the national average. Income growth, nationally, seems to be positively correlated with firms between 10 and 19 employees (see also Fleming & Goetz 2011).

It is also possible to overstate the importance of small business in the local community. David Birch (1987, 1981) was widely credited in the 1980s with bringing prominent attention to the role of small businesses in creating jobs. Politicians widely cited statistics that small businesses are responsible for 80 percent of all new jobs: "Of all the net new jobs in our...sample of...businesses, two-thirds were created by firms with twenty or fewer employees, and about 80 percent were created by firms with 100 or fewer employees" (Birch 1981: 7). Despite decades of critique and clarification of Birch's figures – including by Birch and his colleagues (Birch & Medoff 1994) – similar statistics are still tossed out regularly.

If you represent a low-income community, you probably consider a local firm with 99 employees to be a very big business. Even businesses with the 10–19 employees that Komarek and Loveridge (2014) identify may be considered fairly big players in your local economy. Most of your local businesses likely consist of just a few employees, at most, and some of those may only be employed part time. Definitions of small businesses vary widely in terms of employee numbers and earnings: firms even as large as 500 employees or more may qualify as "small businesses" for some purposes (US Small Business Administration: Contracting). Many of your own "small businesses" may be more appropriately described as "microenterprises" – more on that topic later in this chapter.

As you might expect, the answer to "Who creates jobs?" is much more complex and nuanced than any one simple answer (Haltiwanger, Jarmin, & Miranda 2010; Acs, Parsons, & Tracy 2008; Neumark, Wall, & Zhang 2008). The reality is that small businesses create jobs, but so do medium and large-sized firms. Much depends on the type of business, industry sector, and other factors. Birch & Medoff (1994) coined the term "gazelle" for the type of small business that creates by far most of the jobs. Also called "high-impact" firms, those businesses typically are young, very productive, and highly innovative companies. But the story is always the same: those are not the sorts of companies that will be found in a typical low-income community.

A note on terminology: I use the term "entrepreneur" more or less interchangeably with local business owner, even though they are distinct concepts. An entrepreneur is by definition someone who has an element of their own risk involved in the business, especially their own financial investment. A local businessperson could be a true entrepreneur or have little or no personal financial stake in a local business. The business could be a franchise such as a fast food restaurant, the business could be owned by someone else from outside the community, or both. Even if a manager of a local business does not have a financial stake in the business, to be successful they must have a substantial psychological stake in it, being concerned, at a minimum, with their own job, their reputation, their résumé, the jobs of their employees, and the expectations of their community.

Creating an entrepreneurial environment

Education is the foundation of entrepreneurship. No one who has read to this point in the book will be surprised by that contention. There will always be intuitive shade tree mechanics, but increasingly successful entrepreneurship in a modern economy demands – at a minimum – basic literacy and math skills, a familiarity with computers and other technologies, and social "soft skills" acquired through basic education (Chapter 4). There also are many school-based programs to teach general business skills as well as entrepreneurship. Hanham, Loveridge, and Richardson (1999) evaluate the national K–8th grade Rural Entrepreneurship through Action Learning (REAL) program, active in 43 states and internationally (Gruidl & Markley 2015). Hogarth, Kolodinsky, and Hilgert (2007) review programs and research related to financial education as well as "financial literacy" educational programs in the US. Vorley and Williams (2015) explain entrepreneurial education in the UK school system.

Many professional networks provide entrepreneurs with continuing education and support for building "linking" social capital (Chapter 5), that is, for building networks beyond your community. Examples include regional Small Business Development Centers (SBDCs) (US Small Business Administration: Office of Small Business Development Centers), the Center for Rural Entrepreneurship (Center for Rural Entrepreneurship), and the Initiative for a Competitive Inner City (Initiative for a Competitive Inner City). Chapter 3 mentioned the "economic gardening" movement, which prioritizes the growth of local businesses over industrial recruitment (Edward Lowe Foundation; Kauffman Foundation).

A special issue of *Community Development* contributes to the research literature that "seeks to understand the complex ways that entrepreneurs benefit their communities, and that communities enhance or inhibit entrepreneurship" (Fortunato & Alter 2015: 444). An essay by Lyons (2015; see also Kickul & Lyons 2012) expands the discussion to include "civic and social entrepreneurship," that is, applying the business skills of economic entrepreneurs to help build community civic capacity and address social problems.

In a case study of Halifax, Nova Scotia, Dye and Alter (2015) advocate expanding the concept of "entrepreneurial environment" to a broader context that they term an "entrepreneurial ecology." This greater entrepreneurial ecology encompasses the whole of the community's interconnecting social, cultural, and political influences on an entrepreneur – which can include everything from government efficiency to healthcare. Markley, Lyons and Macke (2015) employ the same terminology and concept in Kansas and Australia case studies of building community and individual capacities for entrepreneurship.

Weinberg and Vaughn (1999) conclude from their research that home-based entrepreneurs are often overlooked, but can be extraordinarily numerous and diverse in their characteristics. The researchers group the home-based businesses they identified and studied – in a New York case study – into five broad categories: 1) professional services, (2) manual labor services, (3) light manufacturers, (4) crafters, and (5) direct consumer sales. Rowe, Haynes, and Stafford (1999) consider various means by which localities can encourage the development of home-based businesses.

A literature review by Fortunato (2014) focuses in particular on the challenges and opportunities for entrepreneurship in rural communities. Fortunato argues that rural entrepreneurship should be considered a distinctive field of study in part because most rural areas are not conducive to the sorts of high-growth, high-tech industries that have attracted much of the scholarship on entrepreneurship. Goetz and Rupasingha (2014: 42) find that "in the 'jobless recovery' from the recession of 2000, self-employment has clearly been vital to the economic survival of many rural workers, households, and the communities in which they reside....It is also associated with reduced poverty rates at the county level."

Henderson and Weiler (2010) note the constraints to entrepreneurship in nearly any rural region. They find in their research that investment capital is likely to have a greater impact when invested with entrepreneurs in urban areas, especially densely populated metropolitan cities. The market for the entrepreneur's business or service is simply richer in an urban area, along with better access to the materials, business services, and other resources the business needs to function. Halstead and Deller (1997) study the specific needs of rural manufacturers, in particular public infrastructure such as roads and other transportation systems, electric power, water and sewer, waste treatment, and telecommunications. From their research in New England and Wisconsin, they conclude that "investment in public infrastructure tends to be necessary for local economic development and growth, but it is not sufficient. Other critical factors such as a quality labor pool, or robust financial markets are equally important....Rather than approaching major investments in infrastructure in an 'if you build it, they will come' frame of mind, local decision makers should be determining which investments will make a community a better place to live. The same investments might be made, but for the right reasons" (Halstead & Deller 1997: 165–166).

From his research on inner-city businesses, Porter (2016) advocates regular, systematic surveys of local business needs. Enlisting the businesses themselves "directly in strategic planning for the inner city will return the same benefits as we have seen from engaging inner-city residents in the process" (Porter 2016: 111–112). Porter also advocates including "anchor institutions" in these business surveys (see also Birch 2014). Anchor institutions are those large, sometimes mysterious enterprises in your community that we often take for granted and often don't think of as businesses or industries at all. Typical examples of anchor institutions include local colleges and universities, hospitals and clinics, and state and federal government offices. Yes, they are local businesses in the sense that they provide jobs, local spending (recall the multiplier effect from Chapter 1), and at least some local tax revenue. They are less likely to go out of business than a local small shop, but it is not an impossibility. Sirkin and Stalk (1990) offer insights into how communities might intervene to prevent major plant closings, rather than simply react to such devastating events. Major anchor institutions can experience cutbacks and layoffs – or, more happily, they have the potential for expanding and adding more employees. With some encouragement, they might improve their record of purchasing locally or hiring local residents. Nelson and Wolf-Powers (2010) consider how hospitals could better encourage low-skilled workers to better "climb the ladder" to gain skills and seek better employment opportunities. Cultivate them, just like any other local business.

Survey work by the Initiative for a Competitive Inner City (ICIC) in 2015 found that "the top five disadvantages facing inner-city businesses were parking and traffic problems, the perception of high crime, negative perceptions of the inner city, actual crime, and higher costs for office space. Labor force issues were cited by 20% of the businesses, and blight (16%) and poor roads (10%) were additional concerns" (Porter 2016: 111–112). Based on a study of small "disadvantaged" businesses – with 20 employees or less – in New York City, Servon et al. (2010) identify five "gaps" facing these entrepreneurs:

- Capital gap, especially startup capital;
- Asset gap, to start and expand businesses;
- Transitional gap, to move from microcredit programs to private sector banking;
- Information gap, e.g., regarding available resources, financial expertise, or management skills; and
- Institutional capacity and service delivery gap, to serve the needs of potential new or growing entrepreneurs.

"Coaching" is a familiar and comfortable metaphor for many businesspeople, and it is used by some in the research literature on cultivating entrepreneurship (Flora, Flora, & Gasteyer 2015; Henderson & Weiler 2010). Phil Hanes, former head of Hanes Industries, later devoted his energies to revitalizing the downtown of his home city of Winston-Salem, North Carolina (Malone & Richard 2007).

Hanes encouraged city agencies to use the term and concept of "coaches" instead of "inspectors" to guide and support local entrepreneurs through building projects, health regulations, employment law, etc. (personal communication). Henderson and Weiler (2010) recommend a "coaching" approach to overcome some of the obstacles that entrepreneurs face in rural, inner-city, or otherwise isolated locations through building social capital, that is, through tapping into more extensive markets and supplier networks at the regional level (Chapter 5).

Business incubators

Business incubators are a popular tool for providing a nurturing entrepreneurial environment (Sutton 2010; Sherman & Chappell 1998; National Business Incubation Association). Incubators usually consist of a physical facility of some sort. Alternatively, they can exist as simply a concept or support organization, in which case they are termed "virtual incubators" (Qian, Haynes, & Riggle 2011). Business incubators can provide tangible needs for small entrepreneurs such as affordable or subsidized rent, shared business equipment (e.g., a photocopier, a broadband connection), shared industry-specific tools or equipment, and shared services (e.g., administrative, legal, accounting). They can also provide informal and intangible support such as advice from and comradery with fellow entrepreneurs.

Incubators take on a wide variety of physical appearances and are set in a range of locations. Rypkema (2005) advocates the preservation and use of available historic buildings for business incubator space, especially in downtown settings where they can provide close access to potential clients and business services. Incubators can provide an adaptive reuse for a shuttered factory or other available facility. Qian, Haynes, and Riggle (2011) report that 72 percent of incubators are located in urban centers and are mostly located in major metropolises.

Stokan, Thompson, and Mahu (2015) review the research literature concerned with the performance of business incubators. Their findings suggest that businesses nurtured in incubators have a significantly higher success rate than those that operate independently – although the success rate depends on the overall local entrepreneurial climate. Their own research indicates that incubators have a positive impact on local job growth. Firms located in incubators also interact with many more business services than other firms – both inside and outside the incubator itself – confirming other research that networking is one of the most valuable contributions that incubators provide for their businesses.

Cooperatives

Cooperatives can provide many functions similar to business incubators. Cooperatives are perhaps most commonly thought of as agricultural, serving members with assistance in purchasing supplies and marketing products. Perhaps it is cooperatives' original association with small family-based farmers and disadvantaged communities (Merrett & Walzer 2004) that engenders a particular reverence for these organizations.

Although traditional farm cooperative membership has fallen steadily since its peak in the 1950s, cooperatives can also serve a wide variety of non-agricultural industries. Many cooperatives are "hiding in plain sight" in our communities. Credit unions, for example, are a form of financial cooperative. Many ACE Hardware stores function as a cooperative of independent retailers (Bhuyan & Leistritz 2000).

Bhuyan and Leistritz (2000) survey the different types of cooperatives, their characteristics, and the challenges they may face. Stofferahn (2009: 177) lists traditional characteristics of cooperatives: they exert "democratic control based on one-member, one vote; they distribute earnings based on patronage with the cooperative; and they have a board of directors elected by the membership." Merrett & Walzer (2004) offer more extensive information about traditional as well as new forms of the cooperative concept in their book. Egerstrom (2004) discusses some of the conflicts and other challenges facing both forms. An example of a relatively recent development is the "new generation cooperative," or NGC (Goldsmith 2004). The most commonly recognized form of NGC is a group of urban residents who purchase a membership in a "farmers NGC", which assures the city-dwellers that they will receive fresh produce and other farm products. The 2005 documentary film *The Real Dirt on Farmer John* helped to publicize this movement (Siegel 2005).

Hoyt (2004) and MacLeod (2004) discuss the potential roles for cooperatives in contributing to overall community development for rural and other disadvantaged communities, beyond just ED. Those roles include helping to build rich networks of social capital, as well as strengthening attachment to local place. Especially in an NGC, "consumers may want to maintain control over an essential local enterprise. They may be concerned about environmental issues and may prefer to conduct business with a firm that shares their values about sustainable development" (Merrett & Walzer 2004: 14–15).

Community development corporations

Community development corporations (CDCs) can serve a variety of ED functions, although typically they are associated with other community development subfields such as healthcare, education, and community organizing. There is a substantial professional and research literature on the topic. I will only provide an overview here, and offer some entrée to the deeper research body related to CDCs and ED. Seidman (2005) and Wiewel and Weintraub (1990) survey the range of CDC functions as they have evolved since the 1970s.

Frisch and Servon (2006: 88) cite Vidal (1992) as a landmark study which "helped to establish community development corporations (CDCs) as models for urban neighborhood revitalization....[Vidal's] *Rebuilding Communities* documented the accomplishments of community development corporations and identified the potential of spreading the CDC model to other low-income communities." Frisch and Servon's (2006: 88) literature review "takes Rebuilding Communities as a starting point to survey the community development literature, the community development field, and external environmental factors, in order to examine what has happened over the [subsequent] fifteen years to shape the context in which urban community development corporations (CDCs) now operate."

Metzger (1998) provides a case study of the Pittsburgh Partnership for Neighborhood Development (PPND), one of the first city-wide networks of CDCs in the country: "No group of CDCs in the country has become nearly so tightly integrated into the complex of financial and corporate leadership in its city as has the PPND" (Metzger 1998: 13). From among the many activities of the PPND partner CDCs, he elaborates on their involvement with and network-building for employment training:

> The partnership CDCs have formed networks with major employers in their communities (such as hospitals and manufacturing companies) to prepare and refer residents to jobs. The access to banks, corporations, and educational institutions provided to the CDCs through the PPND network strengthens their capacity to conduct this strategic outreach for employment training and industrial retention.
>
> *(Metzger 1998: 13)*

Gittell and Wilder (1999) review the research on CDCs and conduct their own analysis of three CDC case studies. They conclude that there are four key factors that influence the success of CDCs: (1) a clear mission, (2) organizational competency, (3) political funding, and (4) adequate funding levels. Each of the successful CDCs that Gittell and Wilder (1999: 58) studied had

> developed missions that engender solid local support and attract the necessary resources....Given the wide array of needs and problems confronting communities, CDCs could conceivably engage in many different initiatives. However...the more successful organizations tend to limit their activities to those that are of high priority for community residents and are most likely to produce tangible results in a relatively short time frame.

Rusk (1999) analyzes the impacts of 34 "exemplary" CDCs over the course of the 1970s and 1980s. He finds that, on average, poverty rates actually rose faster in the neighborhoods in which these CDCs were operating than they did in the metropolitan areas in which they existed. However, there were still some successes – and one can also argue that the neighborhoods might have fared worse in the absence of CDC activity. Still, Rusk (1999) suggests that CDCs might usefully shift to what he terms the "outside game" (Chapter 5): organizing to change the rules so as to share tax resources across metropolitan regions and constrain outward sprawl, and working to deconcentrate the poor by promoting affordable housing in existing suburbs.

Clusters, "third-wave" policies, and anchor industries

Identifying, recognizing, and attempting to develop industrial clusters represents another strategy for creating an entrepreneurial environment in low-income communities (Porter 2016, 1997; Cortright & Langkilde 2014; Cortright 2002; Hill & Brennan 2000). Taylor & Miller (2010: 115) present case studies of two rural agribusiness clusters: local produce production in Maine and catfish farming in Mississippi. They found that the Maine local produce cluster, in particular, showed "potential positive economic impacts of local cluster development. Most significantly, the cluster shows strong economic growth, while capturing many more dollars of economic activity via processing, distribution, and retailing." The authors conclude that locally oriented clusters provide more stability for local businesses and economies than clusters that are more directly export-oriented. Miller and Gibson (1990) and Miller, Gibson, and Wright (1991) employ mixed methods of location quotient analysis and an expert "Delphi" panel to identify industrial sectors that were underrepresented in a remote rural county of Arizona facing the possibility of a major military base closure, and they also identify potential business opportunities for capitalizing on overrepresented, or "clusters" of industries. (At that time, we used the older term industrial "agglomerations.")

Cluster analysis is often used as a way to identify (cynics might say justify) potential industries for recruitment. Such analysis can also provide insight into local businesses which might have promise for growth, or niches for the creation of new local businesses. In traditional economic geography, we refer to "backward linkages," or businesses that serve as suppliers of products to or services for the key industry cluster: electrical components to vehicle manufacturers, for example. "Forward linkages" are businesses that serve as purchasers of the products or services created by the key cluster: furniture manufacturers purchasing lumber from mills, for example. Porter (2016) and others emphasize the importance of building on linkage and employment opportunities related to major "anchor" industries for inner-city ED, such as the ones mentioned earlier: typically "eds and meds," or healthcare and educational institutions (Hartley, Kaza, & Lester 2016; Adams 2003).

Import substitution and localism

Import substitution might be considered a rather "tainted" concept in international development, having been replaced by the almost universal embrace of neoliberal economics and globalization (Todaro & Smith 2014). In an international economics context, import substitution is generally imposed through tariffs (taxes on imports), quotas, or other trade barriers that discourage imports and encourage local industries to produce for the local market. Harley-Davidson is a US example of the use of import restrictions that is generally considered a success story (Duprey 2016). The end results of mandatory import substitution measures instead are often inferior, overpriced locally manufactured products.

The term "import substitution" is not commonly used in a local ED context, with some exceptions (Persky, Ranmey, & Wiewel 1993). Similar concepts may be found, though, of a more voluntary than mandatory nature. Taylor and Miller (2010), cited above, explore the cluster concept as a means of encouraging the local exchange of goods and services: a non-coercive form of substituting local products and services for products and services that might otherwise be imported from outside the local region. Hess (2009: 7) refers to "localism" as a "movement in support of government policies and economic practices oriented toward enhancing local democracy and local ownership of the economy in a historical context of corporate-led globalization." Phillips, Seifer, and Antczak (2013) and Shuman (2007 and 2000) also advocate the importance of local businesses. Hess (2009) notes that a local orientation toward ED can include some or all of these aspects: locally sourced crops and other factors of production, locally crafted or manufactured goods, sales by local stores and other organizations (including "shop local" campaigns), and consumption by a local population.

Fleming and Goetz (2011: 277), analyzing national data, find "a positive relationship between density of locally owned firms and per capita income growth but only for small (10–99 employees) firms." Halebsky (2010), in a case study from rural New York State, compares the impacts of chain retail stores compared with locally owned establishments. He finds that local, independent stores result in less economic "leakage," or a higher economic multiplier (see Chapter 1 sidebar) than comparable chain stores. Beyond economic considerations, Halebsky (2010: 447, citing Green & Haines 2012 and Tolbert 2005) argues that social capital "declines as small merchants, who are traditionally heavily involved in community affairs, become less numerous and less prosperous."

Financing entrepreneurs in low-income communities

Financing ED is a complex, specialized, interdisciplinary area of research with a large literature (White & Kotval 2012; Bates, Lofstrom, & Servon 2011; Seidman 2005). In this section, I hope to provide the non-specialist with an overview of the various financing tools and institutions that are especially relevant to the needs of entrepreneurs in low-income communities, along with references to more detailed research articles and books.

Patraporn (2015) helpfully diagrams the various types of financing institutions for entrepreneurs as a spectrum, paying particular attention to ethnic minority populations. On one end of the spectrum are the savings of the individual entrepreneur, family, or friends, which target the success of that individual. On the other end of the spectrum are large, regulated, private banks, which target the success of the financial institution – but which, of course, also help to create ED in the process through business and real estate loans. In the middle of the spectrum are a number of perhaps lesser-known institutions that have community development as their target, including microbusiness funds, community development loan funds, and community development credit unions. By far, most of the financing for startup entrepreneurs comes from their own resources: individual savings, credit cards, family, and friends. On the other end of the spectrum, by far most of the lending for business expansion and growth comes from conventional bank loans.

Recall the discussion in Chapter 3 regarding the difference between the ED process and ED practice: naturally occurring economic growth as opposed to active intervention by ED professionals and organizations. Especially in struggling low-income communities, there is potential for ED practice – professional intervention – at all points along the spectrum, from beginning entrepreneurs to thriving businesses that potentially could build further on their success. Microfinance, addressed below, is an example of an intervention for the smallest business ventures. Intervention for already large, successful businesses I will leave to standard ED resources and texts (International Economic Development Council; Leigh & Blakely 2013; Seidman 2005). In between those two ends of the spectrum are a large number of innovative policies and tools for financing entrepreneurship in low-income communities.

Porter (2016: 107) maintains that "successful inner-city economic development must be led by the private sector. As I wrote in 1997: 'Our strategy begins with the premise that a sustainable economic base can be created in inner cities only as it has been elsewhere: through private, for-profit initiatives, and investments based on economic self-interest and genuine competitive advantage instead of artificial inducements, government mandates, or charity' (Porter 1997: 12). This approach is also the only one that is politically feasible over the long term. It does not ask people to support wealth redistribution but focuses on expanding the economic pie." Bates (2010), however, warns that the competitive advantages of the inner city heralded by Porter are generally not great enough to support profitable business development lending, except under certain specific conditions.

Various federal lending programs have long but mixed records of support for disadvantaged entrepreneurs. In one of the most notorious cases, a group of Black farmers reached a $1.25 billion settlement in 2010 from a farm finance discrimination suit against the US Department of Agriculture (Etter 2010). Federal housing programs discriminated against minorities for decades (National Public Radio 2015). The federal Small Business Administration (SBA) began in 1953 with a number of lending programs (US Small Business Administration: Office of Small Business Development Centers; see also Bates, Bradford, & Rubin 2006). Immergluck and Mullen (1998) find a pattern of SBA lending concentrated in higher income metropolitan districts dispersed from the city center and located away from lower-income districts closer to the central city. Research on a broad range of small- and micro-business lending programs in the US by Bates, Lofstrom, & Servon (2011: 255, citing Shane 2008) "yields no evidence that financial capital constraints are a significant barrier to small-firm creation." They find that simplistic notions about small- and micro-business lending do not match the reality and complexity of those programs.

The Community Reinvestment Act and community development financial institutions

The modern era of financing ED in low-income communities is perhaps best thought of as beginning with the revolutionary Community Reinvestment Act (CRA) of 1977 (National Community Reinvestment Corporation; Marsico 2005; Dreier 2003): extraordinarily progressive legislation toward "democratizing capital," in the words of Marsico (2005), but a continuing work in progress (Dreier 2003;

US General Accountability Office 1995). The CRA sought to eliminate loan "redlining," or restrictions on loans in minority and low-income communities. The Act also requires banks to extend their loans in some reasonable proportion to reflect the communities they serve. The CRA affirms that "regulated financial institutions have continuing and affirmative obligations to help meet the credit needs of the local communities in which they are chartered" (cited by the National Community Reinvestment Corporation). Immergluck (2004) provides a historical overview of the CRA and its development.

The Clinton Administration, in 1995, "strengthened enforcement of the… CRA. New CRA regulations, enacted in 1995, recognized community development financial institutions [CDFIs] for the first time as qualifying investments and borrowers, giving commercial banks a significant incentive to finance CDFIs" (Rubin 2007: 3). Research by Bates and Robb (2015) and Bates (2010) finds that the CRA has resulted in greater equity in lending, but that discriminatory inequities persist, especially for Black-, Latino-, and Asian-owned businesses. Community Development Financial Institutions (CDFIs),

> are private-sector, financial intermediaries with community development as their primary mission. While CDFIs share a common mission, they have a variety of structures and development lending goals. There are six basic types of CDFIs: community development banks, community development loan funds, community development credit unions, microenterprise funds, community development corporation-based lenders and investors, and community development venture funds. All are market-driven, locally-controlled, private-sector organizations.
>
> CDFIs measure success by focusing on the "double bottom line": economic gains and the contributions they make to the local community. CDFIs rebuild businesses, housing, voluntary organizations, and services central to revitalizing our nation's poor and working class neighborhoods.
>
> *(CDFI Coalition)*

Community development loan funds provide debt capital for entrepreneurs and other business borrowers. Comparable institutions for providing equity capital are called community development venture capital funds. Rubin (2007) provides an overview of both these types of institutions and a variety of other community development financing programs (e.g., New Markets Venture Capital [NMVC] Program, the Rural Business Investment Program [RBIP], economically targeted investment opportunities for public pension funds), and discusses the challenges that these programs face. Hollister (2007) reviews the methods and literature for evaluating the impacts of various CDFIs.

Tax increment financing

Tax increment financing (TIF) is a very popular but controversial tool targeting development in low-income communities (Callies & Gowder 2014; Johnson &

Man 2001). The intention of TIF is to subsidize and encourage development in "blighted" communities – typically urban neighborhoods – by capturing the projected increases in tax assessments that result from development improvements: "TIF can be used to finance general infrastructure improvements, such as extending water and sewer lines, adding or improving roads and viaducts, and general improvements to streetscapes and lighting. TIF can also finance property acquisition, site preparation, and environmental cleanup, as well as the rehabilitation of existing buildings" (Byrne 2010: 13–14).

The use of TIF has expanded to all 50 states, although California has now discontinued new applications (Swenson 2015). The use of TIFs has grown partly in response to the "devolution" of responsibility for ED from the federal to the state and (often-struggling) local levels, and from urban to rural communities (Crowe et al. 2015). The concept of blighted target communities has been extended to include revitalization of "brownfield" sites (Bacot & O'Dell 2006): potentially contaminated properties (covered in Chapter 8).

Bartels and Hall (2012: 31) find wide variation in TIF "program design, implementation, and project monitoring" even within their case study of the Dallas-Fort Worth region. They conclude: "Given the current political and economic climate favoring more rigorous analysis of public sector activities, especially in relation to economic development, cities may be able to maximize the value of their investments by emphasizing risk assessment and performance measurement" (Bartels & Hall 2012: 31). Swenson's (2015) analysis of California's use of TIFs in its now-discontinued redevelopment areas indicates economic impacts that are very limited, at best. Another critique of TIFs is their proliferation beyond true "blighted" communities, to be used as a tool of general ED practice: they are simply another kind of conventional tax incentive. Byrne (2010) finds no evidence that TIFs result in higher employment overall, although employment is often cited as a justification for a proposed TIF.

Microenterprises, microfinancing, and the informal sector

In many parts of the Developing World, the informal sector is recognized as comprising half or more of the economy. The informal sector – also known as the black market, underground, irregular, or unregulated economy – includes a wide range of entrepreneurial activities that operate outside the official, regulated, or "formal" economy. Those enterprises typically operate without permits, licenses, inspections, or business taxes – and without employee benefits, insurance, or collateral for business loans. If you have visited the Developing World, you've likely seen street vendors everywhere, most of them operating in the informal sector – along with taxi and minibus services, daycares, midwives, informal restaurants and bars, gambling clubs, loan sharks, and operators with a ladder who will hook you up to the local electric, telephone, Internet, cable TV, or other utilities for a heavily discounted fee. The informal sector also constitutes a large share of the Developing World's rural economy, especially in the small-scale farming sector.

Many of these activities also operate in the Developed World, as can be seen on the streets of most major US city downtowns, along with the shade tree mechanics, day laborers, and other informal entrepreneurs that can be found in almost any community in the US. Much of this entrepreneurial energy in the US and the Developed World is driven by immigrants from the Developing World – authorized and otherwise – who learned their way around this sector of the economy in their home country, in some cases with a high degree of sophistication and organization. Many Asian immigrants, for example, bring to the US old traditions of "lending circles": successful businesspeople who loan money to trusted family members or other associates to start their own small businesses.

Mukhija and Loukaitou-Sideris (2014) credit Lewis (1954; Chapter 3) with early research on the informal labor market, and Hart (1973) with the first use of the term "informal sector," which he used in his research on Ghana's economy. There has been an extensive research literature on the Developing World's informal sector since that time. Mukhija and Loukaitou-Sideris (2014) point out the relative lack of research attention paid to the informal sector in the US and elsewhere in the Developed World.

Covert and Morales (2014) and Hou (2014) address community gardens and urban farms as growing examples of informal economic activities in the US. Browne, Dominie, and Mayerson (2014) research urban food cart vending. Vallianatos (2014) considers various means to assist street food vendors to transition into the formal sector of the urban economy, including lower permit costs – especially for vendors that offer healthier food. Vallianatos (2014: 218) argues that "legal sidewalk vending can also improve the vitality and walkability of cities by giving people a reason to walk and be outside. Increasing the number of people on city sidewalks can also make neighborhoods safer by ensuring more eyes on the street, and may have a positive spillover effect on local stores as more people are out strolling and shopping."

Valenzuela (2014: 261) examines the extensive market for informal day laborers, in which mainly men "by the thousands and their employers gather daily, usually in public spaces during the early morning, to negotiate an exchange of cash wages for a job" – typically without taxes, benefits, or legal protections. Valenzuela (2014: 265; see also Gonzalez et al. 2006) offers the concept of day labor worker centers as a potentially "important first defense against unscrupulous employers and poor working conditions." Shoup (2014) examines informal parking spaces: another widespread informal industry around many sports and music events.

Most of those informal businesses, both in the Developing and the Developed World, will be "microenterprises" with often a single owner-operator and usually five or fewer total employees. Muhammed Yunus (1999), the founder of the Grameen Bank in Bangladesh in 1976, is recognized as a pioneer in developing an institutional model for financing microenterprises (Grameen Foundation). Yunus and the bank were jointly awarded the Nobel Peace Prize in 2006 for their work. The Grameen Bank concept has served as a model and an inspiration throughout the Developing World as well as the Developed World since that time (Association for Enterprise Opportunity).

There are many variations on the general concept of microlending, but typically a Grameen-Bank-inspired institution will organize lending circles, or small groups of potential microentrepreneurs in need of capital. The amount of the loan may be as little as $100 in the environment of the Developing World: enough to finance a pedal-powered sewing machine for an aspiring seamstress, for example, or a wooden cart and produce to jump-start a street vendor. The borrowers involved are generally women, based on the perception (although this is under some dispute) that women are more reliable than men in terms of carrying out an agreed-upon business plan and not drinking up the profits. The women involved in a lending circle will often vote on who in their circle has the best business proposal, and then keep an eye on and support whoever receives the first loan. The other aspiring borrowers will not be eligible for their own loan until the first woman pays back her loan. Interest rates range from low to significantly higher than commercial bank rates. The microenterprise concept continues to expand and innovate widely in the Developing World, helping to support a new generation of "necessity entrepreneurs" (Brewer & Gibson 2014).

Servon (2007, 2006, 1999, 1997) has written extensively on microenterprises and microlending in the US. Servon (2007) dates active microenterprise development programs in the US to the mid-1980s. According to Servon (2006: 352, citing Edgecomb 2002), "for the most part, U.S. microenterprise development organizations (MDOs) were initiated as locally based responses to a need for better economic options, particularly for people who lacked access to mainstream financial institutions. As a result, a majority of programs have targeted what are often categorized as *disadvantaged* groups such as women, public assistance recipients, displaced workers, and people of color." Tinker's (2000) research on strategies for removing women from poverty largely focuses on microenterprise development.

In the US, "the Association for Enterprise Opportunity defines microbusiness as any business with 5 or fewer employees that can use a loan of $35,000 or less" (Servon et al. 2010: 129). In general, SBA programs focus on businesses larger than microenterprise size – although the SBA does offer the Microloan Program and the 7(a) Program, which serve microenterprises (Servon 2007). Servon suggests that microenterprise development in the US context can be more difficult than in the Developing World, with higher levels of business regulation and an entrepreneurial environment that is less comfortable with the informal economy. In general, microenterprise development programs tend to be relatively small, and so they don't realize the economies of scale of other, larger ED financing programs (Servon 2007). For that reason, mergers and partnerships are among Servon's (2006) recommendations for encouraging microenterprise-based development. Bhatt and Tang (2001) address the management and other administrative challenges facing US microlending programs. Servon (2007) also notes policy obstacles to self-employment that include health insurance (especially prior to the Affordable Care Act) and certain TANF (Temporary Assistance for Needy Families) requirements. Hung (2003) considers the challenges of loan repayment in microlending programs. He recommends expanding the traditional base of US microlending programs from welfare recipients in major cities to include the working poor in small towns and rural communities.

Servon (2007) discusses the challenges of evaluating the effectiveness of microenterprise development programs. There may be different and even conflicting objectives between ED and poverty alleviation (Chapter 3): is a given microenterprise program more focused on creating jobs, for example, adequate household income levels, or both? Servon and Bates (1998) warn against viewing miocroenterprise development as a "panacea" for alleviating poverty. A more fundamental critique of microlending programs – which could be applied to many other small-scale ED programs – is that they provide only "microbandaids" for individuals, and "don't make any sort of a macro-difference" (Cockburn 2006: 9) for large-scale low-income populations: they don't address the root issues of poverty.

Predatory lending

While a variety of credit services represent a form of entrepreneurship in low-income communities, they may run contrary to larger community development objectives. Among these services are pawn shops; check-cashing and money-order services; rent-to-own furniture and appliance stores; and payday, tax refund, and car title loan operations – all of which typically charge interest rates that are high, at best, or usurious at worst. I quote Karger (2015) in Chapter 1, citing the Center for Responsible Lending, regarding the extraordinarily high interest that can rapidly accrue and spiral out of control. Although these financing services are typically targeted toward household rather than business needs, I include them in this section as a general financial caution, and because household and business finances can quickly become entangled for small businesses and microenterprises.

Low-income populations and communities are particularly dependent on these types of services for a variety of reasons. Many of them do not have bank accounts in part because they reside in communities that are poorly served by traditional bank branches. Many low-income individuals do not hold credit cards, or those credit cards that they do hold are already "maxed out." The wealth gap is very deep for Black and Hispanic populations, giving them little collateral or little potential to borrow from family members (Chapter 1).

Growing rapidly into the mainstream from the 1990s, predatory lending services are now nearly ubiquitous in low-income communities. "Predatory lending" is, of course, an intentionally pejorative term, and the industry would prefer more benign terms such as "payday lending" or "title loans." Even though these institutions do provide a business presence and jobs in low-income communities, there is growing concern that they also have a pernicious impact on the low-income individuals who serve as their target market. Usurious interest rates, fraud, deception, lack of transparency, requiring borrowers to waive their rights to legal redress, and exploitative or coercive debt servicing are among common practices in this sector (Engle & McCoy 2007).

Bates and Dunham (2003) edit a special issue of *Economic Development Quarterly* devoted to the "use of financial services by low-income households." The authors contributing to the issue address concerns about the negative impacts of many financial services targeting low-income households (Stegman & Faris 2003), and the nature of the industry as well as the households involved (Bradford 2003; Hogarth, Anguelov, & Lee 2003; McKernan, Lacko, & Hastak 2003). Engle & McCoy (2007) note that one of the challenges of regulating predatory lending is the difficulty of defining it. A number of anti-predatory lending laws passed at the federal and state levels, but with considerable industry challenge. Consumer education and counseling may be the best defense (Engle & McCoy 2007; Hogarth, Kolodinsky, & Hilgert 2007).

Working toward solutions, Sherraden, Schreiner, and Beverly (2003: 95) explore individual development accounts (IDAs), "saving programs targeted to people with low incomes, offering subsidies in the form of matching funds on withdrawal." Karger (2015, citing Caskey 2002) advocates mainstream banks play a larger role in providing low-income populations and communities with better access to credit.

Targeting entrepreneurs in specific populations and communities

Entrepreneurship has been a traditional route forward for many immigrant groups to the US, but it has been a challenging path for Black and Latino minorities. Fairlie and Robb (2008: 1), citing Census Bureau data, state that "[o]n average, black and Latino-owned businesses have lower sales, hire fewer employees, and have smaller payrolls than white-owned businesses....Firms owned by African Americans also have lower profits and higher closure rates than those owned by whites." Bates (1997) notes the importance of education levels (including lower levels of college attainment) and startup capital as key limiting factors for these groups, which is confirmed by Fairlie and Robb (2008). Blacks and Latinos are also much less likely to have a parent or other family member with entrepreneurial experience, inherit a family business, hold a college degree, or have work experience in a family business (Fairlie & Robb 2008). Gittell and Thompson (2001; see also Bates 2009) place the challenges in the context of social capital, in which minority entrepreneurs often lack connections to financing, training, and support services networks. Smith (2005) considers the role of "household resources," such as marriage, in the entrepreneurial success of African Americans.

Research confirms that Black-owned firms tend to hire a higher percentage of Black employees than White-owned firms (Bates 1993; see also Bates 2006). By one estimate, "Black workers comprise almost two-thirds (64 percent) of the workforce in Black-owned firms" (Boston 2006: 163). According to Bates (1993: 77), "Black employers tend to utilize a work force consisting largely of minority workers, and this is true whether they are located in inner-city ghettos, central business districts, or outlying suburban areas."

Entrepreneurs who are low-income individuals themselves or who seek to create a business in a low-income community face a number of challenges: "[D]espite the fact that the poor often provide the source of new ideas and innovations, it is those with the social and financial resources that are able to bring the innovations or new trends to market" (Casey 2015, citing Gans 1971). Most successful entrepreneurs finance their businesses through personal savings and equity, and continued expansion through bank loans and lines of credit (Casey 2015): resources that are typically lacking for those with low incomes. Despite decades of effort to overcome lending discrimination and "redlining" – such as the CRA of 1977 – minority-owned business owners still view financing as a major constraint to business growth, and minority-owned businesses have higher loan rejection rates and pay higher interest rates than comparable White-owned businesses (Bates & Robb 2016 provide a literature review). Research by Bone, Christensen, and Williams (2014) shows that both Blacks and Latinos are treated differently by loan officers than Whites, resulting in a number of discouraging effects on those minority groups.

Blacks in the US have faced many constraints on their ability to access business, personal, agricultural, and household credit since the country's founding, both through outright slavery as well as through informal discrimination, geographic segregation, and a variety of restrictive laws nationwide (Immergluck 2004). Many such barriers continue to date, at least on an informal basis, and the impacts of past discriminatory policies persist today: "It was precisely because blacks had suffered from discrimination in credit, housing, employment, and other markets that they had accumulated less capital, less education, and less business experience, on average, than whites" (Immergluck 2004: 62). The impacts of such historic discrimination against Latino communities have been comparable. Historian Richard Rothstein squarely blames "an explicit, racially purposeful policy [of minority discrimination] that was pursued at all levels of government, and that's the reason we have these ghettos today and we are reaping the fruits of those policies" (National Public Radio 2015).

Where Blacks were allowed to open businesses, often they were restricted through various means to serving only the Black community, rather than having access to the full community market (Immergluck 2004). There was considerable debate among prominent Black leaders at the turn of the twentieth century – Booker T. Washington, W.E.B. DuBois, Marcus Garvey – over the extent to which Blacks should target economic separatism and self-sufficiency through Black-owned businesses and banks. Regardless, the peripheral status of Black-owned businesses kept those businesses in a precarious situation, being especially vulnerable in economic downturns. Only 12 Black-owned banks remained in the country five years after the 1929 stock market crash (Immergluck 2004).

Banks provide the large majority of business lending for all small businesses – including minority-owned businesses, even though minority entrepreneurs tend to rely less on banks than White entrepreneurs. In their study of bank business lending, Bates and Robb (2016) did not find evidence of a pattern of lending discrimination against businesses located in minority neighborhoods – in part, because many of the businesses in those neighborhoods are not minority-owned. Instead, they found evidence of lending discrimination against business owners who are Black or

Latino, as opposed to those who are White. That impact may be further amplified as Blacks and Latinos become discouraged by the experience or reputation of lending discrimination and simply give up applying for loans. The end result – lack of adequate business capitalization – is the single biggest factor in business failure among Black and Latino entrepreneurs (Bates & Robb 2016, Bates 2010; Immergluck 2004; Smith 2003).

Cummings (1999) finds that African American entrepreneurs have greater business success reaching outside of their traditional urban communities than they do within their own "ethnic enclaves." He concludes: "For economic development and equity planners, therefore, it appears wiser to promote minority entrepreneurship within a regional or metropolitan area than to confine such efforts to the enclave....Second, strategies that encourage business networking among minority firms and between minority and majority firms are clearly useful" (Cummings 1999: 59). Casey confirms the importance of networks and other needs of "low-wealth" minority entrepreneurs:

> When low-wealth entrepreneurs connect to a greater stock of social resources, they obtain a greater amount of formal financial resources....Partnering with owners with greater levels of education, more years of industry experience, and greater career prestige yields a higher value of formal financial resources.... [F]or low-wealth African Americans there is an association between racially and ethnically diverse ownership teams and a higher value of formal financial resources.
>
> *(Casey 2012: 263)*

The economic growth years of the 1990s resulted in at least a slowing of the financial hemorrhage from inner cities (Bates 2010, citing Hill & Brennan 2005) – as well as a significant decrease in inner-city poverty concentration, especially among African Americans. According to Bates,

> central business districts in many large central cities were driving economic rejuvenation. Many inner-city areas traditionally plagued by disinvestment and population loss had stabilized in the 1990s (Hill & Brennan 2005). Substantial progress on stabilizing population and even reducing poverty occurred between 1990 and 2000 in census tracts where concentrated poverty had been pronounced....These positive developments, however, did not appear to ease capital constraints impeding business investment in inner-city minority neighborhoods.
>
> *(Bates 2010: 351)*

Bates (2009) addresses the potential opportunities and challenges in appropriately targeting affirmative action programs for minority entrepreneurs (e.g., through public sector procurement programs).

In research on the impact of crime on urban enterprises, Bates and Robb (2008) find that crime is largely not cited as a major concern by existing businesses.

Although high crime rates may dissuade many entrepreneurs from investing in urban neighborhoods, the environment seems to provide a niche for others: "The positive association of crime's severity with a firm's survival prospects most likely reflects the benefits that existing firms derive when concerns over crime scare away most of their potential competitors....Owners speaking Spanish and operating in markets where they serve Spanish-speaking coethnics, for example, may be able to deal with crime in less costly ways than owners lacking empathy with this clientele" (Bates & Robb 2008: 237). From a nation-wide study of Latino entrepreneurship, Wang (2015) finds much variation resulting from the specific location, industrial mix, population diversity, and gender factors.

Some churches and faith-based organizations (discussed in Chapter 5) provide services to support entrepreneurship in a variety of ethnic communities. Choi (2010) provides case study research on the ways in which ethnic Korean Christian churches in Los Angeles serve as incubators of small business development for their congregations.

Native Americans and gaming

The federal Indian Self-Determination and Education Assistance Act of 1975 initiated the current model of ED for American Indians, which is intended to "promote self-determination on behalf of Tribal governments, American Indians and Alaska Natives" (Jojola & Ong 2006: 215, quoting the Bureau of Indian Affairs). For a variety of reasons, though, conventional entrepreneurial ventures on the reservations were often unsuccessful at creating ED. One of the most important issues has been the lack of financial capital and technical expertise. Financial capital can be particularly limited in terms of collateral because of the Tribal ownership of much of the land, housing, and other resources. Dewees and Sarkozy-Banoczy (2013) address the need to grow financial institutions in Native American communities. Many tribes also have suffered from poor management – sometimes by federal agencies such as the US Department of the Interior – of natural resource sales: petroleum, timber, coal, and other minerals. There have been successes, on the other hand: for example, lauded industrial development by the Mississippi Band of Choctaw Indians (Mississippi Band of Choctaw Indians; Martin 2009). Middleton and Kusel (2007: 165) evaluate "how six Pacific Northwest tribes applied Northwest Economic Adjustment Initiative funds to diverse projects, which strategies were successful, and why."

The Mississippi Choctaw's industrial development success was quickly overshadowed by more spectacular success in casino and casino-based resort development, a situation experienced by many other tribes across the US (Benedict 2001). Since the 1970s, nearly half of the recognized tribes in the US have adopted some sort of gaming industry as an ED initiative, ranging from bingo (Cordeiro 1993) to full casino gaming (Jojola & Ong 2006). By 2015, total tribal gambling revenues in the US reached nearly $30 billion (National Indian Gaming Commission 2016). There remain a number of major concerns regarding this explosive industry. For example, the industry has helped contribute to a growing inequality among the American Indian tribes and reservations; much of the success of a gaming operation depends upon the location of the reservation land with regard to major cities and competing operations (Jojola & Ong 2006).

In general, approximately one quarter of the jobs created by the tribal gaming industry have gone to American Indians, and the poverty rate is lower for reservations with gambling operations than those without them (Jojola & Ong 2006). Research by Jojola and Ong (2006) in New Mexico found that the poverty rate was lower on reservations with gambling enterprises than among American Indians living off the reservation in the city of Albuquerque. On the other hand, the 2000 poverty rate on reservations with gambling enterprises remained "over three times as high as the poverty rate for non-Hispanic whites in Albuquerque (24 percent versus 8 percent), and the per-capita income was far less than half ($10,200 versus $27,100). Gaming, by itself, [Jojola and Ong (2006) conclude,] is insufficient to achieve economic self-sufficiency" (Jojola & Ong 2006: 226).

Nor can gambling necessarily provide sustained and sustainable growth. The great recession demonstrated the vulnerability of even the country's largest gambling centers (Las Vegas, Atlantic City) to economic fluctuations. Competition continues to grow, as well, both from new Indian tribes entering the market, as well as from outside competitors: "The non-Indian public does not generally perceive gaming as a legitimate exercise of tribal sovereignty, but instead as an unfair monopoly. This leaves an opening for those who advocate breaking the perceived monopoly" (Jojola & Ong 2006: 227). As among the general population, there are also ethical questions and mixed emotions among tribe members regarding ED based on such a controversial activity as gambling (Jojola & Ong 2006).

Immigrant entrepreneurs

Moon et al. (2014) survey Latino immigrant entrepreneurs in both urban and rural communities of Arkansas regarding barriers to business creation and growth. Startup capital as well as government regulations and tax information were the two primary barriers that the businesspeople cited. In some of the communities studied, "Latin American migrant owners cited their businesses in struggling downtown business districts as contributing to a revitalization of these districts. Growing local businesses will provide additional revenue to local governments for the development of facilities and infrastructure needed to maintain and enhance the viability of these communities" (Moon et al. 2014: 70). In a case study of Asian and Latino immigrant entrepreneurs in the "emerging gateway" metropolis of Atlanta, Liu (2012: 189) concludes that "Latino immigrants living in central city and inner-ring suburbs are significantly less likely to involve in self-employment [and]....Self-employment probability increases with experience, suggesting it takes time for immigrants to find their way in the labor market in a new country and to accumulate the necessary resources and knowledge to start up a business."

The narrative of industrious Asian entrepreneurs holds some truth, although the reality is complex. Hum (2006: 183) found in one study of New York City that "despite the common view that there are extraordinarily high self-employment rates among immigrant Asians, Asian immigrants are actually only slightly more likely than other groups to work for themselves." Contrasts among Asian immigrant groups are also significant in terms of their level of human capital, as measured by educational attainment. Many Asian immigrant entrepreneurs are college graduates, while Chinese entrepreneurs in New York City in particular show marked differences within their ranks: 27 percent have college degrees, while 40 percent do not have high school diplomas (Hum 2006).

A number of articles and books are devoted to affluent immigrant entrepreneurs with significant financial capital to invest and to the EB-5 visa program which is designed to attract those investments to the US (Simons et al. 2016; Herman & Smith 2010; Campbell & Edwards 2008; Saxenian 2002). Patraporn, Pfeiffer, and Ong (2010) examine the various roles that community-based organizations can play to help build working assets for Asian Americans. Bates and Dunham (1993) and Bates (1994) address Asian American self-employment in general and Korean immigrant small startup businesses in particular.

Many immigrant businesspeople require assistance with English language skills, standard recordkeeping practices, and establishing a documented credit history (Hum 2006). In addition, Hum (2006: 198) notes: "Integral to an entrepreneurial support system are 'culturally competent' financial institutions, business assistance programs, and government regulatory agencies" to effectively serve those populations. Support for immigrant entrepreneurs can also focus on broadening their reach beyond their traditionally strong close social capital – or cultural bonds – within their own ethnic group to the world of banks and government agencies that can provide them with greater financial resources and technical support. Hum (2006) suggests that immigrant entrepreneurs can benefit from developing an "export orientation" for their goods or services, rather than their typical focus on food products, restaurants, and other goods or services that target only their own cultural group. Building on cultural strengths as well as an export orientation, cultural tourism enterprises such as ethnic restaurants and markets offer other opportunities for immigrant entrepreneurs.

TAKEAWAY FOR ED ACTION: NURTURING ENTREPRENEURSHIP

- *Value all your local businesses, small, large, and in-between – especially those that are already in place locally and might be nurtured to health or further growth.* Reach out to your local entrepreneurs: talk with them to learn more about their strengths, challenges, and opportunities for growth. Try to prevent established local businesses from going out of business or leaving town. Local governments can help "coach" local entrepreneurs, rather than just taxing and regulating them.

- *Consider organizing a business incubator or cooperative.* These are not tools for every community or every business' situation, but they may hold some promise.
- *Reach out to your local "anchor" industries, such as "eds and meds."* Are there ways that major industries and local communities can work together to create more employment opportunities for local workers, or greater opportunities for local small businesses?
- *Encourage community residents to "shop local."* Maintain that multiplier effect.
- *Examine tax increment financing (TIF) districts and other tools for ED financing*: as always, study carefully before you leap into an incentives program.
- *Don't overlook the potential of local "microentrepreneurs."* Help coach informal entrepreneurs into more stable situations. Even tiny businesses add up, and you never know when a local microenterprise might develop into a "macroenterprise."
- *Assure equity for minority entrepreneurs.* Don't allow the biases of the past to perpetuate themselves.
- *Educate your residents on the costs of predatory lending.* Work with local banks and other organizations to steer low-income borrowers to more reasonable credit alternatives.
- *Reach out to immigrant and other ethnic entrepreneurs.* Exercise patience and honesty to gain their confidence and help encourage their development.

References

Acs, Zoltan, William Parsons, & Spencer Tracy. 2008. High-impact firms: Gazelles revisited. Small Business Association. Small Business Research Summary No. 328: https://www.sba.gov/content/high-impact-firms-gazelles-revisited.

Adams, Carolyn. 2003. The meds and eds in urban economic development. *Journal of Urban Affairs* 25(5): 571–588.

Anderson, Maggie. 2012. *Our Black Year: One Family's Quest to Buy Black in America's Racially Divided Economy.* New York: PublicAffairs.

Association for Enterprise Opportunity. Retrieved August 5, 2016: http://www.microenterpriseworks.org/.

Bacot, Hunter, & Cindy O'Dell. 2006. Establishing indicators to evaluate brownfield redevelopment. *Economic Development Quarterly* 20(2): 142–161.

Bartels, Christopher E., & Jeremy L. Hall. 2012. Exploring management practice variation in tax increment financing districts: Toward an administrative theory of performance. *Economic Development Quarterly* 26(1): 13–33.

Bates, Timothy. 2010. Alleviating the financial capital barriers impeding business development in inner cities. *Journal of the American Planning Association* 76(3): 349–362.

Bates, Timothy. 2009. Utilizing affirmative action in public sector procurement as a social economic development strategy. *Economic Development Quarterly* 23(3): 180–192.

Bates, Timothy. 2006. The urban development potential of black-owned businesses. *Journal of the American Planning Association* 72(2): 227–237.

Bates, Timothy. 1997. *Race, Self-Employment and Upward Mobility: An Illusive American Dream.* Baltimore: Johns Hopkins University Press.

Bates, Timothy. 1994. An analysis of Korean-immigrant-owned small-business start-ups with comparisons to African-American- and nonminority-owned firms. *Urban Affairs Review* 30(2): 227–248.

Bates, Timothy. 1993. *Banking on Black Enterprise: The Potential of Emerging Firms for Revitalizing Urban Economies.* Lanham, MD: University Press of America.

Bates, Timothy, William Bradford, & Julia S. Rubin. 2006. The viability of the minority-oriented venture-capital industry under alternative financing arrangements. *Economic Development Quarterly* 20(2): 178–191.

Bates, Timothy, & Constance R. Dunham. 2003. Introduction to focus issue: Use of financial services by low-income households. *Economic Development Quarterly* 17(1): 3–7.

Bates, Timothy, & Constance R. Dunham. 1993. Asian-American success in self-employment. *Economic Development Quarterly* 7(2): 199–214.

Bates, Timothy, & Alicia Robb. 2016. Impacts of owner race and geographic context on access to small-business financing. *Economic Development Quarterly* 30(2): 159–170.

Bates, Timothy, & Alicia Robb. 2015. Has the Community Reinvestment Act increased loan availability among small businesses operating in minority neighborhoods? *Urban Studies* 52(9): 1702–1721.

Bates, Timothy, & Alicia Robb. 2008. Crime's impact on the survival prospects of young urban small businesses. *Economic Development Quarterly* 22(3): 228–238.

Bates, Timothy, Magnus Lofstrom, & Lisa J. Servon. 2011. Why have lending programs targeting disadvantaged small business borrowers achieved so little success in the United States? *Economic Development Quarterly* 25(3): 255–266.

Benedict, Jeff. 2001. *Without Reservation: The Making of America's Most Powerful Indian Tribe and Foxwoods the World's Largest Casino.* New York: Harper.

Bhatt, Nitin, & Shui-Yan Tang. 2001. Making microcredit work in the United States: Social, financial, and administrative dimensions. *Economic Development Quarterly* 15(3): 229–241.

Bhuyan, Sanjib, & F. Larry Leistritz. 2000. Cooperatives in nonagricultural sectors: Examining a potential community development tool. *Journal of the Community Development Society* 31(1): 89–111.

Birch, David L. 1987. *Job Creation in America: How Our Smallest Companies Put the Most People to Work.* New York: Free Press.

Birch, David L. 1981. Who creates jobs? *The Public Interest* 65: 3–14.

Birch, David L., & James Medoff. 1994. Gazelles, in Lewis C. Solomon & Alec R. Levenson, eds., *Labor Markets, Employment Policy, and Job Creation,* 159–168. Boulder, CO: Westview.

Birch, Eugenie. 2014. Anchor institutions in the Northeast Megaregion: An important but not fully realized resource, in Susan M. Wachter & Kimberly A. Zeuli, eds., *Revitalizing America's Cities,* 207–223. Philadelphia: University of Pennsylvania Press.

Bone, Sterling A., Glenn L. Christensen, & Jerome D. Williams. 2014. Rejected, shackled, and alone: The impact of systemic restricted choice on minority consumers' construction of self. *Journal of Consumer Research* 41(2): 451–474.

Boston, Thomas D. 2006. The role of Black-owned businesses in Black community development, in Paul Ong & Anastasia Loukaitou-Sideris, eds., *Jobs and Economic Development in Minority Communities,* 161–175. Philadelphia: Temple University Press.

Bradford, William D. 2003. The savings and credit management of low-income, low-wealth Black and White families. *Economic Development Quarterly* 17(1): 53–74.

Brewer, Jeremi, & Stephen W. Gibson, eds. 2014. *Necessity Entrepreneurs: Microenterprise Education and Economic Development.* Cheltenham, UK: Edward Elgar.

Browne, Ginny, Will Dominie, & Kate Mayerson. 2014. "Keep your wheels on": Mediating informality in the food cart industry, in Vinit Mukhija & Anastasia Loukaitou-Sideris, eds., *The Informal American City: Beyond Taco Trucks and Day Labor*, 243–260. Cambridge: MIT Press.

Byrne, Paul F. 2010. Does tax increment financing deliver on its promise of jobs? The impact of tax increment financing on municipal employment growth. *Economic Development Quarterly* 24(1): 13–22.

Callies, David, & W. AndrewGowder, Jr. 2014. *Tax Increment Financing*. Chicago: American Bar Association.

Campbell, Boyd, & Judson C. Edwards. 2008. EB-5 foreign investors create new jobs. *Applied Research in Economic Development* 5(1): 69–73.

Casey, Colleen. 2015. The paradox of entrepreneurship as a policy tool for economic inclusion in neoliberal policy environments, in Stephen N. Haymes, Maria V. de Haymes, & Reuben J. Miller, eds., *The Routledge Handbook of Poverty in the United States*, 406–414. New York: Routledge.

Casey, Colleen. 2012. Low-wealth minority enterprises and access to financial resources for start-up activities: Do connections matter? *Economic Development Quarterly* 26(3): 252–266.

Caskey, John P. 2002. *Bringing Unbanked Households into the Banking System*. Brookings Institution. January: http://www.brookings.edu/research/articles/2002/01/01metropolita npolicy-caskey.

CDFI Coalition. What are CDFIs? Retrieved August 8, 2016: http://www.cdfi.org/about-cdfis/what-are-cdfis/.

Center for Responsible Lending. Retrieved June 28, 2016: http://www.responsiblelending.org/.

Center for Rural Entrepreneurship. Retrieved August 5, 2016: http://www.energizingen trepreneurs.org/.

Choi, Hyunsun. 2010. Religious institutions and ethnic entrepreneurship: The Korean ethnic church as a small business incubator. *Economic Development Quarterly* 24(4): 372–383.

Cockburn, Alexander. 2006. The myth of microloans. *The Nation*. November 6: 9.

Cordeiro, Eduardo E. 1993. The economics of bingo: Factors influencing the success of bingo operations on American Indian reservations, in Stephen Cornell & Joseph P. Kalt, eds., *What Can Tribes Do? Strategies and Institutions in American Indian Economic Development*, 205–238. Los Angeles: American Indian Studies Center.

Cortright, Joseph. 2002. The economic importance of being different: Regional variations in tastes, increasing returns, and the dynamics of development. *Economic Development Quarterly* 16(1): 3–16.

Cortright, Joseph, & Lotte Langkilde. 2014. *Clusters and Your Economy: An Illustrated Introduction*. Portland: Impresa.

Covert, Matt, & Alfonso Morales. 2014. Formalizing city farms: Conflict and conciliation, in Vinit Mukhija & Anastasia Loukaitou-Sideris, eds., *The Informal American City: Beyond Taco Trucks and Day Labor*, 193–208. Cambridge: MIT Press.

Crowe, Jessica A., Ryan Ceresola, Tony Silva, & Nicholas Recker. 2015. Rural economic development under devolution: A test of local strategies. *Community Development* 46(5): 461–478.

Cummings, Scott. 1999. African American entrepreneurship in the suburbs: Protected markets and enclave business development. *Journal of the American Planning Association* 65(1): 50–61.

Dewees, Sarah, & Stewart Sarkozy-Banoczy. 2013. Investing in the double bottom line: Growing financial institutions in native communities, in Gary P. Green & Ann Goetting, eds., *Mobilizing Communities: Asset Building as a Community Development Strategy*, 14–47. Philadelphia: Temple University Press.

Dreier, Peter. 2003. The future of community reinvestment. *Journal of the American Planning Association* 69(4): 341–353.

Duprey, Rich. 2016. 33 years ago, tariffs saved Harley-Davidson Inc. – or did they? *Motley Fool.* April 5: http://www.fool.com/investing/general/2016/04/05/33-years-ago-toda y-tariffs-saved-harley-davidson.aspx.

Dye, Bruce, & Theodore R. Alter. 2015. Government and the entrepreneurial ecology: The case of Halifax, Nova Scotia. *Community Development* 46(5): 541–558.

Edgecomb, Elaine L. 2002. *Scaling Up Microenterprise Services.* Washington, DC: Aspen Institute. Retrieved August 12, 2016: http://fieldus.org/publications/#2002Dir.

Edward Lowe Foundation. Economic gardening. Retrieved July 26, 2016: http://edwa rdlowe.org/entrepreneurship-programs/economic-gardening/.

Egerstrom, Lee. 2004. Obstacles to cooperation, in Christopher D. Merrett & Norman Walzer, eds., *Cooperatives and Local Development: Theory and Applications for the 21st Century,* 70–92. Armonk, NY: M.E. Sharpe.

Engle, Kathleen C., & Patricia A. McCoy. 2007. Predatory lending and community development at loggerheads, in Julia S. Rubin, ed., *Financing Low-Income Communities: Models, Obstacles, and Future Directions,* 227–262. New York: Russell Sage Foundation.

Etter, Lauren. 2010. Black farmers, USDA agree to $1.25 billion settlement. *Wall Street Journal.* February 18: http://www.wsj.com/articles/SB1000142405274870426900457507 3820593191804.

Fairlie, Robert W., & Alicia M. Robb. 2008. *Race and Entrepreneurial Success: Black-, Asian-, and White-Owned Businesses in the United States.* Cambridge: MIT Press.

Fleming, David A., & Stephan J. Goetz. 2011. Does local firm ownership matter? *Economic Development Quarterly* 25(3): 277–281.

Flora, Cornelia B., Jan L. Flora, & Stephen Gasteyer. 2015. *Rural Communities: Legacy and Change,* 5th ed. Boulder, CO: Westview.

Fortunato, Michael W-P. 2014. Supporting rural entrepreneurship: A review of conceptual developments from research to practice. *Community Development* 45(4): 387–408.

Fortunato, Michael W-P., & Theodore Alter. 2015. Community entrepreneurship development: An introduction. *Community Development* 46(5): 444–455.

Frisch, Michael, & Lisa J. Servon. 2006. CDCs and the changing context for urban community development: A review of the field and the environment. *Community Development* 37(4): 88–108.

Gans, Herbert J. 1971. The uses of poverty: The poor pay all. *Social Policy* July/August: 20–24.

Gittell, Ross, & J. Phillip Thompson. 2001. Making social capital work: Social capital and community economic development, in Susan Saegert, J. Phillip Thompson, & Mark R. Warren, eds., *Social Capital and Poor Communities,* 115–135. New York: Russell Sage Foundation.

Gittell, Ross, & Margaret Wilder. 1999. Community development corporations: Critical factors that influence success. *Journal of Urban Affairs* 21(3): 341–362.

Goetz, Stephan J., & Anil Rupasingha. 2014. The determinants of self-employment growth: Insights from county-level data, 2000–2009. *Economic Development Quarterly* 28(1): 42–60.

Goldsmith, Peter. 2004. Creating value in a knowledge-based agriculture: A theory of new generation cooperatives, in Christopher D. Merrett & Norman Walzer, eds., *Cooperatives and Local Development: Theory and Applications for the 21st Century,* 165–204. Armonk, NY: M.E. Sharpe.

Gonzalez, Ana L., Edwin Melendez, Nik Theodore, & Abel Valenzuela. 2006. *On the Corner: Day Labor in the United States.* Center for the Study of Urban Poverty. Retrieved August 11, 2016: http://www.issuelab.org/resource/on_the_corner_day_labor_in_the_ united_states.

Grameen Foundation. Retrieved August 12, 2016: http://www.grameenfoundation.org.

Green, Gary P., & Anna Haines. 2012. *Asset Building and Community Development*, 3rd ed. Thousand Oaks, CA: Sage.

Gruidl, John, & Deborah Markley. 2015. Entrepreneurship as a community development strategy, in Rhonda Phillips & Robert H. Pittman, eds., *An Introduction to Community Development*, 2nd ed., 278–295. New York: Routledge.

Halebsky, Stephen. 2010. Chain stores and local economies: A case study of a rural county in New York. *Community Development* 41(4): 431–452.

Halstead, John M., & Steven C. Deller. 1997. Public infrastructure in economic development and growth: Evidence from rural manufacturers. *Journal of the Community Development Society* 28(2): 149–169.

Haltiwanger, John C., Ron S. Jarmin, & Javier Miranda. 2010. *Who Creates Jobs? Small vs. Large vs. Young*. National Bureau of Economic Research Working Paper No. 16300: http://www.nber.org/papers/w16300.

Hanham, Alison C., Scott Loveridge & Bill Richardson. 1999. A national school-based entrepreneurship program offers promise. *Community Development* 30(2): 115–130.

Hart, Keith. 1973. Informal income opportunities and urban employment in Ghana. *Journal of Modern African Studies* 11(1): 61–89.

Hartley, Daniel A., Nikhil Kaza, & T. William Lester. 2016. Are America's inner cities competitive? Evidence from the 2000s. *Economic Development Quarterly* 30(2): 137–158.

Henderson, Jason, & Stephan Weiler. 2010. Entrepreneurs and job growth: Probing the boundaries of time and space. *Economic Development Quarterly* 24(1): 23–32.

Herman, Richard T., & Robert L. Smith. 2010. *Immigrant, Inc.: Why Immigrant Entrepreneurs Are Driving the New Economy (and How They Will Save the American Worker)*. Hoboken, NJ: Wiley.

Hess, David J. 2009. *Localist Movements in a Global Economy: Sustainability, Justice, and Urban Development in the United States*. Cambridge: MIT Press.

Hill, Edward W., & John F. Brennan. 2005. America's central cities and the location of work: Can cities compete with their suburbs? *Journal of the American Planning Association* 71(4): 411–432.

Hill, Edward W., & John F. Brennan. 2000. A methodology for identifying the drivers of industrial clusters: The foundation of regional competitive advantage. *Economic Development Quarterly* 14(1): 65–96.

Hogarth, Jeanne M., Chris E. Anguelov, & Jinkook Lee. 2003. Why households don't have checking accounts. *Economic Development Quarterly* 17(1): 75–94.

Hogarth, Jeanne M., Jane Kolodinsky, & Marianne A. Hilgert. 2007. Financial education and community economic development, in Julia S. Rubin, ed., *Financing Low-Income Communities: Models, Obstacles, and Future Directions*, 72–94. New York: Russell Sage Foundation.

Hollister, Robinson. 2007. Measuring the impact of community development financial institutions' activities, in Julia S. Rubin, ed., *Financing Low-Income Communities: Models, Obstacles, and Future Directions*, 265–310. New York: Russell Sage Foundation.

Hou, Jeffrey. 2014. Making and supporting community gardens as informal urban land-scapes, in Vinit Mukhija & Anastasia Loukaitou-Sideris, eds., *The Informal American City: Beyond Taco Trucks and Day Labor*, 79–96. Cambridge: MIT Press.

Hoyt, Ann. 2004. Consumer ownership in capitalist economies: Applications of theory to con-sumer cooperation, in Christopher D. Merrett & Norman Walzer, eds., *Cooperatives and Local Development: Theory and Applications for the 21st Century*, 265–289. Armonk, NY: M.E. Sharpe.

Hum, Tarry. 2006. New York City's Asian immigrant economies, in Paul Ong & Anastasia Loukaitou-Sideris, eds., *Jobs and Economic Development in Minority Communities*, 176–213. Philadelphia: Temple University Press.

Hung, Chikan R. 2003. Loan performance of group-based microcredit programs in the United States. *Economic Development Quarterly* 17(4): 382–395.

Immergluck, Daniel. 2004. *Credit to the Community: Community Reinvestment and Fair Lending Policy in the United States*. Armonk, NY: M.E. Sharpe.

Immergluck, Daniel, & Erin Mullen. 1998. The intrametropolitan distribution of economic development financing: An analysis of SBA 504 lending patterns. *Economic Development Quarterly* 12(4): 372–384.

Initiative for a Competitive Inner City. Retrieved June 13, 2016: http://icic.org/.

International Economic Development Council. Retrieved February 1, 2016: http://www.iedconline.org/.

Johnson, Craig L., & Joyce Y. Man. 2001. *Tax Increment Financing and Economic Development: Uses, Structures, and Impact*. Albany, NY: State University of New York Press.

Jojola, Ted, & Paul Ong. 2006. Indian gaming as community economic development, in Paul Ong & Anastasia Loukaitou-Sideris, eds., *Jobs and Economic Development in Minority Communities*, 213–232. Philadelphia: Temple University Press.

Karger, Howard. 2015. Predatory financial services: The high cost of being poor in America, in Stephen N. Haymes, Maria V. de Haymes, & Reuben J. Miller, eds., *The Routledge Handbook of Poverty in the United States*, 75–82. New York: Routledge.

Kauffman Foundation. Economic gardening. Retrieved July 26, 2016: http://www.kauffman.org/what-we-do/resources/policy/economic-gardening.

Kickul, Jill, & Thomas S. Lyons. 2012. *Understanding Social Entrepreneurship: The Relentless Pursuit of Mission in an Ever-Changing World*. New York: Routledge.

Komarek, Timothy M., & Scott Loveridge. 2014. Too big? Too small? Just right? An empirical perspective on local firm size distribution and economic growth in U.S. counties and high-poverty rural regions. *Economic Development Quarterly* 28(1): 28–41.

Leigh, Nancey G., & Edward J. Blakely. 2013. *Planning Local Economic Development: Theory and Practice*, 5th ed. Thousand Oaks, CA: Sage.

Lewis, W. Arthur. 1954. Economic development with unlimited supplies of labour. *Manchester School* 22(2): 139–191.

Liu, Cathy Y. 2012. Intrametropolitan opportunity structure and the self-employment of Asian and Latino immigrants. *Economic Development Quarterly* 26(2): 178–192.

Lyons, Thomas S. 2015. Entrepreneurship and community development: What matters and why? *Community Development* 46(5): 456–460.

MacLeod, Greg. 2004. The business of relationships, in Christopher D. Merrett & Norman Walzer, eds., *Cooperatives and Local Development: Theory and Applications for the 21st Century*, 290–313. Armonk, NY: M.E. Sharpe.

Malone, Ken, & Brian Richard. 2007. Linking high tech, arts, & affordable housing – Winston-Salem case study. *Applied Research in Economic Development* 4(1): 112–123.

Markley, Deborah M., Thomas S. Lyons, & Donald W. Macke. 2015. Creating entrepreneurial communities: Building community capacity for ecosystem development. *Community Development* 46(5): 580–598.

Marsico, Richard. 2005. *Democratizing Capital: The History, Law and Reform of the Community Reinvestment Act*. Durham, NC: Carolina Academic Press.

Martin, Phillip. 2009. *Chief: The Autobiography of Chief Phillip Martin, Longtime Tribal Leader, Mississippi Band of Choctaw Indians*. Brandon, MS: Quail Ridge.

McKernan, Signe-Mary, James M. Lacko, & Manoj Hastak. 2003. Empirical evidence on the determinants of rent-to-own use and purchase behavior. *Economic Development Quarterly* 17(1): 33–52.

Merrett, Christopher D., & Norman Walzer, eds. 2004. *Cooperatives and Local Development: Theory and Applications for the 21st Century*. Armonk, NY: M.E. Sharpe.

Metzger, John T. 1998. Remaking the growth coalition: The Pittsburgh Partnership for Neighborhood Development. *Economic Development Quarterly* 12(1): 12–29.

Middleton, Beth Rose, & Jonathan Kusel. 2007. Northwest Economic Adjustment Initiative assessment: Lessons learned for American Indian community and economic development. *Economic Development Quarterly* 21(2): 165–178.

Miller, Mark M., & Lay James Gibson. 1990. A Delphi model for planning "preemptive" regional economic diversification. *Economic Development Review* 8(2): 24–41.

Miller, Mark M., Lay James Gibson, & Gene Wright. 1991. Location quotient: A basic tool for regional economic development. *Economic Development Review* 9(2): 65–68.

Mississippi Band of Choctaw Indians. Retrieved May 27, 2016: http://www.choctaw.org/.

Moon, Zola K., Frank L. Farmer, Wayne P. Miller, & Christina Abreo. 2014. Identification and attenuation of barriers to entrepreneurship: Targeting new destination Latino migrants. *Economic Development Quarterly* 28(1): 61–72.

Mukhija, Vinit, & Anastasia Loukaitou-Sideris, eds. 2014. *The Informal American City: Beyond Taco Trucks and Day Labor.* Cambridge: MIT Press.

National Business Incubation Association. Retrieved August 10, 2016: http://www2.nbia.org/about_nbia/.

National Community Reinvestment Corporation. A brief description of CRA. Retrieved August 10, 2016: http://www.ncrc.org/programs-a-services-mainmenu-109/policy-and-legislation-mainmenu-110/the-community-reinvestment-act-mainmenu-80/a-brief-description-of-cra-mainmenu-136.

National Indian Gaming Commission. 2016. The NIGC announces largest tribal revenue gain in 10 years. July 19: http://www.nigc.gov/news/detail/live-from-indian-country-the-nigc-announces-largest-tribal-revenue-gain-in.

National Public Radio. 2015. Historian says don't "sanitize" how our government created ghettos. *Fresh Air.* May 14: http://www.npr.org/2015/05/14/406699264/historian-says-dont-sanitize-how-our-government-created-the-ghettos.

Nelson, Marla, & Laura Wolf-Powers. 2010. Chains and ladders: Exploring the opportunities for workforce development and poverty reduction in the hospital sector. *Economic Development Quarterly* 24(1): 33–44.

Neumark, David, Brandon Wall, & Junfu Zhang. 2008. *Do Small Businesses Create More Jobs? New Evidence from the National Establishment Time Series.* National Bureau of Economic Research Working Paper No. 13818: http://www.nber.org/papers/w13818.

Patraporn, R. Varisa. 2015. Complex transactions: Community development financial institutions lending to ethnic entrepreneurs in Los Angeles. *Community Development* 46(5): 479–498.

Patraporn, R. Varisa, Deirdre Pfeiffer, & Paul Ong. 2010. Building bridges to the middle class: The role of community-based organizations in Asian American wealth accumulation. *Economic Development Quarterly* 24(3): 288–303.

Persky, Joseph, David Ranney, & Wim Wiewel. 1993. Import substitution and local ED. *Economic Development Quarterly* 7(1): 18–29.

Phillips, Rhonda, Bruce Seifer, & Ed Antczak. 2013. *Sustainable Communities: Creating a Durable Local Economy.* Abingdon, UK: Routledge.

Porter, Michael E. 2016. Inner-city economic development: Learnings from 20 years of research and practice. *Economic Development Quarterly* 30(2): 105–116.

Porter, Michael E. 1997. New strategies for inner-city economic development. *Economic Development Quarterly* 11(1): 11–27.

Qian, Haifeng, Kingsley E. Haynes, & James D. Riggle. 2011. Incubation push or business pull? Investigating the geography of U.S. business incubators. *Economic Development Quarterly* 25(1): 79–90.

Rowe, Barbara R., George W. Haynes, & Kathryn Stafford. 1999. The contribution of home-based business income to rural and urban economies. *Economic Development Quarterly* 13(1): 66–77.

Rubin, Julia S. 2007. Introduction, in Julia S. Rubin, ed., *Financing Low-Income Communities: Models, Obstacles, and Future Directions*, 1–10. New York: Russell Sage Foundation.

Rusk, David. 1999. *Inside Game / Outside Game: Winning Strategies for Saving Urban America*. Washington, DC: Brookings Institution.

Rypkema, Donovan D. 2005. *The Economics of Historic Preservation: A Community Leader's Guide*. Washington, DC: National Trust for Historic Preservation.

Saxenian, AnnaLee. 2002. Silicon Valley's new immigrant high-growth entrepreneurs. *Economic Development Quarterly* 16(1): 20–31.

Seidman, Karl F. 2005. *Economic Development Finance*. Thousand Oaks, CA: Sage.

Servon, Lisa J. 2007. Making US microenterprise work: Recommendations for policy makers and the field, in Julia S. Rubin, ed., *Financing Low-Income Communities: Models, Obstacles, and Future Directions*, 95–122. New York: Russell Sage Foundation.

Servon, Lisa J. 2006. Microenterprise development in the United States: Current challenges and new directions. *Economic Development Quarterly* 20(4): 351–367.

Servon, Lisa J. 1999. *Bootstrap Capital: Microenterprises and the American Poor*. Washington, DC: Brookings Institution.

Servon, Lisa J. 1997. Microenterprise programs in U.S. inner cities: Economic development or social welfare? *Economic Development Quarterly* 11(2): 166–180.

Servon, Lisa J., Robert W. Fairlie, Blaise Rastello, & Amber Seely. 2010. The five gaps facing small and microbusiness owners: Evidence from New York City. *Economic Development Quarterly* 24(2): 126–142.

Servon, Lisa J., & Timothy Bates. 1998. Microenterprise as an exit route from poverty: Recommendations for programs and policy makers. *Journal of Urban Affairs* 20(4): 419–441.

Shane, Scott A. 2008. *The Illusions of Entrepreneurship: The Costly Myths that Entrepreneurs, Investors, and Policy Makers Live By*. New Haven: Yale University Press.

Sherman, Hugh, & David S. Chappell. 1998. Methodological challenges in evaluating business incubator outcomes. *Economic Development Quarterly* 12(4): 313–321.

Sherraden, Michael, Mark Schreiner, & Sondra Beverly. 2003. Income, institutions, and saving performance in individual development accounts. *Economic Development Quarterly* 17(1): 95–112.

Shoup, Donald. 2014. Informal parking markets: Turning problems into solutions, in Vinit Mukhija & Anastasia Loukaitou-Sideris, eds., *The Informal American City: Beyond Taco Trucks and Day Labor*, 277–294. Cambridge: MIT Press.

Shuman, Michael H. 2007. *The Small-Mart Revolution: How Local Businesses Are Beating the Global Competition*. San Franciso: Berrett-Koehler.

Shuman, Michael H. 2000. *Going Local: Creating Self-Reliant Communities in a Global Age*. New York: Routledge.

Siegel, Taggart, dir. 2005. *The Real Dirt on Farmer John*. Collective Eye Films.

Simons, Robert A., Jing Wu, Jie Xu, & Yu Fei. 2016. Chinese investment in U.S. real estate markets using the EB-5 Program. *Economic Development Quarterly* 30(1): 75–87.

Sirkin, Harold L., & George Stalk, Jr. 1990. Fix the process, not the problem. *Harvard Business Review* 68(4): 26–33.

Smith, Danielle T. 2005. Developing self-employment among African Americans: The impact of household social resources on African American entrepreneurship. *Economic Development Quarterly* 19(4): 346–355.

Smith, Geoff. 2003. Small business lending in the Chicago region, 2001. *Reinvestment Alert* 23: 1–17.

Stegman, Michael A. & Robert Faris. 2003. Payday lending: A business model that encourages chronic borrowing. *Economic Development Quarterly* 17(1): 8–32.

Stofferahn, Curtis W. 2009. Cooperative community development: A comparative case study of locality-based impacts of new generation cooperatives. *Community Development* 40(2): 177–198.

Stokan, Eric, Lyke Thompson, & Robert J. Mahu. 2015. Testing the differential effect of business incubators on firm growth. *Economic Development Quarterly* 29(4): 317–327.

Sutton, Stacey. 2010. Rethinking commercial revitalization. *Economic Development Quarterly* 24(4): 352–371.

Swenson, Charles W. 2015. The death of California redevelopment areas: Did the state get it right? *Economic Development Quarterly* 29(3): 211–228.

Taylor, Davis F., & Chad R. Miller. 2010. Rethinking local business clusters: The case of food clusters for promoting community development. *Community Development* 41(1): 108–120.

Tinker, Irene. 2000. Alleviating poverty: Investing in women's work. *Journal of the American Planning Association* 66(3): 229–242.

Todaro, Michael P., & Stephen C. Smith. 2014. *Economic Development*, 12th ed. Englewood Cliffs, NJ: Prentice Hall.

Tolbert, Charles M. 2005. Minding our own business: Local retail establishments and the future of Southern civic community. *Social Forces* 83(4): 1309–1328.

US General Accountability Office. 1995. *Community Reinvestment Act: Challenges Remain to Successfully Implement CRA.* GGD-96–23. Retrieved June 24, 2016: http://www.gao. gov/products/GGD-96-23.

US Small Business Administration. Contracting. Retrieved August 5, 2016: https://www. sba.gov/contracting/getting-started-contractor/make-sure-you-meet-sba-size-standards.

US Small Business Administration. Office of Small Business Development Centers. Retrieved August 5, 2016: https://www.sba.gov/offices/headquarters/osbdc.

Valenzuela, Jr., Abel. 2014. Regulating day labor: Worker centers and organizing in the informal economy, in Vinit Mukhija & Anastasia Loukaitou-Sideris, eds., *The Informal American City: Beyond Taco Trucks and Day Labor*, 261–276. Cambridge: MIT Press.

Vallianatos, Mark. 2014. A more delicious city: How to legalize street food, in Vinit Mukhija & Anastasia Loukaitou-Sideris, eds., *The Informal American City: Beyond Taco Trucks and Day Labor*, 209–226. Cambridge: MIT Press.

Vidal, Avis C. 1992. *Rebuilding Communities.* New York: Community Development Research Center.

Vorley, Tim, & Nick Williams. 2015. Creating and sustaining a model of community-based enterprise learning: A participatory case study of ready hubs. *Community Development* 46(5): 559–579.

Wang, Qingfang. 2015. Foreign-born status, gender, and Hispanic business ownership across U.S. metropolitan labor markets: A multilevel approach. *Economic Development Quarterly* 29(4): 328–340.

Weinberg, Adam S., & Heather Vaughn. 1999. The home-based businesses of Madison County: Creating categories and assessing local mechanisms for local self-development. *Community Development* 30(1): 83–98.

White, Sammis B., & Zenia Z. Kotval. 2012. *Financing Economic Development in the 21st Century*, 2nd ed. Abingdon, UK: Routledge.

Wiewel, Wim, & Jeff Weintraub. 1990. Community development corporations as a tool for economic development finance, in Richard D. Bingham, Edward W. Hill, & Sammis B. White, eds., *Financing Economic Development: An Institutional Response*, 160–176. Newbury Park, CA: Sage.

Yunus, Muhammed. 1999. *Banker to the Poor: Micro-Lending and the Battle against World Poverty.* New York: PublicAffairs.

7

DIVERSIFY YOUR ECONOMY

It is rather sad to drive along a country road and see a faded billboard announcing "Smallville County Industrial Park" sitting in the middle of 160 acres purchased years ago in starry-eyed certainty that "If we build it they will come." Well, 30 years later they have not come. And since more than 15,000 other small town local development groups also dream of attracting one of the few hundred large new industrial facilities built or relocated annually, they are unlikely to come.

(Rypkema 2005: 17)

Among the main objectives of true economic development (ED) efforts – in contrast to simple economic growth – should be to build an economy that is stable and resilient against economic downturns and other community misfortunes. There are a number of ways to try building such stability into a local economy. One important strategy is to solidify the foundation of the local economy, beginning with education (Chapter 4). Another vital strategy is to support the existing base of local businesses and anchor institutions (Chapter 6). Economic diversification is another important strategy for building stability and resilience, providing for a diversity of different types of employers and industries in the community and precluding dependence on a few employers, a few major industries, or a few natural resources.

There are boundless possibilities for new industry options available to creative entrepreneurs and ED-minded communities, with new horizons opening up year by year. A few decades back, for example, who could have imagined there would be a twenty-first-century market for high-tech windmills? This section will focus on a few key, broad industry sectors that have already shown some promise for low-income communities – urban and rural – and that are represented to date in the research literature: retail and services, tourism, local food and agriculture, gambling, arts and crafts, and retirement, bedroom, and second-home communities.

SIDEBAR: THE CURSE OF NATURAL RESOURCES

One of the great mysteries of development – in the US and around the world – is the "curse of natural resources" (Sachs 2015; Le Billon 2008; Gylfason 2001; Ross 1999). What low-income community would not want to discover a massive oil reserve or gold deposit under city hall? Those countries and those communities that are most blessed with natural resources, however – oil, gold, diamonds, rich agricultural land, timber – are those countries and communities that tend to have some of the lowest and least equitable ED over time.

Consider just a few cases, such as Nigeria (oil), the Democratic Republic of the Congo (diamonds), or Mississippi (agricultural land). The opposite is often also true: countries and communities that have scarce natural resources are those that often have higher and more equitable levels of ED. Consider Japan or Connecticut. Albrecht (1995: 155) cites numerous sources supporting the contention that "resource-dependent communities [in the US] appear to have substantially lower levels of community stability…social conflict and well-being…[and] institutional structures." In his own analysis of US counties, Albrecht (1995: 155) finds that "resource-dependent counties were significantly more likely to experience population declines during the 1980s than other types of counties."

There are a number of possible explanations for this tendency. For example, places with great natural resource endowments may become complacent with relatively "easy" wealth – especially for those who control and profit most from those resources. The local farm, mining, or forestry workers may not find extracting those resources to be "easy" at all, but they lack other employment options. Indeed, those who control natural-resource-based industries may actively discourage manufacturing or other alternative industries, since those employers could compete for and raise wages for their labor force. Such was apparently the case for the Mississippi Delta plantation owners for many decades (Cobb 1994). A rural, resource-dependent community can become irreversibly dependent on the economically more dynamic and diverse urban "core" (Smith & Steel 1995). According to Beatley & Manning (1997: 152–153), "in regions that have traditionally been highly dependent on the extraction of natural resources by industries such as timber and mining, it is the economies that have protected their natural environment and diversified away from extractive industry that have thrived."

Another common explanation for the "resource curse" is the tendency for such wealth to be concentrated in relatively few hands, in turn leading to great income inequalities and political corruption. Outsiders, seeking to gain access to exploit local resources, may offer bribes to local power-brokers. Resource-dependent countries (Transparency International) and states (Center for Public Integrity 2015) are frequently found on "most corrupt" lists. True sustainable ED depends upon the rule of law, the fair enforcement of those laws, and political stability.

Retail and services

Most ED activity is concerned with either attracting or cultivating "basic industries" (Chapter 1 sidebar): enterprises that bring in new money from outside the community. Instead, this chapter will begin with "non-basic industries": local businesses that instead receive money from local customers. Examples can include local grocery stores, gas stations, car dealerships, healthcare providers, restaurants, and building contractors. The purpose of starting with this part of the local economy is to re-emphasize the importance of building on your existing local assets – in this case, to recognize, nurture, and, if possible, grow existing local businesses (Gibson, Albrecht, & Evans 2003; Chapters 3 and 6). Existing businesses are the most efficient industries to develop; typically, they don't expect or require expensive incentives or tax abatements just to remain where they are. They are already familiar with the local business environment, and they already have an established local network.

Non-basic industries are also key to stopping economic leakage from your community (Chapter 1 sidebar). When residents of your community spend their money locally, the money "multiplies" in the community economy, creating more employment and more tax revenue for local needs. A customer buys produce from a local grocery store, which had bought the produce from a local farmer, who had bought seeds from a local nursery, and so on. Alternatively, if the customer drives out of town to the nearest Wal-Mart, that money immediately "leaks" out of the community, with no more potential for fueling local employment or wealth. Aiken (1990) diagrams an extreme – but not unusual – example of small rural communities in the Mississippi Delta region that are almost entirely dependent on larger urban centers for retail and services. Such multiplier and leakage effects are relevant to inner-city neighborhoods as well (Nunn 2001).

Large retail and service establishments can also serve as basic, or exporting, industries for a community. Major medical care facilities can serve as major basic industries by attracting patients from outside the community, and when local patients draw from Medicare, private insurance, and other sources of outside-the-community money. Nelson (2009) finds that hospitals can provide an important economic base even for lagging, or slow-growth regions.

Communities that lack retailers and services can and should try to attract those businesses and services, just as they might try to attract a manufacturer. There are many good reasons to want a solid foundation of basic community grocers, retailers, and service providers. Local grocers can help provide residents with better access to fresh produce and other healthy foods. Local businesses often tend to be more engaged in and supportive of the community's social activities. Local entrepreneurs can provide role models for young people in the community. A critical mass of specialized or otherwise distinctive retail and other local market-oriented enterprises can potentially emerge as a draw for tourists and other consumers from outside the immediate vicinity of the community (Markusen & Schrock 2009; Markusen 2007; Cortright 2002). Locally based establishments can also occupy and provide rents for buildings that would otherwise go vacant, including in historic downtowns or other lagging commercial districts (Markusen 2007). Many low-income communities, both rural and urban, have vacant movie theaters and other public spaces that could be occupied by local theater groups, visual artists, or other creative organizations. There are numerous stories of struggling communities that built a critical mass of arts-related activity that led to sustained ED (Seman 2008; Markusen 2007).

Fleming and Goetz (2011) find a positive relationship between the concentration of small, locally owned businesses in a community and growth in per capita income; they find the opposite is true for concentrations of larger businesses such as big box chain stores. Chain stores and particularly the "Wal-Mart effect" have engendered substantial debate in communities as well as in the research literature. In a focus issue of *Economic Development Quarterly* on Wal-Mart (Persky & Merriman 2012), a longitudinal (research over an extended time period) Iowa study by Artz and Stone (2012) finds that retail sales increase in the small towns in which Wal-Mart stores locate, but at the cost of local retail establishments and retail sales in surrounding communities. A study of Wal-Mart locations in Chicago by Merriman et al. (2012) finds similar impacts in an urban setting, with losses of jobs and other establishments in the vicinity being roughly proportionate to the jobs and retail sales created by the Wal-Mart. A literature review by Bonanno and Goetz (2012) finds a broader but more complicated set of impacts from Wal-Mart stores on local economies. For example, a Wal-Mart in a community can help reduce overall retail prices, but it can also contribute to higher poverty rates and lower measures of social capital in the community (Goetz & Rupasingha 2006; Goetz & Swaminathan 2006). Starr (2016) links Wal-Mart's closure of many smaller "Wal-Mart Express" stores to competition with the lower-priced "dollar stores." To date, I have found relatively little published research literature on the widespread phenomenon of dollar stores spreading across the low-income urban and rural landscapes.

Porter (2016: 105) reports significant growth in the inner-city retail sector: "Overall, great progress has been made on many fronts in improving inner-city economies over the last two decades. Inner-city residents now have many more retail options than they did two decades ago…including an increased presence of national retailers." Nunn (2001) presents a case study of an inner-city retail development in Indianapolis framed in Porter's early ED theories. Meltzer and Schuetz (2012) report similar retail growth, but find that most of that growth has occurred in gentrifying neighborhoods; their "research finds that poor and minority neighborhoods currently have much smaller average stores for nearly all the retail categories examined. This implies a smaller range of product choices within each store, and, to the extent that economies of scale exist, may result in higher prices than in larger establishments. Moreover, larger stores by definition offer more opportunities for employment" (Meltzer & Schuetz 2012: 89–90).

"Food deserts," communities without adequate access to healthy, affordable fresh produce and other healthy groceries, have inspired a robust interdisciplinary research agenda and numerous government policies (Otero, Pechlaner, & Gürcan 2015; Lawrence 2015; Pine & Bennett 2014; Walker, Keane, & Burke 2010; Raja, Ma, & Yadav 2008; US Departments of Agriculture, Treasury and Health and

Human Services; Chapter 1). Pothukuchi (2005) studies the relatively rare cases of communities making an active effort to attract supermarkets to inner-city neighborhoods. Pothukuchi suggests several characteristics of successful initiatives of this kind, including, not surprisingly at this point in this book, community networking and building public-private-nonprofit partnerships with private companies, community development organizations, city agencies, and others local actors. On the other hand, Raja, Ma, and Yadav (2008) argue that communities or neighborhoods that lack supermarkets often do have smaller grocery stores and that these might be a better target for ED initiatives.

Sutton (2010) reaches a similar conclusion to that of Pothukuchi (2005) in a case study of Black-owned retail revitalization in a Brooklyn neighborhood: success requires a coordinated community partnership. Sutton contrasts "top-down," chain store, or corporate-led initiatives for commercial revitalization with "bottom-up" initiatives that result from locally led initiatives and local small-business owners. The former may provide greater investment resources and a more efficient model of ED, while the latter may provide more connections (economic, employment, and otherwise) with the local community, as well as a less generic, more place-distinctive appearance. In particular, Sutton (2010) suggests the importance of supportive merchant associations, which may be especially important in communities that lack many typical sources of information and support services for small businesses. Researching inner-city commercial strips in particular, which are typically "characterized by major decay and disinvestment," Loukaitou-Sideris (2000: 165) emphasizes the roles of local retailers and merchants associations in fostering an entrepreneurial environment, especially when working together with local governments and community development organizations. Halebsky (2010) addresses similar issues in a rural context.

Community activity and research work related to the local food movement (Ostrom 2006) and local farmers' markets continues to grow steadily. Alonso and O'Neill (2011) review the literature of the potential contributions that farmers' markets can make to their communities – including helping to develop local social capital – offering a rural Alabama case study. In another rural study in Mississippi, Holland and Thompson (2015) conclude that farmers' markets tend to be under-utilized and could make more effective use of SNAP (Supplemental Nutrition Assistance Program) benefits. Inda et al. (2011) study a farmers market in the relatively isolated rural community of Waianae, Hawaii, and note several successful innovations including electronic benefits processing and networks with local producers. Hardesty et al. (2014) and Brown et al. (2014) continue research work on regional farm and food networks. Economic impact analysis by Brown et al. (2014) on what they term "community focused agriculture" shows mixed but generally disappointing results.

Young et al. (2011) study a number of factors affecting urban farmers' markets in Philadelphia, including the regulatory environment and – again – the effective use of food assistance programs. Lowery et al. (2016: 252), in a study of Los Angeles farmers' markets, find that markets tend to locate in relatively affluent neighborhoods: "Farmers' markets in low-income and non-White communities are smaller and provide fewer fresh fruits and vegetables than markets situated in more affluent communities."

Hou (2014) and Covert and Morales (2014) address community gardens and the potential for conflict in an urban environment. Kashian and Skidmore (2002) and Alterman (1997) consider the challenges of preserving productive farmland in the path of urban development and sprawl. Lewis (2009) examines immigrant farmers as a solution to the growing need for human capital to sustain Iowa's agriculture industry.

Tourism

The research literature on tourism is extensive, as is befitting for the world's largest industry by many measures (Biederman 2007). Tourism has emerged as the leading industry for many countries of the Developing World, as well as for many rural communities across the US and the Developed World. Tourism may also be viewed by some struggling communities as an industry of last resort, where manufacturing, mining, and other more traditional industries have failed.

The tourism industry can serve both rural and urban communities. Marcouiller, Clendenning, and Kedzior (2002) and Marcouiller (1997) review the literature of tourism planning for rural areas. Rural regions are, of course, more likely to enjoy scenic and natural assets for tourism. McGranahan, Wojan, and Lambert (2011) find that rural communities with high concentrations of creative class individuals (Chapter 3) are more likely to experience entrepreneurship and job growth – and especially so if those communities are blessed with outdoor amenities. On the other hand, rural areas also face challenges in terms of basic tourism infrastructure: adequate roads and other transportation modes, well-educated individuals with training in tourism and hospitality, hotels or bed-and-breakfast facilities, and so on. Cohen, Hannah, and Miller (2008, see also Snyder & Stonehouse 2007) provide an extreme example of efforts to develop a rural tourism industry in the Canadian Arctic. Marcouiller (1997: 353) calls for greater emphasis on "a broader, more integrative, and strategic approach" to help rural communities achieve a variety of possible economic, environmental, and social goals through the tourism industry.

Urban centers, on the other hand, may be more likely to be endowed with historic and arts districts, museums, and other tourism attractions reflecting the built environment and human activities (Judd & Fainstein 1999). Many suburban communities have the potential to capitalize on this industry opportunity, although suburbs generally feature fewer historic, cultural, scenic, or other assets typical of tourism development.

There is a wide range of possible subcategories and niche markets in tourism, spanning from the "three S's" (sun, sea, and sand) to sex tourism (Nelson 2013). This section highlights several of the subcategories that may be most relevant to the potential of low-income communities in the US: pro-poor tourism; tourism based on arts, crafts, music, and culture; agritourism and nature tourism; recreational trails; volunteer tourism; "dark tourism," and gambling.

Pro-poor tourism

The "pro-poor tourism" movement has an extensive research presence in reports and proceedings (Ashley & Haysom 2005) and online (Pro-Poor Tourism Partnership; Responsible Tourism Partnership; International Centre for Responsible Tourism or ICRT). The purpose of the ICRT is stated succinctly as: "Making better places for people to live in, and better places to visit." To date, the pro-poor tourism movement is less well represented in the formal research literature (Torres, Skillicorn, & Nelson 2011; Holden & Novelli 2011; Goodwin 2008a, 2008b; Harrison 2008). Most of the research available under this general heading is focused on the Developing World (Jiang et al. 2011; Truong 2011): Africa (Blake et al. 2008) and Latin America (Torres & Momsen 2004) in particular.

Harrill (2004) reminds us that tourism, although seemingly a pleasant and innocuous industry on its face, can have a variety of physical, social, economic, and cultural impacts on local residents, both positive and negative. As usual, it is the low-income residents of a community who have the least control and smallest voice regarding the distribution of those impacts along with their consequences for the local natural environment (Nasser 2003).

Arts, crafts, music, and culture

Rural communities may have preserved some of their traditional cultural practices, heritage, crafts, or other assets that are attractive to tourists (MacDonald & Jolliffe 2003). Loukaitou-Sideris and Soureli (2012) review the research literature on cultural tourism, and remind us that cultural assets for tourism are not limited to rural communities. They provide case studies of four ethnic Los Angeles neighborhoods – in addition to the more well-known "Chinatown" and "Little Tokyo" communities – with potential for tourism growth: artistic, largely Latino Highland Park; the African American cultural center Leimert Park, the "Little Armenia" neighborhood, and "Thai Town."

"Heritage tourism" "affords communities endowed with a rich and attractive cultural, natural, and historical environment the opportunity to capitalize on [those economic assets]. The movement is based on the tenets of sustainable development and seeks to promote tourism in a manner that is respectful of the natural and built environments while relying on local values and beliefs" (Beatley & Manning 1997: 154, quoting from North Carolina Heritage Tourism). Even a community's heritage as a manufacturing or other type of industrial center can provide an asset for "industrial tourism" (Rastorfer 2015).

Cultural or heritage tourism can also include traditional arts, crafts, and music (Phillips 2015; CanagaRetna 2008). Artists may also find a rural or otherwise non-traditional location inspirational for creating or marketing craft products (Tumber 2014) or art in general (Seman 2008). Luckman (2015) connects crafts in particular with the larger creative economy (Chapter 3) of a community. The Americana Music Triangle is an initiative of several Southern states to represent and market

Americana music (Americana Music Triangle), which by one definition is "contemporary music that incorporates elements of various American roots music styles, including country, roots-rock, folk, bluegrass, R&B and blues, resulting in a distinctive roots-oriented sound that lives in a world apart from the pure forms of the genres upon which it may draw" (Americana Music Foundation).

Markusen and Gadwa (2010) review the literature on planning for arts- and culture-based development, including tourism development. Studying the economic impacts of the arts across Canadian cities, Polèse (2012) finds the greatest impacts in the largest cities, but also finds higher impacts for smaller communities that are either within close proximity to major cities or that possess strong natural amenities. He cautions, however, that there is little evidence that the arts per se are a significant factor in creating overall employment or in attracting other creative new workers to the community. Instead, it appears that the same factors that draw artists (e.g., outdoor amenities or a rich cultural milieu) may also draw other residents, including members of the "creative class" (Chapter 3). Grodach, Foster, and Murdoch (2014) and Malone and Richard (2007) study the relationships between arts-based development, neighborhood gentrification (Chapter 2), and the complex impacts on local residents and even on the "Bohemian" artists themselves.

One craft category in the US that is currently experiencing explosive growth is the craft beer industry.[1] Craft breweries and brew pubs are opening daily in cities big and small, as well as in rural communities (Reid & Gatrell 2015; Acitelli 2013; Florida 2012; Brewers Association). Craft breweries represent industrial development, but can also contribute to the environment of a creative community (Chapter 3): "The authenticity of craft brewing is one of the cool things about it. It's one of the things attractive to people – the fact you can come down to the tasting room, and there are the guys who work here, it's all made here, they can have a pint and rub shoulders and talk to them about what they're doing. There is almost a sense of ownership in the community" (Tuttle 2012, quoting Eric Wallace of Colorado's Left Hand Brewing). In some cases, they provide the community with a basic industry that "exports" product outside the community; some craft breweries even export their products internationally (Birnbaum 2013).

The continued growth of vineyards and wineries, along with their impacts on local economies, is a similar phenomenon which is underrepresented to date in the research literature. Porter (2000) diagrams the California wine industry as an industrial cluster, including wineries, grape growers, agricultural equipment, specialized marketing services, and wine-oriented tourism. In their study of small, rural family wineries, Alonso and Bressan (2013: 516) find that "small family wineries are seeking to make an impact on their local community in ways that go beyond monetary benefits. For example, based on the long history many of the wineries enjoy, as well as on their infrastructure, owners and managers perceive their role in the preservation of the local wine culture, landscape, promotion of the rural area, region, and even country." As such, they find that "wineries are significantly contributing to building social capital in their communities, playing the role of community 'hubs'" (Alonso & Bressan 2013: 515).

If any rapidly growing industry is developing ahead of the research literature, it must be legalized marijuana: policies, production, distribution, retail, and the mixed-blessing relationship with tourism. Németh and Ross (2014) provide an early consideration of the planning implications.

Agritourism and nature tourism

Vineyards and cannabis cultivation provided us with a happy introduction to "agritourism," or tourism based on agricultural production, heritage, and landscapes. An early article by Cox and Fox (1991) titled "Agriculturally based leisure attractions" is a classic of the genre. Torres (2003) studies the economic linkages between the agricultural and tourism sectors in the Cancún region of Mexico; I hope to find more research along these lines in the US. "New generation cooperatives" (Chapter 6) often involve urban residents purchasing a membership in a farming cooperative in exchange for fresh farm produce – and often to provide their children (and themselves) with the experience of farm work and rural life. Boone, Shaeffer, and Lewis (2003), based on their study of "consumer-driven agriculture" in West Virginia, conclude that agritourism can capitalize on consumers' interest in flavor and quality in agricultural products, as well as in generally positive attitudes toward environmental issues and family farms. Webster and Chappelle (2001) extend the general concept of agritourism to embrace forestry as well.

Agritourism can also be seen within the very broad category of "ecotourism" (Fennell 2014), which has at least significant overlap with the concepts of "sustainable tourism" (Hwang, Stewart, & Ko 2012; Miller & Cochran 2013) and "geotourism" (Boley, Nickerson, & Bosak 2011; National Geographic Society). Other related terms or niches might include "nature tourism" and "adventure tourism" (Nelson 2013). These very general concepts can embrace hiking, nature tours, birdwatching (Glowinski 2008), bicycling, and much more. Ecotourism, broadly defined, can also include more conventional forms of tourism that utilize environmentally friendly products or conservation methods.

Recreational trails[2]

Recreational trails – including rails-to-trails conversions (Rails-to-Trails Conservancy) – are growing nation-wide through urban and rural communities, with a growing emphasis on low-income communities (League of American Bicyclists 2013). The emphasis of these trails, also called "greenways," is often on the health, transportation, and safety benefits of local residents (Day 2006). Recreational trails, however, can also provide sources of revenue for local communities through tourism publicity and spending (Mundet & Coender 2010). There is also some evidence that recreational trails can enhance property values for nearby residents (Parent & Vom Hofe 2012; Asabere & Huffman 2009), along with opportunities for employment in trail construction and maintenance and more customer traffic for businesses along or related to trails (Peltier 2011).

Based on a research literature review, Day (2006) makes a number of suggestions for promoting biking and walking among "active living" programs to reach low-income and minority populations. Anderson and Lauran (2015) offer several case studies of major cities' efforts to reach the needs of low-income populations, including Atlanta and Harlem. Atlanta's Beltline project is one of the most ambitious urban trail developments in the US; it is projected upon completion to be 33 miles in length and connect 45 neighborhoods with a combination of trails, light rail, and greenspace (Davidson 2011; Atlanta Beltline). Immergluck (2009) confirms the positive impacts on property values of this development, but also warns about the potentially negative impacts of land speculation, gentrification, and the displacement of established residents in the low-income neighborhoods involved. A planning process was finalized in 2013 to incorporate equity concerns explicitly in the Atlanta Beltline development process (Atlanta Beltline Partnership 2013).

Zimmerman et al. (2015) recommend incorporating grassroots planning initiatives into the earliest stages of the process to address more directly the interests of low-income populations in trail development and to help mitigate some of the unintended negative impacts on those communities. Chicago's Bloomingdale Trail will be the city's first east–west trail and greenway corridor; inclusive neighborhood participation along the trail has been built into the process from the beginning of the project, according to Kirk (2013), along with plans for associated affordable housing.

Recreational trails are not limited to foot and bike paths. Pollock et al. (2012) study the economic impacts of the Northern Forest Canoe Trail – a water "trail" that runs from the Adirondack Mountains of New York State through New England to the Newfoundland border – and offer several conclusions regarding how communities can contribute to the development of a paddling-based tourism industry.

Volunteer tourism[3]

"Volunteer tourism" is most common in the Developing World (Nelson 2013; Cross-Cultural Solutions; International Volunteer Headquarters; International Volunteer Programs Association). Explained by Keese (2011: 257–258),

> volunteer tourism has grown dramatically as a form of alternative travel for people seeking a more sustainable, productive and interactive experience than the commercial and leisure-based model of mass tourism….Motivated by a sense of altruism and wishing to make a difference in the world, volunteer tourism typically involves volunteering abroad with a non-profit organization to engage in community or conservation-based development work. The majority of these tourists come from the USA, Canada, Europe, Australia and Japan and most go to developing countries. The experience lasts one to four weeks or more and volunteers pay a fee for on-site support. However, in most cases, volunteers also participate in sightseeing and adventure activities associated with a vacation. Therefore, volunteer tourism is a combination of development work, education and tourism.

Coghlan (2007: 267) emphasizes that volunteer tourism also "may offer a way to support nature conservation through increasing the general public's understanding of science during their tourism experience....It provides sustainable alternative travel that can assist in community development, scientific research or ecological restoration."

A wide variety of volunteer trips also reach out to low-income communities of the US, although they are not typically bundled together under that term. Many universities and other organizations offer service learning experiences for students to work in urban and rural low-income communities, or contribute to environmental projects (Student Conservation Association). Many churches offer similar opportunities for their congregations (Travis 2016).

Dark tourism

Barton and Leonard (2010) emphasize that tourism development can potentially be "sustainable" in multiple dimensions, including the physical environment, culture, heritage, and history – and also in terms of sustaining the social capital of a community. Even some aspects of heritage or history about which communities are not proud can still potentially provide "assets" for tourism development, as well as tools for building or rebuilding social capital. Miller and Cochran (2013) offer a case study of Hattiesburg, Mississippi's segregated World War II-era Black USO Club building, which was restored and repurposed by the city's Convention and Visitors Bureau as the country's only African American military history museum.

The term "dark tourism" (credited to Lennon & Foley 2000) has been applied to tourism in the US and worldwide focused on "contemporary and historic sites associated with death, disaster and atrocity" (White & Frew 2013: 1). White and Frew (2013: 2) describe "experiences of shared grief that can help knit generations together," along with the potential to build an identity for a community, demonstrate commitment to the higher "values and goals" of a place, create an "'imagined community' among a diverse population," and "promote a discourse of national inclusion and a shared past." Sion (2016) takes the dismal terminology a step further with "death tourism."

Barton and Leonard (2010) present another Mississippi case study, which revolves around a community effort to memorialize the violent death of Emmett Till: surely one of the darkest episodes in US history. Skipper (2016) offers a participatory research case study of another Mississippi community attempting to reconcile the history of slavery with traditional plantation tourism focused on the "big house" of the plantation owners. Some dark tourism assets can be epic in nature, such as Civil War or other battlefield sites (Willard, Lade, & Frost 2013). Other potential assets may be more dismal in nature, such as disaster sites (Sion 2016). Former prisons are a niche but growing form of tourism (Strange & Kempab 2003), and even celebrity car crash sites can serve as tourist attractions (Best 2013).

Gambling

Legalized and regulated gambling – or "gaming," as the industry and economic developers prefer to term it – has generated an explosion of expansion and development since the 1980s. Growth has come both in terms of overall industry earnings and tourist numbers, but also in terms of its spread to near-ubiquity across the US. Once concentrated in Las Vegas and then Atlantic City, new centers such as Connecticut's Foxwoods, the Mississippi Gulf Coast, and Mississippi's Tunica County emerged in the late 1980s and early 1990s. American Indian reservation-based casinos continue to proliferate (Chapter 6), along with the expansion of state lotteries, slot machines, sports books, and online gambling sites. Gambling establishments range from opulent casino resorts near major metropolises, such as Foxwoods (Benedict 2001), to relatively small, limited gaming locations in remote communities in need of economic stimulus and physical restoration (Jensen & Blevins 1995).

The lures for states and communities are obvious and hard to resist: relatively easy and extravagant investment financing, stunning physical development in rural or deteriorated urban areas, employment, tax revenues – all with little or no direct demands for conventional tax increases: "It is no mystery why most if not all states in the union adopt lotteries. They are politically feasible forms of...taxation that... [generate] millions and billions for state treasuries. What remains less understood and understudied, however...[are] the social consequences that arise from paying for public services in this way" (Henricks & Brockett 2015: 72).

Robert Goodman (1995, 1994) was an early, critical researcher on the gambling industry. Williams (1999) and Skolnik (2011) tracked growth and changes in the industry in the years that followed. Gross (1998) lists several potential problems related to ED from a legal gambling industry, including:

- Direct and indirect costs of pathological gambling and increased crime,
- Cannibalization of the local economy [i.e., local and tourist spending may be diverted from existing local businesses]...,
- Market saturation and the long-term instability of gambling-dependent economies, and
- The regressive nature of gambling-derived revenues.

There seems to be support in the research for the general belief that low-income populations spend a disproportionate share of their income on the lottery and other forms of gaming, although there are also some contradictory findings (Henricks & Brockett 2015). According to Henricks & Brockett (2015: 72), "in true anti-Robin Hood style, lotteries offer a vehicle for institutionally swindling marginal groups while enriching everyone else....The regressive nature of lotteries means that they generate money from those who occupy marginalized positions of race, income, and educational attainment....It is, in many ways, a process in which 'the house always wins'." Although the revenues, physical structures, and employment numbers can be exciting for a community, the gaming industry is volatile, and the economic and social impacts are unpredictable and often inequitable. Case studies in this regard include Atlantic City around 2016 (McGeehan 2016) and Tunica County, Mississippi, one of the poorest counties in the US before the advent of legalized casino gambling in 1995 – the latter continued to experience deep, persistent poverty and inequity over a decade later (Harlan 2015).

Retirement, bedroom, and second-home communities

The three types of "industries" grouped together in this section are all very distinctive from one another, typically targeting very different populations, but they do share some commonalities. All three depend on a particular location and distinctive amenities of a community (Marcouiller, Clendenning, & Kedzior 2002). All three types represent ED aspirations for many struggling exurban and rural communities: "Many rural American communities…now rely heavily on tourism, recreation, and second-home ownership rather than traditional extractive industries such as agriculture, mining, and forestry" (Schewe et al. 2012: 9). None of the three are well represented in the research literature.

A bedroom community requires reasonable proximity to a major urban center – perhaps 45 minutes to an hour or more – typically with some sort of "small town" environment to attract residents. Residents will often commute to the urban center for work, and the bedroom community prospers from property taxes and retail shopping. Second-home communities will typically be a farther distance from the urban center – perhaps two or three hours – often with a rural environment offering woods, mountains, a lake or ocean, hunting, or fishing. Local community revenue and employment result from property and sales taxes, retail and utility spending, real estate, and construction (Schewe et al. 2012).

All these forms of development can also engender conflict between newcomers and long-time residents. Schewe et al. (2012: 5), in a study of second-home owners in rural northern Wisconsin, find that a critical issue "for many residents was the preservation of rural landscapes. Newcomers preferred to preserve their idealized landscape of rolling hills, farms, forests, and open spaces.…In contrast, many longtime residents supported growth and development, seeing growth as a means to provide jobs for themselves and their children." They also maintain that "communities on the outskirts of an urban area, otherwise called 'exurbia' or 'the fringe,' are particularly contested and conflicted" (Schewe et al. 2012: 45). Conflict can also result from attitudes over newcomer or season homeowners' participation in community affairs and control – or lack thereof – over political power and local resources.

Retirement communities cater to some combination of winter "snowbirds" (and their opposite "seasonal tourists": those who flee hot, Southern summers for northern climates), or permanently relocated residents. Stallmann and Jones (1995: 1) develop a typology of different types of retirement communities based on the amenities that attract retirees to the community. The five types are as follows: "resource amenity, planned, continuing care, old home town and regional center."

The costs and benefits of retirees remain under study and are a matter of some dispute. Retirees shop and pay taxes typically without great demands on city services such as schools or other physical infrastructure. Most seniors have some sustained source of income: social security at a minimum, but also pensions and savings. Since the 1950s, per capita social security expenditures have risen steadily, and the elderly poverty rate has also dropped at a steady rate (Mishel et al. 2012). Nation-wide analysis by Hamilton (2010) and a Maine case study by Deller (1995) suggest that at least the short-run impacts of the retirement industry are significant for local economic growth and employment.

On the other hand, Woods et al. (1997) find very different employment impacts among counties in Arkansas, Oklahoma, and Texas resulting from senior citizens moving in. Some communities complain that retirees are reluctant to support bond bills for education or other services they don't require. Ryser and Halseth (2013) and Loukaitou-Sideris et al. (2016) consider the specialized "infrastructure" needs in which a community must invest to support a successful and sustainable retirement industry, including senior-appropriate housing, expanded healthcare, recreation centers, adequate public transportation, and parks with amenities for seniors. Seniors who lack substantial pensions or savings, who have lost their pensions, or who reach an advanced age may require a variety of subsidized medical and other community services.

In a study of aging retirees, Stallmann, Deller, & Shields (1999: 608), however, through a literature review and economic modeling study of Wisconsin, find: "The results do not support the fear of the 'gray peril.' Although per capita earnings and per-capita incomes decline, this is mainly because the majority of new jobs created for employed elderly people in these households are part-time jobs in the trade and services sectors. Total earnings and total incomes increase, as do total retail sales."

TAKEAWAY FOR ED ACTION: OPPORTUNITIES FOR DIVERSIFYING YOUR ECONOMY

- *More of the same is good for economic growth, but true, sustainable ED requires economic diversity.* Economic diversity can also be a key factor in community resilience through economic transitions and disasters.
- *Abundant natural resources are a blessing, but can also be a curse.* Communities with economies that are highly dependent on natural resource extraction tend to have lower and less equitable growth, along with a greater danger of an economic bust.
- *Don't overlook "non-basic" industries such as retail and services as important components of a healthy local economy.* A robust grocery and food sector provides the community with many health and social benefits and slows economic leakage.
- *What assets can your community build on for tourism development?* Potential tourism assets are often overlooked by local residents. Seemingly mundane

activities such as farming may be fascinating to urban visitors. Even "dark" episodes in your community's past may contribute to tourism appeal and provide an opportunity for strengthening relationships within the community. The needs of a struggling low-income community may be the "assets" that most attract volunteer tourists. Recreation development can both serve the tourism industry and contribute to the local quality of life.

- *Gambling industries are very tempting for low-income communities, but exercise caution and study the examples of other communities with gambling-based economies.* Gambling industries are potentially lucrative, but also present challenges for equitable and socially sustainable ED.
- *Retirement, bedroom, and second-home communities all offer ED opportunities, especially for rural communities and smaller cities.* The aging demographics of the US will ensure growth in these types of "industries," especially retirement communities. Like any industry, however, these industries require specialized knowledge and investment to be successful, sustainable, and in harmony with other community interests.

Notes

1 Katherine Hogan provided research on the topic of craft breweries with her undergraduate Honors College thesis, "Making Mississippi Cool: Craft Beer and the Creative Economy."
2 Joseph Yawn contributed research to the section on recreational trails as a student at the University of Southern Mississippi.
3 Nathan Satcher, Master's student in Geography and Economic Development at the University of Southern Mississippi, contributed scholarly and field research on this topic, and first brought this topic to my attention.

References

Acitelli, Tom. 2013. *The Audacity of Hops: The History of America's Craft Beer Revolution.* Chicago: Chicago Review.

Aiken, Charles S. 1990. A new type of Black ghetto in the plantation South. *Annals of the Association of American Geographers* 80(2): 223–246.

Albrecht, Don E. 1995. Population trends in resource-dependent counties. *Journal of the Community Development Society* 26(2): 155–168.

Alonso, Abel D., & Alessandro Bressan. 2013. Small rural family wineries as contributors to social capital and socioeconomic development. *Community Development* 44(4): 503–519.

Alonso, Abel D., & Martin A. O'Neill. 2011. Investing in the social fabric of rural and urban communities: A comparative study of two Alabama farmers' markets. *Community Development* 42(3): 392–409.

Alterman, Rachelle. 1997. The challenge of farmland preservation: Lessons from a six-nation comparison. *Journal of the American Planning Association* 63(2): 220–243.

Americana Music Foundation. Retrieved August 17, 2016: http://americanamusic.org.

Americana Music Triangle. Retrieved August 17, 2016: http://americanamusictriangle.com.

Anderson, Michael, & May Lauran. 2015. *Building Equity, Race, Ethnicity, Class, and Protected Bike Lanes: An Idea Book for Fairer Cities.* People for Bikes: Green Lane Project. Retrieved March 29, 2016: http://b.3cdn.net/bikes/60e4ef1291e083cada_8ym6ip7pw.pdf.

Artz, Georgeanne M., & Kenneth E. Stone. 2012. Revisiting WalMart's impact on Iowa small-town retail: 25 years later. *Economic Development Quarterly* 26(4): 298–310.

Asabere, Paul K., & Forrest E. Huffman. 2009. The relative impacts of trails and greenbelts on home price. *Journal of Real Estate and Financial Economics* 38(4): 408–419.

Ashley, Caroline, & Gareth Haysom. 2005. From philanthropy to a different way of doing business: Strategies and challenges in integrating pro-poor approaches into tourism business. Proceedings of the ATLAS Africa Conference. Retrieved August 16, 2016: https://www.odi.org/resources/docs/3806.pdf.

Atlanta Beltline. Retrieved March 29, 2016: http://beltline.org/.

Atlanta Beltline Partnership. 2013. *An Atlanta Beltline for All: Equitable Development Assessment*. Retrieved August 10, 2015: http://saportareport.com/wp-content/uploads/2014/09/Equitable-Development-Assessment_FINAL-VERSION.pdf.

Barton, Alan W., & Sarah J. Leonard. 2010. Incorporating social justice in tourism planning: Racial reconciliation and sustainable community development in the Deep South. *Community Development* 41(3): 298–322.

Beatley, Timothy, & Kristy Manning. 1997. *The Ecology of Place: Planning for Environment, Economy, and Community*, 2nd ed. Washington, DC: Island.

Benedict, Jeff. 2001. *Without Reservation: The Making of America's Most Powerful Indian Tribe and Foxwoods the World's Largest Casino*. New York: Harper.

Best, Gary. 2013. Dark detours: Celebrity car crash deaths and trajectories of place, in Leanne White & Elspeth Frew, eds., *Dark Tourism and Place Identity: Managing and Interpreting Dark Places*, 202–216. London: Routledge.

Biederman, Paul S. 2007. *Travel and Tourism: An Industry Primer*. New York: Pearson Education.

Birnbaum, Michael. 2013. In Germany, a U.S. beer invasion. *Washington Post*. May 1: http://www.washingtonpost.com/world/in-germany-a-us-beer-invasion/2013/04/30/0d03f6e6-adf3-11e2-8bf6-e70cb6ae066e_story.html.

Blake, Adam, Jorge S. Arbache, M. Thea Sinclair, & Vladimir Teles. 2008. Tourism and poverty relief. *Annals of Tourism Research* 35(1): 107–126.

Boley, B. Bynum, Norma P. Nickerson, & Keith Bosak. 2011. Measuring geotourism: Developing and testing the Geotraveler Tendency Scale (GTS). *Journal of Travel Research* 50(5): 567–578.

Bonanno, Alessandro, & Stephan J. Goetz. 2012. WalMart and local economic development: A survey. *Economic Development Quarterly* 26(4): 285–297.

Boone, Jr., Harry N., Peter V. Shaeffer, & Jennifer L. Lewis. 2003. Consumer-driven agriculture as a means to promote rural income and employment opportunities: A case study of West Virginia. *Applied Research in Economic Development* 1(2): 19–32.

Brewers Association. Retrieved August 17, 2016: https://www.brewersassociation.org/.

Brown, Jason P., Stephan J. Goetz, Mary C. Ahearn, & Chyi-lyi (Kathleen) Liang. 2014. Linkages between community-focused agriculture, farm sales, and regional growth. *Economic Development Quarterly* 28(1): 5–16.

CanagaRetna, Sujit M. 2008. From Blues to Bluegrass: The economic impact of the arts in the South. *Applied Research in Economic Development* 5(3): 3–11.

Center for Public Integrity. 2015. November 9: https://www.publicintegrity.org/2015/11/09/18822/how-does-your-state-rank-integrity.

Cobb, James C. 1994. *The Most Southern Place on Earth: The Mississippi Delta and the Roots of Regional Identity*. Oxford: Oxford University Press.

Coghlan, Alexandra. 2007. Towards an integrated image-based typology of volunteer tourism organisations. *Journal of Sustainable Tourism* 15(3): 267–287.

Cohen, Janel, Steven Hannah, & Mark M. Miller. 2008. Exploring Nunavut: Extreme tourism and development. *Applied Research in Economic Development* 5(3): 32–36.

Cortright, Joseph. 2002. The economic importance of being different: Regional variations in tastes, increasing returns, and the dynamics of development. *Economic Development Quarterly* 16(1): 3–16.

Covert, Matt, & Alfonso Morales. 2014. Formalizing city farms: Conflict and conciliation, in Vinit Mukhija & Anastasia Loukaitou-Sideris, eds., *The Informal American City: Beyond Taco Trucks and Day Labor*, 193–208. Cambridge: MIT Press.

Cox, Linda J., & Morton Fox. 1991. Agriculturally based leisure attractions. *Journal of Tourism Studies* 2(2): 18–27.

Cross-Cultural Solutions. Retrieved September 23, 2016: https://www.crossculturalsolutions.org/.

Davidson, Ethan. 2011. The Atlanta Beltline: A green future. *Public Roads* 72(2). Retrieved March 29, 2016: https://www.fhwa.dot.gov/publications/publicroads/11septoct/04.cfm.

Day, Kristen. 2006. Active living and social justice: Planning for physical activity in low-income, Black, and Latino communities. *Journal of the American Planning Association* 72(1): 88–99.

Deller, Steven C. 1995. Economic impact of retirement migration. *Economic Development Quarterly* 9(1): 25–38.

Fennell, David A. 2014. *Ecotourism*, 4th ed. London: Routledge.

Fleming, David A., & Stephan J. Goetz. 2011. Does local firm ownership matter? *Economic Development Quarterly* 25(3): 277–281.

Florida, Richard. 2012. The geography of craft beer. *CityLab* (from *The Atlantic*). August 20: http://www.citylab.com/design/2012/08/geography-craft-beer/2931/.

Gibson, Lay James, Barry Albrecht, & Bryant Evans. 2003. Is retail trade focus for real economic development in the knowledge-based economy? *Applied Research in Economic Development* 1(1): 45–56.

Glowinski, Sheri L. 2008. Bird-watching as ecotourism and economic development: A review of the evidence. *Applied Research in Economic Development* 5(3): 65–77.

Goetz, Stephan J., & Anil Rupasingha. 2006. WalMart and social capital. *American Journal of Agricultural Economics* 88(5): 1304–1310.

Goetz, Stephan J., & Hema Swaminathan. 2006. WalMart and family poverty in U.S. counties. *Social Science Quarterly* 87(2): 211–225.

Goodman, Robert. 1995. *The Luck Business: The Devastating Consequences and Broken Promises of America's Gambling Explosion*. New York: Free Press.

Goodman, Robert. 1994. *Legalized Gambling as a Strategy for Economic Development*. United States Gambling Study. Retrieved August 18, 2016: http://citeseerx.ist.psu.edu/viewdoc/download?doi=10.1.1.836.6310&rep=rep1&type=pdf.

Goodwin, Harold. 2008a. Pro-poor tourism: A response. *Third World Quarterly* 29(5): 869–871.

Goodwin, Harold. 2008b. Tourism, local economic development, and poverty reduction. *Applied Research in Economic Development* 5(3): 55–64.

Grodach, Carl, Nicole Foster, & James Murdoch. 2014. Gentrification and the artistic dividend: The role of the arts in neighborhood change. *Journal of the American Planning Association* 80(1): 21–35.

Gross, Meir. 1998. Legal gambling as a strategy for economic development. *Economic Development Quarterly* 12(3): 203–213.

Gylfason, Thorvaldur. 2001. Natural resources, education, and economic development. *European Economic Review* 45(4–6): 847–859.

Halebsky, Stephen. 2010. Chain stores and local economies: A case study of a rural county in New York. *Community Development* 41(4): 431–452.

Hamilton, Karen L. 2010. Impact of retirement populations on local jobs and wages. *Economic Development Quarterly* 24(2): 110–125.

Hardesty, Shermain, Gail Feenstra, David Visher, Tracy Lerman, Dawn Thilmany-McFadden, Allison Bauman, Tom Gillpatrick, & Gretchen N. Rainbolt. 2014. Values-based supply chains: Supporting regional food and farms. *Economic Development Quarterly* 28(1): 17–27.

Harlan, Chico. 2015. An opportunity gamed away: For a county in the Deep South that reaped millions from casino business, poverty is still its spin of the wheel. *Washington Post.* July 11: http://www.washingtonpost.com/sf/business/2015/07/11/an-opportunity-gamed-away/.

Harrill, Rich. 2004. Residents' attitudes toward tourism development: A literature review with implications for tourism planning. *Journal of Planning Literature* 18(3): 251–266.

Harrison, David. 2008. Pro-poor tourism: A critique. *Third World Quarterly* 29(5): 851–868.

Henricks, Kasey, & Victoria Brockett. 2015. The house always wins: How state lotteries displace American tax burdens by class and race, in Stephen N. Haymes, Maria V. de Haymes, & Reuben J. Miller, eds., *The Routledge Handbook of Poverty in the United States,* 56–74. New York: Routledge.

Holden, Andrew, & Marina Novelli. 2011. The changing paradigms of tourism in international development: Placing the poor first – Trojan horse or real hope? *Tourism Planning & Development* 8(3): 233–235.

Holland, Joseph H., & Olivia M. Thompson. 2015. Place-based economic development: Examining the relationship between the US Supplemental Nutrition Assistance Program and farmers markets in Mississippi. *Community Development* 46(1): 67–77.

Hou, Jeffrey. 2014. Making and supporting community gardens as informal urban landscapes, in Vinit Mukhija & Anastasia Loukaitou-Sideris, eds., *The Informal American City: Beyond Taco Trucks and Day Labor,* 79–96. Cambridge: MIT Press.

Hwang, Doohyun, William P. Stewart, & Dong-wan Ko. 2012. Community behavior and sustainable rural tourism development. *Journal of Travel Research* 51(3): 328–341.

Immergluck, Dan. 2009. Large redevelopment initiatives, housing values and gentrification: The case of the Atlanta Beltline. *Urban Studies* 46(8): 1723–1745.

Inda, Christy, Anuenue Washburn, Sheila Beckham, Bryan Talisayan, & Desiree Hikuroa. 2011. Home grown: The trials and triumphs of starting up a farmers' market in Waianae, Hawaii. *Community Development* 42(2): 181–192.

International Centre for Responsible Tourism. Retrieved September 21, 2016: http://www.icrtourism.org/.

International Volunteer Headquarters. Retrieved September 23, 2016: https://www.volunteerhq.org/.

International Volunteer Programs Association. Retrieved September 23, 2016: http://volunteerinternational.org/.

Jensen, Katherine, & Audie Blevins. 1995. Gambling on the lure of historic preservation: Community transformation in Rocky Mountain mining towns. *Journal of the Community Development Society* 26(1): 71–92.

Jiang, Min, Terry DeLacy, Nickson Peter Mkiramweni, & David Harrison. 2011. Some evidence for tourism alleviating poverty. *Annals of Tourism Research* 38(3): 1181–1184.

Judd, Dennis R., & Susan S. Fainstein. 1999. *The Tourist City.* New Haven: Yale University Press.

Kashian, Russ, & Mark Skidmore. 2002. Preserving agricultural land via property assessment policy and the willingness to pay for land preservation. *Economic Development Quarterly* 16(1): 75–87.

Keese, James R. 2011. The geography of volunteer tourism: Place matters. *Tourism Geographies* 13(2): 257–279.

Kirk, Patricia. 2013. Chicago's Bloomingdale Trail takes rail-to-trail concept to next level. *Urban Land*. June 19. Retrieved March 29, 2016: http://urbanland.uli.org/infrastructure-transit/chicago-s-bloomingdale-trail-takes-rail-to-trail-concept-to-next-level/.

Lawrence, Nicole B. 2015. *Feeding the South: An assessment of food availability in rural Mississippi*. Master's thesis. The University of Southern Mississippi. Available online: http://aquila.usm.edu/masters_theses/153/.

League of American Bicyclists. 2013. The New Majority: Pedaling towards Equity. Washington, DC. Retrieved March 16, 2016: http://bikeleague.org/sites/default/files/equity_report.pdf.

Le Billon, Philippe. 2008. Diamond wars? Conflict diamonds and geographies of resource wars. *Annals of the Association of American Geographers* 98(2): 345–372.

Lennon, John, & Malcolm Foley. 2000. *Dark Tourism: The Attraction of Death and Disaster*. London: Thomson.

Lewis, Hannah. 2009. From Mexico to Iowa: New immigrant farmers' pathways and potentials. *Community Development* 40(2): 139–153.

Loukaitou-Sideris, Anastasia. 2000. Revisiting inner-city strips: A framework for community and economic development. *Economic Development Quarterly* 14(2): 165–181.

Loukaitou-Sideris, Anastasia, & Konstantina Soureli. 2012. Cultural tourism as an economic development strategy for ethnic neighborhoods. *Economic Development Quarterly* 26(1): 50–72.

Loukaitou-Sideris, Anastasia, Lené Levy-Storms, Lin Chen, & Madeline Brozen. 2016. Parks for an aging population: Needs and preferences of low-income seniors in Los Angeles. *Journal of the American Planning Association* 82(3): 236–251.

Lowery, Bryce, David Sloane, Denise Payán, Jacqueline Illium, & Lavonna Lewis. 2016. Do farmers' markets increase access to healthy foods for all communities? *Journal of the American Planning Association* 82(3): 252–266.

Luckman, Susan. 2015. *Craft and the Creative Economy*. New York: Palgrave Macmillan.

MacDonald, Roberta, & Lee Jolliffe. 2003. Cultural rural tourism: Evidence from Canada. *Annals of Tourism Research* 30(2): 307–322.

Malone, Ken, & Brian Richard. 2007. Linking high tech, arts, and affordable housing – Winston-Salem case study. *Applied Research in Economic Development* 4(1): 112–123.

Marcouiller, David W. 1997. Toward integrative tourism planning in rural America. *Journal of Planning Literature* 11(3): 337–357.

Marcouiller, David W., John G. Clendenning, & Richard Kedzior. 2002. Natural amenity-led development and rural planning. *Journal of Planning Literature* 16(4): 515–542.

Markusen, Ann. 2007. A consumption base theory of development: An application to the rural cultural economy. *Agricultural and Resource Economics Review* 36(1): 9–23.

Markusen, Ann, & Anne Gadwa. 2010. Arts and culture in urban/regional planning: A review and research agenda. *Journal of Planning Education and Research* 29(3): 379–391.

Markusen, Ann, & Greg Schrock. 2009. Consumption-driven urban development. *Urban Geography* 30(4): 344–367.

McGeehan, Patrick. 2016. "A crisis every day" for the mayor trying to rescue Atlantic City. *New York Times*. February 15: http://www.nytimes.com/2016/02/16/nyregion/a-crisis-every-day-for-the-mayor-trying-to-rescue-atlantic-city.html?_r=0.

McGranahan, David, Timothy R. Wojan, & Dayton M. Lambert. 2011. The rural growth trifecta: Outdoor amenities, creative class and entrepreneurial context. *Journal of Economic Geography* 11(3): 529–557.

Meltzer, Rachel, & Jenny Schuetz. 2012. Bodegas or bagel shops? Neighborhood differences in retail and household services. *Economic Development Quarterly* 26(1): 73–94.

Merriman, David, Joseph Persky, Julie Davis, & Ron Baiman. 2012. The impact of an urban WalMart store on area businesses: The Chicago case. *Economic Development Quarterly* 26(4): 321–333.

Miller, Mark M., & David Cochran. 2013. Telling the story of African-Americans in Hattiesburg, Mississippi: A case study of socially sustainable tourism. *Southeastern Geographer* 53(4): 428–454.

Mishel, Lawrence, Josh Bivens, Elise Gould, & Heidi Shierholz. 2012. *The State of Working America*, 12th ed. Ithaca, NY: ILR.

Mundet, Lluis, & Germa Coender. 2010. Greenways: A sustainable leisure experience concept for both communities and tourists. *Journal of Sustainable Tourism* 18(5): 657–674.

Nasser, Noha. 2003. Planning for urban heritage places: Reconciling conservation, tourism, and sustainable development. *Journal of Planning Literature* 17(4): 467–479.

National Geographic Society. About geotourism. Retrieved August 17, 2016: http://travel. nationalgeographic.com/travel/geotourism/about/.

Nelson, Marla. 2009. Are hospitals an export industry? Empirical evidence from five lagging regions. *Economic Development Quarterly* 23(3): 242–253.

Nelson, Velvet. 2013. *An Introduction to the Geography of Tourism*. Lanham, MD: Rowman & Littlefield.

Németh, Jeremy, & Eric Ross. 2014. Planning for marijuana: The cannabis conundrum. *Journal of the American Planning Association* 80(1): 6–20.

Nunn, Samuel. 2001. Planning for inner-city retail development. *Journal of the American Planning Association* 67(2): 159–172.

Ostrom, Marcia. 2006. Everyday meanings of "local food": Views from home and field. *Community Development* 37(1): 65–78.

Otero, Gerardo, Gabriela Pechlaner, & Efe C. Gürcan. 2015. The neoliberal diet: Fattening profits and people, in Stephen N. Haymes, Maria V. de Haymes, & Reuben J. Miller, eds., *The Routledge Handbook of Poverty in the United States*, 472–479. New York: Routledge.

Parent, Olivier, & Rainer Vom Hofe. 2012. Understanding the impacts of trails on residential property values in the presence of spatial dependence. *Annuals of Regional Science* 51(2): 355–375.

Peltier, Heidi G. 2011. *Pedestrian and Bicycle Infrastructure: A National Study of Employment Impacts*. Political Economy Research Institute. Retrieved August 17, 2016: http://www. peri.umass.edu/236/hash/64a34bab6a183a2fc06fdc212875a3ad/publication/467/.

Persky, Joseph, & David Merriman. 2012. Focus issue: WalMart. *Economic Development Quarterly* 26(4): 283–284.

Phillips, Rhonda. 2015. Arts, culture, and community development, in Rhonda Phillips & Robert H. Pittman, eds., *Introduction to Community Development*, 2nd ed. New York: Routledge.

Pine, Adam, & John Bennett. 2014. Food access and food deserts: The diverse methods that residents of a neighborhood in Duluth, Minnesota use to provision themselves. *Community Development* 45(4): 317–336.

Polèse, Mario. 2012. The arts and local economic development: Can a strong arts presence uplift local economies? A study of 135 Canadian cities. *Urban Studies* 49(8): 1811–1835.

Pollock, Noah, Lisa Chase, Clare Ginger, & Jane Kolodinsky. 2012. The Northern Forest Canoe Trail: Economic impacts and implications for community development. *Community Development* 43(2): 244–258.

Porter, Michael E. 2016. Inner-city economic development: Learnings from 20 years of research and practice. *Economic Development Quarterly* 30(2): 105–116.

Porter, Michael E. 2000. Location, competition, and economic development: Local clusters in a global economy. *Economic Development Quarterly* 14(1): 15–34.

Pothukuchi, Kameshwari. 2005. Attracting supermarkets to inner-city neighborhoods: ED outside the box. *Economic Development Quarterly* 19(3): 232–244.

Pro-Poor Tourism Partnership. Pro-poor tourism. Retrieved May 25, 2011: http://www.propoortourism.org.uk/.

Rails-to-Trails Conservancy. Retrieved March 29, 2016: http://www.railstotrails.org/.

Raja, Samina, Changxing Ma, & Pavan Yadav. 2008. Beyond food deserts: Measuring and mapping racial disparities in neighborhood food environments. *Journal of Planning Education and Research* 27(4): 469–482.

Rastorfer, Darl. 2015. 21st-century smokestacks. *Planning*. October: 40–45.

Reid, Neil, & Jay D. Gatrell. 2015. Brewing growth: Regional craft breweries and emerging economic development opportunities. *Economic Development Journal* 14(4): 4–12.

Responsible Tourism Partnership. ProPoor tourism. Retrieved June 20, 2016: http://www.propoortourism.info/.

Ross, Michael L. 1999. The political economy of the resource curse. *World Politics* 51(2): 297–322.

Rypkema, Donovan D. 2005. *The Economics of Historic Preservation: A Community Leader's Guide*. Washington, DC: National Trust for Historic Preservation.

Ryser, Laura M., & Greg Halseth. 2013. So you're thinking about a retirement industry? Economic and community development lessons from resource towns in northern British Columbia. *Community Development* 44(1): 83–96.

Sachs, Jeffrey D. 2015. *The Age of Sustainable Development*. New York: Columbia University Press.

Schewe, Rebecca L., Donald R. Field, Deborah J. Frosch, Gregory Clendenning, & Dana Jensen. 2012. *Condos in the Woods: The Growth of Seasonal and Retirement Homes in Northern Wisconsin*. Madison, WI: University of Wisconsin Press.

Seman, Michael. 2008. No country for old developers: The strange tale of an arts boom, Bohemians, and "Marfalafel" in the High Desert of Marfa, Texas. *Applied Research in Economic Development* 5(3): 25–31.

Sion, Brigitte. 2016. *Death Tourism: Disaster Sites as Recreational Landscape*. London: Seagull.

Skipper, Jodi. 2016. Community development through reconciliation tourism: The behind the Big House Program in Holly Springs, Mississippi. *Community Development* 47(4): 514–529.

Skolnik, Sam. 2011. *High Stakes: The Rising Cost of America's Gambling Addiction*. Boston: Beacon.

Smith, Courtland L., & Brent S. Steel. 1995. Core-periphery relationships of resource-based communities. *Journal of the Community Development Society* 26(1): 52–70.

Snyder, John, & Bernard Stonehouse. 2007. *Prospects for Polar Tourism*. Oxfordshire, UK: CAB International.

Stallmann, Judith I., & Lonnie L. Jones. 1995. A typology of retirement places: A community analysis. *Journal of the Community Development Society* 26(1): 1–14.

Stallmann, Judith I., Steven C. Deller, & Martin Shields. 1999. The economic and fiscal impact of aging retirees on a small rural region. *Gerontologist* 39(5): 599–610.

Starr, Andrew W. 2016. Big box bust? What Walmart Express closures teach us about retail site selection. *Planning*. July: 25–26.

Strange, Carolyn, & Michael Kempab. 2003. Shades of dark tourism: Alcatraz and Robben Island. *Annals of Tourism Research* 30(2): 386–405.

Student Conservation Association. Retrieved September 23, 2016: http://www.thesca.org/.

Sutton, Stacey. 2010. Rethinking commercial revitalization: A neighborhood small business perspective. *Economic Development Quarterly* 24(4): 352–371.

Torres, Rebecca M. 2003. Linkages between tourism and agriculture in Mexico. *Annals of Tourism Research* 30(5): 546–566.

Torres, Rebecca M., & Janet H. Momsen. 2004. Challenges and potential for linking tourism and agriculture to achieve pro-poor tourism objectives. *Progress in Development Studies* 4(4): 294–318.

Torres, Rebecca M., Paul Skillicorn, & Velvet Nelson. 2011. Community corporate joint ventures: An alternative model for pro-poor tourism development. *Tourism Planning & Development* 11(2): 297–316.

Transparency International. Retrieved September 21, 2016: https://www.transparency.org.

Travis, Mary D. 2016. *Delta Hands for Hope: A Force for Reconciliation and Sustainable Development in the Mississippi Delta?* Undergraduate honors thesis. The University of Southern Mississippi Honors College.

Truong, V. Dao. 2011. Pro-poor tourism: Looking backward as we move forward. *Tourism Planning & Development* 8(3): 228–242.

Tumber, Catherine. 2014. Fields, factories, and workshops: Green economic development on the smaller-metro scale, in Susan M. Wachter & Kimberly A. Zeuli, eds., *Revitalizing American Cities*, 224–241. Philadelphia: University of Pennsylvania Press.

Tuttle, Brad. 2012. Trouble brewing: The craft beer vs. "crafty" beer cat fight. *Time*. Retrieved March 1, 2016: http://business.time.com/2012/12/27/trouble-brewing-the-craft-beer-vs-crafty-beer-cat-fight/.

US Departments of Agriculture, Treasury and Health and Human Services. Food deserts. Retrieved May 6, 2014: http://apps.ams.usda.gov/fooddeserts/foodDeserts.aspx.

Walker, Renee E., Christopher R. Keane, & Jessica G. Burke. 2010. Disparities and access to healthy food in the United States: A review of food deserts literature. *Health & Food* 16(5): 876–884.

Webster, Henry H., & Daniel E. Chappelle. 2001. Tourism and forest products: Twin resource sectors for effective community development in the Lake States. *Community Development* 32(1): 88–105.

White, Leanne, & Elspeth Frew, eds. 2013. *Dark Tourism and Place Identity: Managing and Interpreting Dark Places*. London: Routledge.

Willard, Paul, Clare Lade, & Warwick Frost. 2013. Darkness beyond memory: The battlefields at Culloden and Little Bighorn, in Leanne White & Elspeth Frew, eds., *Dark Tourism and Place Identity: Managing and Interpreting Dark Places*, 264–275. London: Routledge.

Williams, Mary E. 1999. *Legalized Gambling*. San Diego: Greenhaven.

Woods, Mike D., Wayne Miller, Don Voth, Boo-Yong Song, & Lonnie Jones. 1997. Economic impacts of in-migrating retirees on local economies. *Journal of the Community Development Society* 28(2): 206–224.

Young, Candace, Allison Karpyn, Nicky Uy, Katy Wich, & Jonathan Glyn. 2011. Farmers' markets in low income communities: Impact of community environment, food programs and public policy. *Community Development* 42(2): 208–220.

Zimmerman, Sara, Michelle Liberman, Karen Kramer, & Bill Sadler. 2015. *At the Intersection of Active Transportation and Equity: Joining Forces to Make Communities Healthier and Fairer*. Safe Routes to School National Partnership. Retrieved March 29, 2016: http://safer outespartnership.org/resources/report/intersection-active-transportation-equity.

8

SUSTAIN YOUR DEVELOPMENT

We have now entered a fourth wave, or phase, of economic development (ED), according to the model popularized by Leigh and Blakely (2013): sustainable ED, or ED that is sensitive to concerns of the natural environment and also, increasingly, social equity. Personally, I applaud this new phase of the profession, although I have struggled to understand it fully. Apparently, I am not alone:

> The broad concept of sustainability has caught the attention of policy makers and citizens the world over. Much of what the term means today is considerably different from what it conveyed a decade ago. As the broad concept of sustainability has evolved, so too have several of its derivatives: sustainable communities, livable communities, and sustainable cities. Even so, these are not concepts that are susceptible to easy or quick definitions. As Beatley and Manning (1997: 3) point out, "there is a general sense that sustainability is a good thing (and that being unsustainable is a bad thing), but will we know it when we see it?"
>
> *(Portney 2013: 1)*

Jepson (2001) details the origins of the term and concept of "sustainability," beginning in the physical, biological sciences – where some physical scientists believe the concept should remain, exclusively. Clearly, however, sustainability has jumped – imperfectly, perhaps – to the human realms of politics, economics, geography, demography, and ED.

Most of the focus of attention on sustainability and sustainable development has been on minimizing human impacts – or our "ecological footprint" (Portney 2013) – on the natural environment: "A sustainable community is a place that seeks to contain the extent of the urban 'footprint' and strives to keep to a minimum the conversion of natural and open lands to urban and developed uses" (Portney 2013:

20, citing Beatley & Manning 1997: 28). Warner et al. (1999), for example, study how rural New York communities have organized to protect their traditional rural landscapes. Murdock et al. (1998) study community responses to the siting of waste facilities. Protecting communities from economic and social impacts of oil and natural gas "fracking" (hydraulic fracturing) is a more recent and growing concern (Loh & Osland 2016) – including economic equity issues (Crowe & Silva 2015; Hardy & Kelsey 2015) and growing alarm that fracking-related activities may be contributing to seismic, or earthquake events (Bustillo 2006). Traditional planning terms include LULUs and NIMBYs: Locally Unwanted Land Uses along with necessary industries or utilities that must be located somewhere but just Not In My Back Yard. Climate change is an increasing concern, of course, on the global level (Sachs 2015; Bauman & Klein 2014; Rubin & Hilton 1996), with growing impacts at the local level. Not surprisingly, the consequences of climate change are first striking some of the most vulnerable populations, including Native Americans in Alaska (Barth 2016) and Louisiana (Houma Today 2016; Isle de Jean Charles, Louisiana).

An extensive planning literature now addresses sustainability, especially in terms of planning for reconciling urban development and maintaining the physical environment (Jepson & Haines 2015; Chapple 2015; Gough 2015; Daniels 2014; Wheeler 2013). Similarly, there are journals (e.g., *Journal of Sustainable Tourism*) and an extensive literature devoted to sustainable tourism, or ecotourism – although with much of the attention focused on international applications, especially in the Developing World (Bricker, Black, & Cottrell 2012; Sloan, Simons-Kaufman, & Legrand 2012; Chapter 7). Among the many topics at the intersection of sustainable planning and tourism is the protection of ocean-related tourism assets, or what has been termed the "blue economy"[1](Economist 2015; Loomis 2015; Svensson & Pendleton 2014).

The sustainability and sustainable development concept has broadened widely over time to embrace more than the maintenance of the natural, physical environment (Miller & Cochran 2013; Barton & Leonard 2010; Manzi & Lucas 2010). Sachs (2015) lists the three concerns of sustainable development as:

- Economic development;
- Social inclusion; and
- Environmental sustainability.

This triple focus is also termed the "three E's of sustainable development": environment, equity, and economic development (Sachs 2015). Berke and Conroy (2000: 23) review the sustainability literature and suggest six "basic principles" of sustainable development from a planning perspective:

1. Harmony with nature
2. Livable built environments
3. Place-based economy

4. Equity
5. Polluters pay, and
6. Responsible regionalism

Toward these ends, there has been much attention paid to the concept of quantifying, accounting for, and assuring accountability for sustainable development. The "triple bottom line" of economic, social, and natural levels of capital (Roberts & Cohen 2002) is now widely used in the private as well as the public sector (Slaper & Hall 2011; Savitz 2006; Buckley 2003): "Although sustainable development was originally considered a trade-off between social, environmental, and economic values over the use of these three types of capital...it is now being viewed as a way to add value to all three pools of capital" (Roberts & Cohen 2002: 127).

"Environmental justice" is an essential category of concern intersecting environmental and social sustainability. Environmental justice traditionally concerns the "inequitable distribution of environmental risk and contamination" (Anguelovski 2016: 25), especially the historical and present-day toxic outputs of local industries. Schweitzer and Valenzuela (2004) and Forkenbrock and Schweitzer (1999) also address the air quality and noise impacts of transportation systems, respectively, on minority and low-income populations. In a literature review on "ecological sustainability, environmental justice, and energy use," Touché (2004) links the three topics together through the themes of intragenerational equity (what we share with each other in the present) and intergenerational equity (what we pass along to future generations).

Anguelovski (2016) reviews the research literature on urban environmental justice activist movements and looks at how the concept of environmental justice has evolved and expanded over time, examining as well the advent of new concepts and causes such as "environmental gentrification." Inevitably, low-income and minority communities are those most heavily affected by environmental risk and contamination, and those with the least amount of social capital for addressing those concerns – both in the US and worldwide (Bullard 2000; Burtynsky 2006; Sadd et al. 1999; Adeola 1995). Research by Collins, Munoz, & JaJa (2016) centers on "a class of hyper-polluters – the worst-of-the-worst – that disproportionately expose communities of color and low income populations to chemical releases," which may be the most efficient targets for environmental justice efforts. On the general theme of justice for low-income communities, Harris (2015) addresses social and economic justice considerations with regard to the highly charged topic of eminent domain for ED purposes.

Burby and Strong (1997) show how Black populations in the US differ from White populations in terms of their concerns about environmental hazards, and how that may affect communications with those populations in the case of an environmental emergency. Morrone and Basta (2013) use the term "local pollution havens" for economically vulnerable communities that are targets for environmentally hazardous industries. Morrone and Basta's (2013) case study focuses on siting for a federal uranium enrichment facility in Appalachian southeast Ohio, while Harper-Anderson (2012: 162) considers the implications for African Americans as "both environmental and economic epidemics are disproportionally affecting communities of color." Looking at the other side of the causality coin between poverty and environmental justice, Hollander (2003) argues that the most effective way to improve the environment at the community and country levels is to raise people out of poverty.

Sustainability can also be viewed as a means of promoting ED and not simply as a trade-off between economic growth and the environment (Shaffer 1995). Jones (2008) describes the "green collar economy," with particular sympathy toward low-income populations. Chapple et al. (2011) examine the frequently asserted potential of the "green economy" to drive innovation in ED – with mixed outcomes and conclusions. Bradshaw and Winn (2000) point out that there are already many examples of jobs created through sustainability practices, including formal and informal recycling practices. Slowinski (1998: 238), for example, examines "demanufacturing" as an industry for urban communities, explaining it as "the disassembly and recycling of obsolete consumer products such as TV sets, personal computers, refrigerators, washing machines, and air conditioners."

Hula (2001) notes that some aspects of environmental policy – including toxic waste management – now include ED as an explicit policy goal. In the case of toxic waste treatment, this broader focus has occurred in concert with the decentralization – a prevalent theme throughout this book – of authority and resources from the federal to the state and even to the local level (US Environmental Protection Agency 1999). Along with decentralization, according to Hula (2001: 194), has come a significant "movement from a punitive regulatory framework to one emphasizing cooperation, self-interest, and incentives."

Consistent with these trends toward sustainability *as* ED, this chapter will focus primarily on what I will term "sustainability-driven ED." What I mean by that somewhat cumbersome term is the creation of jobs and growth of businesses in the broadly-defined "sustainability industry." More to the point, sustainability is nice, but how do low-income communities create jobs, grow businesses, and build resilience within sustainability-related industries? "Doing well by doing good," as the expression goes. Colgan (1997: 133–134, italics in the original) argues:

> Sustainable development arises out of long-standing concerns for the wise use of resources, but it also is an alternate paradigm for how economic development and the environment relate to one another. The standard paradigm is for economic development to propose and for environmental regulation to oppose. From the resolution of this conflict, economic prosperity and environmental protection are supposed to result. But sustainable development forces consideration of both issues by both sides from the beginning. It does not *by itself* resolve the conflicts... but it may point toward common ground and suggest ways in which to get there.

Note that sustainability-driven ED can be very sensitive to geographic scale. That is, a sustainable industry that may be good for the country or the planet as a whole may have severe negative impacts on particular local communities. The world is replete with examples of low-income communities becoming environmentally toxic while recycling the waste of other, typically wealthier communities or countries (Leonard 2010).

As we will explore in this chapter, sustainability-driven ED can include such industries as solar and windmill farms, manufacturing materials (e.g., solar panels), recovering brownfields, and sustainable tourism. The chapter is organized into the following broad sections: sustainable energy and conservation, redevelopment, and sustainability through social equity.

Sustainable energy and conservation[2]

Windmill and solar fields (real estate, construction, maintenance), biofuels (agricultural production), and nuclear energy (uranium mining, construction, waste disposal): all of these industries have the potential to revitalize low-income – rural, especially – communities with economic revenues and new jobs (Pender, Weber, & Brown 2014). That potential comes with the caveat that many of these industries are based on natural resources and, as such, are subject to the "curse of natural resources" (Chapter 7). Tumbling petroleum prices since 2010 have had a major impact on communities that are dependent on non-sustainable energy industries such as coal and fracking, and they have had a similar impact on the demand for substitute sustainable energies such as biofuels (Kammen, Kapadia, & Fripp 2010; Wei, Patadia, & Kammen 2010; & Isserman 2009). Solar energy continues to battle dropping oil prices with dropping technology costs. Wind energy near populated or tourism-related areas faces challenges of competition for landscapes and land uses (Groth & Vogt 2014). In a Wales study, Munday, Bristow, and Cowell (2011) find relatively low job creation from wind energy in rural areas partly due to low local economic multiplier effects (Chapter 1).

The intention of this section is not to be completely discouraging regarding sustainable energies as drivers of ED. Instead, there is great need for more research on this topic – especially regarding *how* these industries can potentially grow more businesses and create more jobs in rural and other low-income communities. To date, many of these technologies are relatively new in terms of large-scale development compared to the more conventional tools in the ED box. There is some research on this topic in the ED and planning journals (Haddad, Taylor, & Owusu 2010), and there is also some in energy-related and geography journals (Munday, Bristow, & Cowell 2011; Wei, Patadia, & Kammen 2010).

The same applies to the ED potential of conservation-related industries, examples being the construction of greener buildings or the retrofitting of existing buildings for greater energy efficiency. There is an extensive literature on these topics (Kibert 2016), especially in the planning journals (Leland, Read, & Wittry 2015). Szibbo (2016) offers a start toward connecting research on conservation with the needs for ED, housing, and other social benefits in low-income communities.

Redevelopment

If there is anything that almost all low-income communities have in common, it is some combination of derelict, obsolete, disused, and potentially hazardous buildings and real estate. The research reviewed in this section is concerned with repurposing those properties from liabilities to potential assets for ED, including ED which benefits low-income populations and communities. Galster, Tatian, and Accordino (2006), for example, emphasize the familiar topic of citizen participation in assuring that public investments in revitalization are both effective and efficient. This section is organized by the following sub-sections: brownfields, downtown development, historic preservation, and resilience from natural and economic disaster.

Brownfields

"Brownfields" are nearly ubiquitous across rural, urban, and suburban landscapes (Hollander 2009). According to the Brownfield Action website,

> the Environmental Protection Agency (EPA) defines a brownfield as "real property, the expansion, redevelopment, or reuse of which may be complicated by the presence or potential presence of a hazardous substance, pollutant, or contaminant."
>
> Brownfields are often abandoned, closed or under-used industrial or commercial facilities, such as an abandoned factory in a town's former industrial section or a closed commercial building or warehouse in a suburban setting. Brownfields, however, can be located anywhere and can be quite small. For instance, many dry cleaning establishments and gas stations produced high levels of subsurface contaminants during their operation. A second growth forest or a vacant lot may contain contaminated fill or be the site of the illegal dumping of pollutants.
>
> *(Brownfield Action)*

Brownfields are not limited to low-income communities, but they are likely to be overrepresented in low-income and minority communities for a number of reasons related to environmental justice issues (mentioned above). Low-income and minority populations have often been limited to the least desirable real estate and housing options, which in turn are often located in close proximity to industrial sites and storage facilities. Ross and Leigh (2000: 367) review the literature related to inner-city revitalization and racial discrimination or "structural racism." They present the two as "woven together almost inextricably, presenting a complex and seemingly intractable problem for urban and regional planners, scholars, policymakers, activists, and citizens."

The opposite of a brownfield is a "greenfield," typically a previously undeveloped site, or a site that clearly did not have hazardous activities in the past. Remaining greenfield sites tend to be in the suburbs or exurbs of a community, helping to contribute to urban sprawl (Reese & Sands 2007). Ross and Leigh (2000: 374) assert that currently, with regard to minority populations and their communities,

> we have under way a process of "environmental redlining," or "brownlining" (i.e., identifying areas to be excluded from redevelopment consideration), that significantly diminishes efforts to improve the economic status and quality of life of populations residing in areas containing contaminated land (Leigh 1994).

As developers' attention has increasingly turned toward revitalizing city downtowns – or gentrifying low-income urban neighborhoods – urban brownfields represent an asset in terms of available, developable land with growing demand. Kotval-K (2016; see also De Sousa, Wu, & Westphal 2009) argues that public sector investment in brownfield development can be a cost-effective investment for governments, especially taking into account factors such as increased local property values and lower infrastructure costs compared with sprawling greenfield development. De Sousa (2005) finds a growing number of examples of successful brownfield remediation and redevelopment with significant social as well as economic benefits in a Milwaukee case study.

Howland's (2003, see also Howland 2000) case study of brownfields in Baltimore concludes that private sector investment can also be financially viable, depending on market conditions. McCarthy (2009) cautions that public sector investment in brownfields – rather than social needs, especially for minority and other low-income populations – may be prioritized for the most marketable sites. A national study by Meyer and Lyons (2000) and a case study of Charlotte, North Carolina, by Bacot and O'Dell (2006) suggest that the most efficient approach to brownfield development may often be a partnership of the public and private sector working toward "win-win" solutions.

However, Hula and Bromley-Trujillo (2010) assess the challenges of making an accurate evaluation of brownfield investment in terms of redevelopment and economic success. Howland (2007) reviews the literature of the employment impacts, in particular, of brownfield redevelopment, noting some of the research challenges with regard to this topic. Most studies to date are relatively short-term: "We still do not know what happens ten to twenty years down the road. Does crime decline, do local residents improve their economic standing, or does gentrification displace the previous residents? The answers to these questions will take a longer range analysis than we have seen so far" (Howland 2007: 102). The American Planning Association (2010) and Walzer, Hamm, and Sutton (2006) both consider factors related to successful brownfield development, and both emphasize the importance of broad community participation.

Downtown development

The downtowns of many major cities are thriving today, with extensive redevelopment and repopulation. Florida (2010) makes the connection between traditional urban centers and the attractions that can potentially draw in young members of the creative class. Among these attractions or amenities is a community that is densely populated, with a mixture of residential, commercial, dining, and entertainment options, which is typical of the traditional (perhaps nostalgic) downtown that the new urbanist movement seeks to reproduce. Downtowns can also offer unique opportunities as tourism attractions (Robertson 1999).

On the other hand, the downtowns of many smaller cities remain in deteriorated condition – victims of retail and services development that moved out further and further to the outskirts of town and along major highways. Walker (2009) provides a practical guide for "downtown planning for smaller and midsized communities." He echoes Richard Florida in advocating the importance of an appealing, robust downtown to help attract industry in the new ED environment. He cites the case of a major industry that selected Murfreesboro, Tennessee, as its relocation site, after showing an unusually keen interest in the city's recently redeveloped downtown area. The company's executives later explained that they viewed "the condition of a community's historic downtown [as] a litmus test…as it reflects the community's general economic health, progressiveness, and level of civic pride" (Walker 2009: 12).

Walker also notes the importance of downtowns in preserving a community's distinctive identity, or sense of place: "For some communities, downtown is their sole tangible link to the past, their only postcard location to take visitors, and their only source of genuine civic pride" (Walker 2009: 12). In a nationwide survey of small cities, Robertson (1999) emphasizes the vital importance of preserving and building on that sense of place for successful downtown development. Robertson's other conclusions from the study include the critical importance of public-private partnerships and building on existing downtown assets.

Historic preservation

It has been argued that the "preservation of historic properties and historic districts has become an important tool in efforts to preserve central-city neighborhoods and to promote economic development in blighted urban areas" (Coulson & Leichenko 2004: 1587, quoted by Ryberg-Webster & Kinahan 2014). In their research review on the topic, Ryberg-Webster and Kinahan (2014: 119) state: "Historic buildings and neighborhoods are massive existing investments – they are part of the existing infrastructure of cities – and understanding how these resources relate to contemporary urban revitalization is imperative." They conclude: "To forge stronger partnerships, planners and policy makers need to have current knowledge about preservation tools, strategies, and benefits, while preservationists need to be versed in urban economic realities. To overcome ingrained perceptions that preservation is an elitist, niche industry, preservationists must be flexible, willing to negotiate, and come to the table with new ideas and data to support their arguments" (Ryberg-Webster & Kinahan 2014: 132).

The *Journal of the American Planning Association* devotes a special issue to historic preservation (Minner & Holleran 2016): Appler and Rumbach (2016) study the relationship between historic preservation and planning for community resilience against natural disasters such as flooding; Avrami (2016) reviews the research literature related to the sometimes-tense relationship between historic preservation and sustainability goals such as energy conservation, citizen participation, diversity, and equity; and Andrews et al. (2016) study the potential for conflicts – as well as resolutions – between historic preservation projects and energy conservation building codes. Furthermore, in a case study of a designated historic district in New York City, McCabe and Ellen (2016) find that preservation initiatives can adversely affect low-income and minority residents of the district. On the other hand, in a San Francisco case study Buckley & Graves (2016) consider how the preservation of historic landmarks can potentially provide a tool for creating a more inclusive environment for "underserved populations."

Historic preservation often centers on a city's downtown area, but this is not always the case. In the South, for example, many historic structures can be found in former Black business districts prior to desegregation (Miller & Cochran 2013). Rural areas may have buildings of historic interest that were birthplaces of politicians, musicians, or other famous public figures. There may also be historic structures related to tragic events, which have the potential for dark tourism (Skipper 2016; Barton & Leonard 2010; Chapter 7).

Rypkema (2005) provides a guide to "the economics of historic preservation," helping to provide low-income communities with justification for investment in their historic structures and districts. He mentions industrial incubators as being among the potential ED applications of redeveloped historic buildings, especially in central cities. Tumber (2014: 236) advocates the use of such buildings for restoring traditional craft or manufacturing "workshops, which build on a community's historical skill base and infrastructure." Among Rypkema's (2005: 11, 19, 20–21, 81) arguments on behalf of historic preservation investment, many of them echo themes touched upon throughout this book:

- "Dollar for dollar, historic preservation is one of the highest job-generating economic development options available." Preservation construction tends to be highly labor-intensive, for example, and renovation projects are more likely than new construction projects to purchase materials locally.
- "Civic centers, aquariums, and gambling may sound more exciting, but incremental, property-by-property reinvestment is more realistic and will lead to a more stable local economy."
- "Historic preservation can be part of a strategy to attract industrial investment….[A]n increasing number of…companies recognize that their real assets are not the plants and equipment, but the people who work for them, and that these employees want a quality place to raise their families. Good industrial recruiters recognize that their communities' historic resources are a major selling point in attracting new businesses."
- "[F]or heritage tourism to be sustainable…successful small towns have discovered that their strategy must be based on three principles: 1) it must be

real – fake Old West towns or Bavarian villages may work for a while but the appeal won't last; 2) it must have quality if it is to survive as a…success; and 3) it needs to be differentiated. The unique qualities of a community need to be identified, preserved, enhanced, and marketed."

Resilience from natural and economic disaster

We are painfully aware of natural disasters and their devastating impact on communities across the US: tornados, hurricanes, forest fires, earthquakes, tsunamis, floods, droughts. A disaster can be defined as "a sudden, calamitous event that seriously disrupts the functioning of a community or society and causes human, material, and economic or environmental losses that exceed the community's or society's ability to cope using its own resources. Though often caused by nature, disasters can have human origins" (International Federation of Red Cross and Red Crescent Societies).

Although disasters can strike anywhere, including affluent neighborhoods and communities, low-income neighborhoods and communities are often the most vulnerable to devastating impacts from those disasters. Low-income neighborhoods are more likely to be located in flood-prone zones; homes, and commercial and public buildings are more likely to be in poor shape or not built to modern codes; residents are more likely to be un- or under-insured; and local medical, psychological, and other services may be underrepresented and overwhelmed. An already-weak local economy may be devastated by the immediate impact of the disaster, combined with a "flood" of disaster relief supplies and services that compete with existing local businesses.

Disasters can also result from a variety of human actions, according to the International Red Cross definition quoted above. Environmental contamination, discussed above, is more likely to affect minority and other low-income and vulnerable populations. The same may be true of failures in dams or levees, which, most notoriously, we saw was the case with New Orleans during and in the aftermath of Hurricane Katrina. Olshansky et al. (2008; see also Olshansky 2006) summarize the lessons learned for planning from the perspective of a few years after the Katrina disaster. Johnson, Farrell, and Toji (1997) assess the major local employment impacts of the 1992 civil unrest in Los Angeles and the disappointing results of the subsequent rebuilding efforts.

A disaster can also present an opportunity for low-income communities for "building back better," to borrow the phrase used by authors in a special issue of the *Journal of the American Planning Association* (Kim & Olshansky 2014). *Community Development* also devotes a special issue to community responses to disaster (Hales, Walzer, & Calvin 2012). Much of the disaster research should remind the reader of themes that prevail throughout this book. Research by Freitag et al. (2014) on community readiness for disaster, for example, highlights the uses of asset-based community development (ABCD), appreciative inquiry, and capacity-building (Chapter 5). All those tools imply some degree of citizen participatory planning (Chapter 5) to ensure that redevelopment reflects the values and interests of the local population and not those of outsiders or local power brokers. Plans developed for all communities across the Mississippi Gulf Coast following Hurricane Katrina, under the direction of new urbanist Andrés Duany (Chapter 3), involved extensive public participation throughout the charrette (a short, intense planning workshop) processes (Mississippi Renewal Forum; Talen 2008). Those participatory processes included the residents of the predominantly low-income, African American city of Moss Point, Mississippi (Mississippi Renewal Forum: Moss Point; Miller 2006). Duval-Diop, Curtis, and Clark (2010) provide a case study of "enhancing equity with public participatory GIS in hurricane rebuilding," working with faith-based organizations in New Orleans post-Katrina.

Similarly, economic diversity (Chapter 7) is the focus of Xiao and Drucker's (2013: 157) study of flooding disasters, "Does economic diversity enhance regional disaster resilience?" The answer is yes: "The effect of diversity on resilience…was unambiguous. Diverse counties better weathered a disaster-generated downturn and returned more quickly to long-term patterns of economic growth. Diversity was of greater benefit to both employment and per capita income growth following the flood than in normal situations."

Webb (2006) reviews the literature concerned with assessing the long-term "consequences of disasters: sources of resilience and vulnerability," with particular attention to the needs of private sector businesses. Clower (2006) reviews the tools and techniques available to support "economic impact analysis for disaster assessment and planning."

Although abrupt economic downturns in a community are often not recognized as "disasters," the impact of a crisis such as a major plant closure may be similar in its psychological and social impacts for a low-income community (Reese 2006; Minchin 2006; Miller 2006; Mayer & Greenberg 2001). According to a study by Ananat, Gassman-Pines, and Gibson-Davis (2011), "[c]hanges in local economic conditions arising from plant closings in North Carolina had large measurable effects on children's reading and math scores, especially among older kids" (quoted by Putnam & Campbell 2016: 246). Based on their research on paper plant closures, Root and Park (2016, citing Minchin 2006 and Sirkin & Stalk 1990) suggest several ways in which closing industries can help employees – and their communities – make a more successful transition to a new economic future, including counseling on unemployment benefits, retirement options, and career transitions.

Sustainability through social equity

Truly sustainable community ED must include attention to social equity as well as the physical environment (Sachs 2015). The two topics included in this section are the contentious living wage movement and the relatively new reformulation of ED as wealth creation.

Living wages

Glickman (1997), Pollin (2005), and Pollin and Luce (1998) all discuss the complex concept and definition of a living wage. Generally, it is understood to mean a wage that allows a worker and his or her family to live above the poverty level in the community in which they work. In a special issue of the *Economic Development Review*, Pollin (2005) quotes Glickman's (1997: 66) expanded definition of living wage as more broadly motivated by the desire for labor to provide "the ability to support families, to maintain self-respect, and to have both the means and the leisure to participate in the civic life of the nation." Pollin (2005) connects this concept with Sen's (1999; Chapter 3) model of providing people with the basic "capabilities" to live full, productive, and satisfying lives. More challenging, however, are efforts to quantify, provide policy projects for, and operationalize the concept (Neumark et al. 2013; Adams & Neumark 2005; Pollin 2005).

The living wage movement has inspired often-heated policy debates in a variety of cities across the US, from Santa Monica, California (Sander & Williams 2005), to Detroit (Reynolds & Vortkamp 2005). The movement has also expanded from cities to college campus communities (Living Wage Action Coalition). Critiques of minimum wage laws include questions of whether businesses will be driven out of cities with these added labor costs. Lester (2012, 2011) argues that no, they will not. Neither do living wage laws generally add additional costs to already-struggling municipal or nonprofit organization budgets, according to research by Reynolds and Vortkamp (2005).

However, Sander and Williams (2005) find that living wage laws can reduce employment opportunities for low-income workers. It is also likely that living wage laws result in reduced benefits for workers as their wages rise, according to Toikka, Yelowitz, & Neveu (2005: 77): "If society wants to improve the economic status of low income families, it seems to us that the best way to do this [instead] is through targeted tax credits that go to families most in need and do not trigger either additional taxes or losses in benefits from public programs."

Wealth creation

The concept of ED as wealth creation dates back to some of the earliest definitions of local ED, one of which was "the process of creating wealth through the mobilization of human, financial, capital, physical and natural resources to generate marketable goods and services" (American Economic Development Council 1984; Chapter 3). I was surprised and intrigued to find this largely overlooked concept return to the ED debate in a special issue of *Community Development* (Ratner & Markley 2016). Ratner and Markley credit support from the Ford Foundation and early work by researchers at the US Department of Agriculture Economic Research Service (Pender, Marré, & Reeder 2012; see also Pender, Weber, & Brown 2014). The special issue editors explain the concept thus:

> What is needed is a systems approach to the development of communities and economies that explicitly connects economic, social, and environmental opportunities and impacts. Such an intentional approach will help to promote a more equitable distribution of income and financial wealth, and to improve

and increase the other forms of capital required for economic revitalization and sustainable livelihoods.

This framework for rural development recognizes that jobs are not "created" in a vacuum but instead result from investments in innovation, infrastructure, skills, human and environmental health, and the capacity to change regulations and resource allocations to respond to a changing world. Jobs result from new relationships that create new economic opportunities. This framework aims for inclusive, sustainable development based on the following assumptions:

- Wealth, broadly defined, is the foundation of prosperity, not just income.
- Poor places and people will stay poor unless they are connected to larger economies.
- Poor people and places have assets which, if properly developed, can contribute to larger regional economies.
- The economy does better as a whole when more people are doing better.

(Ratner & Markley 2016: 437–438)

The extended quote above reads like a summary of many of the themes that have prevailed throughout this book. Lyons and Wyckoff (2014) connect wealth creation with "social entrepreneurship," or "the application of the mindset, processes, tools, and technique of business entrepreneurship to the pursuit of a social and/or environmental mission" (Kickul & Lyons 2012: 1, cited by Lyons & Wyckoff 2014; see also Lyons 2015).

The *Community Development* special issue is concerned particularly with wealth creation in rural communities (Lyman, Grimm, & Evans 2014). Two of the articles have an international focus, on Pakistan in the Developing World (Aijazi & Angeles 2014) and on remote rural communities in Europe (Alonso 2014). The literature of this new conceptualization of wealth creation, as of the writing of this book, is only a few years old and is still limited in its scope. I find it one of the most promising new paths forward for ED on behalf of low-income communities. I hope to follow the concept in the near future as it is developed further and expanded to include low-income urban communities in the US.

TAKEAWAY FOR ED ACTION: BUILDING SUSTAINABLE ED FOR LOW-INCOME COMMUNITIES

- *Sustainable development is not just for tree huggers.* Truly sustainable development for communities includes concern for the natural environment, social equity, and also ED. Environmental justice is one important way in which those three concerns overlap and can mutually reinforce one another.
- *Sustainability does not have to be a "job killer."* To the contrary, sustainability can be a productive route to creating employment and growing businesses

in your community. Recycling, solar energy, and retrofitting existing buildings for energy conservation are just a few industries with development opportunities.

- *Brownfields can be a huge development headache and public health hazard –* *but also a potential asset for redevelopment in many low-income communities.* Combining public sector resources and private sector investment is generally the most promising route for putting abandoned land to new use.
- *Downtown has new importance, as the cornerstone for building a creative community in the modern economy.* Downtowns contribute to attracting and retaining small businesses and creative people. Vital downtowns can provide your community with a positive image and inspiration for overall ED.
- *A diverse economy and a well-educated population are your community's best investments in resilience against natural, man-made, and economic disaster.*
- *Living wages: pick your fights carefully.* This movement may not be the fight you want to prioritize.
- *Viewing ED as equitable wealth creation, rather than just counting jobs created and businesses opened, may be the next promising framework for advancing ED in low-income communities.* Follow the development of this literature in the near future. The second edition of this book may require a new title!

Notes

1 Research by Chad Miller, Associate Professor of Economic Development at the University of Southern Mississippi, brought this concept to my attention.
2 I would like to thank Nadine Armstrong, a University of Southern Mississippi Geography doctoral student, for contributing her research to this section.

References

Adams, Scott, & David Neumark. 2005. Living wage effects: New and improved evidence. *Economic Development Quarterly* 19(1): 80–102.

Adeola, Francis O. 1995. Demographic and socioeconomic differentials in residential propinquity to hazardous waste sites and environmental illness. *Journal of the Community Development Society* 26(1): 15–39.

Aijazi, Omer, & Leonora C. Angeles. 2014. Community development and other extra-religious functions of Islamic schools: A contemporary perspective from the voices of stakeholders in two madrassas in Pakistan. *Community Development* 45(5): 490–506.

Alonso, A.D. 2014. Socioeconomic development in an ultra-peripheral European region: The role of a food regulatory council as a social anchor. *Community Development* 45(5): 458–473.

American Economic Development Council. 1984. *Economic Development Today*. Chicago: American Economic Development Council.

American Planning Association. 2010. *Creating Community-Based Brownfields Redevelopment Strategies*. Retrieved August 26, 2016: https://www.planning.org/research/brownfields/.

Ananat, Elizabeth, Anna Gassman-Pines, & Christina M. Gibson-Davis. 2011. The effects of local employment losses on children's educational achievement, in Greg J. Duncan &

Richard J. Murnane, eds., *Whither Opportunity? Rising Inequality, Schools, and Children's Life Chances*, 299–313. New York: Spencer and Russell Sage Foundations.

Andrews, Clinton, David Hattis, David Listokin, Jennifer Senick, Gabriel Sherman, & Jennifer Souder. 2016. Energy-efficient reuse of existing commercial buildings. *Journal of the American Planning Association* 82(2): 113–133.

Anguelovski, Isabelle. 2016. From toxic sites to parks as (green) LULUs? New challenges of inequity, privilege, gentrification, and exclusion for urban environmental justice. *Journal of Planning Literature* 31(1): 23–36.

Appler, Douglas, & Andrew Rumbach. 2016. Building community resilience through historic preservation. *Journal of the American Planning Association* 82(2): 92–103.

Avrami, Erica. 2016. Making historic preservation sustainable. *Journal of the American Planning Association* 82(2): 104–112.

Bacot, Hunter, & Cindy O'Dell. 2006. Establishing indicators to evaluate brownfield redevelopment. *Economic Development Quarterly* 20(2): 142–161.

Barth, Brian. 2016. Before it's too late. *Planning* 82(8): 14–21.

Barton, Alan W., & Sarah J. Leonard. 2010. Incorporating social justice in tourism planning: Racial reconciliation and sustainable community development in the Deep South. *Community Development* 41(3): 298–322.

Bauman, Yoram, & Grady Klein. 2014. *The Cartoon Introduction to Climate Change*. Washington, DC: Island.

Beatley, Timothy, & Kristy Manning. 1997. *The Ecology of Place: Planning for Environment, Economy, and Community*, 2nd ed. Washington, DC: Island.

Berke, Philip R., & Maria M. Conroy. 2000. Are we planning for sustainable development? An evaluation of 30 comprehensive plans. *Journal of the American Planning Association* 66(1): 21–33.

Bradshaw, Ted K., & Karri Winn. 2000. Gleaners, do-gooders, and balers: Options for linking sustainability and economic development. *Journal of the Community Development Society* 31(1): 112–129.

Bricker, Kelley S., Rosemary Black, & Stuart Cottrell. 2012. *Sustainable Tourism and the Millennium Development Goals: Effecting Positive Change*. Burlington, MA: Jones & Bartlett Learning.

Brownfield Action. What is a "brownfield"? Retrieved August 24, 2016: http://brownfielda ction.org/brownfieldaction/brownfield_basics.

Buckley, James M., & Donna Graves. 2016. Tangible benefits from intangible resources: Using social and cultural history to plan neighborhood futures. *Journal of the American Planning Association* 82(2): 152–166.

Buckley, Ralf. 2003. Environmental inputs and outputs in ecotourism: Geotourism with a positive triple bottom line? *Journal of Ecotourism* 2(1): 76–82.

Bullard, Robert D. 2000. *Dumping in Dixie: Race, Class, and Environmental Quality*, 3rd ed. Boulder, CO: Westview.

Burby, Raymond J., & Denise E. Strong. 1997. Coping with chemicals: Blacks, whites, planners, and industrial pollution. *Journal of the American Planning Association* 63(4): 469–480.

Burtynsky, Edward. 2006. *Manufactured Landscapes* [documentary film]. Directed by Jennifer Baichwal. Toronto: Foundry Films.

Bustillo, Miguel. 2016. Oklahoma earthquake felt in several U.S. states, as oil wells draw scrutiny. *Wall Street Journal*. September 3: http://www.wsj.com/articles/earthquake-sha kes-swath-of-midwest-from-missouri-to-oklahoma-1472906357.

Chapple, Karen. 2015. *Planning Sustainable Cities and Regions: Towards More Equitable Development*. New York: Routledge.

Chapple, Karen, Cynthia Kroll, T. William Lester, & Sergio Montero. 2011. Innovation in the green economy: An extension of the regional innovation system model? *Economic Development Quarterly* 25(1): 5–25.

Clower, Terry L. 2006. Economic impact analysis for disaster assessment and planning: A review of tools and techniques. *Applied Research in Economic Development* 3(1): 19–33.

Colgan, Charles S. 1997. "Sustainable development" and economic development policy: Lessons from Canada. *Economic Development Quarterly* 11(2): 123–137.

Collins, Mary B., Ian Munoz, & Joseph JaJa. 2016. Linking toxic outliers to environmental justice communities. *Environmental Research Letters* 11(1). Retrieved August 23, 2016: http://iopscience.iop.org/article/10.1088/1748-9326/11/1/015004/meta.

Coulson, N. Edward, & Robin M. Leichenko. 2004. Historic preservation and neighborhood change. *Urban Studies* 41(8): 1587–1600.

Crowe, Jessica A., & Tony J. Silva. 2015. The hope-reality gap: Rural community officials' perceptions of unconventional shale development as a means to increase local population and revitalize resource extraction. *Community Development* 46(4): 329–340.

Daniels, Tom. 2014. *The Environmental Planning Handbook for Sustainable Communities and Regions*, 2nd ed. Chicago: APA Planners Press.

De Sousa, Christopher A. 2005. Policy performance and brownfield redevelopment in Milwaukee, Wisconsin. *Professional Geographer* 57(2): 312–327.

De Sousa, Christopher A., Changshan Wu, & Lynne M. Westphal. 2009. Assessing the effect of publicly assisted brownfield redevelopment on surrounding property values. *Economic Development Quarterly* 23(2): 95–110.

Duval-Diop, Dominique; Andrew Curtis, & Annie Clark. 2010. Enhancing equity with public participatory GIS in hurricane rebuilding: Faith-based organizations, community mapping, and policy advocacy. *Community Development* 41(1): 32–49.

Economist. 2015. The blue economy: Growth, opportunity and a sustainable ocean economy. Retrieved November 4, 2016: https://www.eiuperspectives.economist.com/sustainability/blue-economy.

Florida, Richard. 2010. Building the creative community, in Japonica Brown-Saracino, ed., *The Gentrification Debates*, 345–354. New York: Routledge.

Forkenbrock, David J., & Lisa A. Schweitzer. 1999. Environmental justice in transportation planning. *Journal of the American Planning Association* 65(1): 96–111.

Freitag, Robert C., Daniel B. Abramson, Manish Chalana, & Maximilian Dixon. 2014. Whole community resilience: An asset-based approach to enhancing adaptive capacity before a disruption. *Journal of the American Planning Association* 80(4): 324–335.

Galster, George, Peter Tatian, & John Accordino. 2006. Targeting investments for neighborhood revitalization. *Journal of the American Planning Association* 72(4): 457–474.

Glickman, Lawrence B. 1997. *A Living Wage: American Workers and the Making of Consumer Society*. Ithaca, NY: Cornell University Press.

Gough, Meghan Z. 2015. Reconciling livability and sustainability: Conceptual and practical implications for planning. *Journal of Planning Education and Research* 35(2): 145–160.

Groth, Theresa, & Christine A. Vogt. 2014. Renewable wind farm development: Social, environmental and economic features important to residents. *Renewable Energy* 63: 1–8.

Haddad, Monica A., Gary Taylor, & Francis Owusu. 2010. Locational choices of the ethanol industry in the Midwest Corn Belt. *Economic Development Quarterly* 24(1): 74–86.

Hales, Brent, Norman Walzer, & James Calvin. 2012. Community responses to disasters: A foundation for recovery. *Community Development* 43(5): 540–549.

Hardy, Kirsten, & Timothy W. Kelsey. 2015. Local income related to Marcellus shale activity in Pennsylvania. *Community Development* 46(4): 329–340.

Harper-Anderson, Elsie. 2012. Exploring what greening the economy means for African American workers, entrepreneurs, and communities. *Economic Development Quarterly* 26(2): 162–177.

Harris, Kirk E. 2015. Because we can doesn't mean we should and if we do: Urban communities, social and economic justice, and local economic-development-driven eminent domain practices. *Economic Development Quarterly* 29(3): 245–261.

Hollander, Jack M. 2003. *The Real Environmental Crisis: Why Poverty, not Affluence, Is the Environment's Number One Enemy*. Berkeley: University of California Press.

Hollander, Justin B. 2009. *Polluted and Dangerous: America's Worst Abandoned Properties and What Can Be Done about Them*. Burlington, VT: University of Vermont Press.

Houma Today. 2016. Isle de Jean Charles community to receive $52 million to relocate. January 21: http://www.houmatoday.com/article/20160121/HURBLOG/160129923.

Howland, Marie. 2007. Employment effects of brownfield redevelopment: What do we know from the literature? *Journal of Planning Literature* 22(2): 91–107.

Howland, Marie. 2003. Private initiative and public responsibility for the redevelopment of industrial brownfields: Three Baltimore case studies. *Economic Development Quarterly* 17(4): 367–381.

Howland, Marie. 2000. The impact of contamination on the Canton/Southeast Baltimore land market. *Journal of the American Planning Association* 66(4): 411–420.

Hula, Richard C. 2001. Changing priorities and programs in toxic waste policy: The emergence of economic development as a policy goal. *Economic Development Quarterly* 15(2): 181–199.

Hula, Richard C., & Rebecca Bromley-Trujillo. 2010. Cleaning up the mess: Redevelopment of urban brownfields. *Economic Development Quarterly* 24(3): 276–287.

International Federation of Red Cross and Red Crescent Societies. What is a disaster? Retrieved August 26, 2016: http://www.ifrc.org/en/what-we-do/disaster-managem ent/about-disasters/what-is-a-disaster/.

Isle de Jean Charles, Louisiana. The environment. Retrieved September 11, 2016: http:// www.isledejeancharles.com/the-environment/.

Jepson, Jr., Edward. 2001. Sustainability and planning: Diverse concepts and close associations. *Journal of Planning Literature* 15(4): 499–510.

Jepson, Jr., Edward, & Anna L. Haines. 2015. Zoning for sustainability: A review and analysis of the zoning ordinances of 32 cities in the United States. *Journal of the American Planning Association* 80(3): 239–252.

Johnson, Jr., James H., Walter C.Farrell, Jr., & Dean S. Toji. 1997. Assessing the employment impacts of the Los Angeles civil unrest of 1992: Furthering racial divisions. *Economic Development Quarterly* 11(3): 225–235.

Jones, Van. 2008. *The Green Collar Economy*. New York: HarperOne.

Kammen, Daniel M., Kamal Kapadia, & Matthias Fripp. 2010. Putting renewables and energy efficiency to work: How many jobs can the clean energy industry generate in the US? *Energy Policy* 38(2): 919–931.

Kibert, Charles J. 2016. *Sustainable Construction: Green Building Design and Delivery*. Hoboken, NJ: John Wiley & Sons.

Kickul, Jill, & Thomas S. Lyons. 2012. *Understanding Social Entrepreneurship: The Relentless Pursuit of Mission in an Ever-Changing World*. New York: Routledge.

Kim, Karl, & Robert B. Olshansky. 2014. Introduction to the special issue: The theory and practice of building back better. *Journal of the American Planning Association* 80(4): 289–292.

Kotval-K, Zeenat. 2016. Brownfield redevelopment: Why public investments can pay off. *Economic Development Quarterly* 30(3): 275–282.

Leigh, Nancey G. 1994. Focus: Environmental constraints to brownfield redevelopment. *Economic Development Quarterly* 8(4): 325–328.

Leigh, Nancey G., & Edward J. Blakely. 2013. *Planning Local Economic Development: Theory and Practice*, 5th ed. Thousand Oaks, CA: Sage.

Leland, Suzanne M., Dustin C. Read, & Michael Wittry. 2015. Analyzing the perceived benefits of LEED-certified and Energy Star-certified buildings in the realm of local economic development. *Economic Development Quarterly* 29(4): 363–375.

Leonard, Annie. 2010. *The Story of Stuff: How Our Obsession with Stuff Is Trashing the Planet, Our Communities, and Our Health – and a Vision for Change*. New York: Free Press.

Lester, T. William. 2012. Labor standards and local economic development: Do living wage provisions harm economic growth? *Journal of Planning Education and Research* 32(2): 331–348.

Lester, T. William. 2011. The impact of living wage laws on urban economic development patterns and the local business climate: Evidence from California cities. *Economic Development Quarterly* 25(3): 237–254.

Living Wage Action Coalition. Retrieved September 24, 2016: http://www.livingwageaction.org.

Loh, Carolyn G., & Anna C. Osland. 2016. Local land use planning responses to hydraulic fracturing. *Journal of the American Planning Association* 82(3): 222–235.

Loomis, Ilima. 2015. A "blue economy" for Belize: A modeling program helps coastal zone planners put a price tag on natural resources. *Planning*. June: 28–32.

Low, Sarah A., & Andrew M. Isserman. 2009. Ethanol and the local economy: Industry trends, location factors, economic impacts, and risks. *Economic Development Quarterly* 23(1): 71–88.

Lyman, Martha W., Curt Grimm, & Julie R. Evans. 2014. Community forests as a wealth creation strategy for rural communities. *Community Development* 45(5): 474–489.

Lyons, Thomas S. 2015. Entrepreneurship and community development: What matters and why? *Community Development* 46(5): 456–460.

Lyons, Thomas S. & Barbara Wyckoff. 2014. Facilitating community wealth building: Understanding the roles played and capacities needed by coordinating institutions. *Community Development* 45(5): 443–457.

Manzi, Tony, & Karen Lucas. 2010. *Social Sustainability in Urban Areas: Communities, Connectivity, and the Urban Fabric*. London: Earthscan.

Mayer, Henry J., & Michael R. Greenberg. 2001. Coming back from economic despair: Case studies of small- and medium-size American cities. *Economic Development Quarterly* 15(3): 203–216.

McCabe, Brian, & Ingrid G. Ellen. 2016. Does preservation accelerate neighborhood change? Examining the impact of historic preservation in New York City. *Journal of the American Planning Association* 82(2): 134–146.

McCarthy, Linda. 2009. Off the mark? Efficiency in targeting the most marketable sites rather than equity in public assistance for brownfield redevelopment. *Economic Development Quarterly* 23(3): 211–228.

Meyer, Peter B., & Thomas S. Lyons. 2000. Lessons from private sector brownfield redevelopers. *Journal of the American Planning Association* 66(1): 46–57.

Miller, Mark M. 2006. Disaster and recovery in Moss Point, Mississippi. *Applied Research in Economic Development* 3(1): 48–56.

Miller, Mark M., & David Cochran. 2013. Telling the story of African-Americans in Hattiesburg, Mississippi: A case study of socially sustainable tourism. *Southeastern Geographer* 53(4): 428–454.

Minchin, Timothy J. 2006. "Just like a death": The closing of the International Paper Company mill in Mobile, Alabama, and the deindustrialization of the South, 2000–2005. *Alabama Review* 59(1): 44–77.

Minner, Jennifer, & Michael Holleran. 2016. Introduction to the special issue: Historic preservation and planning in the US. *Journal of the American Planning Association* 82(2): 69–71.

Mississippi Renewal Forum. Retrieved May 28, 2014: http://www.mississippirenewal.com.

Mississippi Renewal Forum. *Moss Point*. Prepared by the HOK Planning Group: Steve Schukraft, Todd Meyer, & Dhaval Barbhaya. Retrieved July 29, 2016: http://mississipp irenewal.com/documents/Pres_MossPoint.pdf.

Morrone, Michele, & Tania B. Basta. 2013. Public opinion, local pollution havens, and environmental justice: A case study of a community visioning project in Appalachian Ohio. *Community Development* 44(3): 350–363.

Munday, Max, Gill Bristow, & Richard Cowell. 2011. Wind farms in rural areas: How far do community benefits from wind farms represent a local economic development opportunity? *Journal of Rural Studies* 27(1): 1–12.

Murdock, Steve H., Sherrill Spies, Kofi Effah, Steve White, Richard Krannich, J.D. Wulf-horst, Krissa Wrigley, F. Larry Leistritz, & Randy Sell. 1998. Waste facility siting in rural communities in the United States: An assessment of impacts and their effects on residents' levels of support/opposition. *Journal of the Community Development Society* 29(1): 90–118.

Neumark, David, Matthew Thompson, Francesco Brindisi, Leslie Koyle, & Clayton Reck. 2013. Simulating the economic impacts of living wage mandates using new public and adminis-trative data: Evidence for New York City. *Economic Development Quarterly* 27(4): 271–283.

Olshansky, Robert B. 2006. Planning after Hurricane Katrina. *Journal of the American Planning Association* 72(2): 147–153.

Olshansky, Robert B., Laurie A. Johnson, Jedidiah Horne, & Brendan Nee. 2008. Longer view: Planning for the rebuilding of New Orleans. *Journal of the American Planning Association* 74(3): 273–287.

Pender, John L., Alexander Marré, & Richard Reeder. 2012. *Rural Wealth Creation: Con-cepts, Strategies, and Measures.* Economic Research Report No. ERR-131. United States Department of Agriculture Economic Research Service: http://www.ers.usda.gov/publications/err-economic-research-report/err131.aspx.

Pender, John L., Jeremy G. Weber, & Jason P. Brown. 2014. Sustainable rural development and wealth creation: Five observations based on emerging energy opportunities. *Economic Development Quarterly* 28(1): 73–86.

Pollin, Robert. 2005. Evaluating living wage laws in the United States: Good intentions and economic reality in conflict? *Economic Development Quarterly* 19(1): 3–24.

Pollin, Robert, & Stephanie Luce. 1998. *The Living Wage: Building a Fair Economy.* New York: New Press.

Portney, Kent E. 2013. *Taking Sustainable Cities Seriously: Economic Development, the Environment, and Quality of Life in American Cities*, 2nd ed. Cambridge: MIT Press.

Putnam, Robert D., & David E. Campbell. 2016. *Our Kids: The American Dream in Crisis.* New York: Simon & Schuster.

Ratner, Shanna, & Deborah Markley. 2016. Rural wealth creation as a sustainable economic development strategy: Introduction to the special issue. *Community Development* 45(5): 435–442.

Reese, Laura A. 2006. Economic versus natural disasters: If Detroit had a hurricane.... *Economic Development Quarterly* 20(3): 219–231.

Reese, Laura A., & Gary Sands. 2007. Sustainability and local ED in Canada and the United States. *International Journal of Sustainable Development Planning* 2(1): 25–43.

Reynolds, David, & Jean Vortkamp. 2005. The effect of Detroit's living wage law on nonprofit organizations. *Economic Development Quarterly* 19(1): 45–61.

Roberts, Brian, & Michael Cohen. 2002. Enhancing sustainable development by triple value adding to the core business of government. *Economic Development Quarterly* 16(2): 127–137.

Robertson, Kent A. 1999. Can small-city downtowns remain viable? A national study of development issues and strategies. *Journal of the American Planning Association* 65(3): 270–283.

Root, Kenneth A., & Rosemarie J. Park. 2016. *Surviving Job Loss: Papermakers in Maine and Minnesota*. Kalamazoo, MI: W.E. Upjohn Institute for Employment Research.

Ross, Catherine L., & Nancey G. Leigh. 2000. Planning, urban revitalization, and the inner city: An exploration of structural racism. *Journal of Planning Literature* 14(3): 367–380.

Rubin, Barry M., & Mark D. Hilton. 1996. Identifying the local economic development impacts of global climate change. *Economic Development Quarterly* 10(3): 262–279.

Ryberg-Webster, Stephanie, & Kelly L. Kinahan. 2014. Historic preservation and urban revitalization in the twenty-first century. *Journal of Planning Literature* 29(2): 119–139.

Rypkema, Donovan D. 2005. *The Economics of Historic Preservation: A Community Leader's Guide*. Washington, DC: National Trust for Historic Preservation.

Sachs, Jeffrey D. 2015. *The Age of Sustainable Development*. New York: Columbia University Press.

Sadd, James L., Manuel Pastor, Jr., J. Thomas Boer, & Lori D. Snyder. 1999. "Every breath you take…": The demographics of toxic air releases in Southern California. *Economic Development Quarterly* 13(2): 107–123.

Sander, Richard H., & E. Douglass Williams. 2005. Santa Monica's minimum wage: Assessing the living wage movement's new frontier. *Economic Development Quarterly* 19(1): 25–44.

Savitz, Andrew. 2006. *The Triple Bottom Line: How Today's Best-Run Companies Are Achieving Economic, Social and Environmental Success – and How You Can Too*. San Francisco: Jossey-Bass.

Schweitzer, Lisa, & Abel Valenzuela, Jr. 2004. Environmental injustice and transportation: The claims and the evidence. *Journal of Planning Literature* 18(4): 383–398.

Sen, Amartya. 1999. *Development as Freedom*. New York: Knopf.

Shaffer, Ron. 1995. Achieving sustainable economic development in communities. *Journal of the Community Development Society* 26(2): 145–154.

Sirkin, Harold L., & George Stalk, Jr. 1990. Fix the process, not the problem. *Harvard Business Review* 68(4): 26–33.

Skipper, Jodi. 2016. Community development through reconciliation tourism: The Behind the Big House Program in Holly Springs, Mississippi. *Community Development* 47(4): 514–529.

Slaper, Timothy F., & Tanya J. Hall. 2011. The triple bottom line: What is it and how does it work? *Indiana Business Review* 86(1): 4–8.

Sloan, Philip, Claudia Simons-Kaufman, & Willy Legrand. 2012. *Sustainable Hospitality and Tourism as Motors for Development: Case Studies from Developing Regions of the World*. New York: Routledge.

Slowinski, Gene. 1998. Remanufacturing: The emergence of an urban industry. *Economic Development Quarterly* 12(3): 238–247.

Svensson, Lisa E., & Linwood Pendleton, eds. 2014. *Transitioning to a New Blue Economy*. *Proceedings of the December 2013 Nicholas Institute for Environmental Policy Solutions*. Retrieved September 23, 2016: https://nicholasinstitute.duke.edu/sites/default/files/publications/ni_cp_14-01_final_0.pdf.

Szibbo, Nicola. 2016. Lessons for LEED® for neighborhood development, social equity, and affordable housing. *Journal of the American Planning Association* 82(1): 37–49.

Talen, Emily. 2008. New urbanism, social equity, and the challenge of post-Katrina rebuilding in Mississippi. *Journal of Planning Education and Research* 27(3): 277–293.

Toikka, Richard S., Aaron Yelowitz, & Andre Neveu. 2005. The "poverty trap" and living wage laws. *Economic Development Quarterly* 19(1): 62–79.

Touché, George E. 2004. Ecological sustainability: An annotated bibliography. *Journal of Planning Literature* 19(2): 206–223.

Tumber, Catherine. 2014. Fields, factories, and workshops: Green economic development on the smaller-metro scale, in Susan M. Wachter & Kimberly A. Zeuli, eds., *Revitalizing America's Cities*, 224–241. Philadelphia: University of Pennsylvania Press.

US Environmental Protection Agency. 1999. *EPA's Framework for Community-Based Environmental Protection*. National Service Center for Environmental Publications. Retrieved June 17, 2016: https://nepis.epa.gov.

Walker, Philip L. 2009. *Downtown Planning for Smaller and Midsized Communities*. Chicago: Planners.

Walzer, Norman, Gisele F. Hamm, & Lori A. Sutton. 2006. Involving brownfields in community development: Preliminary findings. *Community Development* 37(1): 79–89.

Warner, Mildred E., C. Clare Hinrichs, Judith Schneyer, & Lucy Joyce. 1999. Organizing communities to sustain rural landscapes: Lessons from New York. *Community Development* 30(2): 178–195.

Webb, Gary R. 2006. Unraveling the economic consequences of disasters: Sources of resilience and vulnerability. *Applied Research in Economic Development* 3(1): 3–18.

Wei, Max, Shana Patadia, & Daniel M. Kammen. 2010. Putting renewables and energy efficiency to work: How many jobs can the clean energy industry generate in the U.S.? *Energy Policy* 38(2): 919–931.

Wheeler, Stephen M. 2013. *Planning for Sustainability: Creating Livable, Equitable and Ecological Communities*, 2nd ed. Abingdon, UK: Routledge.

Xiao, Yu, & Joshua Drucker. 2013. Does economic diversity enhance regional disaster resilience? *Journal of the American Planning Association* 79(2): 148–160.

INDEX